John Huston as Adaptor

Also in the series

William Rothman, editor, *Cavell on Film*

J. David Slocum, editor, *Rebel Without a Cause*

Joe McElhaney, *The Death of Classical Cinema*

Kirsten Moana Thompson, *Apocalyptic Dread*

Frances Gateward, editor, *Seoul Searching*

Michael Atkinson, editor, *Exile Cinema*

Paul S. Moore, *Now Playing*

Robin L. Murray and Joseph K. Heumann, *Ecology and Popular Film*

William Rothman, editor, *Three Documentary Filmmakers*

Sean Griffin, editor, *Hetero*

Jean-Michel Frodon, editor, *Cinema and the Shoah*

Carolyn Jess-Cooke and Constantine Verevis, editors, *Second Takes*

Matthew Solomon, editor, *Fantastic Voyages of the Cinematic Imagination*

R. Barton Palmer and David Boyd, editors, *Hitchcock at the Source*

William Rothman, *Hitchcock: The Murderous Gaze, Second Edition*

Joanna Hearne, *Native Recognition*

Marc Raymond, *Hollywood's New Yorker*

Steven Rybin and Will Scheibel, editors, *Lonely Places, Dangerous Ground*

Claire Perkins and Constantine Verevis, editors, *B Is for Bad Cinema*

Dominic Lennard, *Bad Seeds and Holy Terrors*

Rosie Thomas, *Bombay before Bollywood*

Scott M. MacDonald, *Binghamton Babylon*

Sudhir Mahadevan, *A Very Old Machine*

David Greven, *Ghost Faces*

James S. Williams, *Encounters with Godard*

William H. Epstein and R. Barton Palmer, editors, *Invented Lives, Imagined Communities*

Lee Carruthers, *Doing Time*

Rebecca Meyers, William Rothman and Charles Warren, editors, *Looking with Robert Gardner*

Belinda Smaill, *Regarding Life*

R. Barton Palmer, Homer B. Pettey, and Steven M. Sanders, editors, *Hitchcock's Moral Gaze*

John Huston as Adaptor

Edited by

Douglas McFarland

and

Wesley King

Cover image: Gregory Peck and John Huston on the set of *Moby Dick* (1956). Courtesy of Photofest.

Published by State University of New York Press, Albany

© 2017 State University of New York

All rights reserved

Printed in the United States of America

No part of this book may be used or reproduced in any manner whatsoever without written permission. No part of this book may be stored in a retrieval system or transmitted in any form or by any means including electronic, electrostatic, magnetic tape, mechanical, photocopying, recording, or otherwise without the prior permission in writing of the publisher.

For information, contact State University of New York Press, Albany, NY
www.sunypress.edu

Production, Eileen Nizer
Marketing, Michael Campochiaro

Library of Congress Cataloging-in-Publication Data

Names: McFarland, Douglas editor. | King, Wesley, 1977– editor.
Title: John Huston as adaptor / edited by Douglas McFarland and Wesley King.
Description: Albany : State University of New York Press, 2017. | Series: SUNY series, horizons of cinema | Includes bibliographical references and index.
Identifiers: LCCN 2016031473 (print) | LCCN 2016041188 (ebook) | ISBN 9781438463735 (hardcover : alk. paper) | ISBN 9781438463728 (pbk. : alk. paper) | ISBN 9781438463742 (e-book)
Subjects: LCSH: Huston, John, 1906–1987—Criticism and interpretation. | Film adaptations—History and criticism.
Classification: LCC PN1998.3.H87 J654 2017 (print) | LCC PN1998.3.H87 (ebook) | DDC 791.4302/33092—dc23
LC record available at https://lccn.loc.gov/2016031473

10 9 8 7 6 5 4 3 2 1

Contents

Illustrations ... ix

Acknowledgments ... xi

Editors' Introduction: Huston as Reader ... xiii
Douglas McFarland and Wesley King

Introduction: Adapted by John Huston ... 1
Thomas Leitch

Part I. Aesthetics and Textuality

1. A Passing Node: *The Asphalt Jungle* ... 23
   Murray Pomerance

2. Adapting Addiction: Modernist Aesthetics in *Under the Volcano* ... 43
   Douglas McFarland

3. Taking Gabriel at His Word: Narration and Huston's *The Dead* ... 57
   Robert L. Colson

4. On Beams and Birds: John Huston's Adaptation of *The Maltese Falcon* ... 75
   Steven Rybin

5. A Screenplay-centric Analysis of Huston's *The Man Who Would Be King* ... 91
   Jonathan C. Glance

Part II. History and Social Context

6. "Proceed with the Execution": Casting, Convention, and the Diminishment of Rose in *The African Queen* 107
   Wesley King and Douglas McFarland

7. John Huston and Postwar Hollywood: *The Night of the Iguana* in Context 125
   R. Barton Palmer

8. "This Has Got to Be a Masterpiece": John Huston's Mangled Adaptation of *The Red Badge of Courage* 139
   Dale M. Pollock

9. Shadowboxing in the Sun: Fighters, Their Bodies, and Their Spaces in *Fat City* 153
   Tom Dorey

10. *Prizzi's Honor*: Greed and Gender in the Beginning of the Neoliberal Era 167
    Betty Kaklamanidou

11. Hints of Modernism, Shades of Noir: Huston's *Maltese Falcon* as Transitional Text 181
    Alan Woolfolk

12. Of Borders and Bandits: *The Treasure of the Sierra Madre* 197
    Camilla Fojas

13. "The Thing behind the Mask": Period, Pacing, and Visual Style in John Huston's *Moby Dick* 211
    Nathan Ragain

Part III. Theory and Psychoanalysis

14. Huston's *Freud*: Adapting the Life of Psychoanalysis 233
    David Sigler

15. Queer Movements: Color, Performance, and Rhythm in John Huston's *Reflections in a Golden Eye* 249
    Kyle Stevens

16. Flannery O'Connor's Symbolic Motif and the Psychoanalytic
    Objects of John Huston's *Wise Blood* 271
    Wesley King

Contributors 291

Index 295

Illustrations

Figure 1.1	Dix crosses through the fallen and baroque landscape of a decaying urban center.	25
Figure 1.2	A faint shadow of uncertainty begins to form on Doc's otherwise fully lit face as he realizes he has been deceived.	35
Figure 2.1	The ex-consul cavorts in the street like a madcap Shakespearean fool.	48
Figure 2.2	Subject and object collapse as Firmin stares at a candy skull.	55
Figure 3.1	In one of several similar shots, Gabriel stands aloof from the others, here rehearsing his speech.	59
Figure 3.2	Gazing into the middle distance, Gretta separates herself and her story from the marginalized Gabriel.	69
Figure 4.1	Brigid O'Shaughnessy dramatically enters Spade's office in the first deep-focus shot of the film.	83
Figure 4.2	All five characters appear in a single shot to re-establish Huston's narrative and visual sequencing.	87
Figure 5.1	The charismatic Dravot is crowned King as Carnehan looks on.	99
Figure 6.1	Rose and Charlie exchange wedding vows with nooses around their necks.	112
Figure 6.2	Rose dutifully maintains decorum, ignoring the potentially disruptive rumblings from Charlie's stomach.	118

Figure 7.1	Richard Burton, as the erstwhile anguished male, pauses for a shave.	134
Figure 8.1	A terrified Fleming runs headlong in panic to escape the battle.	148
Figure 9.1	Tully has a muscular physique that carries the marks of a career in the ring.	156
Figure 10.1	A blond femme fatale catches the eye of Charley at a *famiglia* wedding ceremony.	171
Figure 11.1	Spade leaves Gutman's apartment after cleverly pretending to lose his temper.	187
Figure 11.2	Even Spade falls under the spell of the "black bird."	192
Figure 12.1	Gold Hat's persona adds to a negative portrait of Mexican bandits.	205
Figure 13.1	Queequeg's shrunken head looms in a way that suggests earlier B-film horror movies.	217
Figure 13.2	Ahab tames St. Elmo's Fire.	222
Figure 14.1	Freud bends over a waking patient as Breuer looks on.	234
Figure 15.1	A weakened Weldon grips the banister railing while hopelessly caught between stillness and the desire to move.	258
Figure 15.2	The nude figure of Lenora is reflected in an extreme close-up of Ellgee's eye.	259
Figure 16.1	In the restroom scene and elsewhere, Huston's use of mirrors complicates the relationship between subject and object.	279
Figure 16.2	During Motes's dream, Huston pairs sexual desire with death.	283

Acknowledgments

We wish first to thank all the contributors to this volume. We greatly appreciate the time and effort they have spent on the project and the quality of the work they have produced. The idea for a book on John Huston's adaptations was first suggested to us by Tom Leitch. Tom has quite appropriately, therefore, written the introductory chapter of the book; his essay demonstrates his expertise in the field of adaptation studies and more specifically establishes the importance of adaptation to an understanding of Huston as a filmmaker. Our gratitude goes to Colin McKeown for his invitation to speak at the Huston Film Festival, Dromahair, Ireland. Great thanks are also due to our research assistants whose tireless efforts have been critical in bringing the project to its conclusion. These include James Hastings, Rebecca Short, Laura Henning, Lauren Weber, and Quinn Foerch. And finally we wish to give special thanks to Murray Pomerance, who has been a mentor and friend and without whose advice and aid this volume would not have been possible.

Editors' Introduction

Huston as Reader

DOUGLAS MCFARLAND AND WESLEY KING

In his seminal study, *John Huston's Filmmaking*, Lesley Brill acknowledged the importance of literary adaptation to John Huston's body of work. As Brill pointed out, "it is difficult to imagine any other director . . . transforming works so effectively from such a wide variety of writers," especially considering that much of the literature Huston adapted "is manifestly resistant to such translation" (5–6). But where Brill was setting out to establish Huston as more broadly comparable to the likes of Ingmar Bergman, Alfred Hitchcock, Stanley Kubrick, and Akira Kurosawa, this book focuses on how the director was unique in his engagements with literature. It is significant that thirty-four of his thirty-seven films were adaptations of literary works. In order, therefore, to more fully understand Huston as a filmmaker, we need a better and more comprehensive account of the centrality of adaptation to his work. We argue that Huston maintains a sophisticated and at times intense relationship with the materials he chooses to adapt. To put it differently, Huston's adaptations are serious interpretations of literary works that could only be made by an astute reader of literature. It is Huston's competence as a reader of literature, as well as his skill in the medium of film, that distinguishes him as an adaptor and, indeed, as a director. *John Huston as Adaptor* explores through Huston's films an approach to adaptation studies that has been largely overlooked. How an adaptor reads, the works to which she is drawn, and how her literary interpretations can be brought to the screen without relegating film to a subservient role are the issues that are addressed in the book.

Our assertion that adaptation is germane to understanding Huston's status as a filmmaker necessarily raises the question of the relationship between adaptation and authorship. The title of our collection of essays, *John Huston as Adaptor*, implicitly makes the case that Huston needs to be understood as the author of his films. Although this assessment will be qualified to some extent in several chapters in the collection, the understanding that Huston *authorizes* his films does represent our primary approach to him as a filmmaker. The first to seriously address the relationship between authorship and adaptation were the film critics of *Cahier de Cinema* and the New Wave filmmakers that the journal spawned. In his essay on film adaptation, André Bazin, the founder of *Cahier de Cinema*, argued that there was a deep-seated hierarchical relationship between the source of adaptation and the adaptation itself: "The nineteenth century, more than any other, firmly established an idolatry of form, mainly literary, that is still with us today" (45). To be more specific, in the early years of cinema and on into the 1930s and 1940s, this "idolatry" was manifest in three strategies: to legitimize film as a medium by drawing upon canonical works of literature; to disseminate and inculcate a cultural ethos based on those canonical works; and to turn the commercial successes of popular fiction into the commercial successes of film adaptations. The New Wave filmmakers that Bazin influenced sought to reverse this relationship by selecting materials of limited cultural value in order that their own cinematic signatures would not be erased, or to put it more forcefully, that their authorial identity have precedent over source materials. The awareness of the director as one who authorizes his own work hinges on adaptation. Dudley Andrew succinctly points this out in his overview of François Truffaut: "The cinema *d'auteur* that [Truffaut] advocated was not to be pitted against a cinema of adaptation; rather one method of adaptation was to be pitted against another. In this instance, adaptation was the battleground, even though it prepared the way for a stylistic revolution, the New Wave, which would for the most part avoid famous literary sources" (35). As Andrew argues, emphasis in the adaptation process shifted from the cultural cache of the source to the mise-en-scène fashioned by the filmmaker. Style became the marker of authorship. The veneration of Hitchcock, especially by Truffaut, reflects this. Hitchcock was often dismissive of his source material, sometimes not even bothering to read the original work but simply having the plot described to him. Hitchcock may very well have read for pleasure, but that pleasure in reading would seem to have made little if any contribution to his filmmaking. Although themes appear and reappear in his work, Hitchcock asserts his authorship through a style of filmmaking.

We point this out because Huston has been excluded from the ranks of *auteurs* in large measure because his films do lack a consistent visual style, failing to fulfill the fundamental requirement for authorship. Brill circumvents this problem by arguing that Huston's signature is expressed in thematic content, not style. Although Huston does clearly return to issues and character types throughout his work, we are arguing that adaptation as an approach to filmmaking is the salient element in his authorship. Moreover, what distinguishes Huston as an adaptor is Huston as a reader. Huston once asserted that a director of films should be "well read, widely read, and even deeply read" (*Interviews* 88). He was all of the above. By his own account, Huston was a voracious and sophisticated reader all of his life, boasting in his autobiography that he owned a contraband copy of *Ulysses* before Judge Woolsey lifted the ban in 1933. This deep engagement with literature is borne out in the body of Huston's work. His adaptations range from the noir fiction of Dashiell Hammet and W. R. Burnett to the formally sophisticated modernist works of Flannery O'Connor and Malcolm Lowry. But when Huston said that a director should be well read, he did not mean that a repository of literary works should be on hand, from which the director might readily draw material for adaptation. Huston himself made this point clear: "I never read looking for material. I only read for the joy of reading" (66). This "joy" constitutes the intellectual and emotional basis for Huston as an adaptor. And as ephemeral a quality that "joy" might be, it is his authorial signature.

This encounter between reader and text that Huston deems fundamental is energized by his veneration for many of the novelists whose work he adapted. Having written the screenplay adaptation of *High Sierra* (1941), Huston asserted that he considered Burnett one of the "most neglected American writers" and that "more than once [Burnett's works] had me breaking into a sweat" (*An Open Book* 78). In Burnett's novels, Huston was undoubtedly attracted to figures like Roy Earle in *High Sierra* or Dix Handley in *The Asphalt Jungle* (which Huston adapted in 1950), who, as Brill has described them, had "reached the end of their emotional endurance . . . desperate to make a place for themselves in the world" (94). However, it is the intense experience of reading Burnett, not Burnett's particular thematic concerns, that Huston emphasized in praising his work. The pleasure of reading that Hitchcock so easily dismissed becomes for Huston the crux of his approach to filmmaking.

Such intense engagement is apparent in his adaptation of *Moby Dick* (1956). It has been suggested that Huston was a generic storyteller with no particular visual style—criticisms which the chapters of this volume address and reject—and that he was often more concerned with turning literature into something that could be easily consumed by a general audience. With *Moby Dick*, Huston most certainly reduced Herman Melville's novel—which is itself an eccentric, relentlessly allusive, and baroque farrago—to a linear narrative with a dramatic climax. But although the film makes the novel more accessible, it also registers something else: those elements of Huston's experience of reading which had him "breaking into a sweat." Huston's own maniacal obsession with finding the right cinematic grammar and syntax, a vernacular around which to focus the story, might very well mirror Ahab's single-minded obsession.

To suggest, however, that Huston is ultimately more faithful to his experience of reading *Moby-Dick* than to the particularities of the novel itself should not belie the fact that Huston was an intellectually astute reader of literature, especially modernist literature. In an interview at Cannes for the premiere of *Under the Volcano* (1984), Huston revealed that he had read Lowry's novel some thirty-five years earlier when it was first published and that he had recognized the novel's excessive and undisciplined use of modernist literary conventions. Because of his knowledge of modernist aesthetics—which influenced his adaptation of *Wise Blood* (1979), for example—Huston's more disciplined approach to Lowry's novel was less a strict adaptation than an interpretation. Indeed, it is because of Huston's visceral encounters with literature that his films try to balance a deep respect for the original text with the potential ways that literature, through adaptation, can speak to new sociopolitical contexts. *Moby Dick*, for instance, responds to Cold War anxieties; *Prizzi's Honor* (1985) and even Huston's adaptation of *The Dead* (1987) reflect the feminist backlash against the Reagan/ Thatcher agenda. Moreover, Huston's own experience as a filmmaker speaks to the way adaptation can be a politically risky endeavor. Although his battles with producers and studio heads did not reach the levels of those experienced by Orson Welles, Huston's *Red Badge of Courage* (1951), because of its challenging antiwar message, was dramatically recut without his knowledge in order to make the film more palatable to post–World War II audiences.

Although Huston did not cultivate a consistent visual or narrative style, he did, however, experiment with styles from auteurist cinema in adaptations such as *The Night of the Iguana* (1964) and *Reflections in a Golden Eye* (1967). Also, from the range of literature that he adapted, unique concerns emerge, from the existentialist questions that drive *The Maltese Falcon* (1941) to an abiding interest in psychoanalysis. This latter interest was also deeply literary. In discussing his film *Freud: The Secret Passion* (1962), an adaptation of *Studies on Hysteria*, Huston asserted that "the descent into the unconscious should be as terrifying as Dante's descent into Hell" (*An Open Book* 294). Films like *The Dead* and *The Man Who Would Be King* (1975), which in Huston's rendering emphasize the anticolonial theme, exhibit something akin to a personal signature, especially when considered in light of the fact that Huston became an Irish citizen in 1964.

The chapters in this collection take a wide range of critical approaches to Huston's adaptations. Thomas Leitch makes the case that the films of John Huston, the quintessential Hollywood adaptor, demand thoughtful engagement by adaptation scholars. He argues that as director, writer, and adaptor, Huston should be taken as seriously as those directors typically classified as auteurs. Accordingly, the collection then proceeds to take the contours of Huston's work as a new model for adaptation studies. To do so, the chapters are organized into three areas: "Aesthetics and Textuality," "History and Social Context," and "Theory and Psychoanalysis."

Although every chapter in the collection approaches Huston's work through the critical topoi of *text*, *history*, and *theory*, the first section of the volume, "Aesthetics and Textuality," directly centers on how Huston's adaptations are acts of interpretation. The chapters in this section pose the essential question of adaptation studies: How does the translation from the page to the screen shape, enrich, and fundamentally alter the written text? Although known for his fidelity to the source, these chapters show how Huston's aesthetic was often powerfully and meaningfully *unfaithful*. For instance, Murray Pomerance argues that Huston draws out the eccentricities of characters not fully developed in Burnett's *Asphalt Jungle* through a visually lyric sensibility that focuses on objects and details not as they necessarily contribute to a narrative arc, but as discrete expressions of subjectivity. In his chapter on *Under the Volcano*, Douglas McFarland argues that Huston replaced the densely complex aesthetics of the novel into a linear and spatially unified narrative not to make it more accessible but to offer his own modernist style described by Gérard Genette as "showing" rather than "telling." Other chapters such as Robert L. Colson's on *The Dead* show how Huston adapts Joyce's unique use of narrative focalization, while Steven Rybin argues that in *The Maltese Falcon* Huston creates a patterned play between figures and objects, utilizing close-ups and deep focus to create an existential space of assertion and detection. And Jonathan C. Glance in his analysis of *The Man Who Would Be King* explores the relationship between film and screenplay.

Our largest grouping, "History and Social Context," builds on the first by emphasizing the dynamic between text and contexts: historical, political, and social. Wesley King and Douglas McFarland argue that this dynamic is evident in *The African Queen* where Huston's apparent departure from the gender issues of the novel are reinforced by his casting of Katherine Hepburn in the lead role. R. Barton Palmer argues that Huston's adaptation of *The Night of the Iguana* is the product of two quite different trends that found increasing success in Hollywood in the 1950s: the blockbuster production and the small-scale adult film. In tracing the film's production history, Palmer shows how Huston fused the two into a single film. Dale M. Pollack reveals how *The Red Badge of Courage* was compromised by MGM executives, as well as Huston's own postproduction missteps. And whereas Tom Dorey focuses on the construction of masculinity in *Fat City*, Betty Kaklamanidou addresses gender politics of the 1980s in *Prizzi's Honor*. Alan Woolfolk charts Huston's transformation of the tough and ruthless working-class detective Sam Spade into a more inwardly complicated and self-possessed Baudelairian dandy, while Camilla Fojas examines the popular image of the bandit in the context of the sociopolitical border relations between Mexico and the United States when Huston adapted *The Treasure of the Sierra Madre*. Finally, Nathan Ragain argues that Huston shifts the 1850s context of *Moby Dick* to the 1950s, by utilizing the techniques and capturing the ethos of science fiction during the Cold War.

Where the second section offers a panorama, the third, "Theory and Psychoanalysis," provides a tighter focus on a central motif in Huston's work: his representations of perception and the psyche. More theoretically oriented in their engagements, these chapters interpret Huston's adaptations through questions provoked by psychoanalysis and other studies of desire. This is a critical interest, which—at least since his biopic on Freud—Huston himself shared. David Sigler notes that Huston's *Freud: A Secret Passion* is essentially an adaptation of Freud's and Breuer's *Studies on Hysteria*. While ostensibly a biopic, Sigler argues that Huston turns his back on Freud's biography to grant psychoanalytic ideas biographies of their own. Kyle Stevens looks to the psychosexual elements of Huston's adaptation of Carson McCullers's *Reflections in a Golden Eye*. Stevens demonstrates how the film's rhetorical strategies, such as its use of color and rhythm, elucidate an ideological critique of contemporary sexual politics. And finally Wesley King, drawing upon Lacanian psychoanalysis, argues that although Huston and screenwriter Benedict Fitzgerald deliberately avoided many of O'Connor's symbolic motifs in their adaptation of *Wise Blood*, the film approaches symbolism in a way that explores the depths of the unconscious.

Taken together these chapters demonstrate that adaptation is the salient element in Huston's identity as a filmmaker and that his deep and early attraction to the experience of reading informed his process of adaptation. It has been recognized that Huston was a writer before he became a director. Indeed, prior to directing his first film Huston had written several screenplays, and he wrote or contributed to the screenplays for the vast majority of his own films. But the path he took to both writing and directing began with an intense attraction to the experience of reading, and it is the depth and breadth of his reading that set him apart from other directors.

Works Cited

Andrew, Dudley. "Adaptation." *Film Adaptation*. Ed. James Naremore. New Brunswick: Rutgers UP, 2000. 28–37.

Bazin, Andre. "Adaptation, or the Cinema of Digest." *Bazin at Work*. Trans. Alain Piette and Bert Cardullo. New York: Routledge, 1997. 41–51.

Brill, Lesley. *John Huston's Filmmaking*. Cambridge: Cambridge UP, 1997.

Huston, John. *An Open Book*. New York: Alfred Knopf, 1980.

Huston, John. *Interviews*. Ed. Robert Emmet Long. Jackson: U of Mississippi P, 2001.

Introduction

Adapted by John Huston

THOMAS LEITCH

DESPITE THE OBLIGATORY STUDIES OF his individual film adaptations from *The Maltese Falcon* (1941) to *The Dead* (1987), little attention has been paid to the larger issues arising from John Huston's work as an adaptor. This omission is especially surprising in view of two factors. Huston enjoyed a remarkably long and fruitful career as a writer/director who is credited on the screenplays of more than a dozen of the films he directed. In addition, virtually all Huston's films, whether or not he is credited as a screenwriter, are adaptations.

Although Page Laws has aptly dubbed Huston "King Adapter" (123), he has never had his due as an adaptor. This neglect arises partly from the fact that until recently, studies of adaptation focused on novelists rather than screenwriters or directors. Even when adaptation scholars have turned to examining the careers of those successful in the field, they have focused on one of two sorts. The predominant model is offered by auteur directors such as Alfred Hitchcock, who was well known for his cavalier attitude toward the works he adapted to produce what he and François Truffaut revealingly agreed to call "Hitchcock creation[s]" (71). This model is defined by its disavowal of the filmmaker's status as adaptor, a disavowal that in Hitchcock's case had been virtually complete until the recent publication of Mark Osteen's collection *Hitchcock and Adaptation*. More recently, an alternative model has emerged in critical discussions of English literary classics filmed for British television television. Screenwriter Andrew Davies, whom Graham Fuller called the "auteur" (77) of the 1995 BBC *Pride and Prejudice*, has come under attention for his adaptations of *Middlemarch* (1994), *Moll Flanders* (1996), *Emma* (1996), *Vanity Fair* (1998), *Wives and Daughters* (1999), *The Way We Live Now* (2001), *He Knew He Was Right* (2004), *Bleak House* (2005), and *Little Dorrit* (2008) as miniseries for British television. Just as Davies is less widely known than Hitchcock, the auteurist model he represents has been far less influential than the model associated with Hitchcock, but it is noteworthy for at least one important feature. In the course of a 2004 interview with Davies, Deborah Cartmell tells him, "You're unique in that you're known as an adaptor" (Cartmell and Whelehan 242). If Hitchcock succeeds by imposing his personality on a diverse group of sources, Davies succeeds by tailoring adaptations of novels as different as *Pride and Prejudice*, *Moll Flanders*, and *Little Dorrit* to the "strong group style" (Higson 111) of the BBC and ITV that makes so many British television versions of classic novels "look and feel like chapters of a single interminable Classic Serial" (Brownstein 16; both quoted by Cardwell 77–78).

This apparent subordination of the filmmaker's personality to the source material or the group style might seem the inevitable price Davies pays for his reputation as an adaptor. But Huston's practice as an adaptor represents a third model that is more provocative and revealing than either of the other models. Huston is a seasoned screenwriter-turned-writer/director who repeatedly chose to film adaptations over original screenplays without attempting to shoehorn diverse adaptations into either a single mold of the "Huston creation" or a single "group style" and repeatedly rejected the notion that his films were thematically or stylistically linked. What makes this third model particularly valuable is that it corresponds far more closely than either of the other models to typical Hollywood practice during the half-century of Huston's career. Huston exemplifies, more perhaps than any other single filmmaker, the importance, the adventures, and the vicissitudes of adaptation in Hollywood through the second half of the twentieth century.

This chapter focuses on contrasting Huston with Hitchcock rather than Davies because it aims to make a case for Huston as a quintessential Hollywood adaptor. It is only natural to think of Huston in this way because he was for so long a noted screenwriter/director whose films were generally literary adaptations. But Huston's attitude toward filmmaking, his working methods, and the most distinctive qualities of his films would brand him an adaptor even if he had not written, or co-written, and directed them. Perhaps the simplest way to clear the ground for writing about Huston from this perspective is to observe how seldom the question implicit in the essay's title ever gets asked. Until Douglas McFarland and Wesley King opened this subject, virtually no one cared to debate Lesley Brill's assessment of Huston as "[p]erhaps the most resourceful adapter of complex literary texts in the history of American and British cinema" (5). This is because the status of adaptor, as opposed to that of auteur or director, has been so unworthy and unsought. In the hierarchy of Hollywood filmmaking, adaptors rank even lower than screenwriters. That is why Hitchcock's admirers have been so reluctant to identify him as such, even though most of his films are adaptations. And that is why Geoff Andrews has asserted that since Huston "favoured working from literary sources, [he] seldom made films that seemed at all personal" (Andrews 99, qtd. in Tracy and Flynn 2). Andrew Sarris, essentially waiving questions about the nature of adaptation entirely, resolves questions of cinematic authorship more generally by asking, "That was a good movie . . . Who directed it?" (35).

Sarris's celebrated ranking of Hollywood directors dismisses Huston as "less than meets the eye" (155) because his films lack an overarching, unifying vision. For Sarris, Huston is guilty of the cardinal sin against auteurism: he "displayed his material without projecting his personality" (156). Huston can't be categorized as expressive esoterica, like genre directors Budd Boetticher and Joseph H. Lewis, who rise above routine material, or lightly likeable, like the similarly flexible and resourceful Michael Curtiz and Henry Hathaway, because he gets to choose many of his own projects, and the ones he chooses, like *Freud: The Secret Passion* (1962), are often pretentious bombs. As Arlene Croce trenchantly concluded in reviewing *The Barbarian and the Geisha* (1958) and *The Roots of Heaven* (1958): "It is saddening to think that the director of *The Asphalt Jungle* . . . has gained professional freedom and international celebrity in order to become, at 51, yet another taskmaster who goes out in the midday sun" (qtd. in *The Hustons* 455).

Because Sarris's "strong director imposes his own personality on a film" (31), every director he imagines as making an adaptation strives to make a definitive one—Hitchcock's *Rebecca*, not Daphne du Maurier's—and aims to identify it with himself (all of Sarris's auteur directors are male) as the author. So Sarris is especially disappointed in Huston, who had once seemed to fit the mold of the Hollywood auteur so precisely. The first film he directed, *The Maltese Falcon* (1941), was the paradigm of the definitive adaptation. Warner Bros. had already filmed Dashiell Hammett's 1930 novel twice before as *The Maltese Falcon*, aka *Dangerous Female* (1931), and *Satan Met a Lady* (1936), but Huston's film stopped the rush to further versions dead in its tracks. Although Hammett's novel has been parodied in Hollywood films like *The Black Bird* (1975), no one has had the temerity to follow Huston's film with another straight adaptation.

Since his remarkable directorial debut, Huston has made what seem likely to remain definitive adaptations of B. Traven's *The Treasure of the Sierra Madre* (1948), Maxwell Anderson's *Key Largo* (1948), W. R. Burnett's *The Asphalt Jungle* (1950), C. S. Forester's *The African Queen* (1951), Tennessee Williams's *The Night of the Iguana* (1964), Carson McCullers's *Reflections in a Golden Eye* (1967), Rudyard Kipling's *The Man Who Would Be King* (1975), Flannery O'Connor's *Wise Blood* (1979), Malcolm Lowry's *Under the Volcano* (1984), Richard Condon's *Prizzi's Honor* (1985), and James Joyce's *The Dead*. Even though *The Asphalt Jungle* spawned a short-lived 1961 television series and *Key Largo* and *The African Queen* hour-long television segments, it is hard to imagine anyone reworking any of these stories as feature-length films despite Hollywood's insatiable appetite for recycling its source material that allowed Huston to make *The Maltese Falcon* in the first place.

Moreover, Huston has gone out of his way to impose his personality on many of his films, marking them as his in several different ways. He provides uncredited voiceover narration for the army documentaries *Report from the Aleutians* (1942) and *The Battle of San Pietro* (1945). Later, he returns to narrate *Freud* in the first person, even though his voice is nothing like his star Montgomery Clift's, and *The Bible . . . In the Beginning* (1967), in which his hushed but stentorian voice sounds properly godlike. He favors unsettlingly close shots in which a single abstracted character looks away from others in a group but also away from the camera, a composition that he uses consistently from his earliest films through *The Dead*. He appears as a performer in a dozen of his films, often uncredited, although he took the part of Noah in *The Bible* only after Charlie Chaplin and Alec Guinness both turned it down (Huston 318). He even toys with dynastic ambitions when he casts his more famous father, Walter Huston, in an uncredited bit in *The Maltese Falcon* and in an Academy Award–winning performance in *The Treasure of the Sierra Madre*; his son, Tony, in *The List of Adrian Messenger* (1963); and his daughter, Anjelica, in *A Walk with Love and Death* (1969), *Prizzi's Honor*, and *The Dead*. When Anjelica Huston won an Academy Award as Best Supporting Actress as Maerose Prizzi, Huston, the only person ever to direct his own father in an Oscar-winning role, became in addition the only person to direct his daughter in an Oscar-winning role.

If he has often seemed to comply with the unwritten norms that would establish his credentials as an auteur, however, Huston has even more often flouted them. He has adapted books of negligible value like Pierre La Mure's *Moulin Rouge,* James Helvick's *Beat the Devil,* and Charles Shaw's *The Flesh and the Spirit,* the "very bad novel" (*An Open Book* 260) that became the basis for *Heaven Knows, Mr. Allison.* He has filmed other writers' screenplays in such films as *The Barbarian and the Geisha* (1958), *The Roots of Heaven* (1958), *The Unforgiven* (1960), *The Misfits* (1961), *Sinful Davey* (1969), *A Walk with Love and Death* (1969), *Fat City* (1972), *The Life and Times of Judge Roy Bean* (1973), *Independence* (1976), *Phobia* (1980), and *Victory* (1981). He has often been accused of taking on projects like *Annie* (1982), a film he "wasn't proud of, and totally disowned" (Grobel 729), solely for the money. And he produced his share of adaptations from *In This Our Life* (1942) to *The Mackintosh Man* (1973) that were anything but definitive.

But these disappointments, as Sarris and others have considered them, do not undermine Huston's status as an exemplary adaptor; they merely help to define that status more precisely. If Sarris had looked back over Huston's career before *The Maltese Falcon,* he would have seen the lineaments of a quite different model of screen authorship. Before he ever directed a film, Huston worked on the screenplays of films as different as *Murders in the Rue Morgue* (1932), *Jezebel* (1938), *Juarez* (1939), *Dr. Ehrlich's Magic Bullet* (1940), *High Sierra* (1941), and *Sergeant York* (1941), always in collaboration. He continued to serve as an anonymous team member on *Report from the Aleutians,* which was credited only as "Produced by the U.S. Army Signal Corps" and "produced and exhibited through the Office of War Information under the auspices of the War Activities Committee of the Motion Picture Industry," and *The Battle of San Pietro,* which the army was reluctant to release with or without his name attached. It is no slur on Huston to call him a journeyman adaptor who took on projects to earn the money to finance his often extravagant lifestyle or "to launch my sixteen-year-old as an actress" (Huston 337), as he did in *A Walk with Love and Death.* Long before he directed his first film, Huston had already defined himself not as an independent creator but as a collaborator on a production team who did not live to work but worked to live.

Huston's checkered career throws a particularly penetrating light on several implications of Sarris's position. The most obvious is that the exemplary auteur shows his mettle by the way he establishes his individual authorship within the confines of a more powerful studio. Unlike Curtiz's work, however, Huston's is best examined within the context of the breakup of the studio system, when power is up for grabs. Working as cannily as Hitchcock, though along very different lines, Huston established authorship as something to be negotiated film by film rather than either conferred or withheld once and for all. Although Huston's name provided a certain cachet to projects as different as *Wise Blood* and *Annie*, it carried no guarantee of success. Long after Huston had established himself as a celebrity writer/director, he remained free to fail, and he often did fail. Sarris assumes that significant achievement in the cinema and elsewhere depends on authorial control. The perfect auteur could make great films on assignment because he would draw every project into his personal control. Hitchcock, even though the range of material on which he drew was among the narrowest in the industry, became a legendary auteur in large part because he was reputed to plan his films so meticulously shot by shot that he considered the actual shooting of each film a regrettable formality—even though Bill Krohn's research has revealed that this legend was nothing but a legend (Krohn 11–16). And Andrew Davies made his reputation by his success in conforming to the BBC-TV "group style" he came to embody. Huston, by contrast, doesn't even try to make his films perfect. As he infuriatingly says, "I could have spent three times as long on *The Man Who Would Be King*, but I'm not sure it would have been a better picture for it. It doesn't strive for perfection. . . . The picture has its faults, I suppose—but who gives a damn? It plunges recklessly ahead. It swims toward the cataract" (Huston 360). Huston, seeing the film as a gesture rather than an achievement, values it more highly for what it attempts than for what it accomplishes.

Sarris assumes that an auteur's achievement is based on the ascription of thematic unity and consistency over however wide a range of material the auteur is given. Since "the auteur critic is obsessed with the wholeness of art and the artist" (30), argues Sarris, "the auteur theory values the personality of the director precisely because of the barriers to its expression" (31). The fallacies in the assumption that the most successful films are those whose directors' personalities overcome institutional barriers to their expression have been exposed by many commentators—most notably, in "Circles and Squares," by Pauline Kael, whom Sarris characterizes as "a lady critic with a lively sense of outrage" (26)—but this assumption, like the belief that cinematic achievement depends on directorial control, continues to haunt theories of film authorship.

Huston poses a scandal to Sarris's brand of auteurism for several reasons. As he acknowledges himself in his autobiography, the revealingly titled *An Open Book*:

> I'm not aware of myself as a director having a style. . . . I admire directors like Bergman, Fellini, Buñuel, whose every picture is in some way connected with their private lives, but that's never been my approach. I'm eclectic. I like to draw on sources other than myself; further, I don't think of

myself as simply, uniquely and forever a director of motion pictures.... The idea of devoting myself to a single pursuit in life is unthinkable to me. My interests in boxing, writing, painting, horses have at certain periods in my life been every bit as important as that in directing films. (361)

The scandal here is not merely that Huston makes no attempt to impose a single artistic sensibility on the films he makes, practically all of them adaptations, but that he regards filmmaking itself not as an artistic vocation but as only one among many activities that interest him. Hence Norman Mailer, writing of *The Misfits*, observes that Huston's "life celebrates a style more important to him than film. His movies do not embody his life so much as they emerge out of a pocket of his mind.... It is as if film is an activity good men must not take upon themselves too solemnly" (186). Huston presents himself to Mailer not as a consummate filmmaker but as a man of many interests that happen to include filmmaking.

Instead of seeing his career as a continuous story, Huston emphasizes the discreteness of each project, to which his own life and personality necessarily become subordinate: "Those involved in making pictures from beginning to end, especially on location, come to think of each separate picture as a world and a life unto itself. The actors, the crew, technicians—all are caught up in the little planetary system, which one day simply comes to an end. Suddenly it's over, and you can never go back to it. Thus the picture-maker's life is subdivided into many lives" (Huston 263). When he discusses individual films in his memoir, Huston neither analyzes them nor makes any attempt to extract from them a larger story about his own development but instead mines each of them as a source of anecdote or wisdom and rests with judging them simply successes—like *Heaven Knows, Mr. Allison*, "one of the best things I ever made" (Huston 263), and *Reflections in a Golden Eye*, "one of my best pictures" (Huston 333)—or failures—like *The Unforgiven* (1960), "the only one [of my pictures] I actually dislike" (Huston 284), and *Moby Dick*, of which he said: "The picture, like the book, is a blasphemy" (Huston 251), and in which, instead of attempting to engage the audience viscerally, as Steven Spielberg would do twenty years later in *Jaws* (1975), "I settled for literature" (*Grobel* 429).

In addition, as Sarris points out, Huston's filmography indiscriminately combines hits and misses. Even a more sympathetic observer, Robert Mitchum, notes that "throughout his career, John rarely followed one great film with another" (*John Huston*). It is perhaps fortunate that Sarris is not the gatekeeper to the literary pantheon, for adding consistency of achievement to consistency of thematic concerns might well exclude the likes of Byron, Shelley, Poe, Dickens, Hardy, and Fitzgerald.

When the orientation of film studies shifted from evaluation to analysis in the 1970s, auteurism did not change along with it. It simply remained a popular system of evaluating auteurs that remains in place, largely unaltered, to this day as not only the most powerful way but virtually the only way most filmgoers think about cinematic authorship. Huston's body of work and his approach to his work offer welcome alternative ways of thinking about authorship in analytical terms (how does authorship work?) rather than the comparative, evaluative terms of auteurism (which directors are auteurs?). For all its spottiness—in fact, largely because of its spottiness—Huston's filmography poses several promising alternative models of directorial authorship. When he says, "I always keep hoping that it will be the actor who will show me, rather than the other way around," he presents the director as a *collaborator* whose credo is that "the one thing I always try to experiment with is accepting suggestions from the people who work with me" (Sarris, *Interviews with Film Directors* 267, 272).

Huston's candid admission that he has often taken on projects initiated by others for the money, from *Wise Blood* to *Annie*, positions the director as *salaried hireling*. This status would not necessarily exclude Huston form Sarris's pantheon, for Sarris praises Truffaut's "heresy" in "ascribing authorship to Hollywood directors hitherto tagged with the deadly epithets of commercialism" (28). But Arlene Croce's description of the director of *The Barbarian and the Geisha* and *The Roots of Heaven* as "a taskmaster" shows how virulent the prejudice against such hirelings has been and often remains.

Huston's love for boxing and hunting suggests other models for film adaptation as a conflict between equal or unequal contenders. But a still more provocative model is implicit in James Agee's celebrated 1950 profile of Huston as an "undirectable director" who seemed to make movies "blindfolded, by accident, and largely just for the hell of it" (368). For Agee, Huston represents the director as *adventurer*, a model swiftly confirmed when Huston hired Agee to collaborate on the screenplay for *The African Queen* and then took Humphrey Bogart and Katharine Hepburn to Africa to film it. Here it is especially useful to set Huston against Hitchcock and Fritz Lang, who explore the interior nightmares of the human psyche. Huston is a more literal and extroverted explorer of geographical landscapes shot on location, a director who uses each property as a vehicle for exploring the new places Hitchcock shuns. Hitchcock is ultimately a colonizer who aims to transform each source into a Hitchcock creation in the studio. Huston's selection of projects like

The Man Who Would Be King and *The Dead* reveals an anticolonialist bent already implicit in the cautionary tales of *The Treasure of the Sierra Madre*, in which an obsession with taking a mountain's gold leads to disaster, and *The Asphalt Jungle*, in which the leading characters are admirable precisely to the extent they escape definition by alienating institutions. Huston constantly adapts himself, as well as his sources, to Africa or south Asia. When he visits Ireland or Mexico and decides he likes the place, he is capable of settling there, remaining for years, even taking out citizenship. And he leaves himself open to whatever incidental discoveries he can find along the way, from the extraordinary use of Technicolor in *Moulin Rouge* to Pablo, the orphan he discovered and adopted while he was in Mexico shooting *The Treasure of the Sierra Madre*.

When they think they are about to die in *The Man Who Would Be King*, Peachy Carnahan (Michael Caine) reflects to Daniel Dravett (Sean Connery) that they haven't made the world a better place or done a single good deed, "But how many men have been where we've been, and seen what we've seen?" At the corresponding moment in *The African Queen*, Charlie Allnutt (Humphrey Bogart) tells Rose Sayer (Katharine Hepburn) that even though he expects to die without succeeding in their joint venture of using his boat to torpedo a German ship preventing English forces from entering central Africa, "I'm not one bit sorry I came. It was worth it." These credos stand in stark opposition to the fact that the explorers our culture best remembers and most highly values—cartographers and conquerors rather than ethnographers or tourists—are those working most closely in the service of imperialist projects. Explorer/directors like Huston will always be devalued when their products don't come up to snuff until adaptation studies trades its emphasis on constructive or saleable projects for an emphasis on the process of adaptation.

As the title of *An Open Book* suggests, Huston is a voracious *reader* in at least two senses. For his knack of turning so many of the books he read into film adaptations, Huston is comparable to Darryl Zanuck, whom Rick Altman calls "a gifted critic and Hollywood's ultimate assayer" for his success in spinning so many cycles and genres out of films he was watching and imitating (46). For Altman, Zanuck's sensitivity as a reader of scripts, trends, and the public taste is exactly what makes him a successful producer. In a more foundational sense, Huston represents the reader as grazer or adventurer whose professional interest is secondary. "I don't even read with the intention of finding material, I just read out of interest," he told one interviewer, and added to another that he was moved to direct films in order "to express my pleasure in having read something" (*Long* 76, 143). What Huston adapts, he candidly admits, isn't literary sources like Kipling's story "The Man Who Would Be King" but "my reading of the story at age twelve or fifteen, and my impressions of it. . . . Most of my pictures begin with this kind of inbred idea, something that lives in me from long ago" (Sarris, *Interviews with Film Directors* 255). As this example reveals, Huston's "ideas" are not simply impressions or even epitomes of earlier texts. Instead, they can often supplant those texts in providing a raison d'être for Huston's adaptations.

Some of Huston's ideas are specific to individual projects, like the choice of nonprofessional actors as the leads in *The Red Badge of Courage* and the model of Matthew Brady's Civil War photographs for the film's visuals or the flat, two-dimensional color in *Moulin Rouge*, the desaturated color in *Moby Dick*, and the "diffuse amber color" (*Huston* 332) Huston fought with Warner Bros. to maintain in the release prints of *Reflections in a Golden Eye*. Some are characteristic of a wider range of Huston's work, like the anti-institutional bias that makes him sympathetic to loners as unappealing as Fred C. Dobbs (Humphrey Bogart) in *The Treasure of the Sierra Madre* or the ill-fated criminals of *The Asphalt Jungle*. Such preoccupations illuminate the ways that all adaptations are inevitably mediated, and sometimes dominated, by ideas about the works under adaptation rather than by the works themselves.

We could invert the terms of this last model while retaining its force by saying that Huston represents the director as *writer*, always striving to capture a particular idea. Hence Huston was not drawn to Pierre La Mure's novel *Moulin Rouge* because he thought it an impressive literary achievement that deserved cinematic incarnation, but because,

> I had an idea for the end that made me want to make a picture of it. I imagined Lautrec on his deathbed in the château at Toulouse, his mother and father watching the priest administer extreme unction. He smiles and his eyes open. He is hallucinating; the shades from his beloved *Moulin Rouge* enter the room, come there to bid farewell to their departing friend. The music of the can-can starts and Lautrec breathes his last. It would be a truly happy ending. (*Huston* 205)

Huston generalizes this statement by asserting, "The most important element to me is always the idea that I'm trying to express, and everything technical is only a method to make the idea into clear form. I'm always working on the idea: whether I'm writing, directing, choosing music or cutting. Everything must revert back to the idea; when it gets away from the idea it becomes a labyrinth of rococo" (Sarris, *Interviews with Film Directors* 263). So it is no surprise that he has defined style as "the adaptation of the word or action to the idea" (Sarris, *Interviews with Film Directors* 264).

Huston represents the director as an *adaptor* in three different senses. All film directors necessarily work with preexisting material—if not a novel or play or story, then a screenplay—to the cinema. In addition, Huston regards each script as a blueprint that will be subject to constant revision and improvisation if he is "open to take advantage of the terrain, of the things that the setting can give you," and to change dialogue "when I hear the words first spoken by an actor" in order to "allow my imagination the liberty of play" (Sarris, *Interviews with Film Directors* 259). Finally, all directors seek to utilize their own repertory of tricks, techniques, and trademarks to a range of different projects (Sarris, *Interviews with Film Directors* 259), whether or not those strategies and their results are successful, even if they believe along with Huston that "each idea calls for a different treatment, really" (Sarris, *Interviews with Film Directors* 256). In short, the directorial models Huston's career implies provide an opportunity to study directorial authorship as a *process* that is not necessarily synonymous with the success that Sarris assumes always crowns it.

Instead of asking, Has Huston made enough great films to canonize him as an auteur? or even, Which Huston films are most successful, and what makes them stand out from the others?, adaptation theory bids us ask, What is the nature of Huston's method? What is it like for Huston to adapt a property, from the selection of the property and the performers to the final cut? When we pursue these questions, the hit-or-miss quality of Huston's filmography becomes at worst irrelevant, at best positively illuminating, because it raises questions about the process of adaptation that would otherwise be overlooked. Why did Michael Fitzgerald approach Huston to direct *Wise Blood* when Huston's view of its subject—"how ridiculous Christianity was" (*Grobel* 712)—was so deeply opposed to Fitzgerald's? Did Huston pursue *Heaven Knows, Mr. Allison* in the hope of duplicating the success of *The African Queen*, his earlier study of two unlikely characters thrown together in a wilderness made even more perilous by war? More generally, does Huston's work, whether or not it comprises a genre in the way Hitchcock's work does, include minigenres with which Huston would have had especially compelling associations? When Huston repeats the big close-ups of abstracted faces looking toward the camera and away from their groups or interlocutors in apparently unrelated films, are these shots a sign of authorial vision, stylistic consistency, unconscious habit, or impoverished technique?

As Huston commentators have tacitly acknowledged, none of these questions could possibly be answered by a close comparison between any given Huston film and its literary source. Hence Bosley Crowther, reviewing *The African Queen* on its first release, coyly confessed: "Whether C. S. Forester had his salty British tongue in his cheek when he wrote his extravagant story of romance and adventure, *The African Queen*, we wouldn't be able to tell you. But it is obvious—to us, at least—that director John Huston was larking when he turned the novel into a film" (Nichols 8). No wonder that James R. Fultz's essay comparing the novel, Agee's published screenplay, and the film is titled "A Classic Case of Collaboration." And no wonder that Huston's own reminiscences, like those of Lauren Bacall and especially Katharine Hepburn, all concentrate on the adventures and misadventures of the location shoot in equatorial Africa: the miraculously rapid construction of the filmmaking camp ("eighty-five natives had built it in eight days, from pure jungle," according to Bacall [207]); the logistical hurdles that had to be overcome with relatively primitive resources; the bouts of illness among the cast and crew; their encounters with elephants, snakes, and army ants; the accidental offscreen sinking of *The African Queen;* Huston's suggestion that Hepburn play Rose with a smile like Eleanor Roosevelt's ("I was his from there on in," Hepburn recalls [83]); and the director's sudden determination toward the end of the shoot to add three days to the film's already brutal schedule. All these adventures play some role in making the film what it became, but none of them is essential to its success; most of them involve momentary triumphs over obstacles instead of recipes for success. Hence the most valuable book ever written about a Huston film, Lillian Ross's *Picture,* is not a celebration or defense of *The Red Badge of Courage* as a fully achieved work of art but an unblinking account of the film's production. Huston battled MGM over the casting of lead roles and voiced a belated objection to the studio's wholesale recutting of the film from an original length, variously reported as ninety minutes or two hours, down to sixty-nine minutes while Huston was off shooting *The African Queen.*

A particularly revealing example of Huston's process as an adaptor is *The List of Adrian Messenger,* a project on which Huston served as both director and midwife. No one seems to have an especially high opinion of the film—certainly not Huston, who mentions it in *An Open Book* only in the context of reminiscing about his four favorite fox-hunting horses. Indeed, he seems to have been attracted to the project only because Philip MacDonald's 1959 novel included a scene set on the margins of a fox hunt in its opening pages. The film's art director, Stephen Grimes, a frequent Huston collaborator who described the result as "a throw-away sort of film," recalls: "That's why he wanted to make it . . . so he could get in a bit of fox hunting and work at the same time" (*Grobel*

525, 521). Once he had signed on, it was Huston's idea to transpose much of the story's action from London to Ireland, make fox hunting a more prominent motif in its final third, and stage its unmasking of the killer as the conclusion to a climactic hunt. Yet the resulting film, which Huston evidently took on in the spirit of a busman's holiday, is his most provocative reflection on the nature of adaptation.

This reflection is rooted neither in MacDonald's novel nor in the film's screenplay, which Huston farmed out to his old friend Anthony Veiller. Veiller had collaborated with Huston on the screenplay for *The Killers* (1946) and *The Stranger* (1946), two projects on which Huston had received no screen credit, before working on the screenplays for *Moulin Rouge, Beat the Devil*, and *Moby Dick*. After the critical and financial failure of *Beat the Devil*, Huston had created a rift with Veiller by replacing him with Ray Bradbury on *Moby Dick*, but now he was eager to work once more with "my favorite American screenwriter" (*Huston* 205).

In this instance, it was neither Huston nor Veiller but Edward Lewis, the film's producer, who came up with what Huston called the "gimmick" (*Grobel* 525) that would so subversively illuminate the process of adaptation. The novel featured a killer who assumed a dozen different disguises in order to kill off the relatives who stood between him and the estate of the Marquis of Gleneyre and the potential witnesses to his true identity whose names were on a list its title character passed on to his friend, sometime detective Anthony Gethryn (George C. Scott), shortly before his own murder. So it was only logical that the film swathe the killer, George Brougham, played by Kirk Douglas, in heavy makeup for each of these disguises, turning the novel's intellectual game into a more frankly metafictional question: Can you recognize not only the character but the much better-known star beneath the makeup? Although stars from Douglas Fairbanks and Lon Chaney to Alec Guinness had disguised themselves to play multiple roles, Lewis had the idea of extending the masquerade still further, casting Burt Lancaster, Tony Curtis, Frank Sinatra, and Robert Mitchum in heavy makeup in cameo roles and daring the audience to identify them before the film's climax.

Many of the film's other leading features followed from this idea. The emphasis on makeup so heavy that it would render some of the stars unrecognizable meant that, like *Some Like It Hot* four years earlier, it would have to be shot in black and white, even though Huston had shot seven of his last ten movies in color. The wish to begin dramatically, with a teasing sight of the chameleon killer at work, led to a pre-credit sequence in which the murderer sabotages an elevator in order to dispatch the latest victim on his list, a list that, as the film's title credit shows, also includes Adrian Messenger, whose name does not appear on the roster of potential victims he prepares for Gethryn in MacDonald's novel. The audience's presumed desire to spend time in the company of a recognizable Kirk Douglas necessarily reshaped the last third of the film, in which George Brougham, having dispatched all but the last of his targets, arrives undisguised at Gleneyre's estate in order to establish his bona fides before the climactic fox hunt Huston had insinuated into the story.

The film's most original touch was its refusal to end at the orthodox place. As the words "The End" appeared on the screen after the unmasking of the villain in death, Douglas's voiceover announced: "That's the end of the picture, but it's not the end of the mystery," introducing an epilogue of several brief sequences in which Curtis, Sinatra, Mitchum, and Lancaster successively removed their makeup and grinned into the camera before Douglas himself followed suit in the film's final shot, saying, "Ladies and gentlemen, this *is* the end." By mapping the killer's modus operandi onto the mechanics of its own production, *The List of Adrian Messenger* raised playfully serious questions about the relation between the killer's virtuoso masquerades and Hollywood stardom as simultaneously a construction of identity and a disguise for the performer's true identity.

Neither contemporaneous reviewers nor the paying audience were impressed by the film's cleverness. John Russell Taylor deftly summarized the prevailing opinion when he called it "a small joke of a film" and linked it to *Beat the Devil* as "the Huston films that seem to be made entirely for fun. The director doesn't give a damn—he will amuse himself, and if the rest of us aren't amused, well, that's just too bad." Yet Taylor, returning to the film five years later after watching its television broadcast, clearly found in it new depths in unexpected places, as he attested when he acutely observed that "in *The List of Adrian Messenger* . . . the digressions are the essential: the whole thing is a series of enigma variations on the theme of disguise, both within the film's proper context and beyond" (72).

Although Taylor does not pursue this point, the film's emphasis on the radical metaphor of disguise amounts to an attack on traditional notions of adaptation, since it calls into question the ability of audiences and analysts alike to identify the original object under adaptation. Indeed, the most outrageous revelations about the film's dependence on disguise extended this attack in disconcerting ways. Huston admitted after the film's release that "it was basically only Mitchum who did any acting among the cameo appearances" and confessed: "The rest of them . . . had a mask made of the actor who played them and then they'd peel it off at the end. It wasn't grand theft, but it was pretty close to it" (Grobel 526). Audiences who bridled at the news that the faces beneath the makeup were not even the faces the opening credits had promised were only attesting, more or less unwillingly, to the power of Huston's enigma variations outside the film's proper context. If audiences who had paid good money to see Curtis and Sinatra in heavy makeup were actually seeing stand-ins, were they being cheated of the intimacy, however momentary and attenuated, they expected with the original stars? And if they couldn't tell the difference, how were they being cheated, and what did the cheat reveal about their expectations?

Jan Merlin, the actor who doubled for the stars beneath the makeup and provided at least some of their characters' voices, compounded the accusations against the film when he published *Shooting Montezuma: A Hollywood Monster Story* in 2001. Partly at least because it is "dedicated to John Huston, Bud Westmore, John Chambers, and a number of other Hollywood personalities, who were inspiration for this fictional account, due to our mutual involvement in a vaguely similar enterprise" (9), *Shooting Montezuma* is widely regarded as a *roman à clef* formatted as a film treatment in which Merlin, casting himself as Kurt Mitchell, recounts his travails impersonating the different members of an all-star cast headed by Doug Cowan for *Montezuma*, a film shot largely on location in a glamorous but fearsome Brazil by charming, imperious, blarney-spouting veteran director Hugh Johnston. Merlin emphasizes his hero's long hours and physical suffering as he labors to stay in character under different prosthetic faces, the lack of respect he is accorded by the actors whose job he is doing, and his humiliating lack of recognition by Johnston, who reveals in a climactic scene that he has no idea who Kurt is even though he has just spent several months directing him in heavy disguise.

Shooting Montezuma is generally read as an attack on the callous practices that underlie Hollywood artifice in general and *The List of Adrian Messenger* in particular. Instead of taking Kurt Mitchell's legitimate complaints and Merlin's tell-all novel as undermining the film's claims to authenticity, however, it would be wiser to acknowledge that *The List of Adrian Messenger* makes precious few claims to authenticity and recognize Merlin's novel as still further exploring, developing, and often expressing exasperation with the film's central questions, which are quite remote from the central questions of the novel it adapts, and transforming them from questions about the relation between criminal impersonation and Hollywood impersonation to questions about the nature of Hollywood performance. Can you identify the big-name stars? How can you be sure that they're the real stars you've come to see and not lower-echelon impersonators? Since impersonators like Kurt Mitchell are paid much less money than the stars they are replacing even though what they are doing takes much more skill, what is the nature of stardom, and why are so many people so much more eager to see constructions of characters and stars than the much more interesting people who play them? What makes an actor a star, and what does it matter whether or not an actor is a star?

As its dedication suggests, Merlin's novel poses itself not only as a critique but also as an adaptation of Huston's film, whose entertainment value is greatly increased by some inside knowledge of the film's production. Merlin's unmasking of Hollywood acting as a series of second-order performances in which stand-ins aided by a host of makeup experts and other collaborators act the parts of the stars who are ostensibly acting the film's fictional characters, even though the stars appear only in those scenes in which they unmask themselves, indicates both the failure of Huston's film as a moral enterprise and a popular entertainment and the film's surprising success as an adaptation that keeps its enabling idea alive by provoking another equally subversive adaptation. However successful its products may be judged, the point of Huston's work is that he served as a midwife of the idea he was given by the film's producer, not as its sole, exclusive, and universally identified author.

One reason Sarris's brand of auteur criticism was so successful in America is that it offered both a reliable guide to movies a given audience was most likely to enjoy—a precursor, in its own way, of Netflix's algorithms for generating the most likely film affinities for an audience with a given viewing history—and a powerful counterstrike against Hollywood's general devaluation of authors. In its indifference to questions of authorship, always subordinated to the wish to make money by offering a reliable line of products under a given studio brand, the Hollywood industry reduced the authorship of directors to a verb or process, and a relatively subordinate one at that. Sarris rescued Hitchcock, Lang, and a dozen other pantheon directors from this neglect by anointing them artists in accord with a specifically Romantic notion of authorship. Focusing instead on adaptation offers the promise, not of rescuing Huston by providing a different metric for evaluating his films and his career, but of capitalizing on the status of authoring, or authorizing, as a verb to subordinate evaluation as a critical project to the analysis of adaptation, of filmmaking, of authorship as a process. Like Rick Altman's account of genre, which treats genres as "not the permanent *product* of a singular origin, but the temporary *by-product* of an ongoing *process*" of "genrification" (54, 62), this analysis would treat authorizing and adapting as incessant processes whose relatively transient by-products are the adaptations, works, and authors on which Western aesthetics has traditionally focused. Instead of isolating *The List of Adrian Messenger* or *Shooting Montezuma* as a distinct text to be judged in isolation, placing primary emphasis on authorship as a process would treat MacDonald's novel, Huston's film, and Merlin's *roman à clef* as examples of authorizing—an especially pregnant metaphor for adaptations so fascinated with the relationship between adaptations, disguises, and performances that are authorized and those that are not.

In fact, Huston's career suggests that adaptation, properly understood and emphasized, offers a radical alternative not only to the auteurism developed to address the problem of cinematic authorship but to two more general and venerable principles of Western aesthetics. The first is the classical view of the unity of the work of art as a *Ding an sich*, a discrete aesthetic object defined by its distinctness from the world and other works. Instead of focusing on the analysis and evaluation of these privileged objects, this critical approach focuses on the process through which they come to be. Nor is this process to be understood as *creative* because of the second challenge adaptation study offers romantic aesthetics. Considered as adaptors like Huston, filmmakers—or for that matter novelists and painters and composers and storytellers—are not creators of new objects but rather rereaders, revisers, and refashioners operating in a world in which objects are always less important than processes. As Huston himself has said, reacting to the *New York Times*'s description of him as a "bold visionary": "I'm a bold visionary with other people's work. I haven't originated my films in any true sense" (*John Huston Interviews* 159).

Skeptics may wonder whether this description is really accurate, or why we should take Huston at his word in self-descriptions like this one. What if it is merely a self-deprecating pose rather than an accurate description? In the end, however, it does not matter whether we take Huston at his word because the issue is not whether Huston describes his process accurately, but whether it is an illuminating way of describing him. Even if we resisted the temptation to take his description of the adaptive process as applying to him, nothing would prevent us from applying it to other adaptors.

It is indeed precisely in its application to other director-adaptors that this model proves its usefulness. Most of Ernst Lubitsch's films, for example, are adaptations, but they all come out looking and sounding like Lubitsch films. This thematic and stylistic consistency may or may not make him an auteur, but it certainly makes him an activist adaptor. Billy Wilder directs many adaptations, always works on his own screenplays, and ranges widely across genres. But his films have so many close verbal affinities, even though he has maintained that collaboration is forced on him by his uncertain ear for dialogue, that they would never be mistaken for anyone else's. Howard Hawks is never credited for his own screenplays but works across an even wider range of genres than Wilder—he might indeed be called the genre director par excellence—and sees himself, like Huston, as an adventurer who likes to shoot on location. Not surprisingly, he expressed his satisfaction with *Red River* (1948) by emphasizing his own adventure in making the film: "When you have to shift 3,000 head of cattle every time you shoot a new scene, that's hard work" (25). Rouben Mamoulian offers another analogue, since he is a stage-trained director who continues to serve diverse properties when he works in the movies, just as when he works in the theater. Michael Curtiz may be even more like Huston, although many of his films are not adaptations, because he sees his job as making films, not making Curtiz films. In fact, Curtiz suggests that the figures whose working methods are most likely to be illuminated by the model I have developed here are not auteurs but taskmasters, perhaps even studios rather than directors.

If Hitchcock's unitary, thematically integrated, dictatorial model of authorship, borrowing so liberally from literary models, was necessary to get film studies' foot in the door of the academy, Huston's collaborative, adventurous, variegated, process-oriented model may well be the next developmental step in analyzing both film adaptation and film authorship, and suggesting new ways of thinking about textual production and authorship in general. Toward the end of Huston's life, Andrew Sarris concluded his 1980 review of *Wise Blood*, which he evidently assumed would be Huston's valedictory film: "I shall never be that wild about his total career, but I am prepared to concede at long last that I have grossly underestimated his resourcefulness as an artist" ("Of Blood" 34). Sarris's enduringly low evaluation of Huston's total career is entirely consistent with his critical principles, but his emphasis on Huston's resourcefulness as an adaptor of an important but impossible novel—"I am not sure that Flannery O'Connor's vivid gargoyles belong on a movie screen," Sarris remarked (34)—represents a welcome new sensitivity on the part of Huston's most notable detractor. Only the concluding word, "artist," strikes a false note, one Huston would surely have greeted with a snort of derision.

Works Cited

Agee, James. "Undirectable Director." Agee, *Film Writings and Selected Journalism*. New York: Library of America, 1984. 366–82.
Altman, Rick. *Film/Genre*. London: BFI, 1999.
Andrews, Geoff. *The Director's Vision: A Concise Guide to the Art of 250 Great Filmmakers*. Chicago: Chicago Review P, 1999.
Bacall, Lauren. *By Myself and Then Some*. New York: HarperEntertaintment, 2005.

Brill, Lesley. *John Huston's Filmmaking*. Cambridge: Cambridge UP, 1997.
Brownstein, Rachel M. "Out of the Drawing Room, onto the Lawn." *Jane Austen in Hollywood*. Ed. Linda Troost and Sayre Greenfield. Lexington: UP of Kentucky, 2001. 13–21.
Cardwell, Sarah. Adaptation Revisited: Television and the Classic Novel. Manchester: Manchester UP, 2002.
Cartmell, Deborah, and Imelda Whelehan. "A Practical Understanding of Literature on Screen: Two Conversations with Andrew Davies." *The Cambridge Companion to Literature on Screen*. Ed. Cartmell and Whelehan. Cambridge: Cambridge UP, 2007. 239–51.
Fuller, Graham. "Cautionary Tale." 1996; rpt. in *Film/Literature/Heritage*, ed. Ginette Vincendeau. London: BFI, 2001. 77–81.
Fultz, James R. "A Classic Case of Collaboration: *The African Queen*." *Literature/Film Quarterly* 10.1 (1982): 13–24.
Grobel, Lawrence. *The Hustons*. New York: Scribner's, 1989.
Hawks, Howard. "Gunplay and Horses." Interview with David Austin. *Films and Filming* 15 (Oct. 1968): 25.
Hepburn, Katharine. *The Making of The African Queen: How I Went to Africa with Bogart, Bacall and Huston and Almost Lost My Mind*. New York: Knopf, 1987.
Higson, Andrew. "Re-presenting the National Past: Nostalgia and Pastiche in the Heritage Film." *British Cinema and Thatcherism: Fires Were Started*, ed. Lester D. Friedman. London: U College London P, 1993. 109–29.
Huston, John. *An Open Book*. New York: Knopf, 1980.
John Huston: The Man, the Movies, the Maverick. Dir. Frank Martin. Perf. Robert Mitchum, Paul Newman. Point Blank Productions, 1989. DVD.
Kael, Pauline. "Circles and Squares." 1963. Rpt. in Kael, *I Lost It at the Movies*. Boston: Atlantic Monthly P/Little, Brown, 1965. 292–319.
Krohn, Bill. *Hitchcock at Work*. London: Phaidon, 2000.
Laws, Page. "King Adapter: Huston's Famous and Infamous Adaptations of Literary Classics." *John Huston: Essays on a Restless Director*. 123–35.
Long, Robert Emmet, ed. *John Huston Interviews*. Jackson: UP of Mississippi, 2001.
Mailer, Norman. *Marilyn: A Biography*. New York: Grosset and Dunlap, 1973.
Merlin, Jan. *Shooting Montezuma: A Hollywood Monster Story*. N.p.: Xlibris, 2001.
Nichols, Peter M., ed. *The New York Times Guide to the Best 1,000 Movies Ever Made*. New York: Times Books, 1998.
Osteen, Mark, ed. *Hitchcock and Adaptation: On the Page and Screen*. Lanham, MD: Rowman and Littlefield, 2014.
Ross, Lillian. *Picture*. 1952: rpt. New York: Garland, 1985.
Sarris, Andrew. *The American Cinema: Directors and Directions, 1929–1968*. New York: Dutton, 1968.
———, ed. *Interviews with Film Directors*. 1967; rpt. New York: Avon, 1969.
———. "Of Blood and Thunder and Despair." *Village Voice* 25.8 (25 Feb. 1980): 34.
Taylor, John Russell. "John Huston and the Figure in the Carpet." *Sight and Sound* 38.2 (Spring 1969): 70–72.

Tracy, Tony, and Roddy Flynn, eds. *John Huston: Essays on a Restless Director.* Jefferson: McFarland, 2010.
Truffaut, François, with Helen G. Scott. *Hitchcock.* Revised ed. New York: Simon and Schuster, 1984.

Part I

Aesthetics and Textuality

1

Murray Pomerance

A Passing Node

The Asphalt Jungle

> Changing shadows would flit over his face, and sometimes an almost rational light would appear in his eyes—but nonetheless all that could be said of him was that he was immobile—a distressing immobility, exhausting for the gaze that sought a hint of conscious life in it.
>
> —Vladimir Nabokov, *The Luzhin Defense*

Where

"Say it," wrote William Carlos Williams, "no ideas but in things." Cinema is entirely material, an organization of moving reflections of moving things, and the story of a film is but the career line upon which the reflections of a moment are hung.

We have to find a place to set all this, not just a set of coordinates by a collection of shapes and shadows, passageways, rooms, the penumbra of streetlamps. This setting needs to crackle with faded promise and disappointment, the drooping shadows of industry gone to pasture, empty streets in which civilians no longer wish to parade their hopes, a peculiar kind of darkness: not merely night, but that part of the night which is night's nocturne, the night of night, so that all of the creatures who live there in confederate secrecy can come out from under the rocks. Think of John Sloan's "Six O'Clock, Winter" (1912) or of Philip Church's *Furnace Harbor*, and you'll understand the peculiar, post-Depression, pre-LED darkness:

> This night in Furnace Harbor will give you a morning and empty you for the rest of your life. This is your Cemetery Hill, buddy, and no shrink will ever be able to explain why from this night forward you will imagine nothing more to desire.

It is the very late 1940s. If wartime production is at a halt, still the assembly lines have not perked up again, and the women who made artillery shells have been sent home to bake and sweep and mourn. Producer Arthur Hornblow Jr. to Rudolf Monta of the MGM Legal Department on June 11, 1949: "Answering your memo of June 9th, it seems to add up to a conclusion that committing an act of libel is almost inevitable in the event we place the action of *Asphalt Jungle* against the background of an actual city. Nevertheless, in view of the need for reality, I should like to continue to pursue with you a course which, while protecting us legally, can still perhaps achieve the desired result." Then: "It would be an aid to us if you also could suggest a city, preferably large and preferably in the middle-west, that we might approach on this point. St. Louis, Minneapolis or Kansas City would be acceptable but there are several others that could replace them. . . . John Huston and I would be grateful for your affirmative assistance" (Hornblow to Monta, June 11, 1949). Nota bene: "the need for reality." Certainly in the film, certainly from the point of view of the artists and the marketers, who intend to show the American public a picture of its own most repressed, most nocturnal, darknesses, but also as a general condition of life after the war. The producer identifies a "need for reality," as though the war was a kind of shapeless *cauchemar*, the need to put a clarifying light upon things, and to have them linger in darkness just in order that the clarifying light should best do its work. And note, too, "grateful for your affirmative assistance"; "affirmative" assistance, not just assistance, because having been at MGM already for seven years, Hornblow was no stranger to Rudy Monta's circumlocutions, denials, reproachments, demurrers. The job of the legal deptartment was to tell these creative people why they oughtn't to do things, and Monta was very good at his job.

July 8, he replies: "We will have to find a city that would cooperate, permitting photography in and out of their buildings, etc., and obtaining for us releases of necessary persons, where the facts or their position would give grounds pointing to identification" (Monta to Hornblow, July 8, 1949). This won't happen, says Monta, without a final script we can show them. We have to have a final script. What spurred this was a letter Hornblow had written to the new production chief, Dore Schary, a month earlier, to the effect that he and Huston felt a "fictitious odor" would attach to falsely naming a city; and he shared this concern with Monta. "The *city* itself is a character in this story. The city is the Asphalt Jungle. And it is in the true-to-life and fresh handling of the crime problem of such a city that our picture finds both its theme and its strength. . . . It is our plan to use the background of an actual city" (Hornblow to Monta, June 2, 1949). On behalf of the studio, Monta was characteristically squeamish: "To obtain the reality desired of any actual city it means that everyone will know" (Monta to Hornblow, June 9, 1949).

St. Louis, Minneapolis, Jersey City, Kansas City, and Chicago would not do: rather the once great urban center of the Midwest, now

Figure 1.1. Dix crosses through the fallen and baroque landscape of a decaying urban center.

fallen, with its looming baroque mansions and its railroad skirting the Ohio: Cincinnati. No matter what it looks like in real life, it submits to John Huston's portraiture, through the armature of Harold Rosson's camera; it comes out angular and broken, staggering, stolid—George Tice's Paterson with the sun turned out—a zone of pure intentions: the urgent railroad, the broad asphalt playing field of the streets. This is where things happen. This is where America becomes itself, the clash of personalities making sparks. You don't get realer than this, emptied for the rest of your life; you don't have any unresolved, itching need for reality.

Doc

The story, such as it is—no, it's not really a story, it's a meeting—centers upon Doc Riedenschneider (Sam Jaffe), just out of stir, very much an old hack (an artisan) who has all his tricks in order; a queer old owl whose eyes never stop scanning for approaching goons. He's out, therefore, but he's in; dressed in a hat and necktie as though strapped into striped pajamas, imprisoned for the rest of his life. He breezes into town (one of the prevalent conceits of modernity: denying that the city is a city by calling it "town") and meets the pimp bookie Cobby (Marc Lawrence), a creature who gives new meaning to the word "unctuous," persuading him that he has a great plan for a massive jewel heist if only he can get bankrolled. Cobby consults his puppeteer, the gracile and dirty-handed lawyer Emmerich (Louis Calhern), who buys in. A team is put together, including, as thug, Dix Handley (Sterling Hayden)—a handleyman; as cracker, the loyal Catholic family type Louis Ciavelli (Anthony Caruso); as driver, Dix's pal Gus Minissi (James Whitmore), humpbacked cat lover and staunch loyalist. Police commissioner Hardy (John McIntire) is hot for publicity and aggressive for arrests; his lieutenant Ditrich (Barry Kelley) has been on Cobby's take for some time, but will do anything to save his own skin. As for Emmerich, even bolstered by a suspicious private detective, Brannom (Brad Dexter), he is hopelessly down in the gutter. The involvement with Doc and his team becomes fatal. The girl he has been keeping in a lovers' nook, Angela Phinlay (Marilyn Monroe), is either an innocent waif floating through the filthy channel of the action or a canny, utilitarian grifter; we never have an opportunity to know.

Everything goes wrong except the heist itself. A guard shoots Louis during the escape, and he is brought home to his wife to die. The ambitious Hardy sets Ditrich to prey on Cobby, forcing the names of the robbers from this coward who would trade his mother to avoid pain. Doc and Dix confront Emmerich with their booty, demanding payment, but he begs off, having no money in hand. When Brannom suddenly pulls a gun, Dix kills him, but not before being shot. Gus is arrested, as is Cobby. Creeping around the rail yards at night, Doc and the wounded Dix are confronted by a cop who beats Doc on the head. The two retreat to Dix's girl Doll's (Jean Hagen) apartment for nursing and then Doc makes his way out of town, only to be caught at a roadhouse where he has been entranced by a teenaged girl dancing to music from a jukebox. With Doll as company, Dix drives all the way to his horse farm in Kentucky, dying as he crosses the fields. If in film noir generally, as R. Barton Palmer points out, the detective "remains beyond the reach of the criminal" (84), here at least some of the criminals exceed the reach of the detective.

Doc Riedenschneider is a European gentleman, and perhaps, indeed, something of a doctor—another mystery: does he "doctor" safes and jewel caches, or was he once a medical man, now unfrocked and sent to work on the dark side? He knows his etiquette—how to bow to a lady, how to lay a bevy of nickels on a tabletop so an eager girl can dance all night—knows the way around the social machine. We would peg him as an immigrant from Berlin, probably a man who fled the Nazis, got into trouble in the US of A, never stops feeling hunted. Delivered by taxi to Cobby's book joint, he's got some ideas for a good heist: Cobby (Marc Lawrence) can set anybody up with anybody.

A note about Doc's nationality, since his *echt* Germanity runs considerably deeper than a demonstration of fluid sociability and a sense of decorum: late in the film, fleeing for his life after the jewel heist collapses in its finale, the old man falls into a taxicab and persuades the driver to take him to Cleveland. They get to talking, each, as it turns out, a German émigré. Doc has found his haven in this moving cab—a quintessentially American idea, the merger of *heimlichkeit* and continuous mobility—and we have the sense, now as the plot is almost entirely unwound, that in this flickering darkness, and for the very first time in our view, he is able to relax. While Doc does not actually pronounce the words "They don't understand," Jaffe's delicate performance allows us to grasp his deep thought that American culture is an alien one: the way that when he discovers the driver is German he settles back into his seat; the curling smile on his lips; his casual use of German words to salt his English ones:

Doc: Sie haben Verwandten in Deutschland.

Schurz: Ach, ja. Sie sprechen gut Deutsch.

Doc: I haven't spoken German for a long, long time.

SCHURZ: You have a München accent.

DOC: Naturlich, I was born there! But you know what they say: Home is where the money is.

He addresses the driver, whose license tabs him as Frank Schurz, as Franz:

DOC: Let's not stop here [for gas] . . . Let's wait until we get out of town, then we can do everything at once. Have a little meal, beer, cigar, and go in comfort.

SCHURZ: I can see you're a man who likes his pleasures.

DOC: Well, Franz, what else is there in life, I ask you.

Doc's talk is an appeal to a culture now regarded as decadent and defeated, a place where pleasure rules. (He wants a *German* beer.) Here in America, he implies, where you and I are outsiders, Franz, there is too much strife, too much angst, too much confusion. They can't understand us, can't appreciate the correct and *gemutlich* way of being that allows for a genteel cigar, a moment of patient reflection, a focus on things which are good in life.

The cabbie is by far the younger man, probably in his midthirties (the actor, Henry Rowland, was thirty-six during shooting). We can put Riedenschneider at about fifty-five or fifty-six, and thus imagine that in 1929, he himself was the driver's age. Schurz is thus a living memorial—incitement—and Riedenschneider a fading pointer to a recollection or reconstitution of Germany in 1929, that "année terrible," in Harry Graf Kessler's words. "One piece after another of the world, as I and my generation knew it, disappears," with Hugo von Hofmannsthal, Gustav Stresemann, and Serge Diaghilev all dying and the German economy dropping into "another freefall in the months and years that followed: banks closed; businesses shut; unemployment rocket[ing] skyward" (Eksteins; Kessler qtd. in Eksteins 306). As indicated by the etiquette of their brief conversation, the Germany to which Doc and Schurz implicitly refer in meeting one another is a lost paradise of formalities and décor, even in its underbelly.

Also called up in Doc's pervading *gemutlichkeit* is a shadow of another Germany, the one that would have been most prominent in viewers' minds in 1950 and to which Schurz, in his somewhat porcine personification, makes explicit reference. This is the Germany that Wolfgang

Schivelbusch refers to as a "culture of defeat," the nation that lost World War II (Ekstains shows how the rise of Hitlerianism was a direct response to the cultural agonies of the late 1920s in Berlin). Now working for the "Globe Cab Co.," Schurz gives the distinct appearance, with his fleshy face gaudily overlit (to suggest the glare of oncoming traffic), of a man who fought in the Wehrmacht and later found his way to America or a man related to soldiers back home. He has a fixed stare (at once that of a man watching the road and that of a zealot), and he responds to Doc's requests and hints with a fully registered authoritarian submissiveness (see Adorno), as though still functioning in a rigid vertical hierarchy. After the Second World War, Germans who were established in North America carried an aura of self-protective, always defensive strangeness, as though they were implicitly always enemies in hiding. One sees this spelled out pointedly with the character of Keller in Hitchcock's brilliant *I Confess* (1953): a killer, a liar, a coward, and also (and like both Schurz and Doc) a man whose "bulbous, ravenous eyes . . . see everything not only analytically but with a certain exigent and cupidinous *Weltschmerz*— Nietzschean eyes, certainly; eyes that incorporate and digest; greedy eyes that strain to limit and possess through definition" (Pomerance 186).

Jaffe's huge eyes are the signal operative marks of his personality as Riedenschneider. He sees too much; he cannot see enough. Is he grasping for a vision in his helplessness and alienation, or is he using his eyes to control and dispossess his associates and victims? He recalls Lang's Mabuse in these "occult powers of his vision, his ability to hypnotize victims at a distance, bend them to his will through a focused stare. . . . The gaze operates as a ray of power" (Gunning 106). We see this emphatically when Doc confronts the embarrassed, squeamish Emmerich who hasn't managed to muster the fence money for the robbery take; and when he bids farewell to the wounded henchman, Dix, staring at him hard and sincerely, his hungry eyes wide open, while Dix urges him to take a gun ("You shoot a policeman—ah, bad rap, hard to beat. You don't carry a gun, you give up when they hold one on you"). "That square-head, he's a funny little guy. I don't get him at all," Dix muses to Doll, and with eyes glittering and soft in withdrawal she replies, "Maybe it's because he's a foreigner. They just don't think like us."

Dix

"There are very few actors who can make you believe they think," Orson Welles told Peter Bogdanovich, adding, "not that they're thinking about what they're saying, but that they think outside of the scene" (Welles et al. 302). Of all the members of the very striking cast in *The Asphalt Jungle*, only one manages, here as in his other film appearances, to convey this impression, and that is Sterling Hayden. Partly contributory is his habit with that opened mouth, the way preparation for speech immediately precedes speech, as though he is working out the best syntax. But there is also a peculiar quality to Hayden's gaze, which seems, in a particular way, transcendent. While he is openly and plainly regarding the other persons in a scene, even detecting and manipulating key objects, he is also, and evocatively, engaged in examining a world that is outside the one under presentation. He is seeing consequences, causes, histories, futures, implications, side effects. He has a view of things in a wider frame than the camera can capture, a view of the "greater" reality of which the circumstantial moment, given to us here and now, is but a passing node.

Dix has a looming presence, a tall and ponderous body, a thick gaze. He is to be taken seriously. Indeed, he has been brought onto the Bellatier heist project by that sheister-macher-bookie Cobby as "muscle," since here and there a morsel of aggression might be needed. Late in the film, to be sure, confronting a police guard near the railway yards late at night, he is called upon to be brutal in order to protect Doc, whom the guard has recognized and set upon. But the scene, played with the veteran character player Ray Teal, could have been added to the script merely to give pretext for the characterization of Dix as tough, since what he brings to his appearances more than the ability to manhandle and fight is an indomitable sense of purpose, a fixity of intent, a thrusting forward drive, an entrenched sense of etiquette (thus, for all his relatively inarticulate bluff, an urbane civility), and a poetic tenderness. Doll knows that there is more to Dix than posture and strength, knows that he has feelings.

It is a feeling, feline, furtive Dix we meet at the film's opening, after all; with the cops on his tail, he begs the help of Gus in hiding his gun after a petty crime. It is with moral outrage and an offended sense of propriety that Dix confronts Cobby for having blurted out a comment about Dix owing him money in front of the stranger, Doc Reidenschneider. It is with awkwardness, even reticence, that Dix hits the jewelry store watchman, who, firing his gun, lacks precise aim and hits the safecracker, Louis, by accident. At Emmerich's after the robbery, there is trouble of a different kind. The lawyer hasn't got the money to pay for the jewels, and his private detective/collaborator Brannom pulls a gun on Dix and Doc. Dix kills him, but he is shot in the event, forced now to endure the final act of the film in wounded condition. He reveals his greatest vulnerabilities only to Doll: the memory of a black colt pitching him into a fence. An alien to the city, he pines for the Kentucky horse farm where he grew up (this is in a scene "clearly intended," as James Naremore suggests, "to elicit sympathy by evoking popular memories of the Great Depression" [129]). "One of my ancestors imported the first Irish thoroughbred into our county," he boasts.[1] In a quiet scene, as Doc prepares to leave Doll's apartment where she has been tending to him, Dix goes beyond civility to a kind of inviolable honor as he refuses any payment from Doc at all. He has no use for the jewels he is offered, and he sweetly brushes off Doc's promise of sending him money. The film's final sequence shows him driving frantically with Doll to make it to the horse farm, and as the car pulls off the road he staggers out of it and across the field of high grass only to collapse in his dying moment with the thoroughbreds pausing in their feeding to walk up and, in close shot, nuzzle his tranquil corpse.

For all his pretenses to action, Dix is a country boy trapped in city life, a spirit nourished by sunshine trapped in darkness, until our last moment with him (which is our last moment with all of it).

Lon

This is one of Louis Calhern's really momentous performances. Always an actor of consummate polish and articulateness, one of his hallmarks was a way of holding his tall, portentous frame aloft, with his chin kept high in untrammeled dignity. Consider the king in *The Student Prince* (1954), Caesar in *Julius Caesar* (1953), Zapt in *The Prisoner of Zenda* (1952), Oliver Wendell Holmes in *The Magnificent Yankee* (1950), Buffalo Bill in *Annie Get Your Gun* (1950), the spymaster Preston in *Notorious* (1946), to cite just some. But here he manages through artful pauses, shifting gaze, an obsessive and preening self-regard, and an excess of personal grooming to suggest a creature entirely collapsed inside his dignified-looking shell, "really, on the spot, trying to hide naked nerves with charm," as Budd Schulberg put it (Letter to Huston). The posture, the height, the towering personality, the sense of power: all lies. Emmerich, we come quickly to sense, has always been a liar, always been in flight. His ostentatious home with its wood-paneled study and glowing ornaments is only another shell in his monstrous shell game. But what Calhern brings to this portrait is considerably more than a falsity and self-denial. There is almost a glow to the palpably wormy cowardice of his inner self, so that finally, as he stands with Dix and Doc in the embarrassing position of admitting he has no funds, he gains our pity.

Alonzo (Lon) Emmerich's is surely the most strategic intelligence in the film; while Riedenschneider possesses a relentless practicality, Lon's thoughts are philosophical and sociological. He is an observer of things as they are, able to know (calmly) of the criminals he interacts with that they are citizens like all others, in most ways perfectly normal people, but playing by a different set of rules: "Nothing so different about them. After all, crime is only a left-handed form of human endeavour." In this detached regard, he foreshadows ethnographical approaches to deviance, as typified by Mary McIntosh's study of craft thieving. "The effect of the increased importance of planning in thieving," she writes, "has been the emergence of the role of entrepreneur and team leader and it may be that some men are able to establish themselves in this role by developing contacts that give them access to information; a reputation for successful planning and leadership, and contacts with skilled and reliable colleagues" (124).

This is, of course, a virtual formula for the plot arrangement of *The Asphalt Jungle*, as well as of other heist films of the time, such as Kubrick's *The Killing* (1956). But a clinching comment from McIntosh establishes the moral neutrality of thieving: "The picture is rather reminiscent of the way in which a small builder and decorator gather together a team including plumbers and electricians to carry out a house conversion" (125). In short, thieving is a form of renovation. The "team leader" in the present event is Riedenschneider, not the ostensibly puissant Emmerich; the *echt* as opposed to the assimilated, thus *ersatz landsmann*. Emmerich's impracticality becomes inflamed enough to be visible in a number of scenes. With Brannom he is distinctly ill at ease, although the detective is his flunky. It is as though he fears being attacked, both physically and verbally, so that their conversation is a sparring match. With Cobby he is aloof and condescending, playing out his controlling position, yet the indelicateness of this rubs against Cobby and undermines his questionable position further: Cobby's weakness will prove the faulty keystone in the heist architecture. And in the culminating payoff scene, Emmerich's failure to have arranged for the funds to recompense Doc and his too-eager haste to claim storage rights for the jewels reveal openly to us—but worse, openly to Doc—the man's amateur status, his clumsiness as a professional.

Calhern works through his scenes with a delicious combination of gestures: the moist lips seem always posing; the hungry eyes seem always to be calculating for possession; but the hands, large and fleshy, dangle in the air helplessly. Before his suicide he attempts a note to his wife, but the fingers holding the pen won't do the critical, mundane work of carving out the apology. Lon's one act of dexterity, prefacing his quick withdrawal of the pistol from his desk drawer, is his ripping the note up and tossing it away. "The audience should feel that he [Emmerich] is committing suicide out of disgust and despair at the ruin he has brought on himself," Joseph Breen wrote to Louis B. Mayer (October 6, 1949) and then, a few weeks later, "Emmerich is committing suicide out of disgust and despair, rather than as a means of evading the law. This is essential" (October 24, 1949)—essential, but also illustrative. Even killing himself to evade the law would be an act of skill on Emmerich's part, and he cannot put his hands to such pathetic dexterity. "It was necessary that the man destroy himself; it was an integral part of the story," Huston recollected. He went on to say,

> What made it objectionable to the censors was the fact that the man was in his right mind: no man in his right mind kills himself. . . . I came up with an idea to which they agreed. I had him write the note and—like a writer who is dissatisfied with what he's done—crumple it up. The man is a lawyer, literate and well read, but here he can't get what he wants to say down on paper. He tries again and crumples another sheet of paper; he's incapable of lucid thought. He just shoots himself. This was enough to indicate, for the censors' purposes, that he was not in his right mind. (84)

Lon's housekeeping set-up for Angela is notable for its coziness, its rich décor, and the fact that nothing about it appears to be particularly secret. Although the wife never mentions it, and possibly doesn't know about it, everyone else who needs to reach Lon knows exactly where to go. His disloyalty to the wife is thus coupled with (married to) a sense of high-born privilege, the right to behave as the aristocrats do. In a way, there is something European in the origin of Huston's depiction of this part of Lon's character. Typically, on the American scene, the unfaithful husband enacts his secret love affair furtively and in the dark, but all the scenes with Angela are sumptuous, fully lit, even playful. Except for the fact that Monroe is so much younger than Calhern (this was her first screen appearance; Howard Hawks told Huston she was "a real find" [Hawks to Huston]), they could seem wedded; as it is, only her suggestive clothing blocks us from seeing Angela as Lon's daughter or niece. In fact, her pet appellative for him is "Uncle Lon" (thus invoking the repressive knot of the incest taboo and presenting open sexuality at once).

Emmerich is simultaneously portentous and powerless, the shade of a monarch and the incorporation of a fool. The language of Emmerich and Doc is eloquent, and because of this we find an affinity between the two men, one a poser and the other frank and down to earth but caught in the throes of nostalgia.

Bob

Emmerich's detective "friend" is a youthful and unctuous viper, resentful and chafing over his necessary link to a man he can neither respect nor admire. Emmerich isn't capable as an enforcer or as a man, but Brannom sees himself as talented in both areas. As they wait for Doc and Dix to arrive after the heist, Emmerich says that Angela is at her sister's, and Brannom retorts, with a supposedly knowing smile, "She says!" He's been drinking, perhaps too much, and claims, "Half drunk I've got better wits than most people," revealing an inflated self-estimation. He's been working hard at being a student and says, "I should have been in the money years ago. You big boys—what have you got? Front—nothing but front." His estimation of Emmerich as a standing façade is hardly inaccurate, but he is arrogant in thinking himself a more substantial human being; and it is only resentment that makes him consider "big boys" in relation to himself, crave their stature, and hate them for maintaining a position he values and would like to have himself but does not and cannot, because under his own glossy front he's little more than a gunsel.

Brannom is a man who will be fast on the trigger; which is to say, he is eager to have his finger where it counts, and itching in the finger. Nothing about Brannom suggests the wisdom that calmly evaluates targets and chooses the most strategic ones. He will draw on Dix and pay for it with his life. Emmerich will be left to cart him to the river and drop his body from a high pier into the darkness.

J. H.

Every character we meet in the film is as rounded, as complex, and as desperately incongruent as Lon, Angela, Doc, and Dix. This provides no particular evidence of the way they are drawn in W. R. Burnett's 1929 novel or of the way they have been transposed in the screenplay. "It is very rarely that one comes across such a fascinating group of characters as you have gathered in this script," Huston's correspondent "Hugh" wrote to him late in 1949 ("Gray" memo). However, not everyone associated with the production held this view. "Picture-wise, it leaves much to be desired in the way of construction," wrote Bill Cole. "Interest is vested largely in characterization rather than plot, and its episodic telling destroys any thought of dramatic flow or rhythm" (Cole). I have tried in my way of organizing this little homage to recapture some of this "destruction." What the eccentricity of the characters really speaks to, and quite idiosyncratically in this *noir* of *noirs*, is the viscerally poetic sensibility of John Huston, whose Gaelic roots and enormous personal charm affected all who met him. This is a sensibility touched by "holy madness":

> Our greatest blessings, says Socrates in the *Phaedrus*, come to us by way of madness—provided, he adds, that the madness comes from the god. Our real choice is between holy and unholy madness: open your eyes and look around you—madness is in the saddle anyhow. Freud is the measure of our unholy madness, as Nietzsche is the prophet of the holy madness, of Dionysus, the mad truth. . . . Resisting madness can be the maddest way of being mad. (Brown 1–2)

Yet what makes Huston's filmmaking masterly, and *The Asphalt Jungle* an epitome of his mastery, is his own evocative *handling* of the dramatic material so as to embody his riddling charm upon the screen.

A glowing example of Huston's power to arrange is given by a particular feature of the climactic confrontation scene, where Dix, Doc, Brannom, and Emmerich meet to arrange the payoff for the heist. Doc is in possession of the jewels. Dix is alert and observant, perennially distrustful. He doesn't want to be here at all and would always rather be on the farm with his horses, even when in Doll's arms. Brannom is nervous, a little too expectant. Emmerich has had his mask pulled down. The shooting plan supports an editing structure in which we will cut from

Figure 1.2. A faint shadow of uncertainty begins to form on Doc's otherwise fully lit face as he realizes he has been deceived.

character close-up to character close-up, bouncing around the room in a staccato fashion, although not quickly, as the pregnant lines of dialogue are delivered, opening our awareness point by point of Emmerich's falseness, Brannom's cupidity and incontinence, Doc's shocked but always wise disappointment. But as the shots proceed, we may also discover something Huston has arranged in making them, perhaps keeping in mind one of the prevailing critical myths about film noir: as Paul Schrader influentially noted, "Actors and setting are often given equal lighting emphasis. . . . In *film noir*, the central character is likely to be standing in the shadow." (57) Or as Janey Place and Lowell Peterson reflect, "It is the constant opposition of areas of light and dark that characterizes *film noir* cinematography" (67).

Scene 16 of the Final Shooting Script

We are in Emmerich's cottage, as he paces nervously awaiting Doc and Dix with their haul, and Brannom lies back on the sofa comforting himself with a drink. As Emmerich lets the thieves in, his shadow projected on the inside of the door reduces his head to a long oval with a sharply projecting nose. "Everything go all right?" asks Emmerich, and Doc shakes his briefcase to let the fabulous sound of jewels ring through. Emmerich introduces Brannom. He leads them into the living room but stopping on the way to eye Brannom is Dix, his face fully bathed in light. Emmerich eagerly bets that that "thing" is full of koohinoors [Indian diamonds] and grand moguls. Emmerich's head is at three-quarter angle, screen left. Doc faces him and the camera. Light comes from the left and beneath, on Doc's face, his eyes wide open, his eyebrows furrowed under his homburg. As Doc sits and refuses a drink, the lighting contrast on his face intensifies, with the right side in darkness and the left openly and flatly lit. Emmerich asks for a look, and Doc stands and opens his case as we cut to a medium shot of Emmerich, as he bends over the case, which is in the foreground. Brannom is at rear. There is full lighting on Emmerich, with accentuating hot spots on his forehead (simulating perspiration—to indicate his nervousness) and on his craving lower lip. Brannom stands to look from behind at Emmerich, lit on the left side with hot spots on his ear and temple and his lips drawn. For all his braggadocio, the jewels make him anxious, too.

Doc scoops the jewels back into his briefcase, while Emmerich and Brannom coo at one another, and Dix looks on coldly. Doc is sitting again, with a table lamp at left, but his face is lit frontally with a stronger light than the lamp provides, and there is a gleam in his eyes.

Interaction

With eyelids lifted and frontal lighting, Doc stands in Emmerich's face. "I'd just like to see the color of your money." Emmerich stalls, his mouth open, showing gleaming teeth. The jowls are keylit, the temple still radiant. He is clearly flushed. Brannom, behind him, is in shadow, looking askance. Emmerich: "Gentlemen, I must admit at this moment I, uh . . . I'm embarrassed." He lifts a cigarette to cover his mouth, turning his head to screen right, a shadowed area, so that the hot lighting on his face quickly falls away.

Doc looks worried. His shadowy cheek and temple onscreen right dominate structurally and make his eyes now appear dark. "You mean you haven't got the money, Mr. Emmerich?"

Emmerich admits he hasn't got it. "No!" His mouth is wide open, we are looking from below, and there are no teeth visible; instead a wide, black maw. There is a tighter balance between the light on the left side of his face (as we look) and the darker right side. His face seems to be flattening (in withdrawal, in fear). As he turns his head, the hot flash on his forehead is gone. His blood has gone cold. "That's a large sum of money, you know. Considering present conditions. And considering that we had to have it in cash."

A close shot of Dix follows. He is looking offscreen right to where Brannom is sitting. There is a shadow on the left side of his face and pinpoint hot spots in his eyes to indicate intense concentration. Under the brim of his hat most of his hair is obscured by a halo of darkness. His lips are turned down. Emmerich announces that a few days more are needed.

Cut to Brannom seated on the sofa, a lamp to his right that is lighting the right side of his face. There is also light on his left-side upper cheek. But the lower cheek and the left side of the mouth are in shadow, as is the left of the body and both arms. He looks up and left, at Dix, and his eyes are evenly lit and bulbous.

Doc tells Emmerich courteously that although a few days more may not seem like a very long time, it does to him. As he speaks frankly, directly, and politely, there is full lighting on his face, but keylights accentuate his piercing gaze.

A close shot of Emmerich from below follows as he states, "I understand." He looks genteel with full lighting on his face, but still has a hot spot on the left side of his brow. He asks if they trust him, opening his eyes and mouth together. His lower teeth show dimly. The rest of his mouth is black. His opened eyes are watery, and there are pinpoint key spots in his eyes. There is also key lighting at the tip of his nose and on the bridge of his forehead, making him seem anxious and withdrawn (the eyes themselves lie in a plane behind his "hot" nose and brow). "If you don't, well, there's nothing I can say except that I'm . . . sorry."

Then comes a macroclose shot of Doc, light shining not only onto his chin, mouth, brow, cheeks, and eyes, but also onto the underbrow of his hat (so that he looks civil, cultured, proper). His little moustache, in this flood of light, is diminished, and his lips, dry and drawn tightly, give no hint of his thought. His eyes, keylit, continue to stare off left and a little upward at Emmerich. Doc turns his head slightly. "Mr. Emmerich, what are you trying to say?" With the eyes squinting, there is suddenly a curtain of shadow on his upper left brow and on the lower right side of his face, as though a curtain of uncertainty has been pulled over him.

Emmerich says, "It wouldn't be safe for you to carry that stuff around, you said so yourself." And again there is a macroclose shot of Doc, but now with shadows dropping upon his cheeks and his eyes blazing like coals. Lighting models his jowels so that the lines frame his outraged mouth. Now Emmerich says the police won't be coming to search *his* house. We see him put a cigarette into his mouth, and his head is turned in such a way that the glow on his temple is a crown of superiority; a second glow on his cheekbone makes him seem proud, dignified, peachy, pure. "You, on the other hand, Doc, you're . . . you're just out of prison." Cut to a straight-on macroclose shot of Doc, the hat a saddle of darkness on his head, darkness flooding the right side of his face, and the brilliant key light on the left of him making his ear pop out receptively, passively.

It is not necessary for me to pursue this interaction in order to make plain the central development within it, since the rest of the scene works its way out, albeit with increasing dramatic tension, using the same structural elements of tightly designed lighting and variant camera distance in play with the specific lines of the script. As to those extraordinary close-ups—Francesco Casetti writes about what happens in cinema when on the screen "a face, body, or thing suddenly grows. . . . The face, the thing, the body have come out of their most intimate sphere. They turn themselves over to their observer"; and then he quotes Jean Epstein's remarks on "grossissement" from 1921: "The close-up changes the drama . . . Pain is within one's reach. . . . I have never had a face so close to mine. It follows me from so near, and I seek it face to face" (147–48). In the scene as a whole, what we must see is a feature of the filmmaking standing upon the fact that the conversational quality and the adversarial nature of the relationships involved call for a shot/countershot structure and thus for repeated use of the same character set-ups in edited alternation. The way Huston shoots this, however, involves more than straightforward repetition (as is so often used in films noir of the B-movie variety). With each new visit to a character, he and his cinematographer, Harold Rosson, keep the camera positions more or less identical but make subtle alterations in the lighting design. This allows for two eventualities that mark *The Asphalt Jungle* as a special kind of approach to the problem of cinema.

First, time is allowed to pass explicitly onscreen. While we can always have an implicit sensation of temporality, owing to the progression of the plot, it is also possible in situations like this for a sense of temporal freeze to infect the viewer, each shot of a protagonist being more or less interchangeable with each other shot. While a conversation "progresses," then, it also stagnates; character qualities are expanded; conflicts are magnified, and the poses through which they manifest themselves are made statuesque. Here, however, Emmerich and Riedenschneider maintain their vivacity through the scene; seem to breath from moment to moment; and move forward not only strategically, through the enunciation of variously developed positions, but also personally, through a progression across a continuity of moods. As time becomes more vivacious, the viewer is in suspense not only dramaturgically but also emotionally, and the characters become rounded and fleshy. Another way to put this: Rosson's variable lighting, under Huston's direction, assists the performers in mounting what can be taken as "lifelike" representations. In more static filming designs, the actor must resort to crescendos and diminuendos of vocalization to effect a similar sense of vivacity, but optically nothing changes: even if one isn't really looking, the scene seems alive. Here the liveliness comes through our gaze.

Second, and as a more generalized case of this specific, a greater potential of cinema is brought to the fore than normally is used for conversational scenes. (And I should emphasize that I have arbitrarily chosen one part of one scene; this film is filled with scenes that work in this way or according to some other delicate and infusive plan.) Not only is a plot continued here through shot fragmentation and editorial restitching, but the variation among the shots allows for a parallel line of comment to appear and be interpreted by viewers, in this case a line related to characters' flickering attitudes and alignments, varying and developing states of confidence and fear. All of the mounting tension in the scene is implicit in the dialogue, but here we go far beyond merely having ciphers reading out their lines. As the characters grow and darken, we may come to see that lighting is as much a part of scenic design and of performance as camera placement, actorly expression, and editorial pace. The lighting is coming from the level of the film itself, rather than from the reality being diegetically reproduced; that is, none of the lighting is entirely accounted for by the visible diegetic sources. What we get, then, is filmmaking that depends for its full success on the viewer's optical engagement, filmmaking that goes beyond the script in rendering a circumstance ongoing and a developmental at a level no character is in a position to articulate. The characters speak, but so does the film, simultaneously.

While I would hardly choose to argue that John Huston is the only filmmaker who works this way, it does seem valuable to stress that his poetic engagement is the force that makes *The Asphalt Jungle* distinctive as an adaptation and noteworthy as a marker of his career. By "poetic" I mean not a way of using filmic language to be obscure, esoteric, or unconventional, but a way of using it, with all its capabilities, to say many things at once. The story line of this film—a heist plan, its execution, its collapse, the termination of lives—is therefore only the most simplistic account of its working, its evocations, and its possibilities.

Note

1. This is a gentle tip of the hat, perhaps, to Harold Schuster's *Wings of the Morning* (1937), a paean to the Irish thoroughbred. J. P. Telotte sees this as indicative of a "pattern of broken links with a natural or pastoral world" that "shows up in a number of . . . *films noir*," notably in *The Asphalt Jungle* (87n6).

Works Cited

HER = Margaret Herrick Library, Academy of Motion Picture Arts and Sciences, Beverly Hills

Adorno, Theodor W., Else Frenkel-Brunswick, Daniel J. Levinson, and R. Nevitt Sanford. *The Authoritarian Personality*. New York: Harper, 1950.
Breen, Joseph I. Letter to Louis B. Mayer, re *The Asphalt Jungle*, 6 Oct. 1949, Motion Picture Association of America Production Code Administration Records, HER.
———. Letter to Louis B. Mayer, re *The Asphalt Jungle*, 24 Oct. 1949, Motion Picture Association of America Production Code Administration Records, HER.
Brown, Norman O. "Apocalypse: The Place of Mystery in the Life of the Mind," originally the Phi Beta Kappa Speech at Columbia University, May 1960, *Harper's* (May 1961), 46–49; reprinted in *Apocalypse and/or Metamorphosis*, Berkeley: U of California P, 1991, 1–7.

Casetti, Francesco. *Eye of the Century: Film, Experience, Modernity*. New York: Columbia UP, 2008.
Cole, Bill. Synoptic comments on Script for *The Asphalt Jungle*, John Huston Papers, 1950 Script File 17, HER.
Dixon, Wheeler Winston. *Film Noir and the Cinema of Paranoia*. New Brunswick, NJ: Rutgers UP, 2009.
Eksteins, Modris. *Solar Dance: Genius, Forgery, and the Crisis of Truth in the Modern Age*. Toronto: Alfred A. Knopf, 2012.
Epstein, Jean. *Écrits sur le cinéma*. Paris: Cinéma Club-Seghers, 1974–75.
Gray, Hugh. Memorandum to "Gianni" (John Huston), reacting to a reading of the script for *The Asphalt Jungle*, 18 October 1949, John Huston Papers, *Asphalt Jungle* File 33, HER.
Gunning, Tom. "Fritz Lang's Dr. Mabuse, the Gambler (1922)." *Weimar Cinema: An Essential Guide to Classic Films of the Era*. Ed. Noah Isenberg. New York: Columbia UP, 2009. 95–113.
Hawks, Howard. Note to John Huston, 27 March 1950, John Huston Papers, 1950 Script File 32, HER.
Hornblow, Arthur Jr. Inter-Office Communication to Dore Schary, 2 June 1949, re reception of a memo from Rudolf Monta insisting on a "fictitious name," John Huston Papers, *Asphalt Jungle* 1950 Script File 33, HER.
———. Inter-Office Communication to Rudolf Monta, 2 June 1949, re using an actual city as background for *The Asphalt Jungle*, John Huston Papers, *Asphalt Jungle* 1950 Script File 33, HER.
———. Inter-Office Communication to Rudolf Monta, Dore Schary, and John Huston, re using an actual city for *The Asphalt Jungle*, 11 June 1949, John Huston Collection, File 34, HER.
Huston, John. *An Open Book*. New York: Alfred A. Knopf, 1980.
McIntosh, Mary. "Changes in the Organization of Thieving." *Images of Deviance*. Ed. Stanley Cohen. Harmondsworth: Penguin, 1973, 98–133.
Monta, Rudolf. Inter-Office Communication to Arthur Hornblow Jr., 9 June 1949, re releases necessary if an actual city were used for *The Asphalt Jungle*, John Huston Papers, *Asphalt Jungle* 1950 Script File 33, HER.
———. Inter-Office Communication to Arthur Hornblow Jr., Dore Schary, and John Huston, July 8, 1949, re legal problems with usage of a city in *The Asphalt Jungle*, John Huston Papers, File 34, HER.
Naremore, James. *More than Night: Film Noir in Its Contexts*. Berkeley: U of California P, 1998.
Palmer, R. Barton. *Hollywood's Dark Cinema: The American Film Noir*. New York: Twayne, 1994.
Place, Janey, and Lowell Peterson. "Some Visual Motifs of *Film Noir*." *Film Noir Reader*. Ed. Alain Silver and James Ursini. New York: Limelight, 2003, 65–76.
Pomerance, Murray. *An Eye for Hitchcock*. New Brunswick, NJ: Rutgers UP, 2004.
Scheler, Max. *Ressentiment*. Trans. Lewis B. Coser and William W. Holdheim. Milwaukee: Maquette UP, 2003.

Schrader, Paul. "Notes on *Film Noir.*" *Film Noir Reader.* Ed. Alain Silver and James Ursini. New York: Limelight, 2003, 53–63.
Schulberg, Budd. Letter to John Huston, n.d., John Huston Papers, 1950 Script File 32, HER.
Telotte, J. P. *Voices in the Dark: The Narrative Patterns of Film Noir.* Urbana: U of Illinois P, 1989.
Welles, Orson, Peter Bogdanovich, and Jonathan Rosenbaum. *This Is Orson Welles.* New York: DaCapo P, 1998.

Douglas McFarland

Adapting Addiction

Modernist Aesthetics in *Under the Volcano*

John Huston's adaptation of Malcolm Lowry's *Under the Volcano* (1984) addresses a twofold, contradictory, and yet often accepted assessment of the director's many films. James Agee once asserted that throughout his career, Huston rendered as accurately as possible what his source material "dictated," a critical judgment that would necessarily exclude Huston from the ranks of auteurs who would bring their own distinctive styles and approaches to adaptation (26). But Huston has also been seen as a filmmaker with a single nondistinctive way of telling a story. Regardless of his source material, Huston would shoot films in a naturalistic spatial and temporal setting. He saw himself, so it goes, as a storyteller, a role that Huston himself may have perpetuated with declarations such as those he made on the set of *The Man Who Would Be King* (1975). When asked, he said he was attracted to Kipling's tale because it was a yarn of "high adventure" (*Call It Magic*). A better example of Huston's apparent proclivity for a naturalistic narrative style might be *Moby Dick* (1956). In Huston's adaptation, gone are the eccentric baroque digressions and layering of multiple allusions drawn from a diversity of sources in favor of an ostensibly straightforward linear narrative. We are left with the contradiction that Huston was bound to his source material and yet could tell a tale in only one way. Huston's adaptation of *Under the Volcano* would seem at least superficially to refute the one and substantiate the other assessment. Contrary to Agee's appraisal, Huston has dramatically altered the overtly modernist aesthetics of the novel. Gone from the film are the interior and imagined dialogues, the complex scheme of flashbacks, the mythic underpinnings, the attraction to the primitive, and the allusions to a wide range of other texts, all of which inform Lowry's novel. Huston instead filmed his adaptation in a naturalistic setting and in linear time, seemingly substantiating the notion that he is limited to a reductive style of filmmaking. In what follows I will make the argument that Huston's naturalism constitutes a reimagining, not a reduction, of Lowry's novel, a naturalism that offers what I call an objectifying modernist aesthetic that supplants the layered and intentionally disorienting surface complexity of the novel. Moreover, Huston provides his protagonist with an aggressive and concurrently self-destructive proclivity for irony that looks back to a modernist subjectivity fashioned by Baudelaire and later refashioned by William James.

Huston as Reader

Let me emphasize that Huston does not turn against the formal characteristics of Lowry's novel because of an aversion to complex modernist literary conventions. Nor is it his intention to reduce the novel into a film that might be accessible to a wide audience. Huston was not in any sense an unsophisticated reader that would be frustrated by the surface density of *Under the Volcano*. By all accounts, including his own, he was a voracious reader and certainly did not limit himself to traditional works of fiction. Huston was, in fact, deeply committed to modernist literature. Huston recalls that in the 1930s, when it was still banned in the United States, he owned a contraband copy of *Ulysses*. As he puts it in *An Open Book*, reading James Joyce's novel "was probably the greatest experience that any book has ever given me. Doors fell open" (48). Huston also recalls in his autobiography that he would listen with delight to Joe Glennon recite passages from *Finnegans Wake* in his bar on Third Avenue. No amount of powerful drink could make the language of *Finnegans Wake* accessible were there not a deep sensitivity to Joyce's linguistic experimentations.

When he shot the film in 1984, Huston was not a newcomer to *Under the Volcano*. In an interview at the film's premiere in Cannes, he revealed that he had read *Under the Volcano* more than thirty years earlier, essentially at the time of its publication and that scripts had been submitted to him at various times over the next two decades. When Huston did finally turn to the novel in the early 1980s, it was not necessarily out of admiration for Lowry or for his work. In that same interview,

Huston relegated *Under the Volcano* to at best the second tier of twentieth-century works of literature. He astutely observed that the novel suffers from having everything Lowry knew or had ever known thrown into its mix. He pointedly remarked that if Lowry "saw a cat cross a street or read a sign in a park, the cat and sign would be in the book" (145). Huston's cogent and cutting remarks reveal that he recognized, at least in his own reading of the novel, the essentially solipsistic character of *Under the Volcano*. Huston detected that the formal complexities of the novel are employed by Lowry to fashion his own self-absorbed confessional narrative. Although Lowry draws modernist conventions from T. S. Eliot, Ezra Pound, D. H. Lawrence, and especially Joyce, he does not employ them to move beyond or beneath the social, epistemological, or psychological surfaces of reality. These conventions merely serve to allow Lowry, in a very self-conscious and undisciplined manner, to fall into his own subjectivity. The first chapter of the novel provides a fine example. It begins with an extended nonlinear flashback that moves between first- and third-person narration. Direct and indirect literary allusions are made with little explanation to guide the reader. The chapter concludes with a very long letter, written but never sent, that falls by chance from a collection of Elizabethan plays. The letter functions less as an epistolary device for plot exposition than as a rambling interior monologue in which the protagonist gives himself over to the narcissistic self-pity of an alcoholic—a self-pity that has been drawn from Lowry's own experiences as an addict. Moreover, each of the major characters in the novel bears biographical details of Lowry's own life to an excessive degree. The ex-consul's (Albert Finney) half brother (Anthony Andrews) plays the ukulele and writes songs as Lowry himself did as a young man. The issues Yvonne (Jacqueline Bisset) has with her father resemble those Lowry has with his own father. One might say that Lowry lacked the imaginative ability to create characters, but it would be more accurate to say that Lowry could not see beyond himself. At one point in the novel, Geoffrey Firmin laments that he is enslaved to a "tyranny of the self" (300). The novel suffers from this same malady, and judging by his remarks at Cannes, Huston recognized this. *Under the Volcano* is, in short, a novel about an alcoholic, but it is also a novel written by an alcoholic.

Let me approach this from a different critical perspective. In an attempt to detect the structure that lies beneath what is otherwise a linguistically dense surface, Barry Wood has argued that Lowry's novel can best be understood through Northrop Frye's fourfold categorization of prose fiction (142). In *The Anatomy of Criticism*, Frye asserts that prose fiction has four distinct modes and that these appear in a pure or mixed form: the traditional novel with realistic landscape and dialogue; romance with its set of archetypal mythic patterns; the confession with a first-person autobiographical voice and point of view; and the anatomy with its encyclopedic approach to its subject matter. Frye argues that all four modes can be found in *Ulysses*: the sights and smells of Dublin, Homeric structuring, interior monologue, and an exhaustive and encyclopedic collection of styles. Utilizing this schematic, Wood argues that these four categories also inform *Under the Volcano*. The novel transpires in real time and in a real location, has a multitude of allusions to a variety of myths, offers the fictionalized confession of its author; and is an anatomy of the meaning of love and death. This reading is only partially accurate. Lowry's novel, I would argue and I think Huston would agree, is dominated by the confessional mode to the detriment of the other three. Although not with Frye's critical apparatus literally in hand, Huston strips away traces of romance and anatomy, but more significantly has removed the novel's overriding confessional mode of discourse. He has rendered *Under the Volcano*, almost exclusively, in Frye's understanding of the term novel, into a narrative that transpires in real time and in the bright sunlight of a realistic environment. Although in some particulars I will qualify my assertion, this generic stripping away and re-emphasis is the salient formal characteristic of Huston's adaptation and one that must be addressed in any serious reading of the film as an adaptation.

Huston's Modernist Aesthetics

Huston's first step in adapting the novel is to remove its overt modernist conventions and to erase its autobiographical genesis. Guy Gallo had written an early treatment of *Under the Volcano* in which he utilized the styles of European modernist cinema, but when Huston became involved, he insisted that the film be shot without flashbacks, without unnecessary visual ambiguities, without disorienting editing and cinematography, and without any attempt to represent in visual form interior monologue (*Under the Volcano*, DVD). Although Lowry's novel is more than four hundred pages long, the plot covers a mere twelve hours just prior to the beginning of World War II in the life of Geoffrey Firmin, a former British consul in Mexico, who suffers from acute alcoholism. It is Firmin's death day, ironically coinciding with the day of the Mexican celebration of the dead. Huston expands those twelve hours into twenty-four primarily in order to remove the need for any short-term flashbacks. What Huston no doubt found compelling in the novel is not its literary flourishes but the ex-consul himself, a deeply flawed character of the type to whom Huston was often drawn: Fred C. Dobbs of *The Treasure of Sierra Madre* (1948), the hooligan of *Asphalt Jungle* (1950), Captain Ahab of *Moby Dick* (1956), Hazel Motes of *Wise Blood* (1979), Toulouse-Lautrec of *Moulin Rouge* (1952), and Billy Tully of *Fat City* (1972), to name a few. Lesley Brill identifies these characters as "strikingly individualized" and "complex" figures who "struggle, who occasionally win outright, who manage an unlikely draw, or who in losing still win" (9–10). In *Under the Volcano*, however, there is no question of winning or losing. We know from the start that the protagonist is doomed. The Day of the Dead, in short, looms over the narrative and its protagonist.

It is critical, however, to understand that although Huston has jettisoned the overtly modernist conventions of the novel, he has not done away with a modernist aesthetic. The subject of the film is arguably modern and one that is clearly limited in the scope of its audience. The day in the life of an abject and doomed alcoholic provides subject matter more appropriate for art house cinema. But Huston's film is modern in a way that goes beyond subject matter. Let me explain how an apparently naturalist aesthetic might in fact be modern by turning to Joyce's *Dubliners*. Robert Scholes, drawing upon Genette's distinction between "showing" and "telling" in narrative fiction, argues that Joyce employs the former rather than the latter. Joyce inserts objects, manipulates diction, and plants allusions, before withdrawing into the background. As Scholes puts it, "readers have to exercise considerable ingenuity to detect a narrative persona manipulating voice and perspective" (97). This relationship between narrator, subject, and audience is explicitly articulated by Stephen Dedalus in an often cited passage from *A Portrait of the Artist as a Young Man*: "The artist, like the God of the creation, remains within or behind or beyond or above his handiwork, invisible, refined out of existence, indifferent, paring his fingernails" (181). By "showing" rather than "telling" Joyce creates a space of subtle play between ironic judgment, empathetic response, and cool indifference.

Two examples from *Dubliners* of Joyce's technique occur in "The Sisters" and "Eveline." The former begins, "There was no hope for him this time" (3), an allusion to Dante's inscription on the Gate of Hell. The narrator is not "telling" the reader the state of mind of the character, but rather "showing," in a very subtle and indirect way, his otherwise undisclosed state of mind. Similarly in "Eveline," the protagonist attends an operetta whose plot she absorbs and self-deceptively imposes onto her world. Joyce provides no direct access to the inner life of Eveline and withholds overt judgment of how she has constructed her life. We sense him, however, hovering in the background and, as Stephen puts it "paring his fingernails."

Huston employs a similar technique of "showing" in his adaptation of *Under the Volcano*. The confessional characteristics of the novel are essentially removed through the elimination of subjective point-of-view shots. Audiences familiar with the alcoholic protagonist of the novel would expect that Huston would represent Firmin's disorientation through a variety of cinematic techniques. But there are no tricks, no tilting and off balance camera angles, no steady cam sequences, and only two short point-of-view shots of any significance in the entire film. Huston chooses instead to hold the camera back and to refrain from allowing the audience to see through the eyes of his protagonist. Moreover, Huston openly criticized Lowry's use of "allusions in an almost suffocating way," referring to the multiplicity of references to myth, other literary works, and psychological typologies (145). Indeed, for the most part, these have been eliminated in the adaptation. However, at times, Huston does sparingly and strategically and much in the manner of Joyce, allude to other works to show rather than tell the governing consciousness of the narrative. Early in the film, after leaving his ex-wife and stepbrother, Firmin scampers off to the rear of his house in order to recover a bottle of tequila he had earlier hidden behind some plants. When he is confronted by his neighbor and asked why he is rummaging through the tropical undergrowth, Firmin responds that he is emulating William Blackstone,

Figure 2.1. The ex-consul cavorts in the street like a madcap Shakespearean fool.

a Puritan of early America, who when dissatisfied with the congregation went off into the wilderness to establish his own colony. The allusion resonates in the novel because Firmin's father had one day walked off into the Himalayas, never to be heard of again. The relationship between Firmin and his father is left unexplored in Huston's adaptation, indeed erased, but the reference to Blackstone and the wilderness opens the possibility for Huston to insert a subtle Shakespearean allusion. After Firmin has made the reference to Blackstone, he adds, "unaccommodated man, and that sort of thing." These are the words of King Lear, who, in a moment of frenetic insight during his mad romp across the moors, questions the meaning of human identity. Huston's crafty allusion, absent in the novel, opens up another dimension to Firmin's psyche.

Let me make it clear that Shakespeare is not underrepresented in Lowry's novel. There are twenty-seven direct and indirect references to Shakespeare in *Under the Volcano*. Huston's addition to this scene, however, is critical to understanding his interpretation of the drunken ex-consul. Just as Lear's madness gives him license to rail against the world, to pick it apart and mock its hypocrisies, alcohol bestows on Firmin that same license. Or rather, Firmin—through the fiction of Lear's persona—justifies his alcoholism by granting himself that license. The allusion to Lear, similar to Joyce's allusion to Dante in *Dubliners*, provides a governing consciousness while retaining a naturalism suggestive of third-person narration. The reference shows us, rather than tells us, how Firmin has constructed his world, providing an implicit subjectivity in what is otherwise an objectifying landscape. Under the direction of Huston, Finney gives a subtle performance as a madcap, who, like Lear, is cruel, ironic, repentant, judgmental, destructive of self and others, needy and yet unforgiving, full of regret and recrimination, able to hit the mark and yet babble like a fool. Finney makes maximum use of physical posturing and movement. At times he comically cavorts about, teetering on the brink of a fall but rarely losing his balance. In one scene, he does fall in drunken exhaustion in the middle of an empty road. But when he is revived by a driver who has come upon him, he quickly responds with lively irony. He spots his mark, and without hesitation he mocks the stereotypical Englishman. "Awfully decent of you old chap," he wryly remarks. He then sarcastically alludes to the English class system: "Oxford man?" he asks. "No, Cambridge," returns the foolish butt of Firmin's irony. When his victim drives off, Firmin waves his hand in the air and shouts, "Tally-ho." It is not the conditions of the world that have driven Firmin to drink, but it is rather that drink has given him a means, the license of a King Lear, to mock the world in its many manifestations. This also suggests why there is something oddly endearing about this destructive and self-destructive alcoholic. Remarkably, Finney offers a subversive counterintuitively comic performance, one that plays on our envy of a figure who has cast accommodations aside so that with a kind of impunity he might rail against the world.

The Sick Soul and the Ironist

The implications of Firmin's internalization of Lear's persona go beyond the use of allusion to establish subjectivity. To put it differently, Huston has not merely utilized a modernist narrative technique; he has also addressed modernism itself. There is nothing necessarily modern about the despair from which Firmin suffers. The loss of hope is, of course, an aspect of the human condition and has been the subject of artistic representation since Homer, but the context and response to despair can be modern. I argued earlier that it is not the specific conditions of the public or private world—insofar as these could be externalized into a cause—that have cast Firmin into depression and driven him to drink. Instead, these qualities and proclivities are treated as something innate to Firmin's identity. Consider, for instance, the film that is playing in the local cantina/cinema, *The Hands of Orlac*. Posters advertising the film appear throughout *Under the Volcano*, including in the final set-piece. *At* the beginning of the film, as Firmin makes his way to a Red Cross banquet, he pauses to observe and discuss a scene from the film that is playing in the background through the doors of the theater. *The Hands of Orlac* tells the tale of a concert pianist who loses both hands in an accident. The hands of a deceased murderer are then grafted onto his arms. The pianist, whose art and creativity had flowed through his hands, cannot now control this alien presence and so commits acts of evil against his will. The allegory of Orlac provides a trap into which those who require an objective and external source of evil might fall. For Firmin, as he himself reveals, the despair he experiences is of the heart and cannot be accounted for as an alien appendage. When the cinema owner explains the plot of the film to Firmin, he dismisses it with his typically ironic attitude: "There are some things you can't apologize for." Beneath his flippant response is the recognition that blaming the hands of others for one's own demons does not hold. The evil that besets the ex-consul cannot be excised as if it were a cancerous mole or alien hands that had been surgically attached.

I want to turn to William James to deepen an understanding of Firmin's comprehension of the innate source of evil, or in his own case, despair. In his lectures on "The Sick Soul" from *The Varieties of Religious Experience*, James begins his analysis of despair, the type to which Firmin has apparently succumbed, by establishing a distinction in the concept of evil between polytheism and monotheism. In the religious system of the former, evil can simply be foisted onto any one particular deity. For the monotheist, however, good and evil must reside in a single deity, as if the two were intertwined. James then makes a critical move from models of religion to corresponding models of human identity: the pluralistic and the monistic. For the pluralistic individual, evil is "a pure abomination . . . an alien reality, a waste element to be sloughed off and negated" (126). But for the monistic self, identity is a totality, and its "worst parts must be as essential as the best, so "if any part whatever in an individual were to vanish or alter, it would no longer be that individual at all" (125). Echoing Firmin's own self-assessment, James concludes that, for the monistic individual, evil arises not out of the "mere relation of the subject to the particular outer things, but something more radical and general, a wrongness or vice in his essential nature" (127). Whatever despair, whatever depression, whatever mental sickness that might be experienced, one cannot simply attribute it to an external source. The depressed soul is a monolithic entity, enclosed in its own being. Although the hands of Orlac might very well account for the evil deeds of that film's protagonist, the psychological sickness of the ex-consul is not, in James's understanding of depression and addiction, an alien presence that envelopes him, but an intrinsic condition.

This notion of the sick soul has a counterpart in James's formulation of a model for cognitive psychology. One might speculate that his own struggles with acute depression (he would later admit that one of the examples he used in his lecture on "the sick soul" was drawn from his own personal experiences) shaped his understanding of individual consciousness. In *The Principles of Psychology*, he revises his concepts of the pluralistic and monistic individual by arguing that these contrary impulses reside in every human consciousness: "Absolute insulation, irreducible pluralism, is the law" (221). To take the etymology of "insularity" at face value, every man and woman is a world unto him- or herself. But, consequentially, there exist an inexhaustible and "irreducible" number of islands. So, too, each insularity is constantly sculpted out of a multitude of external stimuli: "The mind, in short, works on the data it receives very much as a sculptor works on his block of stone" (277). James's cognitive model asks us to embrace the absolutist and the pluralistic understandings at once. James's "law" reflects, on the one hand, the reality of pluralism—which, for James, supported his democratic idealism—but, on the other hand, it suggests that each individual is necessarily an absolutist, shaping a world that cannot be shared by another.

Ross Posnack has suggested that there is an "inadvertent echo" of James's conflation of absolutism and pluralism in the modernist deployment of irony (285). Such an echo, for example, is also apparent in

Jean-Paul Sartre's explication of irony in *Being and Nothingness*, an explication which helps to better understand how Huston's Firmin, the sick soul, maintains his absolutism in the face of pluralism. Sartre writes: "In irony a man annihilates what he posits within one and the same act; he leads us to believe in order not to be believed; he affirms to deny and denies to affirm; he creates a positive object but it has no being other than its nothingness" (57). The ironist creates authority as he simultaneously denies authority. Irony asserts a godlike creation of knowledge while it concurrently, in annihilating itself, demands that there is no such thing as absolute knowledge, only a plurality of perspectives. As Sartre suggests here, the ironist is empowered through—to use the Jamesian construction—a specific conflation of absolutism and pluralism. The ironist asserts control over others in his assertion of truth—thus holding himself immutable—but denies a responsibility to others (or to the truth itself) as "what he posits" evaporates, thus also experiencing the freedom of transience.

Such is the case with Huston's Firmin and how he uses irony as a means of exerting control over his world. As I argued earlier, there is something Learlike in Firmin's foolish cavorting; however, throughout the film this quickly gives way to another guise. Through his ironic mockery of others, Firmin establishes himself as an absolutist, a single god in control of knowledge, but one whose status requires the recognition that there is no truth. Firmin's protective and punishing irony is on full display in a scene in which his ex-wife, Yvonne, has just returned to him. While speaking with Yvonne, Firmin suddenly turns and pretends that Hugh, his half-brother and one time lover of Yvonne, has returned. He calls out: "Hugh, come out here . . . I believe she missed you full as much as I . . . Join this council of cuckolds . . . Give the wife a welcome back kiss." After his performance, he then slyly recalls, "Oh, he isn't here." In a manner reflective of Sartre's understanding of irony, this sardonic foray is meant concurrently to attack and to defend, to assert control while denying anyone's authority to control. It is an irony that demands by its very nature alienation, and yet it is awash in the despair of alienation.

From Irony to the Loss of Self

Firmin's performance at the Red Cross ball demonstrates the precarious nature of his ironic game and looks ahead to the final scenes in the film. Firmin is already drunk when he arrives, dressed in formal wear but missing his socks. He proceeds to have a great deal more to drink, and at least initially this does not seem to make him any more drunk.

When introduced to a representative of the German Reich, he begins to mock the Nationalist Socialist Party, building into a rant that he can barely control. He becomes intoxicated more with irony than with drink. Or to put it differently, alcohol facilitates irony. Reaching a crescendo of raving, Firmin ascends the stage just barely maintaining his balance. Finally having recovered his equilibrium and with a more controlled irony, on his way out, he playfully snatches a bottle of wine off the table of a startled dinner guest. In other words, just at the moment of collapse into his own despair, at that moment when irony burns itself out and reveals his pathetic isolation, he catches hold of a defensive ironic stability that restores his command.

In the final scenes of Huston's adaptation, however, Firmin is unable to recover that balance. His ironic objectification of others turns back onto himself. The reversal from attacker to target begins with a sadistic antifeminist diatribe against Yvonne. The heightened degree of cruelty seems to poison him, and he immediately scampers off to seek asylum in the seediest of cantinas and in the foul bed of an abject prostitute. Here he becomes the butt of irony, not its practitioner. He is the objectified other within the narrative context of the film, ceasing to be its governing consciousness. A misshapen pimp identifies him as a mark and offers him his choice from an array of freakish prostitutes. He is passively led into the room of one of these, and after finishing his business with her, he is immediately confronted by a group of fascist mercenaries. They demand that he pay for his time with the prostitute and then ask his name. As he had done earlier in the garden, when he had mocked his neighbor, Firmin replies, "William Blackstone, frontiersman." His tormentors snatch letters from his ex-wife that he is holding in his hand. He demands them back; the mercenaries tell him they are addressed to Firmin, not "Black." One of them, needing no badge and yet having many, mockingly tells Firmin that he is not an ex-British consul (which he is) but rather the head of the Department of Drunkards. His earlier condescending irony is now flung back in his face. And at this moment the ironic mask that he has worn throughout the film completely slips away: he openly accuses the fascists of murder and robbery. They rather nonchalantly shoot him and kick his body into a ravine. Before he falls, in a final moment of self-deprecating irony, he observes in a bemused voice, that this is a "dingy way to die." His earlier objectification of others now morphs into self-objectification, a subtle move by Huston to offer a brief moment in which Firmin is again the governing consciousness of the film just before he falls into the abyss.

This final reversal has a counterpart in Charles Baudelaire's "*l'heautontimoroumenos*." The title means "one who takes revenges on oneself" and comes from a Greek middle participle. I point this out because the Greek middle voice (not used in English) signifies that the subject of the verb is the agent of action but is also the recipient of the action. This grammatical option is apt for a poem in which sadistic irony turns back on the agent of irony. Unlike the distancing modernist irony of a closed and insulated self, Baudelaire articulates a self-destructive irony that looms over the ironist: "She is my piercing voice," Baudelaire writes, "she's my blood, my poison noir; I am her sinister mirror, where the bitch watches herself . . . I am the limbs and I am the rack" (157). Baudelaire removes himself in order to punish himself; whore and poet collapse into one another. This modernist sensibility, this dislocation, and a despair that irony cannot cure but only destroy make up the modernist subjectivity that Huston has bequeathed to the ex-consul in the final scenes of the film.

The dichotomy between virgin and whore runs throughout the film, becoming the means through which we witness the film's decided movement away from an ironic governing consciousness. The virgin and whore dichotomy is not intended to represent the filmmaker, but rather the filmmaker's, again as Joyce operates in Dubliners, representation of the consciousness of Firmin. It is a typology that was introduced at the beginning of the film when Firmin visits a church where he gazes at a statue of the Madonna. This scene creates tension between his dark construction of female sexuality and the purity of the virgin. This typology turns back onto Firmin at the end of the film when the Madonna stares in judgment at Firmin. At the end of the hallway, down past the row of rooms where prostitutes service their customers, a statue of the Madonna has scandalously been placed by Huston. The setup of the scene is reminiscent, again, of concerns of Baudelaire. In *A Beatrice*, Baudelaire smothers Dante's source of divine inspiration in a throng of devils. In the poem that follows, *Les Metamorphoses du Vampire*, the Madonna has been completely erased as Baudelaire awakes on "those mattresses that swoon in ecstasy" and "a flask that overflowed with pus" (255). But unlike Baudelaire who testifies to his own defilement and the erasure of the virgin, Firmin is objectified dramatically in the eyes of the Madonna who bears witness to his fall. The balance or tension between virgin and whore collapses as Firmin falls into the whore's bed. The effect parallels the objectification of Firmin by the mercenaries. In this case, the Madonna stares from her perch from the end of the hallway at Firmin who is the object of her silent judgment. In Lowry's version, Firmin imagines Yvonne while he is having sex with the prostitute, revealing his disgust and self-disgust of his entanglement with his wife. In the film, there is no access to the thoughts of Firmin, no entrance into his psyche, no expression of his own voice and imagination. He ceases to be a governing consciousness within the narrative. And stripped of his self-insulating irony, his person vanishes. He immediately falls into the bed of a prostitute, subsequently into the abyss that the mercenaries toss him, and psychologically into a reified state of pure objectivity, not through the perspective of the camera but through the eyes of the Madonna. It is a fine example of Huston's skill at bringing so many complex elements together in an apparently straightforward, naturalistic style.

Candy Skulls

Let me conclude by returning to the beginning of the film. Strolling through the shops erected for the festival of the dead, Firmin stops, bends closer, and stares downward at a collection of miniature candy skulls. Huston cuts to an extreme close-up of Firmin's face. With this cut Huston fashions a subtle and elusive interplay between objectification and subjectivity. The camera establishes Firmin's point of view because the skulls at which he is peering are reflected in his dark glasses. The camera concurrently stares back at the ex-consul but with the further complication that the dark glasses shroud his eyes, the windows into his soul. The audience sees and does not see and experiences a veiled recognition on the part of the subject but also discerns the mark of death that has been stamped upon him and with which he has now been labeled. To put it simply, as he

Figure 2.2. Subject and object collapse as Firmin stares at a candy skull.

stares at death, death stares back at him. Huston has crafted a cinematic moment worthy of Joyce's own modernist experiments in which a governing consciousness mingles with an objectifying gaze.

Rather than allow his source material to dictate to him, Huston expunged its overwrought and self-indulgent modernist conventions to fashion a human subject whose intense and debilitating despair lies at the center of a matrix of modernist insights into what James calls the "sick soul," and Baudelaire calls the "middle voice." The ostensible naturalistic landscape of the film is used by Huston in the service of that fashioning. It should not be simply a matter of recognizing Huston's sophistication as a filmmaker. Of equal importance is the recognition of his willingness to enter the worlds of deeply damaged figures who have fallen into the depths of confusion and the intensities of need. Huston's ability to probe beneath the formal surface of Lowry's novel, to see past its confessional self-pity and narcissism in order to confront a modern sense of despair, speaks to his affinity for literature, his facility with filmmaking, and at his best moments, his willingness to enter, as Alexander Pope put it, "the toyshop of the heart."

Works Cited

Agee, James. "Undirectable Director." *Life* (18 Sept. 1950), and reprinted in *Comprehending Huston—Five Critical Perspectives*, ed. Stephen Cooper. New York: G. K. Hall, 1994.

Baudelaire, Charles. *The Flowers of Evil*. Oxford: Oxford UP, 1993.

Brill, Lesley. *John Huston's Filmmaking*. Cambridge: Cambridge UP, 1997.

Call It Magic: The Making of the Man Who Would Be King. DVD. Warner Bros., 1997.

Gallo, Guy. "Interview." *Under the Volcano*. DVD Criterion, 2007.

Huston, John. *Interviews*. Ed. Robert Emmet Long. Jackson: U of Mississippi P, 2001.

———. *An Open Book*. New York: Knopf, 1980.

James, William. *Principles of Psychology*. Cambridge: Harvard UP, 1983.

———. *The Varieties of Religious Experience*. New York: Library of America, 1990.

Joyce, James. *Dubliners*. Oxford: Oxford UP, 2000.

———. *Portrait of the Artist as a Young Man*. Oxford: Oxford UP, 2000.

Lowry, Malcolm. *Under the Volcano*. New York: HarperCollins, 2000.

Posmock, Ross. *The Trial of Curiosity: Henry James, Williams James, and the Challenge of Modernity*. Oxford: Oxford UP, 1991.

Sartre, Jean-Paul. *Being and Nothingness*. Trans. Hazel E. Barnes. New York: Washington Square P, 1966.

Scholes, Robert. *Semiotics and Interpretation*. New Haven: Yale UP, 1982.

Wood, Barry. "The Strands of Novel, Confession, Anatomy and Romance." *Under the Volcano: A Casebook*. Ed. Gordon Bowker. New York: Macmillan, 1987. 142–51.

3

Robert L. Colson

Taking Gabriel at His Word

Narration and Huston's *The Dead*

The Joyce critical industry's response to John Huston's *The Dead* (1987) as an adaptation of James Joyce's "The Dead" (1907) has been quite mixed. While critics have praised Huston's film for its fidelity to the period and to the spirit of the story, many of them have criticized the film harshly, seeing it as a misreading of Joyce's story, even "unJoycean" (Naremore, "Return" 199; Barry, *The Dead* 46; Barry, "Tracing" 153). Their disappointment stems, in no small part, from Huston's departure from the frequently featured point of view of Gabriel Conroy in Joyce's story. However, Huston's departure from Gabriel's point of view offers instead an alternative critical reading of the story, one that undermines Gabriel's rather condescending, colonial attitudes about Ireland and Irish culture, while also shifting the focus away from the predominantly male perspective of "The Dead." Gabriel's patriarchal and imperial attitudes are closely linked, since "both the empire and the male ego are employed in the activity . . . of making judgments and hierarchical distinctions between what is central . . . and what is marginal" (Cheng 135–36). Huston's dual shift away from Gabriel shows a more decidedly feminist and postcolonial interpretation of Joyce's story, calling into question the power structures of patriarchy and empire and countering with a celebration of women and of Ireland.

Such an interpretation, though, may not be immediately apparent.[1] The film is subtle in its departures from the source text. For instance, much of the film's dialogue is drawn directly from the source, and as James Naremore observes, "Whenever new speeches are invented . . . it is difficult to detect where Joyce's words leave off and the adaptation begins" (198). Nevertheless, Huston's adaptive alterations transform *The Dead* in significant ways. For example, one of Huston's major additions, the invented character of Mr. Grace (Sean McClory) and the scene focused on his recitation, which I will discuss later, draws attention away from Gabriel (Donal McCann) and focuses the viewer on the young women instead. Such shifts of perspective, which are most evident in the way Huston handles the visual narration of the film and externalization of Gabriel's inner thoughts, are subdued but consistent. They point to a more sympathetic portrayal of the women of Joyce's story—especially Gretta (Anjelica Huston)—and of Ireland as a whole.

In order to illustrate the narrative perspective that Huston deliberately delimits in his film, I want to turn briefly to the mode of narration in Joyce's text that figures prominently in several key moments in "The Dead." In Huston's adaptation these moments are transformed as a result of the shift in point of view away from Gabriel's consciousness. The narration of "The Dead" partakes in what Joyce critic Hugh Kenner has termed the "Uncle Charles principle"—named after a character in *A Portrait of the Artist as a Young Man*—which is a particular way to describe what narrative theorists more generally call "character-bound focalization" (Bal 148). Kenner uses the opening line of "The Dead" as an example: "Lily, the caretaker's daughter, was literally run off her feet" (Joyce 151). Kenner notes that "the 'literally' of the perhaps illiterate Lily . . . wears invisible quotation marks" (17), meaning that her mode of speaking has entered the narration. He extrapolates that, though Joyce's "fictions tend not to have a detached narrator," the narration can seem detached by "detect[ing] the gravitational field of the nearest person" (16). The character that exerts the most gravitational force in the story is, of course, Gabriel Conroy. However, Joyce's narrative technique allows other characters' thoughts and perspectives to influence the narration. The film obviously cannot directly reproduce this technique, leaving us, perhaps, to take Gabriel at his word and his characterizations of himself as a gracious guest, nephew, and husband. For instance, one of Kevin Barry's criticisms about Huston's film is that it lacks Joyce's "scrupulous use of undetermined points of view" (77). Yet, as Leslie Brill has argued, Huston's camera "in effect functions as the central character in the film" due to its "mobility, energy, and initiative" (222). While closely bound to Gabriel's perspective (as is the story), Huston uses the camera to provide an "Uncle Charles principle" of sorts, choosing at significant moments to marginalize Gabriel. For Huston's film, the question of his visual narration is one that turns on the distinction between what François Jost calls "focalization," or the point of view "adopted by the narrative," and "ocularization," or the relationship "between what the camera shows and what the characters are presumed to be seeing" (74). Huston does present Gabriel's and other characters' perspectives, at times, through internal ocularization, but at some key moments Huston resorts to "zero ocularization," where "it is not possible to assign an image to any specific gaze" (75–76). In his use of zero ocularization, Huston visually creates a critical distance from Gabriel's perspective, translating Joyce's use of undetermined points of view, while remaining true to the story's focalization through Gabriel.

The film has four segments that most strongly adapt the story's critical perspective on Gabriel, putting him in relief to those around him and against his own public proclamations and behaviors. Three of them involve his interactions with women (with Lily, Miss Ivors, and his wife, Gretta). The fourth one is the dinner speech/toast that he offers.

Figure 3.1. In one of several similar shots, Gabriel stands aloof from the others, here rehearsing his speech.

The film visually links three of these moments in a single sequence in a way that Joyce's story does not explicitly do, but in the way that a careful reader might. When Gabriel finishes his unsettling dance with Miss Ivors in the film, he immediately turns away from the party to look out of a window, opening up the notes to his dinner speech. In this brief sequence about a third of the way into the film, Huston marks a point of connection between the film's end, Gabriel's dinner speech, and Miss Ivors's critical engagement with Gabriel's attitudes about Ireland early in the party. This set of connections, created visually in the film at this seemingly inconsequential moment, positions Gabriel apart from the party guests and his wife Gretta. Huston heightens this by cutting away from Gabriel at the window, more engrossed in preparing his speech than in the company of others, and cutting to the continued dancing of the party guests for a moment. While the camera follows the dancers, Gretta chief among them, it does so by dancing along with them, only to cut back to the staid, solitary Gabriel at the window. The camera's "movement accentuates its presence," an independent presence that is important throughout the film (Brill 223). We see the party carrying on behind Gabriel and his wife approaching to draw him out of his introspection back into the gathering. Gretta's approach is motivated by a question about the dinner service and their roles in it, but she follows this up with a question about why Gabriel stopped dancing. This brief exchange between the Conroys further underscores the points of connection between these moments in the film that offer a critical reading of Joyce's text.

In fact, the film firmly establishes Gabriel as separated from the rest of the party guests from his first appearance onscreen, his encounter with Lily. The scene with Lily, treated so thoroughly in Joyce's story, accounts for just a brief moment in the film. Yet Huston captures the awkwardness of the moment where Gabriel offers to Lily a gift of a coin for Christmas as the camera lingers with Lily below, attempting to refuse Gabriel's gift, while we see Gabriel rushing up the stairs to join his wife at the party. This scene, with its visuals of the staircase, sets up the later scene where Gabriel observes his wife on the staircase, imagining her as a still-life. When we join Gabriel upstairs, the camera looks over his shoulder onto a scene of dancing partygoers, establishing its zero ocularization or a "cinematic narrator" distinct from Gabriel (Jost 76). Gabriel and the camera pause for a moment, before he turns away from the dancing, returns to the top of the stairs, and takes out his speech for rehearsal. Gabriel's encounter with Lily leaves him "discomposed" and "cast a gloom over him which he tried to dispel by . . . glanc[ing] at the headings he made for his speech" (Joyce, "The Dead" 155). Here at the start of the film we have a scene that proleptically looks forward to later moments of Gabriel's separation from the group. This separation in Joyce's story is marked by a certain sense of class and cultural superiority in this moment as Gabriel worries that "the lines from Robert Browning . . . would be above the heads of his hearers" (155). Gabriel's presentation in the film, as aloof and separated from the activities and sociality of the party, indicate this same thing without giving the viewer the precise motivation for it.

This sense of separation and superiority will shortly draw Gabriel under fire from Miss Ivors when they dance. In this moment of the film, we see Gabriel reading from his speech and we hear him say, "One feels that one is listening to a thought tormented music." Huston's film heightens the contrast between the content of Gabriel's speech, which viewers familiar with the story will already know is about hospitality and good humor, with his actions by setting these lines over the continual presence of the diegetic music accompanying the dancers in the next room, dancers whom we have just observed with Gabriel before he turns away from the gathering to mull over his big moment.

The combination of Gabriel's awkward interaction with Lily, whom he has known since she was a young girl, and this moment apart from the party provides a visual and aural adaptation of Gabriel's private worry in Joyce's text that he would fail with his speech just as he has failed with Lily moments ago. Gabriel's fear of failure is signaled in the text as we have access to his thoughts—"He would fail with them just as he had failed with [Lily]" (155)—but in the film Huston suggests the worry in quite another way. From Gabriel's solitary rehearsal the film cuts to Gretta changing her shoes and talking with Gabriel's aunts. As they emerge and greet Gabriel for the first time, his aunts liken him to a little boy, and Gretta teases him playfully about how concerned he is about his dinner speech. The contrast between the solitary Gabriel and the sociable women and the playful teasing from his aunts and wife serve to critique the way Gabriel's focus on his performance prevents him from participating in the very hospitality and humor about which he intends to speak. This shift also places Gabriel's concerns for his own standing or his fear of failure at the margins of the story, rather than close to its center, giving a place for the stories of the female characters of *The Dead*, particularly Gretta, to occupy a more central position.

Gabriel's position on the sidelines of the social gathering continues as the movie approaches his encounter with Miss Ivors. The film takes greater pains to set up the troubling encounter Gabriel has with Miss Ivors as a dance partner. We first see Miss Ivors during Mary Jane's piano performance. While Gretta and others look on from seated positions in the audience, Gabriel stands at the door, almost entirely out in the hall, not quite joining with the others to hear the music, but also not drinking in the room behind him with some of the other male guests. During the musical performance, we see Miss Ivors seated to listen to Mary Jane's performance, first rather out of focus over Mary Jane's shoulder. Then the camera briefly and clearly adopts Gabriel's perspective as we see Gabriel and then Miss Ivors in a shot reverse shot sequence. Miss Ivors's first appearance in the film is playful, if not provocative. When the camera, apparently from Gabriel's point of view, looks at her, she returns the gaze with a wink at Gabriel, which makes him look down, then back at her, and then away from her. She responds to this with a little smirk to which Gabriel seems to answer by looking up at the ceiling. This sequence without dialogue sets the tone for the conversation the two of them will have only moments later when they are dance partners, a conversation which Gabriel considers a "cross-examination" and an "ordeal" (Joyce, "The Dead" 164). Miss Ivors's actions mark her as strong and independent whereas Gabriel's actions mark him as either aloof or afraid, despite the fact that the two obviously know each other fairly well. This also prefigures the tepid response Gabriel gives to Miss Ivors's challenge to his politics.

The film's introduction of Miss Ivors is separated from their dance and conversation by Huston's major interpolation to Joyce's story, the recitation of Mr. Grace. During Mr. Grace's performance, Gabriel does join the audience, escorting his aunt Julia to a chair and standing at her side. The camera primarily focuses on the reaction of Gretta and other women to Mr. Grace's recitation. The only shots of Gabriel are meant to indicate his observation of his wife, signaled just as with Miss Ivors by a shot reverse shot sequence. Many critics treat this addition by Huston quite favorably. Although Barry characterizes the insertion of Mr. Grace in the film's narrative as one of Huston's "chief infidelities," he astutely recognizes that Mr. Grace's recitation "motivate[s] and . . . determine[s] the response of Gretta to the singing of 'The Lass of Aughrim'" (Barry, *The Dead* 59). Clearly Huston's addition, one of the very few he makes to the story, is motivated by the desire to tell Gretta's story, and this makes the film more hers throughout.

The impact of Huston's addition here not only affects Gretta, however. Barry notes that "Mr. Grace's recitation introduces fascinating new imbalances between gender, class and audience" (Barry, *The Dead* 66). Barry and Gibbons both discuss these class and gender issues in some detail.[2] For my purposes, the invention of this incident and Huston's cinematic presentation of it also have a significant effect on Gabriel and the audience's perception of him. Even though Gabriel participates as more of a part of the group during the recitation, he is still marked as separate. At the close of the recitation various characters comment on its strangeness or loveliness. Interrupting these responses, Gabriel begins to applaud, a gesture which the other characters follow. While this demonstrates Gabriel's politeness, it still marks him as out of step with the others and perhaps less moved by Mr. Grace's recitation about lost love, a tale which certainly has implications for Gretta and Gabriel at the film's conclusion. The gendered element of Mr. Grace's reading and the reaction to it only heighten Gabriel's polite indifference to the matter. This seems to be a way to indicate his attitudes toward women that are expressed in his thoughts about Lily, Miss Ivors, and even his wife, Gretta. Not only does this sequence make a point of connection with the end of the film, but it also draws in Gabriel's encounter with Lily earlier on because Lily appears and lingers in the doorway behind Mr. Grace during his recitation. And Mr. Grace begins his recitation by reading from a paper he has in his pocket, visually linking the recitation with Gabriel's rehearsals and delivery of his dinner speech.

The other connection that few, if any, critics link Mr. Grace's recitiation to is the sequence that follows with Gabriel and Miss Ivors. This not only happens by virtue of their narrative propinquity, as Mr. Grace's recitation separates and links Miss Ivors and Gabriel's interactions during Mary Jane's piano performance and their lancers dance. But it also happens because of the way, at the very end of Mr. Grace's recitation, that the camera lingers briefly on Miss Ivors wearing much the same pleased smile that she gives to the uncomfortable Gabriel moments before. The significance of the linkage between Miss Ivors and the recitation is largely a political one. The Irish political scene, and its relation to culture, is precisely the source of Miss Ivors's friendly, but firm, ribbing of Gabriel during their dance and conversation, an encounter that unsettles him.

Their dance begins at the behest of Gabriel's aunt who politely pulls him out of his solitude into the party and pairs him up with Miss Ivors. As Miss Ivors begins to pluck her crow with Gabriel about his work for what she calls "an English rag," the camera places us off her right shoulder so that we see past her to Gabriel's reactions as she needles him about his lack of sympathy for Ireland and Irish political causes. In a way, the camera places us on Miss Ivors's side. In this way the viewer, like Miss Ivors, occupies a political position, whereas Gabriel is unable to articulate or defend his position that "literature was above politics" or "that he saw nothing political in writing reviews of books" (Joyce, "The Dead" 163). In addition, the camera's point of view lets the viewer see the dancing, in the right side of the frame, providing a potent, critical counterpoint to the tension developing in the conversation between Gabriel and Miss Ivors.

Just as she accuses Gabriel of being a "West Briton," looking to England for salvation rather than to "ourselves alone," she and Gabriel separate and move through the dance on opposite sides and with new partners until they reunite as part of the dance. The phrase "ourselves alone" immediately conjures up the connection to Miss Ivors's politics and to *Sinn féin*, which has been commonly mistranslated as "ourselves alone" when it should be "we ourselves." Their movements through the dance indicate the political distance between Miss Ivors and Gabriel, her commitment and his lack thereof. When they are reunited as partners, the camera now captures them from a distance, from the other end of the room rather than at Miss Ivors's side. We hear the conversations of other dancers and party guests, and we see, but do not hear, Miss Ivors continuing her talk with Gabriel. Cutting away, as a contrast, to two happy dance partners, the film then returns to Miss Ivors and Conroy straight on in a medium shot as she urges him to take a holiday in the west of Ireland. In this sequence, she confronts him about his lack of interest in his native land and in the Irish language, in contrast with his intended holiday plans on the continent in order to keep up on those languages. Gabriel in this scene seems uncomfortable under her scrutiny, yet he retains his quiet composure under her attack for some time until his perturbation spills over when he exclaims that he is "sick of [his] own country, sick of it!" (Joyce, "The Dead" 165). Miss Ivors asks him why, and the film cuts back to the more distanced position the camera occupied moments ago. We can see Gabriel's mouth moving, as if he has an answer, but he does not. We don't know what he might be saying at this moment, but clearly it is unsatisfactory because the film cuts back to the medium shot of the two, and Miss Ivors repeats her question, "Why?" Gabriel has no answer other than his discomfited posture and expression. He hardly even looks at her at this point as he seeks a retreat or refuge from her interrogation. It is at precisely this moment that he withdraws to the window to review his speech, in a moment I have discussed earlier.

Critics of Huston's adaptation often point out that the Ireland of Huston's *The Dead* figures more prominently the changes in Irish politics and culture that ensue between the story and the film. In some instances this is a point of harsh criticism, expressing a desire, perhaps unconsciously, for art, and Joyce's art in particular, to be above politics. Yet study after study has demonstrated, since the postcolonial turn in criticism, that Joyce's art has never been above politics, even if Joyce himself was often cagey about just what his politics might be.[3] The film's treatment of the Miss Ivors's character suggests some level of approval of her political commitment in contrast to Gabriel's lack of commitment beyond being sick of his own country. Barry notes in both his essay and his book on the film that Huston is interested in presenting a different public image of Ireland, what he calls "a serene image of Irish life" rather than the "media profile of endemic Irish violence and renewed Irish poverty" that still predominated perceptions of Ireland in the 1980s (Barry, *The Dead* 3). Given Huston's well-known personal attachment to Ireland, becoming an Irish citizen in 1964 and residing there for much of the next two decades, the choices he makes in *The Dead* take on a particular historical resonance both with the period of the film's creation and with the story's own historical moment. Huston's film emphasizes Miss Ivors's political fervor in contrast to Gabriel's political indifference, which in his case amounts to an acceptance of the colonial order and a denigration of Irish culture. Huston's film also celebrates the qualities of hospitality and good humor that Gabriel praises (somewhat hypocritically) in his speech.

    The dinner and Gabriel's speech are connected to Miss Ivors by another of Huston's additions. Miss Ivors leaves before dinner, despite the polite pleadings of Gretta and Mary Jane, announcing that she is off to a political meeting where James Connolly (who in the decade after the story's setting will be a leader of the Easter Rising) is speaking. The political nature of her plans and her boldness at potentially being the only woman at the meeting cast Gabriel in an ironically domestic role as he turns away to the dinner service and the carving of the goose. As the diners assemble at the table with Gabriel at one head and his aunts at the other, we look on from behind Gabriel first. Then the camera attends to Gabriel, the goose, the diners, and the passing of the plates. The camera follows, almost as if it is dancing, a plate as it moves around the table. Although Gabriel is a part of the scene here, not standing off by a window or in a doorway alone, he is also not the central focus of the action. We hear his voice more than we see his face, and when we hear him speak it is primarily to serve the guests or to chide his aunts into sitting down at the other head of the table to eat for themselves. For most of the dinner sequence, which runs for almost twenty minutes in the film, Gabriel is largely absent or silent or both, unless he is serving in his role as carver or until he offers his speech. Although he is taking part in the conviviality of the dinner table, he is really more of a spectator than a participant, keeping to the solitary and aloof persona that the film has already developed for him.

    This contrasts sharply with Gretta's presence in the scene, where she engages in conversation or actively listens to the conversations going on about singers (and minstrels in Freddy Malins's case). It also contrasts starkly with the loving attention the camera pays to Aunt Kate Morkin as she reminisces passionately about a tenor she once heard sing. Aunt Kate's romantic reverie is heightened by the inclusion of extradiegetic music. Both the image and music connect to Gretta in her own brief moment of reverie in the next shot, a moment which anticipates the end and Gretta's revelation to Gabriel of her youthful love, Michael Furey. With the music still playing in the background the camera then moves to Gabriel, whose own reverie we see is connected to his speech. He removes his notes from his pocket, and we see a close-up that allows us to read his notes. After a bit of interreligious dialogue, the camera shifts to the other end of the table, where the aunts have been sitting.

For the first time in this entire sequence, we see Gabriel facing the guests at the head of the table just at the moment he begins his speech. When he stands to speak in the story, he seems unsure of himself, as he "leaned his ten trembling fingers on the tablecloth and smiled nervously at the company. Meeting a row of upturned faces he raised his eyes to the chandelier" (Joyce, "The Dead" 175–76). His thoughts turn, briefly, to the sounds of skirts dancing a waltz in the drawing room and to the snow falling outside, a reference analeptically to the dancing cross-examination he takes from Miss Ivors and proleptically to the falling snow of the concluding scene in the hotel. The confident air exuded in the performance of his speech is contrasted here by his nervousness and by thoughts of failures past and future. And perhaps this is a reason to long for Gabriel's thoughts to somehow be presented to us in the film. However, there are other ways in which the film presents Gabriel's thoughts and contextualizes, visually and cinematically, his actions in general and his speech in particular. His speech—which celebrates "the tradition of genuine warmhearted courteous Irish hospitality," criticizes the "new generation," referring implicitly to nationalists of Miss Ivors's stripe, as "hypereducated," and honors the dead and the living, in particular the hostesses of the evening—is put into question by the film's presentation of him (176–77).

As he rises, the camera presents him in a medium shot, but is then behind him as he begins to speak before moving back to face him again, in a sort of shot reverse shot with Gabriel's front and back, as if Huston wants to establish the camera's total independence from Gabriel's point of view, much as he does with the first shots of Gabriel standing apart from the festivities early in the film. As Gabriel speaks of hospitality, the camera begins to move away from him, circling the table as it has circled before with the plate, in the dances, and during Mr. Grace's recitation. But as Gabriel speaks in praise of hospitality, the camera moves away from him as if distancing itself from him and disconnecting the message of his speech from the messenger and lingering at the apex of his praise for the spirit of hospitality on the "Three Graces of Dublin," his aunts and niece who are the hosts and hospitable ones, the embodiment of his message.

We see Gabriel again briefly, and the camera begins to move back up the table with him out of frame when his speech transitions from its celebration of hospitality to its meditation on the living and the dead. With this more somber turn in the speech, the camera draws closer to the guests at the table as it moves back toward Gabriel. In this movement it captures Gretta in two moments, framed by guests on the opposite side of the table, heightening the irony of Gabriel's unwitting invocation of the dead, when his wife's thoughts have been or will be about the dead Michael Furey. His speech's final turn is to praise and toast the hostesses of the evening. As he praises each one, the camera moves between medium shots of Gabriel or the "Three Graces of Dublin" and longer shots that show the table at length, often from beside or behind him or his aunts. This moment in the film marks a sharp critique in Huston's reading of the story. Gabriel's praise for Aunt Julia rings false to us or has a "hollow quality" despite its apparent sincerity, undermining his praise of Irish hospitality and good humor (Brill 216). As he extols her "perennial youth," we see her close up and note her age. While this certainly has the potential to be the tender and kind gesture of a loving nephew, what follows resists that reading.

When Gabriel says that Aunt Julia's "singing must've been a surprise and a revelation to us all tonight" the viewer cannot help but think back to her singing performance immediately preceding the dinner service. Although Aunt Julia's performance in the film works to undermine any reading of Gabriel's sincerity in his speech, it is also the one major alteration that might seem to frustrate Huston's promising reading of Joyce's story. Hart finds that the moment of Julia's performance "turn[s] a fine artistic moment into a piece of banal pathos" (11–12). Margot Norris notes that "the Huston film blatantly ignores the narrative descriptions of Julia Morkan's musical performance as stunning, and Bartell D'Arcy's as miserable, and reverses them to make them conform to the very gender stereotypes with respect to art that the text goes to pains to discredit" (Norris 115). For the portion of the film's audience that look at the film "*as an adaptation* . . . allowing the [work] to oscillate in [their] memories with what [they] are experiencing" (Hutcheon 120–21), could Huston's alteration contribute to the critical reading the film provides? This choice seems deliberate on the part of Huston to undermine the position of Gabriel. This alteration is striking because of the way it turns the praise of Aunt Julia's singing in the moment of her performance into a kind of pathetic and polite lie told to dissipate the awkward tension created by her poor voice. But Gabriel's repetition and extension of this polite lie underline his own false hospitality. So where Hart sees this alteration as productive of a banal pathos, the film in fact underscores the banality of Gabriel's praises in his speech. In addition, what Norris does not consider about the Julia/D'Arcy reversal in the film is how Julia's poor performance serves to undermine Gabriel's speech at the center of the film and how D'Arcy's polished performance heightens the impact of the story's climactic moment, a moment that Gretta experiences and Gabriel spectates.

In the film's final third of an hour, from the staircase scene with Gretta through the revelation in the Conroys' hotel room, the film's focus is on Gretta Conroy, even though so much of the focus in Joyce's story in these moments is on Gabriel Conroy's perspective on Gretta. As Gabriel gazes up at his wife, who gazes off into space during D'Arcy's singing of the "The Lass of Aughrim," the camera lingers on each of the Conroys in turn after turn, capturing their reactions. The singing of the song, at some length, invites the viewer to consider what Gabriel's thoughts might be as he watches his wife and what Gretta's thoughts might be as she listens to D'Arcy's singing. Although the film loses the interiority of the story here, what it gains is the magic of the moment for Gretta as she hears the song and is transported by the memories it evokes. The camera places us at the side of Gabriel, the observer, but precludes us from either of their thoughts. But not only do we observe from Gabriel's side, we are gazing upward at Gretta as if we were kneeling at the bottom of the stairs, whereas Gabriel stands. This is reinforced by Gabriel's arm and torso, which frame the shot on the left whenever both Gretta and Gabriel are visible. The camera's position in these shots mirrors the position Lily has just vacated as she helped Gabriel on with his boots. That the camera now occupies the same spot as Lily around the staircase creates a subtle visual echo between this scene and our first encounter with Gabriel and Lily at the beginning of the film. Huston's choice to present Gabriel as the adoring husband could seem to give Gabriel a pass for his patriarchal thoughts in the story, both here as he figures Gretta as a still-life, evoking echoes of Browning's "My Last Duchess," and later when he desires to "overmaster her" when they return to their hotel for the night, but this is not the case (Joyce, "The Dead" 189). Gabriel is shown as adoring but excluded in this moment from his wife's thoughts and affections, a separation that will only be heightened by the final scene between them in their hotel. The film places the emphasis, for both Gabriel and Gretta, on Gretta's enjoyment of the song and the sad, romantic memory it evokes, rather than Gabriel's objectification of Gretta. In this way, the film recaptures the story as Gretta's story.

Perhaps nowhere in the film does Gretta's story come more prominently to the fore than in the final twenty minutes, from the time the Conroys leave the party, traveling by carriage to their hotel room for the night. Whereas in Joyce's text these moments are deeply filtered through the lens of Gabriel's consciousness, in the film Gabriel is moved to a secondary position, as he has been throughout the film. This is significant insofar as the film elides the sexual desire expressed in Gabriel's thoughts in the story, thoughts which present a picture of Gabriel that is, at times, quite unflattering in his desire to master Gretta. While much of this is lost in the film's rendering, what is gained is a representation of how completely unaware Gabriel is of a significant story in his wife's past. Gabriel is shown finally to be at a remove even from his own wife, just as he has been apart from so much of the conviviality of the evening's party.

When Gabriel coaxes Gretta into telling him what troubles her, Huston begins to visually emphasize the importance of Gretta and her experience at the same time that Gabriel is made marginal. The visual image in this scene powerfully suggests the way Gretta's story creates a

Figure 3.2. Gazing into the middle distance, Gretta separates herself and her story from the marginalized Gabriel.

point of separation between the two. Gretta, seated on the bed, is closest to the camera, yet she addresses her story off into the distance. Gabriel is standing behind her, fully presented to the camera and at the center of the shot, but off at a diagonal from his wife. Directly over Gretta's head we see Gabriel's shadow cast on the wall, evoking the shade of Michael Furey as she speaks. Although Gabriel shifts a bit during the first part of the scene, he remains in such a position as to keep this shadow above Gretta. When he moves over to sit on the bed, the shadow moves with him and forms a triangle with the shadow on her left, behind Gretta, and with Gabriel on her right, his body and face largely blocked from our view by Gretta sitting at the apex. As Gretta explains why she thinks Furey died for her, she moves to the window. The camera tracks her, putting Gabriel and the shadow out of the frame. Huston only briefly cuts back to Gabriel to establish his attentive gaze on his emotional wife. Brill notes that these "shots of Gretta from her husband's point of view buil[d] toward the revelation of profound loneliness in Gabriel's concluding internal monologue" (Brill 218). So even as the film largely avoids adopting Gabriel's point of view, Huston manages to imply key elements of it. As Gretta's story reaches its emotional climax, Gabriel draws near to her, and she turns and embraces him, crying on his shoulder for a moment. She then throws herself on the bed, once again leaving Gabriel out of the frame, but his shadow lingers over Gretta, until he moves back into the frame and sits on the bed to comfort his weeping wife. As before, the couple and the shadow form a triangle. This shot is particularly Joycean in that it is both rife with intensity and meaning and highly economical.

When Gabriel reaches out to comfort Gretta, Huston cuts to a close-up of Gretta and his hand, cutting most of Gabriel out of the frame again. He is near to her, yet he is distanced from her in a small, significant way. Gretta's sobbing ends, and she appears to sleep. At this moment Gabriel stands up and begins to move across the room toward the window, looking back on his sleeping wife who is now out of the frame. "The Lass of Aughrim" is heard as extradiegetic music. And so begins the concluding moment of the film with Gabriel's voice-over narration and a montage, first of images of family and death and then of the Irish landscape.

Where Barry sees the concluding montage as the ultimate mark of Huston's failure, Brill offers a more sympathetic reading that engages with the potential interpretive complexity generated by the final montage. Barry sees in the ending of Joyce's story a kind of indeterminacy of point of view, where the reader must determine "from phrase to phrase . . . the status and authority of a volatile narrative voice (third-person, first-person, or both at once)" (Barry, *The Dead* 77). He sees Huston's concluding montage as a kind of totalizing vision, free of the uncertainty of the narrative text, and completely and authoritatively in Gabriel's voice. In contrast, Brill notes that the close of *The Dead* is "more skeptical, richer and more delicately balanced, than it at first seems" (221). He turns to an interesting reading of the agency of the camera throughout the entire film to account for the multiplicity of meanings subtly offered up by the end.

In my own reading of the film, I have tried to show ways in which the camera's independence, particularly from Gabriel, gives it a freedom from the limitations of a character-bound perspective, even if it at times draws closer to the gravitational field of a character (to draw once again on Kenner's description of the Uncle Charles principle.) The camera's consistent demonstration of its independence, beginning with Gabriel's entrance at the party, during the party's various performances and the dancing, over the course of the climactic dinner and after-dinner speech, and especially in the film's final act where the focus shifts to Gretta and her story, should prevent a viewer from making the mistake of assuming that the film's final montage presents Gabriel's totalizing vision. At the end of the film, as in these other moments, it is important not to presuppose, as most critics of the film have, that the camera "assumes Gabriel's point of view" merely because the narration features his voice (Varela 146).[4]

The character-ness of the camera, in Brill's terms, or its zero-ocularization, in Jost's terms, troubles the negative critical appraisal of the final montage, accompanied by its voice-over narration. This negativity stems from a concern that an overly strong linkage to Gabriel's personal perspective is generated and that this perspective is reductive in meaning. Ironically, these critics do not voice similar objections to Joyce's text, where at key moments of the story events are filtered through Gabriel's perspective. In Brill's excellent reading, "The camera is partly identified with Gabriel; but even then it retains a separate identity . . . We are likely to apprehend this last shot as coming equally from Gabriel's imagination and from the independent intelligence that has guided the camera throughout the film" (223). This somewhat paradoxical attribution of vision seems to be precisely the kind of indeterminacy that Barry and others read in Joyce's story but do not see in Huston's film. But Brill is right to connect the montage to Gabriel, even though he also attributes independence to the camera. The montage needs to be connected to Gabriel in order for this "final epiphany" to work as an "act of emotional expansiveness, self-understanding, and generosity" that stands "in contrast to [Gabriel's] patriarchal and imperialistic urge for mastery, domination, colonization, and hierarchy" on display throughout Joyce's story (Cheng 146). While the voice in the film speaking the final lines of Joyce's prose might belong to the actor playing Gabriel, and it might need to be his voice in order to connect with Gabriel, the camera troubles a singular or totalizing reading of the passage. Certainly a few shots in the montage could be ascribed to Gabriel's point of view, but the shots of him from outside of the window and almost all of the shots of the landscape of Ireland suggest zero ocularization. This concluding indeterminacy is subtly faithful to Joyce's text yet also consistent with Huston's critical reading as an adaptation of the text. The final gestures of the camera distance it from Gabriel's perspective, without erasing Gabriel's perspective, while still allowing the perspective on Ireland to be more than just his rather hollow formulation of what Ireland might truly be. In a way, Huston finds a way to take Gabriel at his word without being limited by Gabriel's own words. In addition, and perhaps most importantly, Gretta's story is more fully shared, and the praise Gabriel lavishes on Ireland in his speech is genuinely presented by Huston's *The Dead*.

Notes

1. Clive Hart does argue that Huston's version makes the story "Gretta's story rather than Gabriel's," however (13).
2. In addition to Barry's discussion of it in his book on the film, see Luke Gibbons, "'The Cracked Looking Glass.'"
3. See Cheng, Duffy, and Manganiello on Joyce and politics.
4. I should note that although Varela strongly argues that the camera assumes Gabriel's perspective in the final scene, he also sees it "pla[y] a game of proximity and distance" throughout the film (148).

Works Cited

Bal, Mieke. *Narratology: Introduction to the Theory of Narrative*. 2nd ed. Toronto: U of Toronto P, 1997.
Barry, Kevin. *The Dead*. Cork: Cork UP, 2001.
———. "Tracing Joyce: 'The Dead' in Huston and Rossellini." *Roll Away the Reel World: James Joyce and Cinema*. Ed. John McCourt. Cork: Cork UP, 2010. 149–57.
Brill, Lesley. *John Huston's Filmmaking*. Cambridge: Cambridge UP, 1997.
Cheng, Vincent J. *Joyce, Race, and Empire*. Cambridge: Cambridge UP, 1995.
The Dead. Dir. John Huston. Lionsgate, 1987. DVD.
Duffy, Enda. *The Subaltern Ulysses*. Minneapolis: U of Minnesota P, 1994.
Gibbons, Luke. "'The Cracked Looking Glass' of Cinema: James Joyce, John Huston, and the Memory of 'The Dead.'" *The Yale Journal of Criticism* 15.1 (Spring 2002), 127–48. Web. 1 Feb. 2013.

———. "Visualizing the Voice: Joyce, Cinema, and the Politics of Vision." *A Companion to Literature and Film*. Ed. Robert Stam and Alessandra Raengo. Oxford: Blackwell, 2004. 171–88.
Hart, Clive. *Joyce, Huston, and the Making of the Dead*. Gerrards Cross: Colin Smythe, 1988.
Hutcheon, Linda, and Siobhan O'Flynn. *A Theory of Adaptation*. London: Routledge, 2013.
Jost, François. "The Look: From Film to Novel: An Essay in Comparative Narratology." *A Companion to Literature and Film*. Ed. Robert Stam and Alessandra Raengo. Oxford: Blackwell, 2004. 71–80.
Joyce, James. "The Dead." *Dubliners*. Ed. Margot Norris. New York: W. W. Norton, 2006.
———. *A Portrait of the Artist as a Young Man*. New York: Viking, 1964.
———. *Ulysses*. New York: Vintage, 1986.
Kenner, Hugh. *Joyce's Voices*. London: Faber and Faber, 1978.
Manganiello, Dominic. *Joyce's Politics*. London: Routledge and Kegan Paul, 1980.
Naremore, James. "Introduction: Film and the Reign of Adaptation." *Film Adaptation*. Ed. James Naremore. New Brunswick: Rutgers UP, 2000. 1–16.
———. "Return of the Dead." *Perspectives on John Huston*. Ed. Stephen Cooper. New York: G. K. Hall, 1994. 197–206.
Norris, Margot. *Joyce's Web: The Social Unraveling of Modernism*. Austin: U of Texas P, 1992.
Varela, Manuel Barbeito. "John Huston's vs. James Joyce's *The Dead*." *Books in Motion: Adaptation, Intertextuality, Authorship*. Ed. Mireia Aragay. Amsterdam: Rodopi, 2005. 145–161.

4

STEVEN RYBIN

On Beams and Birds

John Huston's Adaptation of *The Maltese Falcon*

IN DASHIELL HAMMETT'S NOVEL *The Maltese Falcon* (1930), characters work to shape and direct the course of plot through their own social performances and through reading the performative signs displayed by others. Brigid O'Shaughnessy, for example, under the assumed moniker Miss Wonderly, tells a story, upon appearing in detective Sam Spade's office in the first chapter of the book, of Floyd Thursby, who has absconded with her sister. Her story is performed convincingly enough and is interpreted by Spade as *true* enough, to prompt the detective and his partner, Miles Archer, to tail this man, a decision that leads to Archer's and Thursby's mysterious deaths and to the ensuing plot of the book. Brigid, transforming herself into Miss Wonderly through her well-prepared story and finely tuned skills of performance, uses both Archer and Thursby as objects in her quest to attain for herself the titular bird. Sometimes, though, characters in Hammett's novel, rather than effectively controlling the story themselves, give themselves away, make themselves too easily interpretable through their relationship with other objects. Joel Cairo, for example, arrives at Spade's office to offer him five thousand dollars in exchange for an "ornament that has been—shall we say?—mislaid" (43)—an object that will soon be revealed as the main concern of all the characters, the object of all their existential plotting.

Unlike Brigid, however, Cairo does not so much tell his story as he has it forced out of him. After Cairo pulls a gun on Spade, the detective drops an elbow on him, and while Cairo is unconscious, the detective sifts through his belongings for objects and scraps that might tell him the story of who Cairo is:

> There was a large wallet of dark soft leather. The wallet contained three hundred and sixty-five dollars in United States bills of several sizes; three five-pound notes; a much-visaed Greek passport bearing Cairo's name and portrait; five folded sheets of pinkish onion-skin paper covered with what seemed to be Arabic writing; a raggedly clipped newspaper-account of the finding of Archer's and Thursby's bodies; a post-card photograph of a dusky woman with bold cruel eyes and a tender drooping mouth; a large silk hanker-chief, yellow with age and somewhat cracked along its folds; a thin sheaf of Mr. Joel Cairo's engraved cards; and a ticket for an orchestra seat at the Geary Theatre that evening. (47)

That all of these objects should amount to an immediate impression of Cairo's place in this story indicates not only the effectiveness of Spade's rough-and-tumble methods of interpreting his social others, but also the importance of Hammett's objective writing style, which, in eschewing a deeply psychological portrait of any of its characters, tends to approach them from the outside, as something like objects under the watchful eye of a writer who describes them not so much to get to know them, but rather to know their place in his novel's world.

It has often been noted that the novel *The Maltese Falcon* and John Huston's 1941 film adaptation are quite similar; indeed, the director himself has made such a claim, in one interview reporting that he polished off the writing of the script adaptation in just two weeks (see Interview by Dick Cavett). In his autobiography, Huston writes that he took to the project precisely because the previous adaptations of the novel, *The Maltese Falcon* (Roy Del Ruth, 1931) and *Satan Met a Lady* (William Dieterle, 1936), suffered from "new, uncalled-for scenes" by screenwriters who misguidedly "sought to put their own stamp on the story" (78). Despite Huston's ostensible faithfulness to the material, one of the oft-noted contrasts between novel and film is the way the content of the story is treated; while Hammett approaches his characters through a mix of psychological distance and close-up physical observation, Huston prefers to embellish both actor and object through an expressionistic vision, the sort of style that prompted Manny Farber to rather hyperbolically label Huston as the "Eisenstein of the Bogart thriller" (33). What unites Hammett's and Huston's approaches, however, is a commitment, approached from these slightly different aesthetic sensibilities, to situate characters within narratives they themselves craft while at the same time observing how those narratives are complicated by the competing existential projects of other characters in the surrounding space. Lesley Brill has explored this idea by interpreting the characters as crafters of self-consciously theatrical personages, figures who bid for control over social meaning through the carefully cultivated presentation of the private self (see Brill, especially 151–52).

In Huston's film, these attempts by the characters to shape a sense of self, or to detect the selves of others through decoding their means of self-presentation or their relationships with objects in social space, are bids to control the flow of events. The director's nimble use of cinematography and mise-en-scène, in turn, are techniques which inscribe this depth of social space into which characters variously attempt to intervene and within which they strive to shape their existential projects (for most of them, this is to acquire the titular bird). As James Naremore has observed, Hammett's method, whereby he "occasionally lends atmosphere to his tale by listing objects," as in the description of Cairo's pocket contents cited earlier, is echoed in Huston's film through the use of deep-focus lenses that enable the detailed presentation of objects and their place within a setting (154). Within this economically presented narrative space (presented rather objectively in Hammett, and embellished by Huston's own expressionistic flourishes in the film), we see characters speak words meant to signify their relationships with the world around them, as they craft narratives and stories meant as the existential means by which they themselves might possess the bird that is the object of pursuit. Yet as they do so, space and the presence of other characters and other stories within that space, threaten to thwart their goals.

The novel contains two examples of especially lengthy narratives recounted by characters, narratives that work to establish a major character's stakes in the game and that pressure other characters to respond to those stakes. Huston retains part of one of these long narratives in his film version, but he entirely discards the second. The first of these narratives is Gutman's long account of the historical origins of the Maltese Falcon, in which he describes:

> this foot-high jeweled bird made by Turkish slaves in the castle of Angelo. . . . The bird went to Algiers. That's a fact.

> That's a fact that the French historian Pierre Dan put in one of his letters from Algiers. He wrote that the bird had been there for more than a hundred years, until it was carried away by Sir Frances Verney, the English adventurer who was with the Algerian buccaneers for awhile. Maybe it wasn't, but Pierre Dan believed it was, and that's good enough for me. (125)

And this narrative, in the book, goes on to describe the bird's journey from the hands of Algerian buccaneers, to a Sicilian king, to the father of a Spanish count, and finally to a Greek dealer of antiques. In the film, Gutman (Sydney Greenstreet) describes a similar, if condensed, history of the Maltese Falcon to Bogart's Sam Spade, highlighting the bird's origins as a figure created by slaves for a Maltese king and charting its course from Malta to the hands of a Greek. In the novel, the depiction of the space in which this story is recounted is kept to a minimum: "The fat man looked over his shoulders at the three closed doors, hunched his chair a few inches nearer Spade's, and reduced his voice to a husky whisper" (123–24). Here, the secrecy with which Gutman tells the story motivates Hammett to foreshorten the reader's sense of narrative space: the novelist makes no further reference to the surrounding space of Gutman's apartment in the rest of the chapter, having situated our interest squarely, and quite closely, on the words his character is speaking. But in Huston's film, the expressionistic depiction of space acts as an important adjunct to Gutman's words. Throughout the film, we see a play between close shots of characters asserting their will to possess the bird of the title and longer shots that place such desire in a more complicated and contested social form. In this sequence, Huston's low-angle camera, during certain shots of Gutman speaking, situates Greenstreet's character as an imposing, voluminous figure, more solid and compact than the "flabbily fat" man with "bulbous pink cheeks and lips and chins and neck, with a great soft egg of a belly that was all his torso, and pendant cones for arms and legs" (104), that Hammett describes in the novel, but every bit as intimidating. This presentation of Gutman as a powerful, looming figure in space conveys less the authenticity of the story he is telling and more the imposing figure of the man telling it—a kind of visual corollary for the idea, expressed in the last clause of the long Hammett passage quoted above—"that's good enough for me"—that Gutman is less concerned with the validity of the Falcon's history than with his own intensity of belief in it. Yet Huston also cuts to longer medium shots of Greenstreet speaking while Bogart sits on the couch to the right of him, shots in which the former is positioned in front of two windows that let in streams of light, images that remind us that a certain measure of Gutman's forceful narrativity is deflected by Bogart's patient, quiet, stoic listening. The scene, up until the subjective shot of Bogart's Spade feeling the woozy effects of the drugged whisky Gutman has tricked him into imbibing, is presented with a kind of expressive objectivity that grants the characters a degree of autonomy in their presentation of narrative, while at the same time reminding us that these narratives are quite simply that: presentations, existing within a social and expressive space that juts up against the meaning of what they have presented and how they have presented it.

It may be, then, that Huston chose to entirely cut the other lengthy narrative presented by a character in Hammett's book—the recounting of the story of Flitman by Sam Spade to Brigid O'Shaughnessy—because the message of a socially placed existentialism contained within its words was to be implicitly conveyed by his expressive visual style. Retaining the Flitman story would have been redundant. Nevertheless, the story of Flitman, as Spade recounts it for Brigid and as written by Hammett, is worth quoting at some length; despite its exclusion from the film, the story indirectly informs the film's poetic inscription of characters within space:

> Going to lunch [Flitman] passed an office-building that was being put up—just the skeleton. A beam or something fell eight or ten stories down and smacked the sidewalk alongside him. It brushed pretty close to him, but didn't touch him, though a piece of the sidewalk was chipped off and flew up and hit his cheek. It only took a piece of skin off, but he still had the scar when I saw him. He rubbed it with his finger—well, affectionately—when he told me about it. He was scared stiff of course, he said, but he was more shocked than really frightened. He felt like somebody had taken the lid off life and let him look at the works.
>
> . . . What disturbed him was the discovery that in sensibly ordering his affairs he had got out of step, and not into step, with life. He said he knew before he had gone twenty feet from the fallen beam that he would never know peace again until he had adjusted himself to this new glimpse of life. By the time he had eaten his luncheon he had found his means of adjustment. Life could be ended for him at random by a falling beam: he would change his life at random by simply going away. (63–64)

As Spade goes on to recount, Flitman decides to abandon his present life for an alternative existence in San Francisco. He is, for a time, a wanderer, but then he begins to order his life in much the same way he had ordered it before, with a wife and "fair games of golf and bridge" (64). "But that's the part of it I always liked," Spade tells Brigid. "He adjusted himself to beams falling, and then no more of them fell, and he adjusted to them not falling" (64).

What is interesting about the Flitman story, beyond the way in which its existentialist message parallels the efforts of Hammett's characters to control the narrative trajectory of the search for the bird, is that it provides us with something that Hammett and Huston, for the most part elsewhere, do not: a back story for a character. We come to know more about the personal history of this otherwise anonymous Flitman, and why he has done what he has done, in the few paragraphs in which Spade speaks these words to Brigid, than we ever quite learn of Brigid, Gutman, or Cairo. What has led Brigid, Gutman, and Cairo to desire to possess the bird? The answer of "money" is not sufficient: certainly other objects might be desired to be possessed, objects perhaps worth a similar value and perhaps not as difficult to obtain. The long historical recounting by Gutman, as filmed by Huston, only reemphasizes that it is not the bird's unique historical trajectory, but the force of Gutman's individual desire to want to possess an object with such a valued and storied history that drives the narrative. Robert B. Ray, in his cinephilic analysis of the film in *The ABCs of Classical Hollywood*, asks a number of additional questions that point to the film's (and the novel's) relative lack of interest in conveying back story, such as: "How does Spade always know when Brigid is lying? . . . What did Gutman's 'agents' do to Kemidov to 'persuade' him to give up the Falcon? . . . What previous occupation has made Gutman so adept with calculations?" (223). Neither Hammett nor Huston answers these questions through Flitmanesque narrative exposition. Neither author tells us of any metaphorical or literal beam that might have fallen on, say, Brigid's head, to lead her to radically redirect her life in pursuit of a bejeweled bird. Indeed, we never even quite learn if Brigid's pursuit of the Falcon is any kind of radical departure at all: perhaps she has always been an inveterate liar. (Certainly Astor's potent performance effectively suggests a character who has spent a life building skills of deception.)

Yet the presence of the Flitman narrative in the Hammett text, and its absence in the Huston film, nevertheless suggests differences in each text's vision. In the novel, the presence of the Flitman narrative opens up the possibility of reading the characters' actions, and their desire to possess the elusive bird, as if it were a response to a fallen beam, a chance to remake one's life in pursuit of an exotic object. Although Hammett never makes this parallel explicit, certain lines of dialogue and aspects of behavior suggest not only the high existential stakes at play in the pursuit of the bird, but also the caution of characters to avoid stepping into a situation too late or too early, lest they be felled by a beam. There is the way Brigid haughtily and humorously dismisses the meaning of Spade's Flitman story with a flip "How perfectly fascinating" (64), deflecting Spade's own brand of existentialism with a single line of dialogue in a partial effort to retain her own control over the flow and meaning of narrative events. And there is the way Hammett describes Spade as a patient and aloof listener, waiting for the right moment in which to intervene in a narrative unfolding before him: "Spade, propped on an elbow on the sofa, looked at and listened to them impartially. In the comfortable slackness of his body, in the easy stillness of his features, there was no indication of either curiosity or impatience" (88). Spade responds, as if aware of the absurdity of his situation in a way that evokes the absurdity of the Flitman tale, to the one metaphorical beam that literally fells him, the drugged whiskey given him by Gutman, after it begins to take its effects: "He stood up, helping himself up with his hands on the arms of his chair. He shook his head again and took an uncertain step forward. He laughed thickly and muttered: 'God damn you'" (130). And at the end of the Hammett story, Spade, having delivered Brigid to jail, goes home with Archer's widow, Iva, effectively inscribing him in the sort of normative, domestic situation to which Flitman also returns after his wandering through San Francisco.

Most of these moments in the book have parallels in the film. The one significant moment that is missing, of course, is Spade's return to Iva: where the novel ends on the coupling of Spade with Iva, the film ends after the scene in which Brigid is delivered to the cops and in which Bogart famously describes the purloined bird as "the stuff that dreams are made of." As Lesley Brill has commented, this line of dialogue, not present in the novel, is a reference to Prospero's speech in the fourth act of Shakespeare's *The Tempest*: "We are such stuff / As dreams are made on, and our little life / Is rounded with a sleep" (quoted in Brill, 153). For Brill, this reference to the play "emphasizes the artifice of the cinematic performance that the audience has just witnessed and the internal fictions, the lies and acting that its figures have performed for each other" (153). In other words, in Huston's film, there is no normative situation from which the characters depart, nor any to which they return; there is no preexisting situation that throws into relief the existential wandering that takes place after the falling of a beam, nor is there any return to a normative situation after the memory of the beam's impact has been forgotten. Instead, the artifice of each character—as a storyteller, or a liar, and a social performer—is an indicator of a larger human situation, in which we are all social players, never rescued by a comfortable normative situation from our ongoing efforts at impressing or figuring ourselves for others in space. In Huston's *Maltese Falcon*, in other words, the falling beam is not the event that causes departure from the norm. The falling of beams is the norm itself: the guarantee that we will all ultimately be felled ("our little life / Is rounded with a sleep"). Unlike Flitman, who forgets the falling beam and returns to a life much like his former one, the characters in Huston's *Maltese Falcon* are always quite ready for the next beam to fall, having never remembered a time before the first one. They remain, at every moment, responsive to the dangers of the world in which the film inscribes them. Huston has again played up this anxiety through two key elements of his inscription of authorship: the orchestration of relationships, accomplished through staging and cutting, and the occasional close-up or, at certain critical moments, deep-focus shot.

In this respect, what is perhaps most interesting about the novel, relative to the Huston film, is that Flitman never quite sees what falls: as Hammett describes in the first sentence above, all Flitman ever sees, or all Spade, as storyteller, quite remembers of the tale, is a "beam *or something* [italics mine]" that falls suddenly alongside the man as he strolls next to the office building. The object that almost fells him remains just out of the frame of Hammett's sentence, an ambiguous "something" not quite part of the narrative space of Spade's recounted story. For Hammett, objects, when knowable, become part of detection, the gradual accumulation of detail that informs who a character is (as in the example of Spade rifling through Cairo's pockets); but as the Flitman tale reminds us, objects in space become treacherous, and potentially life-altering, when they cannot quite be seen or detected, when their placement in or intrusion into a socially defined spatial context becomes ambiguous or unpredictable. This is a strategy Huston has transposed to his film, through patterned play between figures and objects in close-up and social players positioned in depth of space. In depth of focus, that which treacherously invades social form can be anticipated, prepared for, or at least held at bay through one's social performance and narrative control. In close shot, when one or more planes of the image may be beyond what vision can grasp, these social others and foreign objects threaten to become little more than a beam *or something* that might fall—thus knocking out, removing, or redirecting the course of a social player whose presence in deep space once enabled a promise of narrative control.

These patterns of relationship between a collapse of space in close shot and a depth of positioning in long shot are evident in the first ten

Figure 4.1. Brigid O'Shaughnessy dramatically enters Spade's office in the first deep-focus shot of the film.

minutes. The film begins with a close shot of Bogart rolling a cigarette underneath a window bearing the "Spade and Archer" lettering that will soon be modified once the detective's partner is shot by a scheming bird hunter in the film's next sequence. Spade's secretary, Effie Perine (Lee Patrick), describes this woman as someone Spade will want to see—a "knockout." If Effie's words prefigure the romance that will shortly spark between Spade and Brigid, Mary Astor's entrance into Spade's office motivates the first deep-focus shot in the film, in which Astor, first glimpsed in silhouette behind the frosted windows of Spade's office, enters Bogart's space like a player making her entrance from the wings to the stage, ready to shape her share of the story. But Brigid (under the moniker she assumes for the first part of the film, Miss Wonderly), in spite of her attractiveness, is not quite the knockout, in the literal and dangerous sense of the term, that Effie describes: she is no falling beam that will land on Spade's head and knock him out, or at least not quite yet. Having been fully glimpsed in the social space of Spade's office, she can be viewed, kept at a distance, and understood in terms relative to everything else around her. Spade still has some share of the narrative control. As James Naremore writes, "Our first view of Mary Astor's face is meant to contrast her with the drab walls of Spade's office: Daylight from a window at the upper right of the frame sets off the little black hat perched atop her head, her fur wrap, and the line of her shoulder" (156). As Spade will later confirm, when he tells Brigid, after the death of Archer, that her story about her missing sister was never quite convincing, Miss Wonderly can only take partial narrative and visual control of this space in which she enters; visually distinguished from the workaday environs of Spade and Archer's office, she is narratively distinguished from them, too, a fast-talking dame whose story Spade, as he will later tell her, never quite fully believes.

It is, in fact, Archer (Jerome Cowan) who seems to believe it, or is at least attracted by the woman who tells it. When Cowan enters the scene, he walks right up beside Astor, slouching shoulders pointing down toward her, attention riveted, desire and humor piqued. Cowan himself is ever so slightly distinguished from Spade and the rest of the office by a white carnation decorating the left lapel of his suit jacket, and by his rather fey positioning on Spade's desk as he leans forward less because of his rapt interest in Brigid's story than in the appearance of she who tells it. Where Spade, although intrigued, remains thoroughly ambivalent throughout the scene, Archer seems to want to collapse the space that lies between him and Miss Wonderly, less out of interest in the case and more out of interest in her. "Maybe you saw her first," Archer will tell his partner after Wonderly leaves, "but I spoke first," a suggestive line of dialogue that implies that Archer's inability to *see* this woman enables her to become the beam which will knock him out. And Huston foreshadows his fate, too, at the end of the opening sequence, not only through the fact that his camera tracks in to the expressionistic shadow of the Spade and Archer lettering on the window which is cast across the floor, but also because, in this tracking, the shot becomes a close-up, eliminating the depth of space which allows Spade to see Brigid for who she really is and prefiguring the low-key and shallowly presented space of the close-up in the next sequence, in which we will see Archer shot dead by an unseen assailant.

That Spade seems almost entirely nonplussed by Archer's death, and that he is indeed so quick to replace Archer's name on his window marquee, is less a sign of his hard-boiled detachment (and even less an indicator of his possible culpability in Archer's death, as Ward Bond's diegetic cop suspects), than it is his acute understanding that to place oneself in shallow space is to risk the falling beam. So throughout the rest of the film Bogart's Spade will work to position, and reposition, himself in a depth of space, in which objects and other figures can be apprehended visually and intellectually, rather than just obliquely seen or suddenly felt. The first major threat to Spade's life, in the film, arrives in the first presence of Joel Cairo (Peter Lorre). When Effie introduces Cairo into Spade's office, the first impression is one of a vaguely Eastern European politesse: Cairo thanks Spade for the offer of a seat and offers condolences for Archer's death. In the brief medium two-shot of them together, Joel Cairo is no less a contrast with Spade's office than Brigid in the earlier scene, his curly hair, dainty gloves, and walking cane thrown into relief against the workaday environs of Spade's professional den. And Spade, here, is no less ambivalent than he was in the earlier scene with Brigid; but now, as Huston emphasizes through close shots of both characters as the conversation ensues, the threat with Cairo is much more immediate, his ambiguous visual presence in the scene a little trickier to grasp than Brigid's archetypal femme fatale. These shots of Bogart and Lorre talking, in which we will soon see Cairo pull a gun on the detective so that he may search Spade's office for the falcon, are typical of the "deliberately stylized" (156) close-ups of characters that James Naremore has noted throughout the film, character shots that tend to inscribe the essence of a figure through gestures or details—Bogart's rolling of a cigarette, Lorre's caress of the tip of his walking cane. When in close-up, indeed, characters in *The Maltese Falcon* are able to impress upon us the force of their desire for the bird of the title (again, as with the previously noted low-angle close shots of Sidney Greenstreet, inscribing upon us less the movement of a goal-oriented plot than the force of interest each character takes in that plot), and shot reverse shot close-ups become an implicit battle of wills. To place oneself so, to assert the force of one's desire for an object, is to subject oneself to the threats that lie outside the frame, and outside of one's will. Cairo soon finds this out when, compelling Spade to follow his orders from behind the barrel of a gun, he is overpowered by Spade with a right-handed punch, filmed by Huston and Edeson in a low-key, low-angle medium two-shot that asserts, if only for a moment before Cairo recovers, Spade's control over the events that take place in the space of his office.

Although the aforementioned example is of a two-shot featuring Lorre and Bogart, most of the rest of the film will stage its central conflicts through more complicated three-shots, four-shots, and five-shots, as Spade, Brigid, Cairo, Gutman, and Wilmer (Gutman's gunman, played by Elisha Cook Jr.) all descend upon the same space in search of the bird. Nevertheless, despite this ongoing increase in the number of figures that tend to dominate the space of the film's frame at any one time, its play between close-up and long shot, and between individual will and social performance, continues to pattern the rest of the film. After his initial contact with Cairo, Spade will journey to Brigid's apartment, ostensibly to deliver Brigid news of Cairo's search for the bird, but in reality to begin to unpack Brigid's own intentions. In this sequence, and in something of an inversion of Brigid's salient visual presence in Spade's office, Spade's black suit jacket and wary stare are thrown into contrast against the flowered drapes and gray walls of Brigid's apartment. Brigid herself is no more a confident social player in this space, however, given that her nervous pattering, "blushing, stammering" are read by Spade as a "schoolgirl manner" that is performatively unconvincing. This is perhaps why Spade feels comfortable kissing Brigid in close-up; he has peeled away enough layers of her performance to know that no threat lies in wait for him in this scene, quite yet.

But in the next scene, when Spade brings Cairo to his apartment to meet Brigid, the play between close-up and long shot becomes more complex and, for those in the diegesis, more dangerous. As the sequence begins, Brigid and Cairo settle into their chairs, while Spade, positioned between them and with his back to the camera, listens closely, watching the performances unfolding before him. Most of the ensuing conversation between Cairo and Brigid unfolds in a series of shot-reaction shots, punctuated by occasional cutaways of Bogart, quietly listening, in an intense low-angle that prefigures the subsequent presentation of Gutman. In all of these images we remain persistently aware that when characters perform in *The Maltese Falcon*, they perform in a social space, a character always looming out of frame or in the foreground; and this is why when metaphorical beams fall in this scene—when Brigid suddenly slaps Cairo, or when Cairo reaches into his jacket pocket to pull out a gun in response, or when Spade leaps out of his chair to prevent Cairo from firing—they are not quite able to completely knock out their target, given each figure's heightened awareness of the potential threat every other social player in a narrative space that all three, and Spade above all, carefully views.

Some shots thrown at characters eventually begin reaching their targets: when Gutman knocks Spade out with laced whiskey, the detective's woozy fall is complemented by a violent kick to the face from Wilmer. As the knockout drops begin to take their effect, we are briefly presented with a point-of-view shot taken from Spade's perspective of an out-of-focus Gutman. But the greater visual percentage of this narrative event takes place in, first, a two-shot—Bogart gets up, drowsily, from the couch, knocks over an end table and the vase of flowers—and then a three-shot, as Wilmer enters the frame at Gutman's beckon, to knock Spade over and kick him in the face. (That last touch, as a kind of punctuation mark to the violence, is Wilmer's own little touch.) But the fact that a falling beam, in the form of laced whiskey to the gut and a kick to the face, has finally hit Spade directly where it counts, throws into relief the fact that it has taken a degrading of his visual perception, through the knockout drops administered by Gutman, to do the trick. In Huston's film, one is truly and coldly knocked out when one has lost one's view of space and one's position within it.

The film's climax—and its final patterning of relationships between close shots and longer views—occurs in a complicated set of shots, many of them long five-shots, in which the presumed Maltese Falcon makes its first appearance and in which our five main figures (Spade, Brigid, Cairo, Gutman, and Wilmer) occasionally gather in the frame together. When the sequence begins, all five characters are in the same shot: Spade and Wilmer first quarreling, and then positioned on opposite sides of the frame; Brigid, back to the camera, seated, watching the men; Gutman, perched on his large leather chair; and Cairo, behind Gutman, gun pointed at the detective. After this establishing five-shot Huston will transition to a variety of closer four-, three-, and two-shots, and

Figure 4.2. All five characters appear in a single shot to re-establish Huston's narrative and visual sequencing.

the occasional close-up on a single character: tracking in past Brigid to frame the four men as a quartet; in a three-shot, as Bogart leans forward to persist in his explanation of plan to Gutman, with Cairo lingering behind; in a two-shot as Bogart walks over to Brigid to ask his "precious," his "angel," how she feels about his plan; and cutting close on Bogart as he explains his plan to pin the murders on a fall guy (and then close on an uncomfortable Wilmer, as Bogart explains that Wilmer is the best choice for a ringer). In other words, *someone* is almost always out of frame, perched to view and perhaps ruin the intentions of the other scheming characters. Only occasionally will Huston return to a five-shot, reestablishing all of our figures in the same image, and usually only then when some point in the narrative demands it; this happens when Spade, after having his plan of framing Wilmer rejected by Gutman, moves over to Brigid's side, gazing toward Gutman's gang as if thinking how best to approach them next. Throughout this sequence, as throughout much of the film, Bogart's Spade is the motivating force behind the cutting: the one whose crafting of plan (to frame Wilmer; to have his secretary bring the bird to the apartment at a certain time; to check with Brigid about how she feels) motivates cuts to closer shots of the other figures as they respond variously to the machinations of his plan.

And, of course, his machinations unwittingly set up the revelation of the inauthenticity of the film's titular object of pursuit, the fake bird, kept offscreen throughout most of the duration of the movie, which will serve as the figurative beam that spoils the narratives each character has tried to craft. As we learn, the Maltese Falcon that Effie Perine brings to the apartment is not the real Falcon at all but a fake lead version. When the parcel is unwrapped in a close shot, layers of padded stuffing pulled back to reveal the bird, all the characters are kept out of frame, the bird not seen with them until Gutman carefully cradles it in his hands, lifting it up to its standing position—but even then, the bird commands its own shot until Huston tracks the camera back to reveal Cairo, Brigid, Gutman, and, in the background, Wilmer, watching patiently as Gutman checks its authenticity. Bogart watches all of this, out of frame. He is not seen in the same shot as the bird until the camera tracks back to reveal him, on the left side of the frame, watching as Gutman discovers his object of desire is a fake. But the characters quickly recover from this knockout punch. Gutman refuses to be dissuaded from his search, insisting that a seventeen-year journey will not be ended by the revelation of one mere fake. And then he leaves, and so does Cairo, and the cops are called, and Brigid is reluctantly given over to the authorities. Bogart leaves the movie with the beam in his hand, speaking of "the stuff dreams are made of." If only that fake bird, cradled in Bogart's arms as he makes his way back out into the dark world to further adventures in future crime films, could prevent the next knockout punch from landing.

Works Cited

Brill, Lesley. *John Huston's Filmmaking*. Cambridge: Cambridge UP, 1997.
Hammett, Dashiell. *The Maltese Falcon*. New York: Vintage, 1992.
Huston, John. Interview by Dick Cavett. *The Dick Cavett Show: Hollywood Greats*. DVD. Originally broadcast 21 Feb. 1972.
———. *An Open Book*. New York: Knopf, 1980.
Naremore, James. "John Huston and *The Maltese Falcon*." *The Maltese Falcon*. Ed. William Luhr. New Brunswick, New Jersey: Rutgers UP, 1995. 149–60.

5

Jonathan C. Glance

A Screenplay-centric Analysis of Huston's *The Man Who Would Be King*

THE CURRENT FIELD OF ADAPTATION studies strives to explore issues beyond the mere fidelity of the film adaptation to its source text. One issue worth considering is the role of the screenplay in the process. When available, a screenplay provides a significant record of the writer's vision and enriches our understanding of both the process and the product of adaptation. When the screenwriter is also the director, as in the case of John Huston's 1975 adaptation of Rudyard Kipling's "The Man Who Would Be King" (1888), even greater attention is warranted. Huston co-wrote and directed this adaptation, and while each role has received some attention, Huston's contributions as screenwriter have been least explored. Huston's screenplay for *The Man Who Would Be King*, co-written with Gladys Hill, is extant, and a version dated November 15, 1974, will be the one discussed here.[1] Huston's screenplay reveals a wide range of intertextual influences, his deeply personal relationship with Kipling, and divergences from Kipling's story and Huston's final edit of his film.

After two decades of failed attempts to adapt Kipling's story,[2] Huston recalls how in 1974 he and Gladys Hill[3] finally completed the screenplay by

> incorporating a number of good things out of the other scripts, wrote yet another screenplay, sticking this time a little closer to the story by Kipling. The original story was too short to be adapted in itself, but it struck themes that lent themselves to expansion—for instance, the Masonic motif, reflected through the emblems on Kipling's watch fob, the altar stone and the treasure. Using such material as springboards, we did a lot of invention, and it turned out to be good invention, supportive of the tone, feeling and spirit underlying the original short story. Kipling's glossary served me well. I liked this script as well as any I ever wrote. (351)

Huston's recollection points to several factors informing the adaptation process: the screenplay resulted from a collaborative effort; it was an accretive process; the new draft was "a little closer" to Kipling's story, more closely reflecting its "tone, feeling and spirit" (351); and Huston was quite satisfied with the final script.

Although the variant screenplays of *The Man Who Would Be King*—whose named writers and co-writers include Peter Viertel, Aeneas MacKenzie, Tony Veiller, Steve Grimes, John Huston, and Gladys Hill—are not accessible, Huston does mention some changes that differentiate this November 15, 1974, version from the previous ones that apparently followed the expectations and clichés of the films of their day. According to Huston, "In one script both men were in love with the girl and their quarrels were over her. . . . I felt that was wrong but in those days you had to have a boy-girl romance in it" (quoted in Madsen 245). Perhaps because of the success of *Butch Cassidy and the Sundance Kid* (1969), also produced by John Foreman, Huston and Hill replaced the "boy-girl romance" with more of a buddy-picture bromance, a change incidentally more faithful to Kipling's protagonists. In addition, Joseph McBride reports that Huston "relied on ideas and phrasing from other works by Kipling, of whom he is an aficionado" (57). Madsen asserts that Huston and Hill's contributions included "replacing Kipling's fictitious storyteller with Kipling himself" and omitting an "exotic princess leading lady" role (245). The elevation of Kipling's anonymous narrator to the author himself and the interpolation of references to his works point to Huston's deep affection for and familiarity with the matter and tone of that author's works.

Huston had immersed himself in Kipling's poetry and stories as a child and maintained a very personal understanding of Kipling. Indeed, the screenplay reflects his knowledge of Kipling's tropes, terminology, and cultural milieu. In a 1965 interview Huston referred to his tendency to make his films from "something I read 25 or 30 years ago, or when I was a child, and have played around with in my thoughts for a long time"; he added, referring to *The Man Who Would Be King*, "The first script of this film . . . was based on my reading of the story at age 12 or 13, and my impressions of it, that have remained with me" (Bachmann and Huston 3–4). Expanding on the effect his childhood reading of Kipling had on him, Huston declared in his autobiography, "I've read Kipling since I was a kid. I know miles of his doggerel. You can start a line of Kipling verse, and it's an even bet I can supply the rest of the stanza. I studied a Kipling glossary instead of algebra" (345). Axel Madsen discusses Huston telling reporters during the filming of *The Man Who Would Be King* that he had, at age twelve, "been confined to a sanatorium with both heart and kidney ailments" and developed a passion for Kipling's "world of adventure, high honor, mystery"; Madsen goes on to quote Huston as asserting, "I read so much Kipling, it's in my unconscious" (244). According to Huston in a 1976 interview, Kipling was so deeply embedded in his psyche that it spoke through him: "I've got reams of Kipling verse stored away in my unconscious to be tapped on drunken occasions" (Bachmann, "Watching Huston" 61). Besides finding it appealing as an adventure story, Huston thought "The Man Who Would Be King" to be a "splendid tale of two tough and likable rogues who are loyal to each other and to their ideals such as they are" (Madsen 244). It is evident that Huston drew on his deep knowledge of and affection for both Kipling and the Kiplingesque in composing his adapted screenplay, which, while not always loyal to the text, expresses a fidelity to the author's works more generally.

The film, nevertheless, was praised by many critics for its fidelity to Kipling's story, though Huston made significant changes to the structure, tone, language, characters, and actions of his immediate source, and often drew upon several of Kipling's poems and stories to make these changes. For example, Huston and Hill's script opens with the customary establishing shot, but with a greatly expanded and at times metaphorical visual description of the opening scene:

FADE IN

1   LAHORE

A city of beggars, prophets, untouchables, fakirs, tribespeople, British soldiers, starving dogs, holy cattle, camels and hovering kites. In her streets, marriage rites are performed over five-year-olds. Squatting barbers shave their squatting clients. Readers of Sanskrit sit, cross-legged, in the center of enchanted circles. Dentists draw teeth and surgeons take blood. Rouged corpses, tied to flimsy thrones, are carried by ecstatic mourners to pyres by the river.

As the sun goes down, life drains out of the City through her Gates. The quarreling, the crying of wares, the praying, the wailing subsides. The City puts her finger to her lips at nightfall. Silence takes over—such a silence as no Western City, where beasts and men go shod, can ever know. Listen to the SOUND of a single heavy raindrop falling on a leaf. Listen to the YELPING of the pariah dogs outside the City walls. Her streets are empty—except for derelicts, and they hide themselves in shadows. Whatever moves—animal or human—predator or prey—moves furtively, in secret. (Huston and Hill 1)

In this conflation of East and West, human and animal, high and low, Huston establishes an immediate energy in the scene. The opening sentence's unordered list of peoples and animals reflects Huston's view of Kipling himself. Drawing upon his early readings, Huston once asserted that Kipling was "a profound observer of the extravagant doings of his fellow men and fellow beasts, between which he makes no strong distinction" (Huston and Hill 1). Some elements seem intended to render for the viewer the alien Orient, such as the child wedding and the funeral procession, but others seem more neutrally descriptive, such as the barbers, dentists, and surgeons practicing their trades. The crowds in daytime seem intended to portray not so much squalor as activity and noise.

Although Kipling has no such scene or description at the beginning of "The Man Who Would Be King," a close analogue appears later when Dravot and Carnehan set off for their adventure, in a vivid but brief passage describing the Kumharsen Serai as "the great foursquare sink of humanity" where all the peoples of Central Asia meet: "Balkh and Bokhara there meet Bengal and Bombay, and try to draw eye-teeth" (255). Huston and Hill even quote these lines in the screenplay (23). At the caravanserai, Kipling continues, you "can buy ponies, turquoises, Persian pussy-cats, saddle-bags, fat-tailed sheep, and musk . . . and get many strange things for nothing" (255). In the screenplay, Huston captures Kipling's tone of neutral observation by borrowing the listing of sundry and diverse items.

Audiences watching this opening in the film, however, may perceive the imagery as less than objective. Julie F. Codell attacks the opening sequence for its "vermin-like masses of people in excessive close-ups"

(39) and asserts that it, like the other scenes Huston added to Kipling's story, are consistently "problematic, even racist and ethnocentric" (37) and seem intended to "keep the natives as Othered as possible" (38). The opening few minutes of the film do contain several striking shots, none of which is in the script, that support her point: a snake charmer, a fakir hanging scorpions on his face, another drinking and rubbing his face with boiling water. The majority of the shots in this sequence, though—all but a few seconds of the two minutes preceding the credits—portray artisans and shopkeepers at work or the devout in prayer. The portrayal here is, at times, shocking, but ultimately sympathetic, one that aims at depicting the aural and visual richness of a lost world.

Huston's familiarity with Kipling's texts recurs throughout the screenplay. One notable example introduces Kipling himself, literally sweating over his verse as he pens the opening stanza to "The Ballad of Boh Da Thone" (Huston and Hill 1–2). Kipling's mock-heroic ballad, published in 1889, depicts a cunning bandit looting the Burmese countryside, evading Captain O'Neill and the Irish troops of the Black Tyrone until a fat, fearful babu (a Bengali clerk named Harendra Mukerji) falls off his cart, crushing the bandit's head. Mukerji sends the severed head back to O'Neill for the reward. The selected verse has relevant (and perhaps ironic) connections to *The Man Who Would Be King*, notably in Dravot's severed head at its conclusion. The hapless and abused babu in the screenplay, Mr. Clutterbury Das ("Writer of correspondence for the illiterate general public" [Huston and Hill 6]), whom Carnehan ejects from the railway carriage, resembles Mukerji in temperament, size, and downward trajectory, if not in success. The ballad may even comment on the banditry of Carnehan and Dravot, whose agenda is to "loot the Country four ways to Sunday" (Huston and Hill 20). Certainly the two rogues resemble bandits more than they do the stalwart O'Neill. Moreover, the poem substantiates Kipling as a journalist who aspires to be a poet, grounds the character in ostensibly historical reality, and conjures through its echoes a Kiplingesque milieu.

Huston's oft-repeated claim that Kipling had entered his unconscious seems substantiated by intertextual echoes, allusions, and references to that author throughout the screenplay. When Carnehan and Dravot travel through the Khyber Pass, disguised as a mad Muslim priest and his servant, they recognize the British sentry on duty as Private Mulvaney. Dravot identifies him as "that loud-mouthed Mick from the Black Tyrone"—that is, Captain O'Neill's division in "The Ballad of Boh Da Thone." Mulvaney is a well-known character from a dozen other Kipling stories, in *Plain Tales from the Hills* and *Soldiers Three and Other Tales* (both 1888). The screenplay explicitly references the latter source:

"The big rawboned Irishman of Kipling's 'Soldiers Three,' standing negligently at ease, chewing a quid of tobacco, idly watches the passing caravan" (Huston and Hill 31). A more obscure allusion from Kipling is to Billy Fish, a Kafiristani who eventually counsels the two adventurers. The screenplay makes him an English-speaking Gurkha soldier in Er-Heb, the sole survivor of Colonel Robertson's geographic party. It benefits both the adventurers and the audience to have a translator, so the alteration is functional. But it is also character that reflects Kipling's admiration for the bravery of Gurkhas. Moments before their first major battle, while the Bashkais are streaming out of their walled city, Dravot and Carnehan "have assumed the customary air of weary indolence reserved for such occasions," while "Billy Fish, on the other hand, is quivering with anticipation—waiting like a terrier for a ball to be thrown. Fighting is the Gurkha's raison d'etre. Siva so bred him" (Huston and Hill 66). The canine simile is a reference to Kipling's story "The Drums of the Fore and Aft" (1888), which describes a Gurkha regiment anticipating battle in a similar way.[4] More significantly, references to Kipling's "Young British Soldier" (1895) recur at key moments in the screenplay. Kipling's alternately affectionate, ironic, and chilling ballad advises the novice soldier on how to live, serve, and die. In the screenplay, Dravot boldly sings the opening lines, "When the "arf-made recruit goes out to the East, / 'E acts like a babe an' 'e drinks like a beast," as he and Carnehan cross the frozen mountains into Kafiristan; warned he'll start an avalanche, Dravot replies, "If a king can't sing, it isn't worth being king" (Huston and Hill 40). Later Dravot sings the final refrain of the poem while awaiting execution for his presumptions to be king and god. Tossing his crown into the chasm beneath the rope bridge on which he sways, Dravot exclaims "to the world" his final words: "We are not little men! Do you think we don't know how to die? Cut, you beggars, cut!" before singing, "Go, go, go like a soldier . . ." as Carnehan joins in the refrain (Huston and Hill 125). Carnehan, shambling out of Kipling's office after completing his narrative, sings the poem's full refrain: "And go to your God like a soldier, Go, go, go like a soldier, Go, go, go like a soldier, Go, go, go like a soldier, Soldier of the Queen!" (Huston and Hill 131).

These rousing lines conclude the chilling last verse of Kipling's poem; the stanza instructs the English soldier in Afghanistan, wounded in battle, to blow out his brains before the Afghani women come to mutilate him. The screenplay concludes, "His quavering voice dies away as he exits. CAMERA MOVES IN CLOSE, to center on the CROWN" and fades out on that image (131). Kipling's ballad effectively underscores the screenplay's ambivalent attitude toward its protagonists, with their mix of high ideals and low behavior, naive wonder and cynical opportunism.

Just as Kipling's novice soldier navigates the perils of bad grog, cholera, sun, marriage, and battle, only to die "on Afghanistan's plains" (Kipling "The Young British Soldier" 72–74), the two adventurers navigate dangers and temptations and strive for and achieve boundless wealth, only to end up dead or broken. The ballad's use in the screenplay epitomizes what Gaylan Studlar called "Huston's distinctively ironic stance toward the relationship between masculinity, violence, and . . . success" and Huston's "self-evident fascination with failed masculinity" (182). The screenplay's recurring succession of conflicting terms for the protagonists—man, beast, god, devil, king, soldier—enact that ironic stance, with Kipling's ballad providing a fitting accompaniment.

The poem, however, cannot be found either in Kipling's story or in Huston's film. Instead, in source and adaption, a quite different song appears:

> The Son of Man goes forth to war,
> A golden crown to gain;
> His blood-red banner streams afar—
> Who follows in His train? (278–79)

These lines slightly misquote Reginald Heber's 1812 hymn "The Son of God Goes Forth to War," set to the Irish tune "The Minstrel Boy." Huston's film uses that tune extensively in Maurice Jarre's score, and features both Dravot and Carnehan singing those messianic lines (Dravot in the mountains and both together at Dravot's death). Julie Codell notes that their "final duet is thus part of their ambiguous redemption," adding that through the tune and lyrics, "Huston economically layers the characters' class, rebelliousness, and fate, with a Christianizing overlay" (43). Another possibility is an ironic, even blasphemous nod to Dravot's presumption of godhood and Carnehan's resurrection from the cross.

Huston does not end his film with either song but somewhat anticlimactically has Carnehan wander off "to meet a man at Marwar Junction," leaving Kipling in possession of the rotting skull and glowing crown of Daniel Dravot. While both the film and the story end with the vivid, lurid image of a golden crown surmounting the rotting skull of Dravot, Huston and Hill's screenplay notably does not. All Carnehan's bag contains in the script is "the arched misshapen circlet of gold studded with raw turquoises: The Crown of Kafiristan" (130). As director, Huston perhaps decided the film's long hold on the crowned skull would more effectively symbolize the aspiration, the prize, and the punishment of the title character than the screenplay's empty crown and song. The change tends also to undercut any remaining hero worship of Dravot at the end.

Perhaps the most intriguing intertextual moment in the screenplay is the depiction of Dravot's arrow: in the midst of the battle for Bashkai, Daniel Dravot charges the enemy alone when his Er-Heb cavalry fails to advance, is struck by an arrow, and yet lives. Although the Kafiristanis perceive this as a miracle, the arrow has actually stuck in the bandolier under his tunic. Huston and Hill highlight the mythic, intertextual moment in their screenplay:

> An arrow hits Dravot solidly in the chest—imbeds itself over his heart. He falls backwards in the saddle then, grabbing a handful of mane, slowly straightens himself.
>
> DRAVOT: After me you sons of cowardly bastards!
>
> He jerks the arrow free—holds it aloft. It might be Ahab's harpoon, or Excaliber, or a splinter from the True Cross. His Troop follows him. He leads them where the enemy stands thickest, cuts through them back and fourth—crisscrossing—dividing them into fleeing segments. (Huston and Hill 70–71)

This pivotal moment of both the battle and the plot determines the fates of Dravot and Carnehan. If they lose their first battle, or if Dravot dies from the arrow, their hopes of conquest are over, yet not only do they win, but Dravot's seeming invulnerability begins the rumors that he is the son of Alexander the Great, returning to Kafiristan to take the place of his father, now worshipped as a god. Perceived as divine, Dravot easily gains power. The tension now mounts as to when the Kafiristanis will discover the sham.

Kipling's story has no such arrow incident—the natives think Dravot and Carnehan are gods because they know the Third Degree of the Masonic rituals, since only the Second Degree had survived in Kafiristan. Dravot's arrow is thus the screenwriters' invention and visually engages the audience more than Kipling's Masonic explanation. Moreover, Huston and Hill integrate Dravot's arrow into key moments in the film to indicate the rising and falling fortunes of the protagonists. After Carnehan scolds Dravot for rushing "like some green lieutenant" into battle, he then notices the arrow and asks, "What're are you carrying that around for?" Dravot, "hiding it under his arm," replies like an embarrassed boy, "No particular reason" (72). Yet almost immediately Dravot uses it to impose authority when he "raps Ootah sharply over the knuckles" with it (72), disarming him and displacing him as chief. Realizing that the tribes think he is a god because of the arrow, Dravot plays up the symbolism:

A Screenplay-centric Analysis

Figure 5.1. The charismatic Dravot is crowned King as Carnehan looks on.

"As each worshipper kneels before him, Dravot waves his arrow with benign condescension" (80). Upon first seeing Roxanne, however, "his arrow [is] arrested in mid-gesture" (80). Proceeding to his confrontation with Kafu Selim, the high priest, Dravot confidently bears "his arrow swagger-stick tucked under one arm" (88). The priest inspects the arrow and demands a repetition of the alleged miracle; only Carnehan deflecting the shot and Kipling's Masonic emblem avert disaster. The priests crown Dravot as their god-king: "The arrow, now gilded, and Kipling's emblem are handed to him by Kafu Selim as though they were orb and scepter" (96). The screenplay links the gilded arrow to Dravot's infatuation with power: he gives "an imperious wave of the arrow" (101) to dismiss a plaintiff, and later the Chieftain from Agatsi "bends to kiss Dravot's arrow" (103) just before Dravot demands that Carnehan bow before him, too. Dravot, "arrow in hand" (114), awaits his disastrous wedding to Roxanne, and after his followers realize he is "not a god, not a devil but a man" (117), he is reduced to powerlessly "waving his golden arrow, and roaring maledictions" (118) in the face of their furious insurrection. The script's final reference to Dravot's arrow shows it uselessly "dangling from a thong at his wrist" (118), thereby reducing the divine symbol and scepter to a useless accessory.

An earlier appearance of the arrow in the screenplay deserves particular attention. When Dravot is shot, the script's action block states, "He jerks the arrow free—holds it aloft. It might be Ahab's harpoon, or Excalibur, or a splinter from the True Cross. His troop follows him" (71). These three allusions add significant depth to the scene. Surely Huston, having directed and co-written an adaption of Melville's novel in 1956, could not miss the deeply ominous resonance of the allusion to Ahab's doomed obsession with the White Whale. Excalibur points to Arthurian legends, and ironically bestows on Dravot—the man who would be king—the emblem of the rightful sovereignty of the greatest of English monarchs. Dravot, however, only seeks the throne for the riches. The allusion to the cross creates an even deeper irony. The splinter from the cross is perhaps the holiest of Christian relics, symbolizing the death and resurrection of the son of God. Dravot only impersonates a god, and Carnehan descends shattered from his crucifixion "like a hermit crab without his shell" (Huston and Hill 1).

The screenplay suggests that the arrow should be a richly allusive icon, with heroic and divine references, only to be undercut. However, the final version of this scene in the film jettisons the heroic iconography of the arrow altogether. The battle for Bashkai occurs in almost the exact center of the film, suggesting the centrality of the event. A long succession of shots depicting preparations for battle builds anticipation, deflated by an incongruous procession of priests from the holy city of Sikandergul who pass between the opposing forces. Excitement again builds with the ebb and flow of the battle, until the camera finally holds our attention on a medium-long shot of Dravot, mounted, surrounded by and hacking away at Bashkai soldiers. Huston cuts to a medium-close shot of an aiming archer and then to the arrow entering Dravot's dark, padded vest over his red jacket. Briefly off balance, Dravot soon continues hewing the enemy until he perceives, shortly after the audience does, that the Bashkais are no longer resisting, but bowing down around him. Huston shoots the action from behind Dravot in a medium-long shot capturing the scope of the event, but not the protagonist's response. No close ups provide reaction shots for Dravot or his opponents. The usual film syntax to indicate great emotional significances is missing. Huston finally cuts to a medium shot of Dravot anticlimactically pulling out the arrow. The potential for a deeper meaning is further undercut by the action (horse and rider repeatedly turn, preventing any close appreciation of Connery's expression) and the editing (rather than lingering on

Dravot, the film cuts to a reaction shot of Carnehan, looking merely confused).

The screenplay's focus on the arrow seems an attempt to capture the allure and romance of the adventure by evoking a multilayered mythology, while at the same time showing this mythology to be ultimately hollow when it is paired with the questionable motives of Dravot and Carnehan. Perhaps finding it difficult to translate this compressed set of references to film, Huston instead employs a visual rhetoric of distance and objectification that communicates a conflicted vision. The battle is ostensibly a heroic moment in the narrative, but it is filmed in such a way that the audience is encouraged to be emotionally disinvested in the plight of the characters (even Carnehan models for the audience confusion rather than pathos). As Studlar has argued, "The robust, manly quest for material success is exposed as a dubious grail" throughout Huston's films (184). Bringing the screenplay and Huston's writing process to bear on this interpretation, though, helps us to better understand not only the breadth of Huston's literary interests and attachments, but also the depth of Huston's own ambivalence over traditional male heroism. Steeped in stories from childhood on of "going into strange latitudes where reckoning ceases to count" or of "embarking on a voyage where you can't see the end" (Madsen 244), Huston, in his films, retains the power, mystery, and pleasure of these endeavors even as they give way to a more mature vision. His quests rarely end in glory; rather, they lead—like Kipling's "Young British Soldier"—to self-destruction or, even worse, to meaninglessness as the myths unwind.

A screenplay-centric approach to adaptation studies can offer closer attention to the web of intertextual strands revealed in the script as an alternative to traditional questions of a film's faithfulness to its source. We must be careful not to replace one demand for faithfulness with another, though, by expecting fidelity of the film to its screenplay. As a screenplay adapts a source text, so too does a film adapt a screenplay. Extraneous matters—budget, location, an editor's choices, the performances captured by the camera—and essential differences in words and images may reasonably explain changes in the final film. Yet a closer examination of a screenplay and a consideration of it as a significant record of the writer's developing vision of the adaptation enrich our understanding of both the process and the final visual manifestation. In the case of *The Man Who Would Be King*, attention to the script deepens our understanding of the film. Further attention to screenplays as a central component of the process of adaptation may expand the discipline of adaptation studies, particularly in the cases of writer-directors such as Huston.

Notes

1. Previous scripts adapting Kipling's tale had been written, and there were likely subsequent drafts prior to the shooting script, as there are significant differences between this script and the film.

2. Madsen's biography of Huston details aborted projects in 1955 for Allied Artists, with a screenplay by Peter Viertel (151–52), in 1959 for Universal Studios, with a screenplay by Huston and Aeneas MacKenzie (223), and in 1963 for Seven Arts, with a screenplay by Huston and Tony Veiller (196). Finally in 1973 producer John Foreman, while visiting Huston, came across sketches Steve Grimes (Huston's longtime art director and production designer) had produced in 1956, as well another attempt at the script which Grimes had written (Madsen 239). Foreman ultimately produced the 1975 film.

3. Hill, described by Madsen as "Huston's angel-secretary-assistant-screenwriting-companion-chaffeur" (192–93), had previously worked as Huston assistant or associate on eight films, beginning with *Freud* (1962).

4. In "The Drums Fore and Aft," the Gurkhas "gaped expectantly at their officers as terriers grin ere the stone is cast for them to fetch."

Works Cited

Bachmann, Gideon. "Watching Huston." *John Huston: Interviews*. Ed. Robert Emmet Long. UP of Mississippi, 2001. 60–64.

———, and John Huston. "How I Make Films: An Interview with John Huston." *Film Quarterly* 19.1 (1965): 3–13. CrossRef. Web. 10 Mar. 2014.

Booth, Howard J. *The Cambridge Companion to Rudyard Kipling*. Cambridge, NY: Cambridge UP, 2011.

Boozer, Jack. "The Screenplay and Authorship in Adaptation." *Film and Literature*. Ed. Timothy Corrigan. London: Routledge, 2011. 199–219.

Canby, Vincent. "The Man Who Would Be King." *New York Times* 18 Dec. 1975. Web. 14 Mar. 2014

Cocks, Jay. "Rogues' Regiment." *Time* 106.26 (1975): 38. Academic Search Complete. Web. 14 Mar. 2014.

Codell, Julie F. "The Ideological Adventure of *The Man Who Would Be King*." *John Huston Essays on a Restless Director*. Ed. Tracy, Tony, and Roddy Flynn. Jefferson, NC: McFarland, 2010. 33–46.

Cohen, Morton, ed. *Rudyard Kipling to Rider Haggard; the Record of a Friendship*. London: Hutchinson, 1965.

Cooper, Stephen. *Perspectives on John Huston*. New York: G. K. Hall, 1994.

Corrigan, Timothy. *Film and Literature*. London: Routledge, 2011.

Hammett, Dashiell. *The Maltese Falcon*. New York: Random House, 2010.

Huston, John. *The Maltese Falcon*. Screenplay. The Daily Script. Web. 14 Mar. 2014.

———. *An Open Book*. New York: Knopf : Distributed by Random House, 1980.

———, and Gladys Hill. *John Huston's The Man Who Would Be King*: [screenplay]. N. p., 1974.

Kipling, Rudyard. "The Ballad of Boh Da Thone." *The Kipling Society.* Web. 14 Mar. 2014.
———. "The Drums of the Fore and Aft." *The Kipling Society.* Web. 14 Mar. 2014.
———. "The Man Who Would Be King." *The Man Who Would Be King, and Other Stories.* New York: Oxford UP, 1999. library.mercer.edu Library Catalog. Web. 10 Mar. 2014. Oxford World's Classics. 244–79.
———. "The Young British Soldier." *Kipling's Poems.* N. p., 1901.
Long, Robert Emmet. *John Huston: Interviews.* UP of Mississippi, 2001.
McBride, Joseph. "John Huston Finds That the Slow Generation of King Has Made It a Richer Film." *John Huston: Interviews.* Ed. Robert Emmet Long. UP of Mississippi, 2001. 56–59.
Madsen, Axel. *John Huston.* Garden City, NY: Doubleday, 1978.
The Man Who Would Be King. Dir. John Huston. Perf. Sean Connery, Michael Caine, and Christopher Plummer. 1975. Warner Home Video, 1997. DVD.
Meyers, Jeffrey. *John Huston: Courage and Art.* New York: Crown Archetype, 2011.
Palmer, R. Barton, and David Boyd. *Hitchcock at the Source the Auteur as Adaptor.* Albany: SUNY P, 2011. Open WorldCat. Web. 11 Mar. 2014.
Studlar, Gaylyn. "Shadowboxing: Fat City and the Malaise of Masculinity." *Reflections in a Male Eye: John Huston and the American Experience.* Ed. Gaylyn Studlar, and David Desser. Washington: Smithsonian Institution P, 1993. 177–98.

Part II

History and Social Context

6

Wesley King and Douglas McFarland

"Proceed with the Execution"

Casting, Convention, and the Diminishment of Rose in *The African Queen*

John Huston's 1951 adaptation of *The African Queen* differs from the vast majority of those he undertook. Huston chose to adapt a novel by a mainstream author that strikingly violates the ethos of its social context. While not modernist in form, C. S. Forester's novel is modernist in its aims to represent a complex and compelling female character and the discovery of her own sexuality. Published in 1935, *The African Queen* is an overtly protofeminist work. It tells the story of a protagonist who suffers under the traditional social oppression of women and how she came to free herself—for a time at least—from those constraints. In her thirty-third year, Rose Sayer (played by Katherine Hepburn in the film) has escaped her father's house in England only to become the domestic caretaker to her brother, who is a missionary in German-controlled central Africa. Upon the outbreak of World War I, and the forced conscription of the native people, Rose's brother dies. The morning of her brother's death, Charlie Allnutt (played by Humphrey Bogart in the film), who is an acquaintance of Rose and the captain of the steamboat the *African Queen*, offers to help by burying her brother and providing a means of hiding from the German army. After taking to the boat, Rose—motivated in part by her brother's death, in part by English nationalism, and in part by a burgeoning feeling of liberation—quickly devises a plan: she and the reluctant Charlie will navigate the unnavigable Ulanga River to Lake Wittlesbach. Using provisions on the boat that Charlie was ferrying for mining operations, they will turn the *African Queen* into a steam-powered torpedo and destroy the German ship, the *Königin Louise*, which guards the lake.

Against this epic framework, the novel chronicles Rose's release from her patriarchal captivity into a world of risk, self-expression, leadership, and passion. The novel is so emphatic in its sympathies with Rose's liberation that one would be hard pressed to think that Huston would not have recognized its iconoclastic stature, perhaps seeing it as a novel closer to the social modernism of Anaïs Nin than to a run-of-the-mill historical novel or adventure story. Huston was an astute reader, comfortable with the eccentricities of Flannery O'Connor, the experiments of James Joyce, and the risqué sexuality of Carson McCullers's *Reflections in a Golden Eye*. It is, therefore, difficult to understand why in his adaptation he would strip his source of its salient point of view. And indeed this is what he did. Huston's film version is much more muted in its portrayal of the passionate release of a woman into the world than what is depicted in the novel. The social modernism of Forester's novel is given a traditional, both socially and aesthetically traditional, comic treatment. Lesley Brill, in his discussion of the film, notes that unlike the psychologically rich films Huston made either before or after, "the straightforward romance and comedy of *The African Queen* suppress such complexity" (50). Brill, nevertheless, finds in this suppression a "special clarity," and, in fact, he comprehensively traces a set of visual and conceptual motifs in the film that inform Huston's other work.

However, our purpose in this chapter is one guided by concerns specific to the film as an adaptation, concerns which present different complexities. For a reader of the novel, the diminishment of Rose is difficult to ignore, and we are left with two possibilities: either Huston was oblivious to the innovative and transgressive mode of the novel, or he intended quite purposefully to erase it. When this question is viewed with respect both to the directed performance of Katherine Hepburn and the context of her casting—a context developed from her personal biography and her career trajectory up until that point—the latter most certainly seems to be the case. Hepburn's casting not only reinforces the film's deliberate departures and suppressions from the novel, but it provides further insight into the film's aesthetics. Despite its light and humorous tone, the film, when read against the novel, proves to be in deeper conflict both with its source and the Hollywood tropes and clichés that the film otherwise embraces. The diminishment of the character of Rose shows at best a pessimism on Huston's part with regard to his audience's ability to identify with a more liberated female protagonist. At worst, it shows a less flattering portrait of the director with regard to his desire to portray such a protagonist.

Happily Ever After

The film's embrace of Hollywood narrative tropes and its ambivalence over the story's female protagonist is most clear in the ending of the film. The concluding scenes offer the most direct departure that Huston takes from the novel's plot, and hence, are critical in understanding his adaptation. In the novel, Rose and Charlie fail in their personal mission to destroy the *Königin Louise*. They discover, instead, that the British navy had already been preparing to take on the *Königin Louise*, and at the conclusion of the novel the British do, in fact, dispatch it rather quickly. Although the novel can be comic and blasé at times throughout, the narrative tone toward Rose and Charlie changes in the last few pages. This is especially true regarding their love relationship. If their journey allowed them a solitary fantasy space to work out their erotic love, and—for Rose, at least—to achieve a greater level of self-actualization, by the end, we learn that, for Rose, her "feelings toward [Charlie] had changed" (245). When she insists to Charlie, "We've got to get married," she displays little of the urgency that informed her plan to destroy the *Königin Louise* or the leaps of faith, beyond rational calculation, she takes in discovering her previously inhibited capabilities and sexuality. Rather, her insistence on marriage is based on fear, on the calculations of loss she would suffer, and on her failure to meet the quotidian demands of social respectability. Although Forester characterizes the potential loss of her relationship with Charlie as akin to "losing a limb," the emphasis there is on the functionality of their relationship and on what Rose now takes for granted. Her attitude toward her relationship—unlike her other decisions in the novel—constitutes a failure of her imagination: "she could not contemplate this unforeseen future of hers without Allnutt." Moreover, her insistence on marriage seems just as driven by mundane social pressures from the "censorious people and prying aunts" that she imagines encountering upon returning to London.

This failure of imagination, which signifies a return to normalcy, is shared with Allnutt and the narrative voice, as well. After Rose directs Charlie to get married, Forester writes, "This was an aspect of the situation [Charlie] had actually not thought of" (246). Although, throughout the novel, Charlie—with the encouragement and support of Rose—often transcends his need to be mothered (more precisely, his tendency to search out a protective, dominant mother is replaced in these moments by a liberating mother), it is clear at the end that he has returned to his will-less, suggestible character. Moments before agreeing to get married, for instance, Charlie is ready to join the British military after the off-hand suggestion of the naval officer. Forester further reinforces the unreformed aspects of Charlie by pointing out that he, in fact, is already married to an estranged wife, a fact that Charlie blithely does not believe will have ramifications. His denial of the significance of his current marriage echoes the casual way the narration refuses to imagine what the future of Charlie and Rose will be. Forester writes, "Whether or not they lived happily ever after is not easily decided," and this is the last line of the novel.

By the end of the novel, epic romance has given way to cool realism. Forester has stripped from the audience much of what has motivated the story. Forester undermines the expectation that two unlikely individuals could intervene in the course of history and that there would be compensation for this failure through the guarantee of a blissful marriage. Instead, we are forced to speculate how Rose's time aboard the *African Queen*, a time when she was able to free herself from three decades of patriarchal oppression, might provide a pathway into a future life that she herself fashions.

The ending of the film, on the other hand, embraces the expectations of Hollywood narrative by reversing these two key plot points. In the film, the couple not only are successfully married but are also successful in destroying the *Königin Louise*, thus intervening in a small but significant way into the course of World War I. While the explosive-laden *African Queen* lies half-sunken just below the surface of the lake, Rose and Charlie are captured by the German navy and are about to be executed by hanging. Charlie, as a last request, asks the captain of the *Königin Louise* (Peter Bull) to marry him and Rose. The captain quickly indulges the couple, but just as the execution is about to proceed, the ship runs into the *African Queen*, which causes catastrophic damage to the ship. In the commotion, Charlie and Rose are able to abandon the ship along with the captain and much of the crew. In the final shot, treading water but otherwise apparently free from further harm, Rose and Charlie celebrate the success of their plan. Gleefully referring to each other now as "Mr. Allnutt" and "Mrs. Allnutt," they begin to swim to shore, singing together a sailor's song.

Not only does this ending contradict the ethos of the novel, which is, at best, conflicted about the possibility of their future marriage, but also it undermines more significant moments in the film's portrayal of

Rose's independence. For instance, shortly before the scenes of their wedding, the attempted execution, and the destruction of the ship, Charlie has been captured, and while thinking perhaps that Rose has drowned, he has denied his planned sabotage. During his interrogation, a motorboat arrives with Rose. Thrilled to be reunited with Charlie, Rose unabashedly admits to and accepts responsibility for the plan, ignoring Charlie's signals to hush her. She contradicts Charlie to the captain and approaches her possible execution with defiance. Had the ship run into the explosives on the *African Queen* at this moment, it would leave us with a very different message, one stressing the transformation of Rose's character. Instead, the film proceeds with a wedding, but unlike the novel, it deliberately takes the proposal of marriage away from Rose and hands that role to Charlie. In fact, it does more than reverse these roles: Charlie never directly asks Rose to marry him. Although clearly under the pressure of the impending execution, Charlie's proposal is directed through the captain with whom he discusses the captain's official capacities and then requests that the couple be wed. During this exchange, the film frames Charlie and the captain together intimately and in close proximity; it positions Rose on the outside, framing her alone as we watch her emotional response to overhearing the indirect proposal. Although she voices her approval, "Why, Charlie, what a lovely idea," she speaks to the back of Charlie's head, further bolstering his agency. Otherwise, Rose simply fawns and preens during the exchange, gestures which are soon after reinforced by her relishing of her new appellation, "Mrs. Allnutt." The film adopts the conventions of marriage in its more patriarchal dimensions.

 Besides contributing to the diminishment of the character of Rose, the film's ending further replicates what Slavoj Žižek describes as "the Hollywood procedure of staging great historical events as the backdrop to the formation of the couple" (58). For *The African Queen* what is immediately lost in this procedure are the more psychologically complex demands of the novel's conclusion. This differs from the endings of Huston's other films that involve couples: *The Maltese Falcon* (1941), in which Sam Spade (Humphrey Bogart) foregoes the possibility for love by handing Brigid O'Shaughnessy (Mary Astor) over to the police; *Reflections in a Golden Eye* (1967), in which we leave the dysfunctional couple falling apart over the dead body of an army private; or *The Dead* (1987), where the story concludes with Gabriel Conroy (Donal McCann) coming to understand that he will never be able to share in the passionate love his wife, Gretta (Anjelica Huston), still feels for the memory of a young man she lost in her youth. *The African Queen*, however, might be better compared to James Cameron's *Titanic* (1997), which also depicts a couple against a historical background involving a shipwreck. If, as according to

Žižek, the accident in *Titanic* works narratively to preserve the couple by "sustain[ing] the illusion that, had [the accident] not happened, they would have lived 'happily ever after,'" Huston's film reverses the correlation between marriage and history, marriage and catastrophe. Rather than having the shipwreck preserve the idea of the couple, Charlie and Rose's marriage instead seems to guarantee the meeting of the *Königin Louise* and the *African Queen*; their wedding triggers the against-all-odds intervention of fate. The film visually reinforces this narrative correlation when, right after Rose says "I do," Huston quickly cuts to a shot that positions us at the location of the upended and mostly submerged *African Queen* where we face the bow of the *Königin Louise*. The shot prepares us for a second coupling: the ship is on track to collide with the protruding explosives still attached to the steamboat. Having failed in their political, albeit nationalistic, action on its own terms, their marriage rehabilitates their intervention into history, making marriage, which reaffirms the social and symbolic order, the couple's ultimately consequential act—an act that, for Rose, is utterly passive.

Figure 6.1. Rose and Charlie exchange wedding vows with nooses around their necks.

One might argue, nevertheless, that despite the archly conservative aspects of the ending, there is something more wry and critical in the way the film treats traditional order even as it strives to reproduce it. For instance, just before we are brought to the concluding moment before Rose and Charlie swim to shore, we briefly get a shot of the captain, who has just jumped from the fiery, sinking ship into the lake. Struggling in the water himself, the captain is awkwardly saluted by a floundering officer. This moment makes the rituals of order ridiculous and points back to the way that the film unexpectedly pairs marriage with execution. One of the most humorous moments in the film is when the captain, concluding the brief wedding ceremony, says, "I now pronounce you husband and wife," and without skipping a beat adds, "proceed with the execution." The couple, sharing a moment of wedded bliss, do not notice the nooses being slipped around their necks. Perhaps the suggestion here is that marriage is putting Rose back into the noose of patriarchal control, but if this is the case, the film provides no pathos for this underlying message. Unlike the novel, in which Rose contemplates marriage as the only way to address her fears, the film in its portrayal of Rose registers no loss. Marriage might be putting Rose back into the noose, but it leaves us to consider whether in Huston's version of the story Rose ever truly left the noose.

The Casting of Hepburn

The choice of Katherine Hepburn to play the protagonist of the novel constitutes arguably the most important factor in the diminishment of the character of Rose in the film. The rights to *The African Queen* were first purchased by Columbia as a vehicle for Charles Laughton and Elsa Lancaster. The project languished until Warner Bros. bought it from Columbia with the intention of casting Bette Davis as Rose.[1] Casting is one of the most significant of the many critical decisions that influence the film adaptation of a literary work,. The selection of a specific actor transforms what a reader must imagine into what an audience necessarily sees. The mental representation of Rose shaped through the reader's encounter with multiple descriptions, perspectives (first and third person), and interactions with other characters becomes in the film adaptation much more concrete and dependent on physical characteristics, intonation of voice, the mannerisms of a specific screen presence, and a body of previous roles. In the case of *The African Queen*, Bette Davis would seem to be an actress particularly well suited to a narrative of the transformation of a thirty-year-old, sexually inexperienced missionary's sister into the passionate woman in Forester's novel. She had made just such a transformation in *Now, Voyager* (1942), whose main character goes from a spinster virgin bullied by her mother to a fully realized and physically transformed woman of the world. But Warner Bros. never did make the film, so in 1950 Sam Siegel, with John Huston's encouragement, bought the rights to the book. In a critical move, Huston chose Katherine Hepburn to play the part of Rose. In his autobiography, Huston coyly hints that she was chosen in part because her name would help secure a loan for the production. But the choice turns out to be also a highly strategic one. Huston uses Hepburn's personal history, her previous roles, and especially her onscreen mannerisms to undermine the proto-feminist point of view of the novel, an endeavor to which Hepburn herself seemed oblivious.

Hepburn was born into a relatively wealthy and liberal family. Her father was a physician and her mother a college-educated suffragette. Hepburn attended Bryn Mawr College and emerged as a progressive, well-educated woman of her class. This carried over into her status as a screen actor. Hepburn rejected the public role of the traditional screen goddess. She wore slacks, eschewed makeup, avoided movie magazine spreads, gave few interviews, and was particularly athletic. Hepburn had the aura of an upper-class feminist whose social status provided her with the freedom to play golf and tennis, as well as to pick and choose her causes and endeavors. Her persona as "Mayflower in heels" (Pierpont) was reinforced by her adoption of what has been called a mid-Atlantic accent, one that falls between an American and British manner of speech, suggestive of the "linguistic behavior of the upper class" (Taylor). Hepburn would retain this style of elocution throughout her career, even after World War II when onscreen accents became more colloquial. This persona of strong-willed independence with aristocratic trappings effectively informed Hepburn's portrayal of powerful female characters in several of her other roles. In *Bringing Up Baby* (1938), for example, Hepburn (as Susan Vance) draws Mr. Bones (Cary Grant) into a fluid, disarming, and playful world of fast-paced adventure. In this quintessential screwball comedy, Hepburn drags the inexperienced academic professor, devoted to dinosaur bones, into a world of real life animals, energetic women, and the social milieu of the country club. Hepburn's dynamism expresses itself on the members-only golf course, the private bar and lounge, and by implication, the bedroom. Moreover, the process of transforming Grant from a socially awkward academic ensconced in his ivory tower into one fit for marriage and a larger social sphere requires, on the film's terms, his humiliation. Grant is the comic butt in *Bringing Up Baby*. As the director, Howard Hawks, succinctly put it: "Anything we could do to humiliate him, to put him down and let her sail blithely along, made it what I thought was funny. I think it's fun to have a woman dominant" (DiBattista 192). This domination, both social and sexual, drives the comic narrative. With her self-confidence, her familiarity with upper class social institutions, and her sophisticated mannerisms, Hepburn is perfect for the part of Susan Vance. Hepburn's association with this typological female figure is replicated in her role in Shakespeare's *As You Like It*. In perhaps a telling coincidence, Hepburn was touring in the part of Rosalind when she was approached to play Rose in *The African Queen*. Like Susan Vance, Rosalind prepares an unsophisticated man for marriage through a process of comic play. Empowered by her ease in manipulating gender identities, her facility with language, and her wit and sense of irony, Rosalind presides over the fluid landscape of Arden Forest and instructs her inexperienced and underdeveloped young man in matters of love. Humiliating to the male or not, Shakespeare's strong woman outpaces the man in this sixteenth-century version of a screwball comedy.

In this vein, one might naturally imagine Hepburn bringing the kind of playful dominance of Hawks' Susan Vance or the imaginative resourcefulness of Shakespeare's Rosalind to her portrayal of Rose in *The African Queen*. Such would be in keeping with Forester's novel. In a telling moment, after they have made their way down the river, Rose refers to Allnutt as "her crew" (63), explicitly establishing herself at the top of the shipboard hierarchy. A newfound sense of her own abilities to master the natural world results from her maneuvering, essentially without help from Allnutt, the steamboat through dangerous rapids. As Rose establishes more control of her environment and more direction over Charlie, she also emerges more clearly as the governing consciousness of the novel. Whereas Charlie, though skilled, is portrayed to be in constant struggle with the boat, Forester most directly underscores Rose's transformation in the moments where she exists more fluidly between her mind, her body, the machine, and the river. At one point when she takes control of the boat, Forester writes: "The flutter of her bosom was caused by elation and excitement—the mere act of taking hold of the tiller started her heart beating faster" (103). In this passage, Forester not only pairs her mind with the workings of the machine, but her emotive "elation" is counterbalanced by the way that the rhythms of her body ("her heart beating faster") are grounded on her interactions with the external world. That Rose's liberation is dependent upon a new relationship with her body is a recurring motif in the novel. As Forester writes, "Rose was really alive for the first time in her life," when "her body told her so" and "when she stopped to listen" (61).

Compared to the novel, the film significantly downplays how Rose's independence turns on her embodiment. In fact, Huston, in his casting of Hepburn, seems to be more intent throughout the film on emphasizing Rose's disjointedness with her body, her relationship to others, and the external world, a Rose that wouldn't notice that her neck is in a noose. More precisely, it seems that what Huston was looking for with Hepburn was an out-of-place aristocrat. This element of her persona comes through, for instance, in her memoir, *The Making of* The African Queen. Having arrived in Africa and before completing the final leg of the journey to the Congo where the film would be shot, she confidently and independently sought out a local golf course. Her recollection of the young Africans who approached her and her fellow golfers on the course is strikingly condescending: "The caddies are tiny black boys . . . they are wildly anxious for the job . . . each time we played we had to fight them off . . . finally after much shooing away and waving of golf clubs, they would depart" (27–28). The picture of privilege and class conflict created in her account of the golf course seems exactly the version of Hepburn that Huston sought to cast. Huston deposits Hepburn, with her condescending social attitudes and upper-class mannerisms, into the heart of Africa in order to create a comic incongruity between actor and environment.

This incongruity is apparent from the first scenes in the film. The Rose we encounter at the beginning of Forster's novel feels overcome by the oppressive humidity of the African forest: "She could feel the streams of sweat running down beneath her clothes" and "went back to her own room and lay on her string bed in a torment of heat, although she wore only her thin nightdress" (3, 6). Huston gives his audience a much different Rose. The upright and prim Hepburn presides with her brother over a congregation of Africans who are oblivious to the words of the hymns they are attempting to sing (indeed, there is no indication that they understand or can speak English). With her classic cheekbones, her hair in a well-fashioned bun, her naive and yet condescending earnestness, and her body covered in an immaculate Victorian dress, tightly and ornately laced around her neck, Hepburn seems oblivious to the heat and humidity of central Africa on a hot day in a closely packed church. Although brother and sister have been doing this for ten years, there is less a sense of futility than a kind of mindless self-serving perseverance. Moreover, in these opening scenes, Rose seems not at all dominated by her brother, who is played preposterously by Robert Morely. He seems befuddled and unable to lead himself, let alone anyone else. Hepburn's Rose is more out of place than oppressed by weather, domestic hierarchy, or Victorian morality. This incongruity between character and place, established in large measure through the casting of Hepburn, results in an objectification of Rose. Unlike the reader of the book, the audience of the film does not experience Rose's subjectivity. Huston pulls us back so that we can do little other than observe and judge, not experience and empathize. To put it differently, it is Katherine Hepburn, Bryn Mawr graduate and upper-class feminist, who seals off the inner life of Rose. There is a comic cruelty in all of this, most of which is directed toward Hepburn herself. Huston nastily turns his leading actor's public and professional identity back upon her as if he had been privy to her shooing away the "black boys" from the golf course and decided to punish her for it.

In her memoir, however, there is little indication that Hepburn recognized the powerful feminist point of view of the novel. There is, however, the implication that she was afraid that Huston and his friends had concocted something in the script commensurate with Huston's reputation as having chauvinistic qualities. She recalls that in the days after she had agreed to star in the film, Huston repeatedly delayed giving her a copy of the script. When she deplaned on location in Africa, she repeated her request, suspicious that Huston was purposefully keeping something from her. When Huston again put her off, Hepburn's response was oddly not anger or frustration. Instead, she felt embarrassed that she had brought it up at all, afraid that she had made a pest of herself and had alienated the men that were running the show. She even berates herself: "What a lovely start. Oh Hell—Oh Hell. Now, why did I have to bounce that out? There. Of all the moments. Why? What an ass! How dumb can you get. Not even out of the car. And pick pick pick! 'What about the script?' Like an old fusspot" (37). This is a remarkable attitude of a woman about to play the lead in the adaptation of a novel in which a woman escapes male domination.

Covering Rose, Uncovering Male Desire

As we have shown, Huston eliminates the powerful feminist element of Forester's novel, diminishing the impact of its protagonist through the use of Hollywood clichés and his choice of Katherine Hepburn to play the lead role. But in a balanced pair of scenes, Huston takes two further steps: containing the erotic desire of his protagonist within a traditional social hierarchy and subtly shifting his focus away from Rose herself to the male gaze cast upon her by Allnutt. Soon after his arrival at the village, Allnutt is invited into the missionaries' sitting room to have high tea. The scene provides a foreshadowing of Rose's first sexual encounter later in the film. The procedures of this late afternoon English ritual appear ludicrous in the context of the Congo of 1914. With her perfectly postured body and that intonation of voice that is hers alone, Hepburn presides over the ceremony. The scene almost immediately turns comic when Allnutt, already uncomfortable in this social context, unsuccessfully attempts to suppress the growls emanating from his stomach. Here we have what is elemental to comedy: the visceral release of the body from the control of the mind. In this scene, the control comes in the form of social decorum and civil manners. In response to the repeated murmurs of Bogart's stomach, which he is repeatedly unable to control, Hepburn does not express condescending disapproval, but rather soldiers on, dutifully maintaining her physical and social high-mindedness in face of these bodily utterances.

Rose and Allnutt will return to this ceremony later in the film in the aftermath of Rose's loss of her virginity. Forester's version of Rose's first sexual experience is quite remarkable for its candor and willingness to express this almost solely through Rose's point of view. At the moment of consummation, Rose does not passively *give* her body over to masculine desire but meets that desire with her own: "She was conscious of pain which made her put up her arms round Allnutt's *slight* body and

Figure 6.2. Rose dutifully maintains decorum, ignoring the potentially disruptive rumblings from Charlie's stomach.

press him to her, holding him to her breasts while he did his will—*her will* upon her body" (109, our emphasis). To put this differently, Rose does not lose her virginity; she willingly discards it, happy she no longer lives in the "nunnery," as she calls it, that had been her life (99). Rose feels no remorse or self-doubt over what she had done. Instead, her newly discovered sexuality energizes her and propels her ahead to seek further liberation.

This moment of sexual liberation is represented quite differently in Huston's adaptation. Although it would be difficult under any circumstances in a film produced by a major studio in the early 1950s to show a genuine sexual appetite of a woman, Huston goes to extremes in putting his version of Rose back in her place. Rose's mature sexual experience does not result in the independent control of her own body. The release she experiences is almost immediately contained with a traditional patriarchal definition of the proper relationship between a man and a woman. She is, in short, with her own willing complicity, yanked back into domestic subjugation. After their first night together, Rose arises early and busily prepares tea for her unawakened lover. Hepburn beams in the pleasure of satisfying her lover, happily enveloping herself in the role of cook and help-mate. In a manner that is quite similar to Huston's staging of marriage as an inherent containment of the woman, there is no room in this scene, with its light comic tone, for empathy over Rose's fall into the reactionary limitations of the domestic bliss of the morning after. Whether it be late afternoon or early morning, tea time, as Huston would apparently have it, retains its efficacy as a socializing ritual. This morning-after scene also marks an important movement away from Rose's own contextualization of her sexual desire. When Allnutt awakens and discovers that his bed mate has prepared his morning tea, he stretches out and comments, "Breakfast in bed . . . this is more like it." Huston adroitly employs a reverse point-of-view shot of Charlie so that we see the staging of Rose in his self-satisfied face as he gazes upon the object of his desire.

The erotic objectification of Rose has been expressed earlier in the film through the motif of uncovering. At the onset of her journey down the river when Hepburn makes her way to the boat, she is wearing the outfit she had worn earlier, an outfit that miraculously is never soiled. She brings along a parasol and wicker basket and has covered her body with the additional protection of a full-length coat. This is hardly the equipment or the dress required to escape the German army and sink one of its battle cruisers after a perilous journey down a river in Central Africa. But this does introduce a motif that recurs in the film: the covering and anticipated uncovering of the female body. The film is set up in such a way to suggest that as Rose moves downriver, becomes more experienced in the world, and escapes the influence of God and her brother, she will shed her Victorian clothing along with her Victorian manners. But this never really happens. The possibility of a literal uncovering of Hepburn's body hangs over the film and is underscored in one critically important scene. At a certain point in the journey it becomes necessary for the protagonists to bathe. This is accomplished in the only way possible: a dip in the river. In Forrester's novel this proves to be a transformational release for Rose: "Rose found herself stripping herself naked right out in the open, with a man only a dozen feet away doing the same . . . she sat naked on the low gunwale in the stern and lowered her legs into the water . . . The fast current boiled around them, deliciously cool, tugging at her ankles, insidiously luring her further" (45). She feels herself seduced by the depths of the waters and gives herself over to this almost erotic experience. When she has difficulty in pulling herself back onto the boat, she thinks to call to Allnutt for assistance but instead lifts herself back on board with "her powerful hands." Huston's version of this thinly veiled erotic release is dramatically different. The focus is on Hepburn's unsuccessful attempt to climb back into the boat and not her experience in the water. Huston titillates the audience with the possibility that none other than Katherine Hepburn will be offered up if not completely in the flesh at least only partially covered. But when she pulls herself out of the water we discover that she is essentially fully clothed in the equivalent of a 1920s bathing suit. What ensues is a simplistic silent film shtick. She tries repeatedly to lift her leg up onto the boat but comically is unable to do so. It is classic physical comedy in the style of Buster Keaton, in which a character struggles. Finally she must call to "Mr. Allnutt" for assistance. He covers his eyes and helps her on board with his own "powerful hands" not hers. The scene is a microcosm of Huston's strategy of adaptation. He turns a highly charged protofeminist moment into screwball farce. Exploiting once again her persona and career, Huston mocks Hepburn's well-known athleticism, reversing the physical comedy of *Bringing Up Baby* in which she is at ease on the golf course, while Grant makes a fool of himself in what for him is an alien environment. Moreover, Huston has staged Hepburn's body for his audience, teasing those watching with the possibility of its uncovering.

Ten years after directing *The African Queen*, Huston did something similar to his female star in *The Misfits* (1961). He used the personal and professional history of Marilyn Monroe in order to fashion a character who is the object of masculine desire. Hepburn and Monroe seem worlds apart. But both Hepburn and Monroe in their respective films come under an external governing consciousness. Georgiana Banita has astutely recognized that in *The Misfits* masculinity is turned back on itself and that the objectification of Monroe as a sex object becomes a critique of a failed "masculine fantasy that she is supposed to incarnate" (99). The seed of this strategy, we would argue, was first planted in *The African Queen* and is particularly evident in the scene of Hepburn bathing in the river. The titillation of seeing a naked Hepburn is subtly directed back upon its male audience that is aroused by an erotic expectation. While in the *The Misfits*, the male characters objectify the female, *The African Queen* assumes this of its audience. The male viewers of the female become ensnared in their own desire to uncover Hepburn. This plays out somewhat differently in the morning-after scene when Hepburn brings Bogart his breakfast in bed. It is not the male gaze that is operative here, but the self-satisfying pleasure of a male audience witnessing the containment of female sexuality within a gendered social context. The resonance of the scene is augmented by the ease with which Hepburn takes on the role, as if the traditional role of woman as helper had been inculcated into her psyche to the extent that it becomes an instinctual response. Unlike Monroe, whose own identity as a sexual object had come to define her as an actor and hence could be openly appropriated by Huston, Hepburn had a much different screen persona, one that Huston turned against itself. Male desire is generated not by attraction to a woman, but by the pleasure of giving a woman a new identity as an object of desire. The critique of a flawed masculinity, perhaps overt in *The Misfits*, is a subtle gesture in *The African Queen*, but nonetheless effective.

Put on a Smile, Whatever the Situation

Both Huston and Hepburn recall the advice the director had given her during the filming of *The African Queen*. Huston apparently felt things weren't going well, so he took Hepburn aside and explained how she should play the part of Rose: "You put on a smile. Whatever the situation. Like Mrs. Roosevelt—she felt she was ugly—she thought she looked better smiling—so chin up. The best is yet to come—onward ever onward. . . . the society smile" (Hepburn 82). Hepburn's response is extraordinary in its utter lack of critical engagement with Huston, her obliviousness to the Rose of the novel (that she had herself read), and her willingness to be seduced by the charm of her director: "This is the goddamnest best piece of direction I have ever heard . . . Well, he's just told me how to play the part . . . Such fun . . . I was his, from there on in" (83). Yes, the "society smile" amongst the natives, the "society smile" after guiding a boat through treacherous rapids, and a "society smile" after one's first sexual experience at age thirty-three in the stern of a weather beaten boat in the heart of Africa. Huston, with Hepburn's breezy approval, erased the remarkably transgressive subject matter of the novel. Surely, Huston must have realized the ridiculousness of his advice to his star. And surely he must have chuckled at her airy response and quick capitulation to his wiles, she the upper-class dynamo of *Bringing Up Baby* gently deposited into Central Africa at the onset of World War I. The resulting incongruity marks an equally gentle shift, though nonetheless radical, from the transgressive action of the novel to the regressive gestures of the film.

We have argued that Huston, through the manipulation of traditional Hollywood typologies and the strategic decision to cast Katherine Hepburn in the lead role, made the decision to eliminate the powerful feminist point of view of the novel. Huston's film seems innocent enough: a romantic comedy with two established stars playing an odd couple that falls in love. But when the film is approached as an adaptation, such innocence falls away. The discipline of adaptation studies is crucial, therefore, in understanding what Huston's intentions were in making the film. The radical departure that Huston makes from the social modernism of the novel does not raise the issue of fidelity to a source as a criterion for judgment. Instead, it causes us to wonder why Huston has done this and what his intention was in so doing. And once this step has been taken, the film can be studied on a deeper level. Huston was an astute reader of fiction who did not shy away from formally difficult and thematically transgressive works. It is highly dubious that he would have missed the overt feminist treatment of the protagonist of Forester's novel. But it is not enough to say that he has deliberately asserted his own directorial mastery over an impassioned and ultimately liberated woman. Huston turns back against his own apparent patriarchal control of Rose to offer a subtle critique of the masculine gaze. He insidiously makes the audience, especially its male members, complicit in their enjoyment of this ostensibly comic romance. What results is a complex play of perspectives, not simply those of Rose and Charlie, but of Forester, Huston, and the audience. To put this differently and rather succinctly, those who would see *The African Queen* as nothing other than an enjoyable love story set in an exotic location and in turbulent times could not have read Forester's novel. If they had, the sensitive ones might have been made uncomfortable by Huston's aggressive treatment of Forester's Rose, but with more thought they might have become appreciative of his deft commentary on the flaws of masculine identity.

Note

1. On the history behind the production of *The African Queen*, see Huston, pp. 187–205.

Works Cited

Banita, Georgiana. "Re-Visioning the Western: Landscape and Gender in *The Misfits*." *John Huston: Essays on a Restless Director*. Ed. Tony Tracy and Roddy Flynn. Jefferson, North Carolina: McFarland, 2010. 94–110.
Brill, Lesley. *John Huston's Filmmaking*. Cambridge: Cambridge UP, 1997.
DiBattista, Maria. *Fast Talking Dames*. New Haven: Yale UP, 2001.
Forester, C. S. *The African Queen*. 1935. New York: Little, Brown, 2000.
Hepburn, Katherine. *The Making of* The African Queen. New York: Alfred A. Knopf, 1987.
Huston, John. *An Open Book*. New York: Alfred A. Knopf, 1980.
Pierpont, Claudia Roth. "Born for the Part," *The New Yorker* 14 July 2003.
Taylor, Trey. "The Rise and Fall of Katherine Hepburn's Fake Accent." *The Atlantic* 8 Aug. 2013.
Žižek, Slavoj. *In Defense of Lost Causes*. New York: Verso, 2008.

7

R. Barton Palmer

John Huston and Postwar Hollywood

The Night of the Iguana in Context

Pressured by its small-screen rival, the American cinema in the 1950s and 1960s found some success in a generally declining marketplace by exploring two production strategies that seemed to push the industry in quite opposite directions: outsized event films (the antecedent of contemporary tent-pole productions) and small-scale realist projects, usually literary adaptations, and "adult" in theme. These films were long on drama and very short on action, spectacle, and glamour. Many, perhaps most, of the small-scale films of the era were directed by a younger generation of professionals who trained or worked in Broadway theater and prime-time television drama (most notably, Sidney Lumet, Robert Mulligan, Fielder Cook, Delbert Mann, Daniel Mann, Frank Perry, Jack Smight, and John Frankenheimer) and by sojourners from other national cinemas (such as Guy Green, Peter Glenville, and John Schlesinger). But other small-scale projects were undertaken by experienced professionals who had never fit easily into the studio system, such as Elia Kazan, Robert Rossen, Stanley Kramer, Martin Ritt, and John Huston, whose acclaimed late-career films can be seen as continuing this tradition into the 1970s and 1980s.

Although they were meant to compete with what was being offered for free on the new medium, the era's small-scale films, almost always in black and white (there are exceptions such as Kazan's *Splendor in the Grass* [1961]) reflected aesthetic/dramatic conventions then regnant in prime-time live televisual drama, which reflected the challenges then being raised by the international art cinema against the entertainment model of visual narrative long promoted by Hollywood. This highbrow end of a demotic medium also enjoyed strong connections to the contemporary Broadway theater, which was then flourishing with the rise to prominence of a new generation of important playwrights, such as Arthur Miller, Tennessee Williams, and William Inge, whose stage successes often enjoyed live broadcast production in such noted television "playhouses" as *Kraft Television Theatre*, *The Philco-Goodyear Television Playhouse*, and, most famously, *Playhouse 90*.[1] This emergent theatrical venue featured its own star writers, including Rod Serling, Paddy Chayefsky, Mark Harris, J. P. Miller, and James Costigan.

Those directing small-scale films constituted a group with whom Huston must have felt a growing kinship as the postwar era unfolded. To some degree, they were, like him, all rebels against the system who were eager to make films that were more than satisfying entertainment and aspired, in some sense, to be art. Huston had early on shown his interest in the provocative adaptation of literary properties with *The Maltese Falcon* (1941) and *The Treasure of the Sierra Madre* (1948). These novels by Dashiell Hammett and B. J. Traven offer biting critiques of the values that undergird the American system: a fascination with wealth in the abstract; an indifference to those immaterial things that make life most worth living; and the ruthless pursuit of advantage that inevitably turns paranoid and self-destructive. In their honest and moving exploration of these ethical and political issues, Huston's screen versions went far beyond conventional Hollywood moralism, announcing that a distinctive voice, *engagé* and often shrill, had risen to prominence in Tinseltown.[2]

The same abhorrence of conventional pieties dominates the documentaries he produced for the US Army during and after the war. These films reflect Huston's irrepressible interest in using all the resources of cinema to locate and communicate psychological and political truth, avoiding jingoistic propaganda. Huston's contributions to the war effort, filmed at great risk to himself, eschew the triumphalism of what other Hollywood professionals produced to enlighten filmgoers at home. *Report from the Aleutians* (1943), *The Battle of San Pietro* (1945), and *Let There Be Light* (1946) aroused considerable ire, as well as outright condemnation, in official circles for their searing portrayal of the human costs of World War II. *Pietro* and *Light*, as Gary Edgerton observes, developed in comparison to other official cinematic records of the war "a newer, more probing and observational film style that was necessary to let these veterans, in a sense, speak for themselves . . . The vérité aspects of these interviews were frankly ahead of their time and downright taboo" (50, 42).

Huston's interest in dramatic self-revelation and unvarnished realism would be well served by the evolving shape of the small-scale film, which tended to be more theatrical than novelistic, taking advantage of a Broadway that had taken a turn away from comforting entertainment toward serious drama. The production trend began with Elia Kazan's screening of Tennessee Williams's *A Streetcar Named Desire* (1951) and would reach its apogee with Mike Nichols's sensational adaptation of Edward Albee's *Who's Afraid of Virginia Woolf?* (1966). The adult themes of Nichols's film, with its uncompromising and at times darkly obscure portrait of a marriage in deep crisis, challenged the Code even more stridently than had *Streetcar*, which was seen at the time by those at the Production Code Administration as truly groundbreaking. *Who's Afraid* would only receive clearance for nationwide exhibition when those standards were modified; the film's profitable release, limited to those eighteen and older, demonstrated to the industry that releases niche marketed to adults would be successful.

In refusing to compromise in adapting the social, psychological, and intellectual themes of a provocative Broadway hit, Nichols followed a path that had been blazed two years earlier by John Huston with his screen version of the Tennessee Williams play *Night of the Iguana*, which was first produced in 1961 and enjoyed a successful run in New York of 316 performances, ultimately being nominated for a Tony award. In 1958, Huston signed a five-picture deal with producers of Seven Arts Productions, Ray Stark and Elliot Hyman, who had been impressed by his directorial skill in both *Moulin Rouge* (1952) and *Moby Dick* (1956), films in which Stark, to his own satisfaction, had invested, even though the Melville adaptation turned out to be a financial fizzle. Seven Arts had produced Huston's *The Misfits* (1961) and *The Roman Spring of Mrs. Stone* (1961), based respectively on novellas by Arthur Miller and Tennessee Williams. He would do yet another Williams adaptation in 1966: *This Property Is Condemned*. Stark was the creative half of the duo, and although Seven Arts backed occasional productions that were standard industry fluff (e.g., the 1961 Pat Boone vehicle *The Main Attraction*), he was interested in a literary cinema that featured well-known performers in roles that would show off their dramatic talents. These included the following: Kirk Douglas in John Frankenheimer's political thriller *Seven Days in May* (1964), with a screenplay by Rod Serling, based on the novel by Knebel and Bailey; Sean Connery, then world famous as James Bond, in Sidney Lumet's *The Hill* (1965), based on the play by Rigby and Allen; and Jackie Gleason, as screenwriter and star in *Gigot* (1962), an unusual French/American co-production. Based on a superb script by Hollywood professional Anthony Veiller, to which the director made significant contributions, *Iguana* would meet with as much success as had the play, becoming one of the top ten most profitable films of 1964 and paving the way for the more famous *Who's Afraid* two years later. For Nichols, Burton would reprise the character he had created for Huston: a middle-aged man who is dissolute, anguished, experiencing a profound spiritual crisis, and disappointed not only in himself but also in his world, which he finds corrupt and hypocritical. In both films, Burton's character comes to the end of the line only through his own perseverance to find a way forward to a renewed romantic attachment.

Iguana's substantial earnings were unusual for a black-and-white production that, although it featured established stars (Richard Burton, Deborah Kerr, and Ava Gardner), was no star vehicle. One of the era's most handsome leading men found himself in a production emptied of glamour. Burton's leading lady, Deborah Kerr, had a decade before wowed audiences with her portrayal of a sexually hungry army wife in *From Here to Eternity* (1953, Fred Zinnemann). But in *Iguana* she is cast as a spinster, often wearing something like a nun's bonnet, who resists Burton's considerable charms, opting for a wandering, solitary life instead of a rooted and committed relationship with a man she recognizes as her soul mate. If Huston's films normally offer suspenseful and engaging action sequences, *Iguana* is centered on an intensely dramatic, psychological rather than physical confrontation among three souls who are more or less lost and spend the course of a single evening discovering new directions for their lives. The film's ending, to be sure, is only problematically conventional and "happy," involving a significant but slight modification of Williams's less optimistic original. This conclusion, however, promotes a view of human resiliency with which Williams had shown himself elsewhere to be much in agreement. As Huston would put it, the play traces the struggle of "loose, random souls trying to account for themselves and finally being able to do so through love" (Brill 94). Its main themes, as Lesley Brill has noted, "are among Huston's own lifelong preoccupations" (94). It is, in fact, hard to determine where Williams leaves off and Huston begins in a film whose authorship is complexly shared, even as its themes (the difficulty of sexual fulfillment and orientation, the scourge of rootlessness, and the continuing anguish of lost faith) must have been found provocative, perhaps even offensive, by most mainstream filmgoers.

Even so, *Night of the Iguana* brought in more than $12 million ("Big Rental Pictures of 1964"), prompting Stark, not incorrectly, to proclaim that "this one's a real blockbuster" (Nolan 217). Here was a film that succeeded in transferring relatively intact to the screen the difficult vision of suffering and its transcendence purveyed by America's most famously sensational playwright at the time, while producing a film that the public eagerly flocked to see. It seemed to many that with this project, Houston had regained an artistic focus he had lost in his three previous releases, none a box office winner and two of which had been artistically overambitious: *The Misfits* (1961), adapted from a novella by Arthur Miller; and *Freud: The Secret Passion* (1962), with a script by Jean-Paul Sartre. Both Sartre and Miller were very unhappy with Huston, who while shooting *Misfits*, drank heavily and sustained huge gambling losses, which the production company was called upon to pay. Sartre's disagreements with Huston over the script of *Freud* resulted in the removal of his name from the credits; their acrimonious quarrel became public, and French filmgoers stayed away, ruining the film's box office performance in a lucrative market and poisoning its reputation among European cinephiles. A stylish but entirely predictable whodunit, *The List of Adrian Messenger* (1963) retreated from the realm of high art. Although it featured some excellent performances, the film seemed pedestrian compared to the thrillers produced during the era by the two acknowledged masters of the form: Alfred Hitchcock (*Psycho* [1960], *The Birds* [1963], and *Marnie* [1964]) and John Frankenheimer (*The Manchurian Candidate* [1964] and *The Train* [1965]). Costing about $3 million, *Messenger* did not perform well in its North American release despite the substantial popularity of such films at the time.[3]

It seemed that Huston was unable to repeat the success of his other genre pieces in the previous decade, such as *The African Queen* (1951) and *Heaven Knows, Mr. Allison* (1957). Ray Stark's offer to direct a film version of Williams's Broadway hit took the career of the somewhat floundering director in another direction. According to *Films and Feeling*, Huston had been "merely resting his grasp," but with this project he was now able to bring his talent to bear on "really appropriate material" (Nolan 217). The truth of this judgment will be explored in detail later, with *Iguana* pointing the way toward the artistically serious films of his later period, a literary cinema of mostly small-scale projects, upon which his high standing among classic Hollywood *auteurs* largely rests: *Wise Blood* (1979), *Under the Volcano* (1984), and *The Dead* (1987).

Nothing, however, illustrates better the ironies at work in the divided film culture at the time than that *Iguana*'s success attracted the attention of international producer Dino de Laurentiis. Huston was persuaded to direct, of all things, a biblical epic as a follow-up to *Iguana*'s success (the film was eventually titled *The Bible: In the Beginning* [1966]) that would take him into very different filmmaking territory, for which, as the results make clear, he was not well suited. *The Bible* bitterly disappointed those who expected more from Huston, who was arguably then the industry's most noted maverick director, already with a demonstrated flair for adaptation. As Bosley Crowther, the era's most influential tastemaker, sourly observed, "The misfortune of *The Bible* is that it does not live up to hopes . . . It simply repeats in moving pictures what has been done with still pictures over the centuries" ("The Bible According to John Huston"). High art on a grand scale proved to be a risky business, and Huston can be forgiven if he hazarded an ironic smile when his uninspired screen version of Genesis made considerably more money for all involved by catering to a well-established vein of middlebrow taste.

Huston's talents were generally better suited to the blockbuster's stylistic and thematic other—the small film that through the course of the 1960s pushed the envelope in terms of the representation of sexual and related themes, riding the rapidly cresting wave of a thoroughgoing transformation of traditional mores, while adopting, if only in part, the aesthetic richness of the international art film. Catering more, if not exclusively, to filmgoers eager for something more sophisticated and intellectually engaging than the fairly predictable, mostly genre-based entertainment that had long been the mainstay of Hollywood production, the small-scale adult film tended to be more "literary" in several senses, exploring a model of cinematic entertainment also then promoted by the international art cinema, whose anti-Hollywoodism Huston must have found congenial.

As an indication of the deep division then developing between the two areas of Hollywood production, consider that the year before Mike Todd was making millions with the entertaining wide-screen spectacle that was *Around the World in Eighty Days*, Academy members voted Delbert Mann's *Marty* as the year's Best Picture. Amazingly, this low-budget ($340,000) production also won the Palme d'Or at Cannes, as well as many other accolades.[4] *Marty* also turned a handsome profit for its producers (Hecht-Hill-Lancaster), with a domestic box office of about $3 million.[5] In the manner of the Italian neorealist films that had been, since 1945, key to the development and flourishing of the international art cinema, the film's exteriors were shot at various well-known locations in the New York borough, including the Grand Concourse, Arthur Avenue, and Gun Hill Road.[6] A thirty-something, "heavy set" Bronx butcher, Marty Pilletti (Ernest Borgnine), finds living with his mother increasingly miserable. He meets Clara (Betsy Blair), who is likewise socially awkward and unattractive. The long night of the "date" they then enjoy whets their deep needs for companionship, even as it uncovers their manifold insecurities and fears. This undramatic personal drama, with its slice of ordinary life, was not suited to the stage, where a more declamatory or combative style is usually necessary to hold audience attention. *Marty* requires the intimate camerawork with which Mann carefully records it. Also indispensable to its effect is the realism of its many exteriors, street scenes filmed in a glamourized, seemingly unprepared fashion that look backward to neorealist works like Vittorio de Sica's *Bicycle Thieves* (1948) and forward to New Wave productions like *The Four Hundred Blows* (1959).

Despite these international affinities, *Marty* is thoroughly American and provided Huston with a useful model for adapting *Iguana*, which is also structured around an extended dramatic encounter between a man and the two quite different women with whom he might form a relationship. In the style pioneered by Mann, Huston's camera is intimate, making excellent use of the cinema's ability to record the smallest details of expression and manner. *Marty*'s plain and unconcluded story, like the mundane intrigue de Sica offers in *Bicycle Thieves*, strikes a note of universality. At the same time, the film reflects deeply the particularities of Italian American life and is firmly rooted in a Bronx that is filled with an older generation whose English is shaky and accented, as well as their children, who are thoroughly Americanized.

The counterpart in the theater to the deglamourized realism and emphasis on the discontents of personal relationships, evident in *Marty* and many international art films, were the plays of Tennessee Williams. Moreover, beginning with *Streetcar* (first Broadway production 1947), Williams put the erotic life at the center of a revitalized American drama.[7] *Iguana* is not just about sex, to be sure. The play explores religious and intellectual themes that resonated with many at the time, including Huston himself: meeting death bravely; pursuing the creative life to the very end; drawing comfort from others and thus escaping loneliness; pushing beyond simple understandings of the conflict between flesh and spirit; and exploring one's own truth, no matter how disagreeable. With its quartet of finely drawn characters, Williams made it possible, as Gene Phillips suggests, to overlook the play's religious and philosophical implications since there were "enough melodramatic elements . . . to hold their attention" (301). Upon its Broadway opening late in 1961, *Iguana* struck New York critics as a welcome, new direction for Williams's theater, providing, according to Howard Taubman, a deep change in the "tone of the Broadway season," which thereby "gain[ed] greatly in quality." Here was a play that abandoned the "explosive and shocking gestures" of the playwright's earlier successes and turned the stage into a place "where the sources of man's nature may be explored with boldness and wonder" (109). Williams concurred with such judgments. He commented to an interviewer at the time: "I didn't feel like writing a 'black play'" (Taubman 109).

The setting is simple: a broken-down, off-the-beaten-path Mexican seaside hotel, where, having come to the end of their line in various ways, are a defrocked Episcopal minister, T. Lawrence Shannon, who is in the process of failing at his job of last resort, conducting guided tours for American Baptist ladies; an aged poet, Nonno, working on his final poem, accompanied by his granddaughter, Hannah, a forty-year-old spinster, who supports the pair by selling caricatures and drawings to tourists; and Maxine, a blowsy, middle-aged widow, who owns the establishment and entertains herself with a pair of local beach boys. Two of Shannon's erstwhile clients complicate his attempts to escape from the existential trap to which his sexual weakness has brought him: Charlotte, the young girl whom he, offering but an ineffective protest, allows to seduce him; and Miss Fellowes, a tightly closeted lesbian schoolmarm, who is hysterically obsessed with protecting Charlotte from a man she sees as a ruthless predator.

Brought together by accident, these characters provide one another with spiritual companionship and understanding, leading to a series of more or less happy endings. Miss Fellowes (Grayson Hall) succeeds in cooling the lust that Charlotte (Sue Lyon) has for Lawrence, but she takes up with the tour's bus driver, Hank (James Ward), instead. Nonno (Cyril Delevantias) finishes his last poem (which, in part, celebrates a nature that countenances "no betrayal of despair") and dies, to be buried by the sea he had always loved. Hannah determines to carry on, reaffirmed in her knowledge that the future, however uncertain and apparently unpromising, must be faced with equanimity; the play does end with her kissing Nonno's forehead and seeming confused about her next step, but everything that precedes this moment of doubt speaks to her continuing survival. Learning from Hannah to be tolerant of his own weakness and accept the fleshly part of his nature, Shannon emerges from a deep psychological crisis (at one point he is tied up by Hannah and Maxine so he can do himself no harm) to accept the possibility of a new life with Maxine. As Taubman puts it, in *Iguana* Williams declares "his respect for those who have to fight for their bit of decency" (109). Like Shannon, the iguana of the play's title is also confined, tied up so that it can be fattened up before being slaughtered for a tasty meal. After Hannah releases the ropes that bind him to the hammock, Shannon cuts loose the unfortunate beast in a gesture that provides a fitting correlative for the play's commitment to freedom and deliverance.

If lacking the energetic, forward-moving plot and focus on romance that was thought necessary in the standard Hollywood product, *Iguana* lent itself to being reworked with relative ease into a profitable and artistically successful art film that drew deeply on the intimate mundanity of the small film tradition. Crucial was the play's focus on an anguished male, the Reverend Shannon (Richard Burton), who could readily be transformed into the main character, altering the play's emphasis on the ensemble. Typically male (consider the major films of Truffaut, Godard, Bergman, Fellini, and Antonioni), the art film protagonist provides the structural frame for the narrative, especially if, as in the case of *Iguana*, it is devoted principally to tracing his biography, which means that, to quote David Bordwell, "events become pared down toward a picaresque successivity" (96). Such a focus on male angst was to be found in the small realist films of the 1950s, such as *Patterns* (Fielder Cook, 1956), which traces the moral revulsion felt by a newly promoted business executive forced to make a place in a New York of red tooth and claw, and *Days of Wine and Roses* (Blake Edwards, 1962), with its portrait of an alcoholic salesman struggling for sobriety. All three releases, it bears remarking, were based on critically acclaimed live TV productions. This concentration on maleness *in extremis* is fitting because, as Bordwell goes on to suggest, "characters of the classical narrative have clear-cut traits and objectives, [while] the characters of the art cinema lack defined desires and goals" (96). Such formlessness gives them the representational space to "express and explain their psychological states," which Hannah (Deborah Kerr), Lawrence (Richard Burton), and Maxine (Ava Gardner) do at affecting length, spending a long night of the soul together in which they separately and together confront the largest of questions: how to go on living in the face of disappointments, dead ends, and death. At the end, Hannah is bravely confirmed in her self-containment, while Maxine and Lawrence agree to the exploration of a life together (in the rewritten ending confected by director and screenwriter).

If Bordwell is correct that in the art cinema "characters and their effects on one another remain central," then *Iguana* nicely exemplifies the type (96). The adaptation did not attempt to confect plot elements to stretch out what on stage was essentially an extended talkfest, but, instead, added episodes to deepen the portrayal of Shannon's fall from grace and inability to resist the advances of lustful young women. Almost the first third of the film was added by experienced screenwriter Anthony Veiller, with the close collaboration of Huston, but the narrative of how

Shannon manages to wind up in Maxine's hotel with a passel of angry tourists simply expands on the back story presented in the original stage dialogue, remaining faithful to Williams's conception. Bosley Crowther, however, complained that the film, like its source, fails to explain its characters adequately: "But who are these dislocated wanderers? From what Freudian cell have they been sprung, and why are they so aggressive in punching their loneliness home to the world? These are the basic revelations that are not communicated by the film, which follows fairly closely the dialogic substance of the play" (42). And yet, the film traces Shannon's desperate journey to Maxine's hotel, as he tries to prevent Miss Fellowes from contacting his employer and arranging for his dismissal. Huston and Veiller thus dramatize Shannon's headlong, energetic fall into the dead end from which escape seems improbable, the entrapment the play begins with, later to be actualized by the captured iguana and the suicidal protagonist tied to a hammock for his own safety.

Though an avid fan of the international art cinema, Crowther here judges *Iguana* as if it were a standard Hollywood product, committed to characters who, as Bordwell puts it, possess "clear-cut traits and objectives" (96). However anatomized at length and provided with

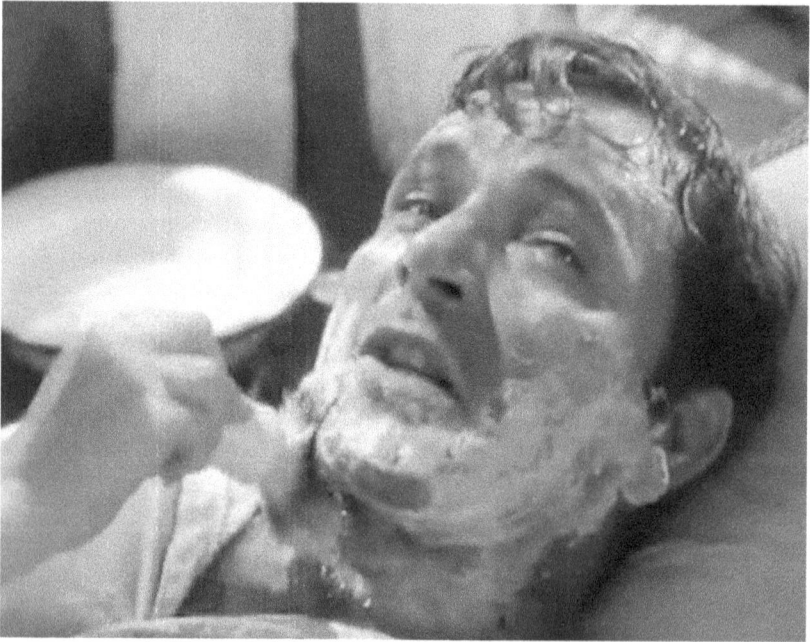

Figure 7.1. Richard Burton, as the erstwhile anguished male, pauses for a shave.

episodic narratives that require them constantly to adjust to changing circumstances, characters in the art cinema always "lack defined desires and goals." We never discover "who they are." Bordwell sees this vagueness or unknowability as essential to what art films of the period, made under the spell of existentialism, always have to say about human experience, which is nothing less than to "pronounce judgments on 'modern life' as a whole. . . . During the film's survey of its world, the hero often shudders on the edge of breakdown. There recurs the realization of the anguish of ordinary living, the discovery of unrelieved misery." Under Huston's skillful direction, and working with a fine script that remains true to the spirit of Williams's conception, the film provides what Howard Taubman terms "the tender, futile gropings of its characters" and the struggle of Hannah, Maxine, and Shannon to "slash the rope that tethers them to their grim, lonely destinies" (109). Arguably, no other Williams property lent itself so readily to the art cinema's commitment to explore (but never explain or explain away) the experience of those shuddering "on the edge of breakdown." It is hard to imagine what Hollywood director of the era, except John Huston, could have brought it so successfully to the screen.

Huston, of course, was fortunate to be working with Ray Stark, who played a central role in packaging the project, in accordance with their original deal, finalized in 1958, just a year after founding Seven Arts. In July 1962, the company announced an unusual agreement with M-G-M to co-produce and co-finance as many as twenty feature films over the next five or six years. Several of these were, interestingly enough, to be produced first by the noted David Merrick on stage, and only then, having earned their presold *bona fides*, to be made into films. In order to acquire properties with proven appeal to the educated and sophisticated, Seven Arts thus connected the theater and the Hollywood cinema in a fashion never attempted before or since, at least on this scale.[8] Seven Arts, however, was interested in literary cinema in its largest sense. As part of his deal with Seven Arts, Huston would direct the adaptation of an honored (if not well-known) property, Rudyard Kipling's fable of the discontents of British colonialism, *The Man Who Would Be King*, a project that the director had been planning for nearly a decade. The resulting film, released many years later, in 1975, is acknowledged as one of Huston's finest. For Seven Arts, he was scheduled to do another novelistic adaptation, bringing to the screen Brian Moore's novel about the drab existence of a middle-aged piano teacher (Maggie Smith) searching for direction in her life: *The Lonely Passion of Judith Hearne* (1987). The financing fell through, and Huston was replaced on this project by Jack Clayton, a director also deeply interested in literary adaptation, who produced an affecting, authentic version of Moore's character study. One cannot help but think, however, that Huston's version would have constituted a fitting sequel to *Iguana*'s exploration of spinsterhood, whose themes would also be explored in the three small films of Huston's later career: *Wise Blood*, *Under the Volcano*, and, preeminently, *The Dead*.

As a sophisticated exploration of American modernity and its discontents, *Iguana* anticipates the more celebrated works of that second wave of auteurs, the directors of the Hollywood Renaissance in the late 1960s and early 1970s. Probably too ambitious, the overall aim of Seven Arts to form an intimate, enduring connection between the theater and Hollywood was not to be realized, save for the remarkably profitable eleven films that Stark made from various Neil Simon properties, including the celebrated *The Goodbye Girl* (1977), *The Sunshine Boys* (1975), and *California Suite* (1978), and several other plays, including most notably *Funny Girl* (1968). But Stark showed wisdom and sound judgment in assigning the project of making *Iguana* to the finest literary adaptor of the era. Who else can claim to have filmed, often with great success, works by Stephen Crane, Herman Melville, James Joyce, Rudyard Kipling, Carson McCullers, and Flannery O'Connor?

Stark may have sensed more than a commercial opportunity in pairing Huston with Tennessee Williams. The two artists seem to have had much in common. Speaking of the adaptation of *Iguana*, Maurice Yacowar expresses the contrary view, observing that "John Huston has always expressed a more robust spirit than Williams has, a vision less bleakly in line with defeat and destruction and one where the joys of life and the quest make up for loss and defeat" (94). In response, we would point to the ending of Huston's *Iguana*, which need alter the original only slightly in order to provide the sense that the characters, while not delivered to what would in the 1940s have been termed a happy ending, are now able to glimpse clearly a future in which their isolation and emotional poverty might end. The play ends with Shannon's agreement to make himself the object of the desire Maxine has always felt for him and with Hannah left alone with Nonno's corpse. In the film, these two sequences are reversed and their sense of irresolution removed, with Hannah's courageous departure for parts unknown (after a gracious refusal to accept Shannon as a traveling partner) followed by a scene in which Shannon accepts Maxine's offer to stay and help run the hotel. She suggests that they share a swim before embarking on this new life together (a connection that may, but need not, be romantic). Shannon admits that he could descend the hill to the beach, but would be unable to climb back up to the hotel. The film ends with Maxine's response: "I'll get you back up, baby. I'll always get you back up." If this moment of comradeship is thoroughly Hustonian, it also fulfills the commitment of Williams in this play, as Howard Taubman puts it, to "transcend the raging pessimism that has permeated so much of his work" (109).

Notes

1. For details, see Boddy and Anderson.
2. Many would agree with critic Martin Rubin that *Treasure* "did the most to enhance his reputation as a Hollywood 'rebel' and 'maverick'" in Studlar and Desser 143.
3. http://www.imdb.com/title/tt0057254/business?ref_=ttfc_sa_3 (accessed 3/4/2014).
4. http://www.filmsite.org/mart.html (accessed 3/4/2014).
5. http://www.imdb.com/title/tt0048356/business (accessed 3/4/2014).
6. On the American enthusiasm for neorealism, see the excellent account in Balio 3–61.
7. This issue is treated at length in Palmer and Bray.
8. Some of these projects were as follows: Paul Osborn's adaptation of Max Druon's Paris hit *La Contessa*, retitled *Film of Memory*; *French Street*, noted playwright Norman Krasna's translation of Jacques Deval's *Romancero*; and *Mrs. 'Arris Goes to Paris*, a musical adaptation of Paul Gallico's book. See Zolotow 18.

Works Cited

Anderson, Christopher. *Hollywood TV: The Studio System in the Fifties*. Austin: U of Texas P, 1992). "Big Rental Pictures of 1964." *Variety*, 6 Jan. 1965: 39.

Balio, Tino. *The Foreign Film Renaissance on American Screens 1946–1973*. Madison: U of Wisconsin P, 2010.

Boddy, William. *Fifties Television: The Industry and Its Critics*. Urbana: U of Illinois P, 1992.

Bordwell, David. "The Art Cinema as a Mode of Film Practice." *Film Criticism* 4.1 (Fall 1979): 56–64.

Brill, Lesley. *John Huston's Filmmaking*. Cambridge: Cambridge UP, 1997.

Crowther, Bosley. "The Bible according to John Huston." *New York Times* 29 Sept. 1966.

Crowther, Bosley. "John Huston and Melville's White Whale." *New York Times* 6 July 1956.

Crowther, Bosley. "Night of the Iguana Has World Premiere." *New York Times* 1 July 1964.

Edgerton, Gary. "Revisiting the Recordings of Wars Past: Remembering the Documentary Trilogy of John Huston." *Reflections in a Male Eye: John Huston and the American Experience*. Ed. Studlar and Desser. Washington DC: Smithsonian, 1993.

Huston, John. *An Open Book*. New York: Knopf, 1980.

Nolan, William F. *John Huston: King Rebel*. Los Angeles: Sherbourne, 1965.

Phillips, Gene D. *The Films of Tennessee Williams*. Philadelphia: Art Alliance, 1980.
Studlar, Gaylyn, and David Desser. *Reflections in a Male Eye: John Huston and the American Experience*. Washington DC: Smithsonian, 1993.
Taubman, Howard. "Changing Course." *New York Times* 7 Jan. 1962.
Yacowar, Maurice. *Tennessee Williams and Film*. New York: *Frederick Ungar, 1977.*
Zolotow, Sam. "Seven Arts Plans to Offer Shows." *New York Times*, 31 May 1962.

8

Dale M. Pollock

"This Has Got to Be a Masterpiece"

John Huston's Mangled Adaptation of *The Red Badge of Courage*

John Huston chose many difficult books to adapt, but none more challenging than Stephen Crane's 1884 novel *The Red Badge of Courage*. That he succeeded in making an intensely personal Civil War drama about a terrified young soldier for a major Hollywood studio is impressive on its own; but its failure to live up to the vision of both Huston and Crane was due to unrealistic expectations, outdated politics at MGM, and a final reluctance by Huston and the studio to accept Crane and his story on their own terms.

Despite its consideration as one of the strongest depictions of the Civil War, Crane's literary impressionism in *Red Badge* was thought to be largely unfilmable. The lack of a narrative plot, the interior nature of the protagonist's dilemma in choosing courage or cowardice on a confusing battlefield, and the total absence of female characters doomed Crane's period story from serious filmic consideration by any major Hollywood studio (Higham 400). Yet Huston was able to take advantage of a confluence of studio power struggles and post–World War II internal reflection by a new generation of film moguls to make his film adaptation of *The*

Red Badge of Courage (1951) into a stinging antiwar Civil War drama, starring an American hero as a sometimes-abject coward.

The experiences of filming his emotional World War II documentaries still fresh in his mind, Huston also intended *Red Badge* as a visual example, set during America's greatest internal battle, of the traumatic aftereffects of war that he documented in *Let There Be Light* (1946). His purpose, if never clearly articulated, seemed to be to offer a withering example of the absurdity of war, and in particular, the extreme toll war enacts on sensitive individuals. In the end, however, Huston backed away from the ambitiousness of his undertaking, unwilling to engage in and fight for the elements of the story he initially insisted were so important to him.

The Red Badge of Courage emerged from its own battles at MGM as a sorry and reduced sixty-nine-minute entity, the celluloid equivalent of the Tattered Soldier whose poignant death scene was the greatest Huston felt he had ever directed and was cut from the final version by Dore Schary, ironically a liberal who had made his reputation writing and producing social problem movies (DeBona 118). When in 1975 MGM came to Huston with a request for a print of his original cut of *Red Badge*, he said, "It doesn't exist" (*Huston* 180). Reminded of the lesson he should have learned, Huston then instructed his agent, Paul Kohner, to include in all his future contracts a stipulation that he be given a 16 millimeter print of the first cut of any film he made (180).

The Artist and the Studio

In his autobiography, Huston is remarkably candid about what he termed one of the worst episodes of his career. Since its release, *Red Badge* has been described in most critical works about Huston as an artistic disaster (Hammen 55). Many have recognized that *it* was an ill-fated project inadvertently caught up in a titanic studio power struggle—the wrong film at the wrong time for an audience sated on World War II movies and worried about a new conflict breaking out in Korea. The film's dire fate was not helped by the fact that Huston, rarely fully engaged in a project following the completion of principal photography, had abandoned *Red Badge* with alacrity following its first two catastrophic public previews in February 1951. Huston wrote in his autobiography, "During the preview you could actually feel the audience stiffen against the film. That's an experience I don't look forward to reliving, and when it happened I knew the picture had no future" (179). Louis B. Mayer, the vice president of MGM, who always waited for the first public preview to see an MGM production, also had his opinions confirmed. *Red Badge* was the antithesis of everything Mayer admired in a film (Higham 402). Where were the warmth and drama inherent in other MGM Civil War sagas, such as *Gone with the Wind* (1939) and *Of Human Hearts* (1938)?

At the time, Huston had a much more commercial film to start, *The African Queen* (1951), with real movie stars, Humphrey Bogart and Katharine Hepburn, for a veteran producer, Sam Spiegel. Huston had worked on *Red Badge* for nine months, was broke, and had too many projects piling up on his plate (Nolan 93). The African jungle in the Republic of the Congo was a convenient place to forget all about the Civil War and the flawed creation he had fashioned from Crane's tale of unwilling maturation in the heat of conflict. Huston's producer Gottfried Reinhardt, who had first brought him the project, said to Lillian Ross, "John doesn't care any more about the picture. John doesn't care about anything, and I am left here to listen to Louis B. Mayer" (*Huston* 193). It is unclear if Huston had stayed and fought for the picture, it would have made any difference. In his own defense, Huston claimed, "I had made what I thought was a good picture. In fact, in its original version it was a very good picture, but audiences were not prepared to accept it" (179). But to many of his associates Huston's failure to fight for his version was a sign of weakness. "It is a startling irresponsibility in so good an artist," his frequent collaborator James Agee wrote (28).

Even prior to the studio's unauthorized cutting of the film, problems were arising. As the screenplay underwent a series of revisions—Albert Band now assigned to help with the rewrites—that pulled it farther and farther away from Huston's vision and Crane's story, it became a fulcrum in the final throes of the struggle for control of production at MGM (Ross 81). In his new appointment as West Coast head of production, Schary was using *Red Badge* as the lead spear in his insurgency against Mayer, who had opposed the project from the outset. The chairman of Loews Incorporated, Nicholas Schenck, would eventually force out Mayer and anoint Schary the new studio chieftain. When Schary learned of Mayer's withdrawing his objections to making the film, he saw it as a tactical victory: "So that battle was won," he wrote in his autobiography (208). But ultimately Schenck would use the failure of *Red Badge* to teach Schary a lesson about getting too involved in artistic projects that didn't make money for the shareholders.

The production of *Red Badge* in the summer and fall of 1950 was plagued with compromises and problems and went significantly over budget (Ross 185). Huston's career-long cavalier attitude toward film directing is typified by his declaration in preproduction that he would direct on horseback—a decision overturned by lunchtime on the first day of filming (Ross 22). Huston downplayed how significantly he took any directing assignment: "It never seems to me that my films start off with much preparation. In fact, I often get the feeling that my films make themselves" (Bachmann 100). That might have been news to producer Reinhardt. More significantly, Huston was under constant pressure to impose a stronger narrative structure on Crane's impressionistic prose and make the novel into more of a traditional war story than Huston wanted to tell but that MGM wanted to release.

The conflict between Hollywood and great art, whether literary or cinematic, grew exponentially in the postproduction process, as preview screenings of *Red Badge* validated Mayer's predictive dismissal of the project as a commercial failure. "It will be ugly and will not make money," he reportedly told Huston and Reinhardt before preproduction commenced (Nolan 86). Audiences were not interested in the tortured emotions of a raw army recruit in a war they last thought about in high school, if at all; those who had read *The Red Badge of Courage* were probably required to. Huston's decision to cast World War II's most decorated hero, twenty-six-year-old Audie Murphy (another decision Mayer opposed) did not make *Red Badge* any more interesting or compelling for 1951 movie audiences, who could not figure out why they were watching the last war's greatest hero turn yellow and flee at the first bad turn in battle.

Huston was stunned by the failure of the audience to identify with the film: "I think it's my best picture. How could they hate it so much?" (85). His goal had been to demythologize the American soldier, as he recalled images of the broken men he had interviewed on Long Island following World War II and saw the gulf between the patriotic war propaganda Hollywood created and the sad reality of the shattered lives of veterans. Huston had come to the realization that it was a fraud to portray soldiers as dashing, devil-may-care heroes who fought for glory and God. In retrospect, Huston felt that making and releasing the film while the Korean War was growing magnified the problems in adapting Crane's antiwar message. In an interview in *Film Culture*, Huston recalled, "The worst frost I ever had was with *Red Badge*. "It was too much for audiences," Huston continued, "and they wanted no part of it." He felt that all their reactions were magnified by the Korean War. The film was ultimately a victim of bad timing (Anonymous).

Schary was committed to saving *Red Badge*, and he resented Huston's quick abdication. He recounted Huston's phone call to him the morning after the disastrous preview: "He asked me to take over the film, assuring me that I could fix it. He was in a hurry. He wished me good luck. I wished him the same. I guessed he had found a usable raft but that we were to go down with the ship" (Schary 226). Schary's instincts proved fatal to Huston's cut of the film. Even though Crane and Huston had opted clearly for rendition over narration, Schary and Reinhardt retreated to the Hollywood default setting of a narrator to tell the audience what was happening and how to feel about it. The decision to use Crane's prose, distilled personally by Schary to pretentious sound bites, and read aloud by the mid-American voice of James Whitmore, a World War II Marine veteran and a star of Huston's *The Asphalt Jungle* (1950), failed to vitiate the damage done (Ross 216).

Huston's choice to eschew a traditional linear narrative structure frustrated Reinhardt and Schary in their attempts to recut the picture; abetting their problem was Huston's career-long strategy of cutting in the camera and thus not permitting alternate versions because the footage doesn't exist to constitute them. The results of Schary and Reinhardt's editing were not always pretty. In the eyes of Mayer biographer Charles Higham, "Reinhardt castrated the picture, then Dore Schary cut its arms and legs off" (402). For MGM, the theatrical failure of the film wasn't that expensive of a lesson. *Red Badge* ground out some revenue as the bottom half of a B-picture double bill featuring *Texas Carnival* (1951), an Esther Williams musical. There was no serious attempt to release it abroad. Huston still made films for the studio in the future, such as *The Night of the Iguana* (1964). Audie Murphy's movie career flourished, although he never starred in a prestige title again. Producer Gottfried Reinhardt, while bemoaning his fate to anyone who would listen, would go on to direct thirteen films himself after determining how little fun it was to be a producer. James Agee, Huston's collaborator on *The African Queen*, wrote a screen adaptation of Crane's short story "The Blue Hotel" (1899) with the understanding that it would be one of the director's next projects at MGM. But the disastrous commercial performance of the first Crane-Huston combination would preclude a second (Hammen 62).

Grappling with Crane

Could any filmmaker have successfully transferred Crane's largely interior story to the big screen? Huston considered Crane a genius: "I rank his book with the great war chronicles of Thucydides, Caesar, Tolstoy, Stendahl, and Norman Mailer" (Kaminsky 76–77). Huston's three World War II documentary films for the U.S. Army Pictorial Services offer evidence of the approach he would employ in realizing Crane's impressionistic story. Two of these, *San Pietro* (1945) and *Report from the Aleutians* (1943), gave Huston both narrative and visual strategies for addressing the battle sequences in *Red Badge*, while *Let There Be Light* dramatically prepared the director for capturing the stress and anxiety the Youth experiences before and during his skirmishes. "Fear in a man is something tragic or reprehensible," Huston is quoted as saying about *Red Badge* while still in preproduction, "We'll show this. Our film should have real humor in it along with the horror of battle. And I want to put in some things I've learned about war" (Nolan 87). In Crane's novel Huston found something that deepened and validated the message of his war trilogy. Rarely discussed in the corridors of MGM were the problems inherent in adapting a work of literature that presaged both the personal war novel and the psychological fiction of F. Scott Fitzgerald and Ernest Hemingway, who followed Crane as popular American novelists. Huston was drawn to Crane's semirealistic approach to depicting war, which the author achieved by what Milne Holton calls "a parodic irony, by a form of denial of all the heroic and romantic attitudes which established the conventions of the war novel" (87). Huston had taken on a literary project that the studio chiefs were not oriented to understand.

But Huston also recognized the challenge of adapting a work characterized by fluidity and change. Much of *Red Badge* is composed of brief, one- or two-sentence paragraphs, presenting rapidly successive sensations, thoughts, feelings, and observations. There is little structure to the tumble of ideas and emotions; rather than the string of events that befall the protagonist, the way Crane tells his story is decisive to its meaning. Huston felt that Crane's sudden and illogical transitions between the Youth's experiences captured the nervousness and abruptness of his wartime personality (Bergon 2). This depiction exactly mirrored what Huston had witnessed on Long Island while shooting *Let There Be Light* (he likened making the film to "having a religious experience" [Jameson 50]). At the same time, Crane did deal in cinematic imagery throughout his narrative; he zooms in on one scene, pulls back abruptly from another as if his writerly eye is tracking back. The prose often moves from a wide-angle view to a close-up on one or more significant details (Bergon 13). In the Youth's first taste of combat, the battle is a never-ending, always-evolving trial, a blur of events and marches "so that afterward, everything was pictures and explained to him, save why he himself was there" (Crane 359). "Everything was pictures": Crane anticipated a cinematic style that reflected the growing impact of photographic depiction as America transitioned from a strictly print-oriented culture to a more visual one. Photography, magazine illustration, and political cartooning all helped build a more modern visual consciousness in which the pictorial held sway over literary description.

For all the filmic potential Huston and Reinhardt perceived in Crane's pointillist rendering of war, the pitfalls were obvious and plentiful. The novel is inherently an interior story, one of thoughts and emotions impossible to communicate, at least as Crane wrote them, in a traditional Hollywood narrative. Fleming's character spends the first third of the book explaining his cowardice and the second third justifying it to himself. In the finale, he magically absorbs an unconscious form of bravery that finds him bearing the regimental colors and urging his comrades forward without quite understanding how he got there. "The Youth really has nothing to do with the outcome of the Civil War," Huston is quoted as saying. "He simply gets tossed on the roulette wheel of battle, gets thrown off and, of his own free will, jumps back on again. This could happen to a boy in any war, anywhere, and that's what we'll show. That's what the picture will be about" (Nolan 87). Huston wanted a film that would speak to the alienation and trauma of all wars.

To do this, the challenge for Huston was to make sure the audience saw the battle not only through Henry's eyes, but also through their own. The experience of war, as in Crane's novel, is presented through subjective impressionism, which Crane saw as "pure" writing and Huston saw as "pure" cinema (Holton 89; Agee 26). Most of the book consists of Fleming's stream-of-consciousness ramblings, primarily on his own status as soldier, man, coward, and hero. Near the end of the story, the total insignificance of his experience begins to dawn on the Youth. Thus, it seems of little consequence when he becomes the heroic flag bearer, since the battle itself is worthless to him. However, something takes over Henry in the process, a feeling he had never before experienced. "He felt himself the daring spirit of a savage, religion-mad. He was capable of profound sacrifices, a tremendous depth" (Crane 431). When he is leading the charge, he can see all parts of the battlefield for the first time. He finally possesses the ability to be a true voyeur in his own story. "He was deeply involved as a spectator" (420). It's difficult to find another protagonist in a war story who sees the battle as if he's in the audience, rather than the center of the conflict. Crane manages to achieve the simultaneous perspective, at the cost of minimizing the triumph of Henry's courage.

Before the novel is over, Henry has led his comrades to victory, although the prize is but a humble stone wall. Crane writes, "He had been where there was red of blood and black of passion, and he was escaped" (448). The stakes were low but the cost was high, and Henry remains haunted by his experience, especially because he deserted the Tattered Soldier on the battlefield. He felt it was the defining moment of his cowardice and lack of gumption. The final image Crane leaves us with could have been entered into the psychiatric file of one of Huston's subjects in *Let There Be Light*: "He has been to touch the great death, and found that, after all, it was but the great death" (455). Several literary critics interpret this is in a religious context and consider spiritual change to be Henry Fleming's red badge, one that is his conscience reborn and purified (Stallman 134). Cinema, of course, has difficulty in portraying such inner emotions with any other device than the close-up. *The Red Badge of Courage* consists of nothing but interior feelings: shame, loss, pride, and exhilaration are just a few of the emotions the Youth experiences. The successful translation of these to the screen remained questionable, even after the efforts Huston and Band applied to their adaptation.

Adaptation and Failure

Huston certainly believed that a film version could work. "I don't seek to interpret, to put my own stamp on the material," Huston said of his professed fidelity to Crane. "I try to be as faithful to the original material as I can. . . . In fact, it's the fascination I feel for the original that makes me want to make it into a film" (Bachmann 102). Huston felt that Crane's mixture of impressionism and subjective realism was exactly his strength as a director. He had a look in mind, a romantic mixture of D. W. Griffith's *The Birth of a Nation* (1914) and Matthew Brady's legendary Civil War photographs, reportedly the model for many of Crane's descriptions of the battle landscape. Huston even owned a Brady photograph of his great-grandfather, Colonel William P. Richardson, whose sword also makes it into the movie on the belt of the General, played by Tim Durant. Huston's long shots in the film, the result of close collaboration with veteran cinematographer Harold Rosson, do indeed evoke Brady's classic photography. The black-and-white images contrast the bloodshed in the foreground against the clear gray sky in the background. By varying long shots with close-ups and then extreme close-ups, Huston and Rosson achieve pathos, rather than the formal stiffness of Brady's staged photographs. The close-ups undercut the film's pseudo-photographic, sharply photographed realism, shifting its tenor from an objective war story to a largely subjective domain of terror and bravery.

It is the unknown that haunts the Youth. Until the final charge near the end of *Red Badge*, the enemy remains largely unseen. Instead, Huston tries as much as possible to have the film shot from Henry's point of view (Ross 53). When a Union rifle fires, the focus is always on the shooter rather than the intended target on the Confederate side. Huston is not taking sides in the conflict, but rather determined to maintain the perspective on Henry Fleming, his fellow soldiers, and their collective fears and prejudices about what constitutes heroism and cowardice. Huston keeps the camera low whenever around the Union soldiers who congregate in clumps so that the filmmaker can eavesdrop on their conversations. He ennobles his characters by shooting from below them, and his use of deep focus to achieve a close-up of the Youth in the foreground, with a deep background of campfires and shadows, gives the individual and the group equal weight in the frame. Huston often keeps the Youth in the foreground even when the action in the background goes in and out of focus, amplifying the attention paid to the Youth's face, eyes, and body language to pick up his never-ending stream of emotions. The constantly shifting feelings on Murphy's face helped establish the essential tone of the film.

Huston also wanted to capture a neorealist version of the rural Americans who did the down and dirty fighting in the Civil War: the upper- and middle-class urban residents could easily buy their way out of military service. Crane focused on the dialogue of his soldiers, laboring for realism and poetry in their unaffected drawls. Huston had a similar obsession: "It seems to me that the word contains as much action as a purely visual scene, and that dialogue should have as much action as physical motion" (Bachmann 101). Although the small bantam Lieutenant has a memorable way of speaking and conducting himself in the novel, Huston did not succeed in re-creating his voice in the film. Consistently, Huston falters in translating the words uttered by Crane's characters to the screen. He was frequently limited in his attempt at realism by Joseph H. Breen, the head of the Production Code, who found each use of "damn," "Lord," and "Gawd" objectionable, along with "hell to pay" (Ross 33–34). Huston can be forgiven somewhat when his attempts at mimicking Crane's invented 1860s naturalism, which is tolerable on the page, fall flat onscreen, coming off as contrived and unconvincing Hollywood ruralspeak (Georgakas).

Raw and rugged faces still existed in the post–World War II era, and Huston used them to great effect in *Red Badge*. He had seen the World War II versions of these soldiers when making his war documentaries, and he strove for a similar realism in the faces he filmed. The casting of John Dierkes as Jim Conklin, the Tall Soldier, Royal Dano as the Tattered Soldier (who also possessed a wonderful voice), and Bill Mauldin as the Loud Soldier gave Huston a documentary version of Hollywood's traditional foxhole movie, that invariably contained a WASP, a Jew, a second-generation ethnic immigrant, and never a black soldier.

African Americans are totally absent from this film, as from Crane's novel, and *The Red Badge of Courage* may be the Civil War film the least concerned with slavery, race, or any of the political reasons for fighting the war. Huston essentially depicts his protagonist fighting with near-suicidal bravado for an undefined cause, but his goal was specifically to surmount the restrictions he felt were inherent in the traditional war film: the glorification of battle and the unquestioning heroism of the protagonist(s). Huston made one of the most personal accounts of war put on film, certainly since *All Quiet on the Western Front* (1930), one that deemed the conflict to be ultimately meaningless on the larger level, while still transformative personally. Fleming has crossed the threshold into manhood and has learned something important about his own capabilities and his weaknesses.

Huston is at his best when depicting Fleming in his moments of total animal fear. Rosson's highly effective tracking shot of the Youth running, falling, slipping, and sliding as he retreats in panic keeps us in synch with Fleming at his wildest moments. We understand his dread at encountering either Confederate or Union forces, and Huston works hard to develop a strong sense of empathy for the Youth's impulsive behavior and subsequent guilt. The impact is undercut, however, by Murphy's weakness as an expressive performer. He displays primarily three expressions: fear, concern, and determination. Any gradations of these seem beyond his capabilities, and he frequently fails to capture the complex emotions that Crane and Huston wrote for him, much less his

Figure 8.1. A terrified Fleming runs headlong in panic to escape the battle.

transformation from fear to daring. In addition, by casting inexperienced or nonactors such as Mauldin, Huston lost an opportunity to have his supporting cast lift some of the burden off Murphy's performance, with the exception of Andy Devine as the Cheery Soldier. The death of the Tall Soldier, for instance, is not nearly as dramatic on film as it was in Crane's description. Dierkes certainly looks the part, but he falters in the believability of his admittedly strange death scene. The film further sentimentalizes the moment by playing "Taps" softly in the background, a rare concession to overt emotional manipulation by Huston.

Crane repeatedly used sound imagery in *The Red Badge of Courage*, which has been described as a very noisy book (Holton 89). This created a great temptation for composer Bronislau Kaper, who needed little encouragement to overscore. There are, however, scenes that Kaper scores evocatively, such as the cue that begins with a crane shot of the Union troops asleep in camp. The camera tracks through the camp, beginning on a fire, panning from one soldier to another, and ending on a wide-eyed Audie Murphy. He looks as if a fire is still burning in his panicked brain, despite his bizarre journey back to his comrades. It seems as if years have gone by, but the action has been confined to two days. Too often in the film Kaper's score is bombastic and overly reinforces the emotional state Huston is trying to establish for the Youth. But in the sequence cited above, the cue starts out as slow and solemn, and then a jarring outburst of brass communicates the nightmare one commanding officer has in his sleep. For once, we learn about the uneasiness of an officer, and not just the Youth and his fellow infantrymen.

Despite the pressure from MGM, Huston kept the actual war-making to a minimum. He stages *Red Badge's* only major battle for the finale, and this is probably Murphy's finest moment in the film, not surprising given its similarity to his actual wartime experiences. He charges ahead without any order to do so, possessed by the first great passion of his life. Huston's experience with filming *San Pietro* is vividly utilized here in the bloody charge sequence, as soldiers abruptly drop to the ground, killed or wounded by the bullets whizzing through the befogging smoke of battle. *San Pietro* is also obliquely referred to at the end of *Red Badge*, as the camera sits and watches the troops march away, growing smaller and smaller until they disappear from the camera's eye. As in the final shots in *San Pietro*, when Huston the narrator remarks upon the now-legendary status of the warriors who restored the town to its people "and then moved on with the passing battle," Henry Fleming watches his comrades march off to the next battle and its inherent futility.

Although the mixture of score and sound plays an important role in *Red Badge*, it nevertheless remains one of the quietest war films ever made: battles are few, and the emphasis is always on the soldiers and their interactions. An exception is Huston's use of the drum beating throughout the ending of the film, an approximation of what Crane wrote: "Their thunder swelled loud and valiant" (388). This makes Huston's (or Schary's) choice to play "The Battle Hymn of the Republic" over the final charge seem contradictory to the drumbeat; one is ominous, and the other is clichéd and melodramatic.

Henry is not the same at the end of the film, nor is he at Crane's finale, which is famously cryptic. The transition to manhood is acknowledged by the final line of one chapter: "And they were men" (391). But it is not the real focus of either Crane or Huston. Crane writes, "He has been to touch the great death, and found that, after all, it was but the great death" (455). Huston's conclusion feels more ambiguous. Have we seen the Youth's soul change? Have we grown significantly from participating in his personal experience? The emphasis Huston places on the irrelevancy of the stone wall captured at tremendous loss of limb and life undercuts the Youth's arrival at a naturalistic pantheon where death is equally important as life: "We begin with a big thing and end with a little thing" (Ross 109).

In this sense, Huston's adaptation of Crane's novel captures its vital essence, the idea that sometimes we die, and sometimes we survive and even triumph, and one or the other of these outcomes has precious little to do with what we think or fear or worry about. There is an ironic tension between what a character learns and what he thinks he has learned, so both Huston and Crane give us an experiential war encounter, not concerned with battlefield strategy or logistics, but focused intently and intensely on the mind of one young, confused, and intimidated man. From this example, both artists extrapolate to identify aspects of all men under the stress of not only battle, but also life itself.

Crane and Huston serve as anonymous narrators, one with his breathless prose, and the other with his roaming, subjective camera. They present experience directly to the reader and the viewer, while dramatizing the Youth's subjective reaction to it. But this changes at the end, when both filmmaker and author seem to make value judgments they have previously withheld. The process of gaining his manhood, his courage, and, for the first time, his self-respect requires Henry to strip away certain delusions about his own importance as an individual and as part of the regiment he ends up inspiring.

The final judgment on the adaptability of Red Badge may have come from New York-based MGM executive Si Seadler, who summed up the situation for Ross after the film was just a red-lined loss for the studio: "It doesn't pay to be so faithful to a book, the way John Huston did," Seadler patiently explained. He continued, "*The Red Badge of Courage* is a great novel. As a movie, it's too fragmentary. There's no story . . . The picture was beautiful, but it's just a vignette. As soon as Mr. Schenk saw the picture, we knew it was a flop" (Ross 262). *The Red Badge of Courage* remains a qualified failure. Huston bears partial responsibility for that failure, especially given his upbringing in the Hollywood studio system, first with his father, actor Walter Huston, and then his own career as a writer and director, during which he became thoroughly familiar with major movie studio practices. MGM played the principal role in gutting Huston's version of *Red Badge* and thus deprived anyone outside of the studio from seeing the director's complete vision realized, as his original cut no longer existed.

The implacable foe Huston faced throughout the writing and making of *The Red Badge of Courage* was Crane himself and his experimental exploration of the human psyche under the stress of battle. Some works of literature, particularly those focused on mental and emotional wrestling with the fear of imminent death, stubbornly resist cinematic adaptation. Whether through naiveté (unlikely) or hubris (in character), Huston thought he could lick the problems inherent in turning *Red Badge* into a movie; instead, they licked him. The interaction of arrogance, capitalism, and high culture proved disastrous for Huston, MGM, and the future of Crane's work as source material for films.

Works Cited

Agee, James. "Undirectable Director." *Agee on Film*, vol. 1. New York: Grosset and Dunlap (1958).

Anonymous. "An Encounter with John Huston (Excerpts from a Conversation)." *Film Culture* 2.8 (1956).

Bachmann, Gideon. "How I Make Films: An Interview with John Huston." *Film Quarterly* 19.1 (Fall 1965).

Bassan, Maurice, ed. *Stephen Crane: A Collection of Critical Essays*. Englewood Cliffs, NJ: Prentice Hall, 1967.

Bergon, Frank. *Stephen Crane's Artistry*. New York: Columbia UP, 1975.

Brill, Lesley. *John Huston's Filmmaking*. Cambridge: Cambridge UP, 1997.

Combs, Richard. "The Man Who Would Be Ahab: The Myths and Masks of John Huston." *Monthly Film Bulletin* 52 (December 1985).

Cooper, Stephen, ed. *Perspectives on John Huston*. New York: G. K. Hall, 1994.

———. Introduction. "The Critical Coming of Age of John Huston," *Perspectives on John Huston*, New York: G. K. Hall, 1994.

Crane, Stephen. *The Red Badge of Courage* (1895). iTunes. E-Book.

Crowther, Bosley. "The Screen in Review: The Red Badge of Courage." *New York Times* 19 Oct. 1951.

DeBona, Guerric. "Masculinity on the Front: John Huston's *The Red Badge of Courage* (1951) Revisited." *Cinema Journal* 42.4 (Winter 2003). Austin: U of Texas P.

Eberwein, Robert, ed. *The War Film*. New Brunswick: Rutgers UP, 2005.

Eyman, Scott. *The Lion of Hollywood: The Life and Legend of Louis B. Mayer*. New York: Simon and Schuster, 2005.

Georgakas, Dan. "From the Archives: The Red Badge of Courage." *Cineaste* 34.1 (2013).

Gossett, Sue. *The Films and Career of Audie Murphy: America's Real Hero*. Madison, NC: Empire, 1996.

Hammen, Scott. *John Huston*. Boston: Twayne, 1985.

Higham, Charles. *Merchant of Dreams: Louis B. Mayer, MGM and the Secret Hollywood*. New York: Donald I. Fine, 1993.

Holton, Milne. *Cylinder of Vision: The Fiction and Journalistic Writing of Stephen Crane*. Baton Rouge: Louisiana State UP, 1972.

Huston, John. *An Open Book*. New York: Knopf, 1980.

Jameson, Richard T. "John Huston." *Film Comment* (May 1980).

Kaminsky, Stuart. *John Huston: Maker of Magic*. Boston: Houghton Mifflin, 1978.

Let There Be Light. Dir. John Huston. 1946. Amazon Instant Video.

Long, Robert Emmett, ed. *John Huston: Interviews*. Jackson: UP of Mississippi, 2001.

McCarty, John. *The Films of John Huston*. Secaucus, NJ: Citadel, 1987.

Nolan, William F. *John Huston: King Rebel*. Los Angeles: Sherbourne P, 1965.

The Red Badge of Courage (1951). Dir. John Huston. 1951. MGM. DVD.

Reisz, Karl. "Interview with Huston." *Sight and Sound* (Jan.–March 1952).

Report from the Aleutians. Dir. John Huston. 1943. Amazon Instant Video.

Robinson, David. "The Innocent Bystander." *Sight and Sound* (Winter 1972–73).

Ross, Lillian. *Picture*. New York: Da Capo, 1952.

San Pietro. Dir. John Huston. 1945. Amazon Instant Video.

Schary, Dore. *Heyday: An Autobiography*. Boston: Little Brown, 1979.

Stallman, R.W. "Notes toward an Analysis of *The Red Badge of Courage*." *Stephen Crane: A Collection of Critical Essays*. Ed. Maurice Bassan. Englewood Cliffs: Prentice-Hall 1967.

9

Tom Dorey

Shadowboxing in the Sun

Fighters, Their Bodies, and Their Spaces in *Fat City*

"For some reason people don't want fighters just to be fighters," Gary Willis declared in his 1975 profile of Muhammad Ali (66). If John Huston, self-described as a "'philosophical atheist' with existential ideas" (Kaminsky 168), wants boxers to be anything, it is not paragons of near-superhuman strength, success, and celebrity such as Ali at the height of his fame, but rather to embody Joyce Carol Oates's assertion about the true nature of being a boxer, that it is, contrary to popular stereotypes, "primarily about being, and not giving, hurt" (60). Oates's point is that boxing externalizes psychic pain: boxers bear the masses of scar tissue that we all carry on the inside outwardly, on their brows and the bridges of noses for all to see. *Fat City* (1972) finds Huston exploring the lives of amateur boxers in much the same way as he returns to a distinctly American milieu in his first film produced in the United States since 1960. Adapted by Leonard Gardner from his 1969 novel of the same name, Huston's film depicts a world far removed from the glitz and glamour of the high-profile title fight. As with *The Asphalt Jungle* (1950) and *The Misfits* (1960), Huston's focus is on those left out of the American Dream: the downtrodden who populate the postindustrial wasteland's neon-lit dive bars and squalid hotels and the depressed, disenfranchised men whose hunched shoulders and stooped postures embody their failures.

Shot on location in Stockton, California, *Fat City* met favorable critical reviews and was hailed as a return to form for Huston after a string of disappointments. The film, however, failed at the box office despite stunning realist cinematography by Conrad L. Hall and compelling acting by Stacy Keach, Jeff Bridges, and Susan Tyrrell, who was nominated for an Academy Award for her work in the role of Oma. *Fat City* would present a picture of boxing in America that ran counter to Depression-era boxing narratives and their successors, films that upheld the notion that success in the boxing ring, enabled by the support and belief of family and friends, could triumph over barriers to achieve masculine self-determination. Instead, it was one of the first films to directly acknowledge what other, more pessimistic fight films had only been hinting at since the 1930s, that larger circumstances could and would present insurmountable obstacles.[1] *Fat City* is very much about a transitory time in the life of the white working-class American male left out of the postwar prosperity, attempting to redefine himself against the offscreen horrors of Vietnam. Huston approached his subject matter from a social realist perspective, refusing to offer any grand narrative of redemption of the lower-class white male body as would be seen only four years later in Sylvester Stallone and John G. Avildsen's *Rocky* (1976). Betraying a sociological fascination with the novel's lower-class setting of Stockton, California, Huston approaches this story with an existential humanistic lens. Boxing becomes, in his adaptation, a window into masculinity in American society—in particular, blue-collar, white masculinity—and the damage done to it by contemporary social and economic systems.

Gardner's *Fat City*

Joyce Carol Oates describes Gardner as having "a remarkable gift for realizing, as if from the inside, the psychology of the man born to fight, the man who knows nothing *but* fighting, no matter the suicidal nature of his calling," while calling *Fat City* "everyone's favorite boxing novel" (55–56). A Stockton native, Gardner threw himself into boxing in his youth, fighting seven matches as a welterweight. Boxing in the area provided Gardner an intimate knowledge of the milieu he would depict in this work. Set during an unnamed year in the latter 1950s, the novel is a lean 183 pages, with muscular, sinewy prose carefully and thoughtfully shaped. Gardner follows the parallel lives of two central characters: Billy Tully, a worn-out twenty-nine-year-old third-string veteran prizefighter gone to seed over the last two years, and the eighteen-year-old Ernie Munger, whom Tully catalyzes into the boxing world after a chance encounter at the local YMCA. Gardner penetrates their thoughts and feelings with an impressionistic intimacy. At the periphery of the two main characters are Ernie's Lido Gym teammate Wes Haynes; the ailing, workmanlike Mexican fighter Arcadio Lucero; and Mexican American manager and gym-owner Ruben Luna. Oates describes the novel as "less about boxing than the strategies of self-deception; a handbook of sorts in failure, in which boxing functions as the natural activity of men totally unequipped to comprehend life" (55). Leo Litwak's 1969 review of the novel similarly foregrounded the "dream of self-transcendence" shared by the fighters and their managers as they exaggerated victories and made excuses for defeats, unable to fully understand why they occupied the positions they did. The bulk of the novel remains outside of the ring as Gardner sketches his characters' internal lives, exploring the forces that motivate them rather than describing the mechanics of throwing punches and absorbing blows.

Huston Arrives in *Fat City*

Huston had himself boxed in and around Stockton during his youth, earning a record of twenty-three wins in twenty-five fights and winning the Amateur Lightweight Boxing Championship of California title in 1924. As he became a writer, he would use what he knew of boxing in his short stories. In "Fool" (1929) and "Figures of Fighting Men" (1931), Huston depicts the world of boxing as one of "lower-class camaraderie" where ethnic divisions fall away and where young fighters remain unaware of the costs of a sport in which men must beat each other into submission.[2] The stories reflect Hemingway's spare style of writing, his stoicism, and his thematic concern with finding victory even in defeat (Meyers 7).

More than two decades later, impressed by Gardner's novel, Huston hired the author to adapt *Fat City* for the screen. Huston's background in boxing had persuaded Gardner, who was troubled by Hollywood's tendency to "turn to the same schlock clichés" whenever it entered the ring (Kimball). Huston and Gardner narrowed the focus of the novel, omitting Ernie's (Jeff Bridges) nonrelationship with his parents and bouts of jealousy over Faye's (Candy Clarke) previous relationships. While retaining much of the novel's parallel structure, greater emphasis is placed on the long-suffering Tully (Stacy Keach). Ernie maintains his role as an initiate into the punishing world of amateur boxing.

Boxing and the White Male Body

The body of the actor is central to Huston's exploration of the labor of boxing, particularly in its two male leads. One of Huston's cardinal principles as a filmmaker was the casting of actors himself, believing firmly that convincing performances came not so much because of his direction but because an actor embodied the character himself (Studlar 80). For a character such as Tully, living with a handful of shabby possessions in decrepit hotel rooms, his body is his primary possession and his primary means of exercising agency. Huston first offered the role of Tully to Marlon Brando, whose noncommittal response led Huston to believe that the actor was uninterested. Huston was impressed after seeing Keach in *The Traveling Executioner* (Jack Smight, 1970; Kaminsky 188). The softness of Keach's voice suggested to Huston a tenderness and sensitivity beneath Tully's scarred and broken exterior. Moreover, the scar on Keach's upper lip, his thinning hair, and his rugged handsomeness gave his character the appearance of someone who has lived hard.

Figure 9.1. Tully has a muscular physique that carries the marks of a career in the ring.

Six months prior to shooting, Keach moved to New York to train with Puerto Rican light-heavyweight José Torres (Meyers 334). Keach toned his body into that of a boxer yet left it pliable enough to communicate muscular power reduced by the weight of the blows he absorbed over the course of his career.

The film begins with a montage of Stockton's Skid Row. The bright sunshine of the exterior world then dissolves into Tully's darkened room. A model of wasted masculinity, the unemployed Tully lies propped up on a messy bed, the frame of the bed suggesting the self-enclosed space of the boxing ring. He is clothed in a soiled shirt and stained briefs. In a long take, we see Tully rouse himself to search his room for a match with which to light his cigarette. The camera tilts up and down his body from a low angle in the dim room, emphasizing his slumped shoulders. Pulling on wrinkled pants, he leaves through the halls and stairwells of the hotel. Once outside, he begins to shadowbox in the bright sunlight, rehearsing footwork patterns and broadcasting through muscle memory how deeply he identifies himself as a boxer.

Fired from his job as a short-order cook and unable to keep pace with African American and Latino farm laborers, Tully gravitates to two familiar locales: the gym and Stockton's dive bars. Without a body that would provide longevity in the ring, Tully's only success in the film comes against the secretly ailing Lucero (Sixto Rodriguez) in a local fight venue. Although looking lean and clad in blue trunks with gold trim rather than his usual stained and torn clothing, Tully's thin hair is disheveled, and his body seems tired. In the third round of the fight when Tully is declared winner, he seems dazed, and his right brow is smeared with blood. He asks Babe (Art Aragon), "Did I get knocked out?" and Babe replies that he has won. He retains the dazed, far-away look after he has changed into street clothes, robbed of any real self-acknowledgment of his victory.

In contrast to Keach, twenty-two-year-old Jeff Bridges has an almost preternaturally smooth face full of unbroken, flat planes and a smooth, hairless body. In their first scene together, Tully recognizes the potential in Ernie's youthful athleticism. Bridges brings a detached, relaxed quality to Ernie, his vocal inflections tinged by his coastal upbringing. Although his long, lithe limbs give him a greater reach, he remains clumsier and less fluid than either Tully or the boxers with whom he spars in the Lido Gym.

When Tully and Ernie themselves begin to spar, both clad in dingy whites as though stripped to their underwear, the camera holds them in a tight close-up. As they begin throwing punches, a medium shot shows their bodies at work before a long shot frames their bodies against the expanse of the empty gym; Tully stands more firmly, reacts more patiently, and allows the eager, younger fighter to lean in toward him and close the distance. The mouthpiece Tully wears gives his lips a peculiar smile, suggesting emotion that he has earlier failed to express. The camera moves closer, careful to leave space between itself and the men's bodies, holding the fighters in a medium close-up when Tully throws up his hands to stop the fight because of a pulled muscle.

This scene marks the only time in the film that either character boxes with a white opponent in the ring. Richard Dyer, in discussing how the white male has been the center of attention in Western culture, identifies three main cycles of films prominently displaying the seminaked white male body: the Tarzan films, mid-twentieth-century Italian films featuring characters of classical antiquity played by bodybuilders, and the muscle star vehicles featuring actors such as Arnold Schwarzenegger, Sylvester Stallone, and Jean-Claude Van Damme. These "champion/built" (146) white bodies are frequently pitted against the less-impressive bodies of nonwhite characters in order to visually reinforce white superiority. However, as Dyer points out, the racial superiority of the ideal white body punishes the nonideal white males as well:

> The possibility of white bodily inferiority falls heavily on the shoulders of those white men who are not at the top of the spirit pile, those for whom their body is their only capital. In the context particularly of white working-class or "underachieving" masculinity, an assertion of the value and even superiority of the white male body has especial resonance. (147)

While Huston's focus on two white boxers is perhaps suggestive of the long-standing racial bias that Dyer identifies, the bodies of Ernie and Tully are antithetical to "champion/built" bodies. Huston is more interested in the frailties, the awkwardness, and the vulnerability of the "white working class," and, in a reversal of film tradition, juxtaposes these bodies to stronger and more experienced bodies of nonwhites.

On his first visit to the Lido Gym, Ernie spars with Wes, an African American fighter played by local amateur boxer Billy Walker. Wes moves from the waist with much more fluidity than Ernie, bobbing and weaving with ease against his stiffer opponent. Although Ernie's prowess does grow throughout the film, he never looks entirely coordinated inside nor outside the ring. His inferiority when matched with an African American fighter mirrors Tully's difficulty matching the efforts of the African American and Latino day laborers depicted earlier in the film.

Moreover, although Ernie, in an effort to reinforce his male prowess, manages to take his girlfriend's virginity the night before his first bout, he soon discovers that his car is mired in the mud on the rural lovers' lane. When Ernie tries to push the vehicle free, he slips in the mud, falls on his face, and coats himself in filth. His girlfriend laughs at his plight. The miasma into which Ernie has fallen and its association with female sexuality foreshadows the difficulty that Tully will later experience in his attempt at domesticity with the drunk and belligerent Oma. Male-female relationships are "muddier" than the clean, white, masculine space of Ruben's (Nicholas Colasanto) gym. The threat of the female is expressed more explicitly when Ernie loses this first fight, apparently because he has broken the boxers' superstition about remaining celibate before a bout. This misogynistic belief positions the female body as a threat to masculine power and virility while further emphasizing the conflicting emphases on virile heterosexual masculinity and masculine agency over one's own body.

But Ernie's initiation into the exclusive male domain of boxing is violent and disabling. The bridge of Ernie's broken nose is a bloody mess. In his next and final bout of the film, Ernie lasts mere seconds before he is knocked out. Ultimately, both Ernie and Tully look more awkward than their competitors. The audience recognizes that they are doomed to repeat this awkwardness within and beyond the male confines of the ring.

The Nonwhite Body in *Fat City*

Huston's belief in the importance of actors embodying their characters influenced the casting of not only Tully and Ernie, but also the nonwhite characters such as Earl (Curtis Cokes). In a 1972 interview for *Sight and Sound*, Huston described how, after auditioning many black professional actors for the part of Earl, he attended a bout of the welterweight champion Cokes. The boxer's natural melancholic quality and worldliness inspired Huston to ask him if he would consider acting in his film (Robinson 21). Huston no doubt enjoyed the irony of having a champion boxer playing a character who states that he has never boxed himself, but to his credit, Cokes gives a captivating performance. Like many other of the boxer-actors in the film, he bears the physical scars of a lifetime of fighting, including a broken nose and scar tissue above his brows; he concurrently communicates an underlying strength in his musculature and physicality. Moreover, Earl is patient and impassive under Oma's harassment when they first meet Tully at the bar. He calmly ignores the insults Oma shouts from offscreen at both men as Tully collects his things after his victory over Lucero. Earl expresses assurance and a quiet confidence as he talks with the man who had so recently taken his place.

At the suggestion of Gardner, Huston hired then-retired former California light-heavyweight champion Sixto Rodriguez to play Lucero (Kimball), who gives a haunting performance as the stoic and disfigured fighter. His nose, like that of Cokes, has seen its bridge obliterated over the course of his boxing career, sitting flat against his face, permanently skewed to the side. While he speaks only a few lines in the film, his damaged posture and face are visual manifestations of internal wounds that he hides in order to continue in the only line of work he knows. Ruben's second is also played by an ex-boxer, Art Aragon, who is also a first-time actor. He also sports the hallmark smashed-in nose, a testament to his professional career as a lightweight in New Mexico. His hoarse voice is the result of too many unprotected punches to the neck and matches Colasanto's own raspy vocalizations.

Local amateur boxers were cast as well. For instance, Stockton's Wayne Mahan plays Buford, the cocky teenager who encourages Ernie with a Muhammad Ali-like speech full of braggadocio. Dispelling the superstition that a boxer should not have sex prior to a fight, Buford tells Ernie that winning is all in the mind. So true was his performance that, when Huston held a private screening of the film for Ali, the boxer stood up, shouting, "Stop the picture! That's me up there! Listen to that . . . that's me! You hear me?" (Huston 338). His bravado proves impotent as both he and Ernie lose their fights.

All boxers, white or otherwise, are here configured as negative ids, driven to fight not necessarily because they are good at it, but because they can find nothing else to do. The expression of the naturalness or rawness of that drive, enhanced here by the nonactor supporting cast, also positions them as needing the shaping guidance of older men. Ruben embodies paternalism as he assesses the prospects of Ernie's career as a heavyweight boxer: "Maybe he can if he'd just listen to me and let me put everything I know in 'im." Elsewhere, after Ernie first spars with Wes, Ruben instructs the novice on how to move and build combinations of punches, after tenderly wiping away the blood from Ernie's cut brow, the camera crossing over the ropes to present the tender moment in close-up. There is a decidedly racial element to Ruben's paternalism alongside his misogynistic suspicion of women. As he speaks to his sleeping wife in the following scene, Ruben points directly to the fact that Ernie is "a nice *white* kid," acknowledging that boxing audiences actively seek white fighters to watch and that they are more of a rarity—indeed, all of the fighters that Ernie and Tully face or train with at the gym are either black or Latino. Ruben's warmth extends to them as well, though, as he attempts to cheer his group of losing fighters under the warm chiaroscuro light of a Monterey bar's overhead lamp, a father presiding over his sons at a dinner table. While characters of other ethnicities are featured, and Huston approaches them with the same stoic dignity he celebrates in Ernie and Tully, the film, like the novel, remains centrally concerned with the white, male characters.

Stockton's Own Bruised Body

Stockton is nearly as important to Huston's film as the actors. The city provides a space in which extreme dispossession and hopelessness are shared by a cross-section of ethnicities. Christopher Lehmann-Haupt calls it "Steinbeck country in the nineteen-fifties," populated by "the mid-California of fruit-pickers and farm pieceworkers, of wetbacks and drifters, of onion-toppers, tomato thinners, and fourth-rate prizefighters" (27), all stripped of social power. The city and its location operate as a metaphor for stalled American progress, the westward expansion of Manifest Destiny reaching its limit at the Pacific and curling back in upon itself, festering and cracking under the harsh sun without anywhere else to go. Action moves between the grimy hotels Tully occupies—Gardner's novel begins with Tully in his room in the tellingly named Hotel Coma, where "smudges from oily heads darkened the wallpaper between the metal rods of his bed" (3)—to the dive bars that Tully frequents; to Ruben's car as the hopeful boxers and their handlers drive to Monterey and return again, dozing and dejected; and the fields where Tully and then Ernie work as day laborers, picking vegetables in the scorching hot sun, outpaced by the Latino, Chinese, and African American laborers. There are also the boxing venues: the dingy and dangerous stairwell of the YMCA and its basement's cracked concrete floors; Ruben's modest Lido Gym, also located in a basement and suffering from a clogged shower room drain; and the arenas where the men fight.

Huston's film begins with an aerial shot of a neighborhood full of flat buildings, followed by a sun-filled, impressionistic montage of the grimmer side of the city. Camera shots fade in and out of each other, capturing dilapidated storefronts and bars lit with neon signs, chipped and peeling paint beside plywood covering doors and windows, the site of a building demolition indistinguishable from the smoldering remains of a fire, a shabby mission with a "For Sale" sign hanging on its side, as well as gnarled, tired old men—white, Latino, African American—gathered together, leaning against walls and sitting on crates, passing a bottle of liquor between themselves, shoulders stooped and shaped by years of hard physical labor capped with nights hunched over the counters of all-night restaurants. Hall's documentary-style cinematography captures the rough beauty of the straight streets and squat, utilitarian buildings as

Kris Kristofferson's melancholic "Help Me Make It through the Night" plays on the soundtrack. Hall describes how, for this sequence, Huston sent him to Stockton's Skid Row in order to find examples of "life running down the drain." Hall recalls, "I got a camper and covered the rear and side windows with black curtains . . . I had quick-set mounts on tripods in each window and just moved my Arriflex from window to window depending on what I saw. . . . When John, the crew and the actors sat down to look at the footage I'd compiled, you could have heard a pin drop. Some of it was devastating. It really gave you the sense of the harshness of these lives that we were recording, and it provided an all-too-real reference point for the actors" (Pizzello 40–41). This is the sociocultural milieu of Stockton that will provide the landscape in which the characters will act out their lives.

Huston utilizes the powerful Central California sun to provide bright, washed-out visuals that the studio complained were overexposed portions of the film. The film's lighting is a study in contrasts—brilliant, almost blinding natural light outside, and dimly lit spaces within. The exterior light renders the audience's eyes disoriented and punch-drunk like the characters in the film who, as Vernon Young points out, can do little more than "squint" (172). In Tully and Oma's second bar scene, Huston eschews artificial light for the dim lights of the bar itself, rendering characters barely distinguishable from the shadows of the scene's opening. Huston likened the effect to stumbling into a "dark theater" (Kaminsky 189) with only silhouettes at first visible.

The disorienting light-dark dynamic is employed again by Huston and Hall as they explore Stockton's migrant work economy. Barrel fires and street lamps barely light the crowd of day laborers trying to be picked for jobs in the fields before the scene abruptly cuts to their arrival in the sun-drenched fields themselves. The filmmakers saturate the image with blown-out light, causing the viewer to squint along with the overwhelmed and unconditioned Tully, who staggers, swaying from side to side and raising his arm in a weak defense against the sun's rays. Close-ups in the bright white-yellow sunlight show sweat rolling down the side of Tully's reddened face; he stands up straight in the middle of a row, rubbing his back, and takes a furtive swig from a small bottle as the workers move ever onward past him. The scene presages how he will look in the final round of his fight against Lucero.

The places in which light and dark find their most comfortable balance remain the places where Tully and Ernie are continually drawn, hoping to regain what Oates calls the lost "religion of masculinity" (72). From the YMCA gym canvas where the two meet to the raised arena ring in which Tully fights Lucero, these rings represent sane, tidy places removed from the filth and chaos surrounding them and exhibit a balance between the dizzyingly bright sunlight and the dim interiors. The YMCA gym is lit by high windows like those of a church, with softened natural white light streaming in through them, in stark contrast to the dank basement gym of the novel. A large white diamond of canvas lies in the center of the gym floor as Ernie moves from the heavy bag to the speed bag. In the distance behind him Tully enters, grabs a skipping rope, and begins hopping, the ring a gentle white shape between them before they come together in a form of communion. The busy, homosocial Lido Gym is a boxer's monastery. As Ernie enters this male-dominated space, the camera follows him into a room with windows lining the eggshell walls and soft midafternoon, refracted light permeating the space. There is a neatness to the room, giving it a sense of organization and order, befitting of Ruben as the most organized and responsible of the film's characters. We watch Ernie take in the low ceilings and the clean, bright white walls.

Finally, a high-angle shot reveals the large volume of space above the white, pulpit-like ring in the center of the arena where Tully and Lucero will fight, offering up blood in a ritual sacrifice. A four-sided scoreboard and light rig hang above this ring, bathing it in a soft, uniform yellow-white light. It seems small by virtue of the size of the space, but the off-white of the canvas draws the viewer's eyes to its relative brightness against the shadowed spectator areas surrounding it. As the fight begins, Huston's camera remains almost exclusively outside the ropes. The ring becomes a rarified space, informed by a secular sacredness and set apart from the audiences within and outside the film. When Huston does penetrate the ring before the final round, it is for a long close-up of Tully's impenetrable, vacant stare, reinforcing our physical and psychological distance from the boxers as they work.

"Maybe we're all happy"

Reviewing Gardner's book in *the New York Times*, Christopher Lehmann-Haupt wondered why he repeatedly felt the urge to put down Gardner's book, hypothesizing that it was Gardner's clear intention to bring his characters "nowhere but down" (27). Huston's adaptation departs from the novel's dark ending, providing the faintest glimmer of hope. Huston brings back together the beaten white bodies in the context of other nonwhite bodies to emphasize their shared human condition. At the film's conclusion, Tully is again on the street, dazed and futilely panhandling for another match, recalling his unsuccessful search for one at the film's opening. When he spots Ernie walking to his car, Tully is pulled from his stupor. Ernie tells Tully that he's just won a bout in Reno, but when asked by Tully to join him for a drink, he reminds him that he doesn't drink. Ernie does finally agree to have coffee with Tully, and they enter an all-night diner, the whitish-blue light from its overhead fluorescents recalling those above the arena's boxing ring. A horizontal metal bar mimicking a boxing ring's ropes separates Ernie and Tully from groups of African American patrons who sit scattered amongst the tables in the seating area. Across the counter, Tully stares at an ancient Chinese man working the kitchen. Each of the two boxers looks worse than when we had met them earlier in the film. The bridge of Ernie's nose now has a crooked lump and back bruises lie under his eyes. Tully seems filthier and more slack-jawed than he was in his hotel room following the opening's montage of Skid Row. Referring to the Chinese cook, Tully asks Ernie, "How'd you like to wake up in the morning and be him?" He responds: "Maybe he's happy." Tully thinks for a moment and says, "Maybe we're all happy," before asking Ernie if he thinks the cook was ever young. Ernie momentarily pauses and then answers, "No." Tully, turning his back to the counter and looking across the metal bar, is suddenly in rapt attention. The soundtrack fades to silence as Tully stares at the groups of men on the other side of the bar just as he stared across the ring while in the corner during his fight. The camera then pans quickly to the left, from one group of immobile men to another, as a car's headlights streak past outside. After returning to Tully's stunned eyes, the camera moves again to the frozen men before the ambient sound floods back in and the men begin moving again. The stylized representation of this moment following Huston's employment of realist, documentary-influenced filming earlier underscores the significance it has for Tully. In this moment of pure affect, he almost—but not quite—grasps his situation, how he is and will keep being drawn to these boxing rings because that is who he is. Outside of the ropes of the squared circle, he is hemmed in by the dim, hopeless desolation of Stockton and his lack of fitness for the too-bright fields beyond. Ernie shakes Tully out of his brief epiphany reverie by telling him he is leaving, but Tully asks Ernie to stay and talk a while, and the younger man agrees, though neither says anything. Tully seems to be again accepting the Sisyphean task to return to the sacred space of the boxing ring without any expectation of reward.

Huston's camera has suggested that we can never be close enough to understand what it is like to be these boxers—their internal codes are as personal and inaccessible as the detective's morality that motivates Sam Spade (Humphrey Bogart) in the *The Maltese Falcon* (1939) or the sociopathic religious devotion of Hazel Motes (Brad Dourif) in *Wise Blood* (1979). Here the humanist Huston asks that the audience join him in accepting, without irony or mockery, that there is a shabby nobility to these men's almost existential resolve to continue their quests for fulfillment in the only spaces their bodies are fit to occupy.

Notes

1. See Baker, 69–70.
2. Both short stories were published in H. L. Mencken's literary magazine, *American Mercury* (Studlar 179).

Works Cited

Baker, Aaron. *Contesting Identities: Sports in American Film*. 2003. Urbana: U of Illinois P, 2006.
Brill, Lesley. *John Huston's Filmmaking*. Cambridge: Cambridge UP, 1997.
Ford, Dan. "A Talk with John Huston." 1972. *John Huston Interviews*. By Robert Emmet Long. Jackson: UP of Mississippi, 2001. 21–29.
Gardner, Leonard. *Fat City*. New York: Farrar, Straus and Giroux, 1969.
Grindon, Leger. *Knockout: The Boxer and Boxing in American Cinema*. Jackson: U of Mississippi P, 2011.
Heiskanen, Benita. *The Urban Geography of Boxing: Race, Class, and Gender in the Ring*. New York: Routledge, 2012.
Huston, John. *An Open Book*. New York: Knopf, 1980.
Kaminsky, Stuart. *John Huston: Maker of Magic*. Boston: Houghton Mifflin, 1978.
Kimball, George. "Fat City and Fat City: An Appreciation." *The Sweet Science*. TheSweetScience.com. 16 Sept., 2009. Web. 10 Jan. 2014.
Lehmann-Haupt, Christopher. "Rats in a Maze." *The New York Times* 29 Aug., 1969: 27. Proquest. Web. 29 June 2013.
Litwak, Leo. "There was always a fighter to fill out the card: *Fat City*." *The New York Times* 31 Aug. 1969: BR18. Proquest. Web. 20 Aug. 2013.
Mewshaw, Michael. "Vidal and Mailer." *South Central Review* 19.1 (Spring 2002): 4–14. *JSTOR*. Web. 6 July 2013.
Meyers, Jeffrey. *John Huston: Courage and Art*. New York: Crown Archetype, 2011.
Murray, Donald. "Write before Writing." *College Composition and Communication* 29.4 (Dec. 1978): 375–81. *JSTOR*. Web. 10 Aug. 2013.
Oates, Joyce C. *On Boxing*. 1987. New York: HarperCollins, 2006.
Pizzello, Stephen. "Artistry and the 'Happy Accident': Conrad L. Hall." *American Cinematographer* 84.5 (May 2003): 34–38, 40–43. *International Index to the Performing Arts*. Web. 20 Aug. 2013.
Robinson, David. "The Innocent Bystander." *Sight and Sound* 42.1 (Winter 1972/3): 20–21. *International Index to the Performing Arts*. Web. 20 Aug. 2013.

Sammons, Jeffrey T. *Beyond the Ring*. Chicago: U of Illinois P, 1988.
Studlar, Gaylyn. "*Fat City* and the Malaise of Masculinity." *Reflections in a Male Eye: John Huston and the American Experience*. Ed. David Desser and Gaylyn Studlar. Washington: Smithsonian Institution P, 1993. 177–98.
Thomson, David. "Wild Animal." *New Republic. The New Republic Mag.*, 21 June 2012. Web. 10 Jan. 2014.
Willis, Gary. "Muhammad Ali." 1975. *I'm a Little Special: A Muhammad Ali Reader*. Ed. Gerald Early. London: Random House, 1999. 66.
Young, Vernon. "Fat Shakespeare, Fat City, Lean Wilderness." *The Hudson Review* 26.1 (Spring 1973): 170–76. *JSTOR*. Web. 29 June 2013.

10

Betty Kaklamanidou

Prizzi's Honor

Greed and Gender in the Beginning of the Neoliberal Era

The majority of gangster/crime films, including a number of film noirs, equate, in one way or another, the illegal transactions of crime syndicates to a legitimate business and include subtexts that relate their plots to the sociopolitical circumstances of their time; *Little Caesar* (1931), *The Public Enemy* (1931), and *Scarface: The Shame of the Nation* (1932) were produced not only because of the advent of sound and the invention of the necessary technology, but because the sociopolitical environment—the Great Depression, the existence and operation of crime syndicates, and the inability on the part of the authorities to control the situation—was part of America's everyday life.[1] In the case of film noir and within a larger critique of American society, gender roles came under particular scrutiny.

In 1985, John Huston directed his penultimate film, the noir crime-comedy *Prizzi's Honor*, based on the novel by Richard Condon, who co-wrote the screenplay along with Janet Roach. Set in contemporary times, both novel and film narrate the story of Charley, an assassin working for the powerful Prizzi family, who faces the dilemma between his love for a woman and his loyalty to the Prizzis. Although the subject matter clearly belongs to the dramatic form of the crime genre and Huston is responsible for some of the genre's paradigmatic texts (*The Maltese Falcon* [1941], *Key Largo* [1948], *The Asphalt Jungle* [1950]), *Prizzi's Honor* adds a heavy dose of satire and comedy to the expected conventions of sinister characters, violence, illegal transactions, dangerous women, and treacherous relationships. Following the literary source's satirical vein, the cinematic *Prizzi's Honor* is not only a hybrid crime-comedy, but it also marks the beginning of the mafia comedy subgenre.

The film became a significant commercial and artistic success, was nominated for seven Academy Awards (Huston received his last of five Oscar nominations as a director), and won the Oscar for Best Supporting Actress (Anjelica Huston, the director's daughter, received the award for her portrayal of Maerose Prizzi). Both the film and the novel were born in the 1980s. Since the time between the publication of the book and its film adaptation is quite short and considering the screenwriters not only followed the novel's structure but managed successfully to convey the spirit of the literary source, this chapter will focus primarily on Huston's black comedy from a gender perspective, with the use of textual analysis as analytical tool. I will also examine how Huston, a director who was always interested in the negative "side of humanity" (Giannetti and Eyman 203), comments on the contemporary sociopolitical atmosphere, mainly the insistence on the neoliberal principles (individualism, accumulation of wealth, private enterprise) put forward by the Reagan administration and their impact on gender politics. Centering on the characters of Irene Walker (Kathleen Turner) and Maerose in the context of a decade which witnessed a feminist backlash, I will begin by placing both the film and the novel in their sociopolitical context and discuss how the film treats the novel's overt social commentary.

The 1980s: The Novel, Reaganism, and Gender

The 1980s was a significant decade in American history, politics, and popular culture, marked by the eight-year Reagan administration and the return to rigid conservatism both domestically and in matters of foreign policy. More importantly, however, the decade is also associated with the consolidation of neoliberalism, championed by Margaret Thatcher in the United Kingdom and Ronald Reagan in the United States. Consequently, William J. Palmer argues that *Prizzi's Honor* belongs to what he calls the "yuppie" cinematic texts of the 1980s and examines "the consequences of the obsession with money . . . in one of America's most profitable companies, organized crime" (294). At the same time, both the film and its literary source use satire and humor in order to criticize the greed—whether it is greed for money or power—that characterizes their protagonists.

Prizzi's Honor was published in 1982 and is the first novel in Condon's tetralogy of the Prizzi dynasty (the other three novels being *Prizzi's Family* [1986], *Prizzi's Glory* [1988], and *Prizzi's Money* [1994]). The film adaptation was released in 1985, and the plot revolves around Charley Partanna (Jack Nicholson), "the Prizzis' enforcer" (2), who falls in love with and marries Irene, a freelance contract killer, not knowing that she has stolen money from the family. When the truth is revealed with the help of Maerose Prizzi, a woman with whom Charley once had a romantic relationship, he has to decide between his love for Irene and his loyalty to the Prizzis.

Condon's novel is a satirical account of contemporary mores. In the tradition of the author's earlier work,[2] *Prizzi's Honor* is a morality tale disguised as an action-romance narrative infused with comic interludes, creating a cosmos where money and power are the ultimate goals for both female and male characters. Literary works are, for the most part, condensed when they are adapted for the screen, and Condon's novel is no exception. The viewer never learns all the names of the Prizzi family, minor characters vanish, and series of actions are condensed. On a macronarrative level, though, the basic functions remain intact. The film retains the comic elements as well as the financially driven desires of its protagonists and places Charley's relationship with Irene at its center.

The main difference between the two texts is the absence in the film of explicit police and government corruption, as well as the Prizzis' involvement in the heroin trade. These are secondary events in the novel, yet they accentuate the corrupted universe Condon creates and leave no doubt as to the decadent world the characters inhabit. Due to either industry conservatism or the profit motive, film adaptations tend to subdue explicit views on politics. Huston's *Prizzi's Honor* does not deviate from this pattern and only implicitly comments on the close relationship between the authorities and the mafia family; for instance, a brief close-up of three rows of police officers sitting in uniform and solemnly attending the marriage of Prizzi's granddaughter in the first scene after the film's credits only implies their potential illegal transaction with the Prizzi family. Also absent from the film are the explicit ties between "senators and congressman," the media, and the mafia that Condon describes in his novel (2).

However, as Peter Bondanella and Rebecca Bauman each have recently pointed out, both novel and film are unique in attaching significance to the woman's viewpoint in a crime narrative.[3] Although both literary and cinematic texts focus on the mafia Prizzi *famiglia*, a family of Italian descent run entirely by its male representatives, two powerful women become central to the story and are not simply relegated to the periphery as mere love objects: Irene and Maerose. Irene is of Polish descent and has a freelance relationship with the Prizzi family as a contract assassin;, Maerose, the daughter of Dominic Prizzi, is ostracized by her father and the family due to a past sexual escapade.

The power these two female characters accrue is quite significant to the evolution of both the literary and the film genre of crime stories and provides a direct commentary aimed at the sociopolitical context in which they were created. The 1980s were not kind to the feminist movement. Not only were young women largely indifferent to the cause because they believed that everything had already been achieved by the feminists of the 1970s and there was no need for additional struggle, but, more importantly, the Reagan administration cultivated a feminist backlash. Sara M. Evans explains:

> The Reagan administration was overtly antagonistic to most of the women's rights initiatives that had made some headway in the 1970s, and the political atmosphere of the 1980s authorized more open expressions of hostility toward women and minorities. Battles to eliminate language demeaning or belittling to women, for example, that seemed to have been won in the 1970s, turned out to be only partially achieved. Growing violence against abortion clinics accompanied an increase in hate crimes . . . and a greater tolerance for overt expressions of prejudice. (86)

John Huston and his screenwriters, Condon (the author of the novel) and Roach (a screenwriter, lecturer, and documentary filmmaker for CBS and PBS), do not deviate much from the original text regarding the female characters and their personal narrative agendas. Nevertheless, as I will show, some changes in what may seem minor or even trivial actions do in fact influence how female figures are characterized in the film.

Irene—The Blonde Femme Fatale

The cinematic Irene appears in twenty-three scenes, and her total screen time is 37.8 minutes; in other words, she occupies 29.3 percent, or near one-fourth of the 129-minute duration of the film. Portrayed by one of the most beautiful and talented actresses of the 1980s, Kathleen Turner, the character is very close to Condon's literary vision, described as a

Figure 10.1. A blond femme fatale catches the eye of Charley at a *famiglia* wedding ceremony.

very beautiful woman who attracted Charley's attention just sitting "as reposefully as a swan" (3). For their first flirtatious encounter, Houston uses brief alternate shots between Irene and Charley. When Charley first notices Irene during a wedding ceremony of his *famiglia*, she is seated on the second floor of the church among ten other guests that frame her in two rows. Irene is front and center and stands out; her blonde hair and lavender blouse are in stark contrast with the Italianate people who surround her, only two of whom are women (and the one seated beside her is visibly older). After the first, very brief, glimpse of Irene, Charley casts his glance at her five more times. The second time, the camera zooms in a little more, and the third time, a close-up of Irene that lasts five seconds permits Charley and the viewers to observe the pearls around her neck, her black gloves, and her smart black hat. Irene touches her pearls as she realizes Charley is watching her, and she smiles invitingly back to her admirer. At the same time, she listens attentively to the words of the priest, conveying the impression she believes in the institution of marriage. When she runs away, Charley is left wondering who she is and how he could meet her again.

The mysterious Irene falls into the tradition of the 1940s film noirs' femmes fatales; the epitome of beauty, dangerously addictive and enigmatic. Turner's beauty, classical facial features, and clothes remind the viewer of the great noir femmes fatales of the 1940s, such as Gene Tierney, Lauren Bacall, Veronica Lake, and Lizabeth Scott, and even her hairstyle echoes that of Lana Turner in *The Postman Always Rings Twice* (1946). Furthermore, the mise-en-scène, which does not appear in the book—where Irene is seated "across the aisle, two rows up" (3)—accentuates Irene's narrative importance as her position on the church's second floor obliges Charley to keep looking up at someone who is literally in a higher position and unattainable, at least momentarily. The empowering spatial positioning of Irene suggests an intertextual play/homage between *Prizzi's Honor* and the celebrated noir *Double Indemnity* (1942), where Phyliss Dietrichson (Barbara Stanwyck) appears at the top of the stairs wearing only a towel around her body in her first encounter with insurance salesman Walter Neff (Fred MacMurray).

Irene, however, differs from the 1940s noir femme fatale in that she is not aiming to seduce and/or entrap a man in order to enlist his services for a sinister plan; on the contrary, she is an active agent, a freelance, highly skilled assassin, a pragmatic and intelligent professional, who enjoys the luxurious life her job offers without ever questioning its morality. Irene, therefore, also presents affinities with the action heroine, foreshadowing such cinematic characters as Sarah Connor in *Terminator 2: Judgment Day* (1991) and Catwoman in *Batman Returns* (1992).

After Irene's first dramatic appearance, Charley begins his pursuit, which ends rather quickly as he spots her sitting at one of the tables at the reception. As Charley approaches her, a point-of-view shot steadily focuses on Irene, who fixes her own stare without hesitation or sign of shyness, only to turn her head when he is beside her. They eventually dance, and while Charley can't seem to stop talking, Irene only asks his name. Their dance is interrupted by a boy who informs Irene she has a telephone call waiting, and Charley for the second time is left alone abruptly wondering how he can see her again.

Prizzi's Honor, nevertheless, does not continue to follow the traditional dichotomy of femme fatale and male victim of film noir. Although Irene does finally call Charley, ending his frustrated search for her name and phone number, her motive, at least initially, is not to lure him into a sinister plot. Irene is among the guests of the Prizzi wedding because she has been hired by the family to murder Louis Palo, an employee in a Vegas casino, who was suspected of embezzling a large sum of Prizzi money. Charley becomes enchanted by her presence, and Irene seems to also be genuinely interested in him. In both the literary and the cinematic texts, there is no suggestion that she enters a relationship with Charley as a kind of insurance against the powerful Prizzis. Just like her film noir counterparts, Irene is in charge of her relationship with Charley. It is he who flies to her home in Los Angeles; it is he who first declares his love; it is he who confides stories from his past (although he leaves out the family business); and, finally, it is he who proposes marriage. Nevertheless, Charley's proposal is a satirical take on the era's mores. After their first date in Los Angeles, Irene and Charley finish making love in an intense thirty-second scene, rolling around, gasping, and finally falling off the bed, accompanied by Gioachino Rossini's highly energetic "Overture to Semiramide." Irene lands on top of Charley, who looks at her and asks her to marry him, now that "everything is equal." With this phrase, Charley clumsily acknowledges that men and women have equal status in contemporary society, and that the struggles of the second feminist wave were certainly not in vain. Nevertheless, the viewer can detect the semblance of wry sarcasm in his intonation that negates what their relative positions on the floor imply. On the other hand, Charley's proposal in itself signals a violation of the custom of the Italian mobster marrying Italian woman. It also confirms his love for Irene. As the conventional male protagonist of film noir, Charley is entrapped by his emotional response to femme fatale.

The next scene holds a significant surprise: Irene is revealed to be the wife of Marxie (Joseph Ruskin). Charley breaks into Marxie's house with the intention of killing him and taking the money he owes to the Prizzi family, but when Irene is caught by Charley entering the house, she is forced to reveal that Marxie had helped her become a tax accountant and that he was ready to give her a divorce so that she could marry Charley. Her fake tears and obvious insincerity regarding Maxie's dealings with the Prizzis and her efforts to concoct yet another story to conceal her part echo Mary Astor's confrontation with Humphrey Bogart in Huston's archetypical noir *The Maltese Falcon*. The scene validates Irene's femme fatale characteristics and also unites her with Huston's directorial debut in an amusing intertextual play.

Although the film certainly implies Irene's genuine love for Charley, it is also clear that she loves power and money. For instance, she drives an Excalibur, a hyperluxurious, red convertible, which, as she tells Charley, is made in Japan for the super rich Arabs. Her LA apartment seems trendy and expensively furnished, and her clothes and makeup are stylish and elegant. Charley, however, marries Irene in Mexico, away from his family and business, knowing that Irene might very well be a liar and a thief. Her treatment as other or beneath the family's standards is confirmed by Houston's mise-en-scène choices the first time Irene—the married lady—is seen in Charley's apartment preparing dinner for his father. While father and son are planning their next hit, dressed in casual, earthy tones, Irene stands, visibly separate, wearing black and white, in clear contrast to the color-palette of both the apartment and the cinematography. When she starts talking about an addition to the plan that Charley's dad applauds, she occupies the whole frame, once again expressing her position of superiority and distance from both the Prizzi family and the Partanna family.

Irene is a contract killer with no moral dilemmas regarding the nature of her job; when Charley and his dad start planning the next hit, she comes up with the idea of holding a baby to distract the body guard of the man they target. During the actual raid, she is calm, collected, and betrays no sign of doubt, remorse, or second thoughts. When their mission is accomplished, Charley and Irene, experienced and serious professionals, kiss each other, and Irene nonchalantly tells her husband, "See you at dinner," before she walks off the elevator of the building where the crimes took place. The abduction and unplanned killing of an innocent eyewitness do not trigger any moral or ethical compass in either of the characters. Irene's lack of compassion and cynical use of a baby reveal the absence of any traditional female attributes. Instead, Irene operates as a cold, detached individual, a mixture of femme fatale and ruthless male gangster.

Even when, near the climax of the film, she is hired by Maerose's father to murder Charley, she remains calm and collected, accepting the assignment without a second thought. When she realizes that despite her efforts—her meeting with the don and her confiding to Charley about the contract on his life—she will not be able to get away with keeping the money she stole from the Prizzis, she decides to go ahead with Dominic's assignment. In the film's penultimate sequence, which follows exactly the actions of the literary characters, Irene and Charley meet for the last time, each knowing they will never see each other again. Irene is wearing a virginal white satin negligee, as if she were trying to summon a more innocent version of herself while concurrently making herself ready for a night of passion. But as she prepares to kill, she does not know that Charley is preparing to kill her. Huston films their duel and Irene's ensuing death in slow motion, intensifying the action and the drama of a man and a woman who love each other but who are forced to kill each other in the name of their work ethic. The close-up of Irene's profile with the knife across her neck not only signifies Charley's and the Prizzi's victory against a free agent who dared to steal money from them, but it is also a patriarchal victory of a male-dominated business which was almost defeated by a female newcomer. Female entrepreneurship, initiative, ability, and sexuality are punished in the character of Irene, who dared antagonize such a powerful male-established and run business. *Prizzi's Honor* ends with Irene's death at the hands of the man she dominated sexually and intellectually for the greater part of the narrative. The message is clear: women of the 1980s, be careful; you can work alongside men, even have better ideas than them, but you will never actually become number one.

Maerose—Patience and Intelligence

Maerose appears in just ten scenes of *Prizzi's Honor*, with a total screen time of approximately seventeen minutes, roughly 13 percent of the total duration of the film. Despite her limited appearance, Maerose is the only character who in the end triumphs, thanks largely to a meticulously orchestrated and ingenious plan. Maerose's entrance into the film, however, does not approach the almost majestic appearance of Irene. At the opening reception, Maerose wears an extravagant black gown with intense fuchsia details, her hair held up high in an elegant chignon. Maerose's father, Dominic Prizzi (Lee Richardson), finds her attire quite risqué for the occasion and shuns his daughter once more, despite her aunt's protests. Maerose is considered the black sheep of the family because of a sexual indiscretion that occurred a few years earlier. In the context of a conservative Italian family, Maerose is required to repress any sexual desires she might have. The Prizzis conform to a strictly patriarchal code that respects and protects women, whose duties are to bear their children, clean their houses, and prepare their favorite dishes. The Prizzis, however, do attempt in their business dealings to adapt to the changes the new era has brought to the traditional gender roles. Dominic hires a woman to assassinate Charley, while Charley's father appreciates the ingenuity of Irene's abduction plan, thus acknowledging in a dark way the changing professional roles for women in the 1980s.

Maerose's and Irene's respective paths to independence and self-realization are both similar and different. Although they both lead luxurious lives, Irene has had to work harder in her ascent up the professional ladder and acquisition of the material possessions that signal the yuppie success of the 1980s. Maerose, on the other hand, comes from a privileged home and despite her isolation from the rest of the family, leads a glamorous life as a Manhattan interior decorator. Irene must penetrate the intricate levels of the Prizzi family structure to achieve her goals; Maerose also must fight through her father's resistance in order to be accepted into the family once again. But while money and financial security seem to be Irene's ultimate goal, Maerose, as the conclusion of the film shows, is more interested in empowering herself over the males who have mistreated her in one way or another.

In the novel, Maerose introduces Irene to Charley, whereas in the film the two women do not know each other. This alteration is significant because it precludes the violation of the bonds of sisterhood. As I mentioned earlier, the 1980s saw a feminist backlash, evident in a variety of films, such as *Working Girl* (1988) and *Dangerous Liaisons* (1988). Palmer points out that "sexploitation is an exercise of power, but irony accrues when one woman is exerting exploitative power over other women" and that "women should not use other women as objects in their power games" (258). Huston avoids this female opposition by making Irene simply another obstacle that Maerose has to face and not a woman she knows and decides to destroy, which could lead to a different and probably antifeminist reading.

Maerose is forced to operate then as a solitary agent, without any allies, against her father and the male relatives who cannot forgive her human instincts. As her old flame and cause of her exile, Charley tells her at the wedding reception at the beginning of the film: "You're still beautiful . . . Find someone away from the family, practice your meatballs." Maerose's expression may reveal the disgust at Charley's attitude toward the role the women of the Prizzi family are expected to have, but her actions superficially follow his advice. While Maerose encourages Charley to marry Irene, despite her being an outsider and a thief, she also secretly visits the don and receives forgiveness, playing the role of the repentant daughter. After the don's acceptance of her atonement, her father, Dominic, does not have any choice but to try to also make amends. Maerose manipulates him with ease and "expertly exploits her father's mafioso obsession with "honor" to get what she wants" (De Stefano 195). She reveals she has been sexually violated by Charley, infuriating Dominic and almost causing him to have a heart attack.

Not only does Maerose convince her father that Charley is responsible for her dishonor, but she actually triggers a series of events that lead to her final victory. Ostensibly obeying gender rules that relegate females to housework and motherhood, Maerose actually operates as a neoliberal individual subject, diplomatically facing every opponent until she gets what she wants. Maerose is welcomed back into the family, her father is murdered, and Charley is free after murdering Irene and decides to return to her arms. The last frame of the film validates her supremacy. Once Charley kills Irene, he returns to his Brooklyn apartment, takes a shower, and calls Maerose to ask her to dinner. Maerose answers the phone while sitting on her bed in her dim-lit bedroom. As she stands and walks to the window, the viewer notices her demure, yet elegant floral dress, her hair worn down in waves, accentuating her femininity. More and more light comes in from outside until the whole room and Maerose's face literally are bathed in light. Huston's heroine has overcome the final obstacle and realizes that the Prizzi power and respect, the Prizzi money, and Charley all belong to her.

Concluding Thoughts

Most scholars agree that film noir offers a grim commentary on the social instability that reigned after World War II[4] and that the image of the femme fatale is associated "with sexual and social anxieties particular to postwar America" (Harris 8). Not noir per se, but more of a hybrid which combines comedy with noir overtones in its themes and mise-en-scène decisions, *Prizzi's Honor* aims at an audience three decades later and addresses issues germane to the 1980s. While neoliberal forces such as individualism, consumerism, and private entrepreneurship began to infiltrate American society, concurrently traditional values associated with family, religion, and gender reassert themselves. In *Prizzi's Honor*, these sets of values are exemplified by the divergent paths of Irene and Maerose. Irene is an independent young woman who was obliged to become her own protector and guide from an early age. Utilizing her feminine charms and acute intelligence, Irene attained a privileged position. At the same time, Irene is the perfect neoliberal subject: an enterprising individual who methodically runs her own business, driven by the need to acquire and consume.

Maerose is also an independent working woman, but unlike Irene, she comes from a privileged background. However, Maerose has been marginalized by her family and has had to reinvent herself. Relying on her wits and knowledge of the Prizzi operations, she also transforms herself into a neoliberal individual. Both women finally avenge the male oligarchy they have had to endure. However, while Irene begins as an established contract assassin who enjoys material luxuries, she ends her journey stabbed to death by the man she had hoped would lead her to a life of security and comfort. Maerose enters the film as a disgraced and weak individual who triumphs in the end. The cinematic choices Huston and his filmmaking team made, with respect to mise-en-scène, cinematography, camera work, and subtle but important changes to the story, highlight the power of both Irene and Maerose and also comment on the role of women in contemporary society. Such a cinematic statement is surprising for a director most known for his explorations into the vicissitudes of the male psyche.

Notes

1. Today, this link between crime organizations and capitalism is made explicit. For instance, in the last scene of the 2012 critically acclaimed crime film *Killing Them Softly*, Jackie (Brad Pitt), a professional assassin who has just accomplished his mission for the mafia, demands that he be paid the prearranged amount and tells the mafia connection that gave him the assignment: "America is not a country. It's just a business. Now, fucking pay ME"; these are the last lines of the film, which is one of those rare crime films that explicitly and unabashedly links organized crime to a well-oiled corporate machine driven simply by financial greed. Many is the time during the narrative that criminal negotiations take place in seedy bars while television screens host Presidents W. Bush and Obama talking about the country's economy. *Killing Them Softly* ends with the abovementioned lines, full of cynicism and pessimism, which underline that irrespective of your career "choice," the United States is a country forged on the ideals of individuality and entrepreneurship, where class and status are measured in dollars, whether inherited or earned, and not necessarily actual merit.

2. For a discussion on Condon's main themes and accomplishment as a writer prior to *Prizzi's Honor*, see Smith 221–29.

3. Regarding *Prizzi's Honor*'s promotion of active female characters in the crime syndicate, Bondanella notes that the 1988 mafia comedy *Married to the Mob* "continues this novel interest in viewing the Italian Mafia from a woman's viewpoint. Women in the first two Coppola *Godfather* films were largely superfluous appendages to male characters that were at the core of the action. In *The Godfather Part III*, Michael's sister Connie, however, becomes one of the cleverest and most powerful of the Corleone family, eventually supplanting Michael and sponsoring the rise of Sonny Corleone's illegitimate son to head the family" (285).

4. See Vivian Sobchack's and Elisabeth Bronfen's observations on the societal commentary of film noir in the latter's article "Negotiations of Tragic Desire" (104).

Works Cited

Bauman Rebecca. "The Sexual Politics of Loyalty in John Huston's Prizzi's Honor." *Mafia Movies: A Reader*. Ed. Dana Renga. Toronto: U of Toronto P, 2011.

Bondanella Peter E. *Hollywood Italians: Dagos, Palookas, Romeos, Wise Guys, and Sopranos*. New York: Continuum, 2010.

Bronfen, Elisabeth "Femme Fatale: Negotiations of Tragic Desire." *New Literary History: Rethinking Tragedy* 35.1 (Winter, 2004): 103–116.

Condon, Richard. *Prizzi's Honor*. New York: Berkeley Books. 1983.

DeMartino, George. *Global Economy, Global Justice. Theoretical Objections and Policy Alternatives to Neoliberalism*. London: Routledge, 2000.

De Stefano, George. *An Offer We Can't Refuse: The Mafia in the Mind of America*. New York: Faber and Faber, 2006.

Evans, Sara M. "Feminism in the 1980s: Surviving the Backlash." *Living in the Eighties*. Ed. Gil Troy and Vincent J. Cannat. Oxford: Oxford UP, 2009. 85–97.

Harris, Oliver. "Film Noir Fascination: Outside History, but Historically So." *Cinema Journal* 43.1 (Autumn 2003): 3–24.

Giannetti, Louis, and Scott Eyman. *Flash-Back—A Brief History of Film*, 4th edition. New Jersey: Prentice Hall, 2001.

Palmer, William J. *The Films of the Eighties*. Carbondale: Southern Illinois UP, 1993.

Smith, Julian. "The Infernal Comedy of Richard Condon." *Twentieth Century Literature* 14.4 (Jan. 1969): 221–29.

11

ALAN WOOLFOLK

Hints of Modernism, Shades of Noir

Huston's *Maltese Falcon* as Transitional Text

> Who is the Dandy? . . . We still feel the power of this myth, of this figure still staking himself upon a passive potency . . . Our most brilliant representatives of the type are the Western hero and Bogart.
>
> —Stanley Cavell, *The World Viewed*

> Noir heroes are endlessly reluctant to act, and when they do, they are mostly responsive and often halfhearted. The issue of destiny or fate in Westerns is framed as a question of national historical destiny, and it is, at least on the surface, progressive and meliorist, whereas the issue of destiny in noirs is largely framed in psychological or social or existential terms, and the relevant possibilities are severely constricted. The standard picture is of people "trapped" either (somewhat paradoxically) by themselves (by who they have become), or by an anonymous and autonomous social order or societal machine, or by a vast purposeless play of uncontrollable fortune, chance.
>
> —Robert B. Pippin, *Fatalism in American Film Noir*

Director John Huston's film adaptation of Dashiell Hammett's detective novel *The Maltese Falcon* (1930) arguably marks the beginning of the classic noir era, which is frequently defined as commencing with Huston's film in 1941 and ending with Orson Welles's *Touch of Evil* in 1958.[1] More precisely, Huston's adaptation is best viewed as a transitional film that played a critical role in defining the emerging noir worldview because it transformed the popular modernism of Hammett's hard-boiled detective story into a protonoir film, while at the same time it also transformed the genre of the American detective film in the direction of noir. In the former instance, Huston's adaptation was a technically faithful rendering of much of the novel that employed what would become classic noir themes (e.g., the cynical detective with dubious ethics; the seductive and dangerous femme fatale) and noir techniques (e.g., low-angle close-ups; shadowed and cramped interior scenes), yet it also radically altered the popular modernism of Hammett's novel by transforming the tough and ruthless working-class detective, Sam Spade, into a more inwardly complicated and self-possessed Baudelairean dandy who would serve as a would-be role model for the noir heroes to come. In the latter instance, Huston's film helped to transform the conventional detective melodrama into a darker drama of unredeemed deceit and desire, but the very self-possession and self-control of Huston's Sam Spade (Humphrey Bogart) kept the film from depicting the full-blown fatalism and failure of individual agency that came to define the essential noir films and many of the neonoir films that followed. More pointedly, neither the novel nor the film explores what became the most significant marker of noir films—the "dark past" of the protagonist and antagonist(s). This chapter will explore the development of the noir worldview, including its relation to the social and cultural context, through an analysis of the presence and absence of modernist and noir motifs in Huston's adaptation and their relation to one another, looking backward to Hammett's novel and forward to the definitive noir films to come.

Resisting the Fate of the Philistines

As an *ex post facto* genre, classic film noir drew upon the long-standing conflict between what Matei Calinescu has called "two distinct and bitterly conflicting modernities," a conflict that has been largely resolved with the rise of a postmodern, therapeutic culture during the last half of the twentieth century. On the one side, modernity was conceived as a moral and political project grounded in the doctrine of progress, scientific and technological advancement, and capitalist economics centered on the bourgeoisie, especially the morality of the bourgeois family. On the other side, an oppositional cultural, explicitly aesthetic, modernity arose out of the romantic movement that was "inclined toward radical antibourgeois attitudes," a modernity that led to the rise not only of modernism, but also eventually of the political and artistic avant-gardes (Calinescu 41–42). Originally, film noir drew upon the modernist heritage of aesthetic modernity, exploiting its critique of bourgeois modernity at a time when the tension between conventional morality and modernism, bourgeois and bohemian, was weakening. Indeed, as James Naremore has argued, following Fredric Jameson, American film noir is "both a type of modernism and a type of commercial melodrama." Naremore clarifies the affinity between noir films and modernism, as well as the close ties between this variety of cinematic modernism and commercial culture, with Graham Greene's notion of "blood melodrama" (45).

With the concept of "blood melodrama," Naremore points to the influence of European art cinema on American directors and genres, specifically the films of Weimar Germans who specialized in "gothic horror, criminal psychology, and sinister conspiracies"; French films about "working class crime"; and English films by Hitchcock on international intrigue. "What united the three types of cinematic modernism," according to Naremore, "was an interest in popular stories about violence and sexual love, or in what Graham Greene once called 'blood melodrama.'" Naremore also contends that the influence of blood melodrama may be seen in the literature of Anglo-American high culture (e.g., Joseph Conrad, Henry James) as well as in the rise of a "countertradition" to the traditional detective story that built on the rapid rise of American working-class pulp fiction during the 1920s and the growth of novels about crime in the late 1920s and 1930s that appealed to the middle class. According to Naremore, this "second generation modernism" interacted with mass culture and eventually made its way into the respectable realms of New York publishing, Broadway theatre, and Hollywood," resulting in the rise of film noir (45–46). In a similar vein, R. Barton Palmer, while emphasizing the dominance of the established Hollywood system and downplaying the influence of cinematic modernism, identifies the increasing appeal of working-class pulp fiction *and* the growth of a fatalistic noir worldview within that literature as critical for the advent of film noir (35–37).

Nonetheless, the rise of a "countertradition" to the traditional detective story, which is best represented in the work of Dashiell Hammett, Raymond Chandler, and James Cain (with Hammett's *The Maltese Falcon* being the least fatalistic of the major works), must be placed within the context of rapidly changing definitions of what was permitted and not permitted, the shifting dialectic of yes and no, in American culture during the 1920s and 1930s. The expansion of "second generation modernism" into mainstream American culture is another way of describing what Lionel Trilling has characterized as the growth and spreading influence of an "adversary culture," which originated in a long line of artists and intellectuals at the center of aesthetic modernity and reached its spiritual height during the first quarter of the twentieth century. "The adversary intention, the actually subversive intention" of modern literature, according to Trilling, had the "clear purpose of detaching the reader from the habits of thought and feeling that the larger culture imposes, of giving him a ground and a vantage point from which to judge and condemn, and perhaps revise, the culture that produced him" (*Beyond Culture* preface). Indeed, Trilling, writing in the 1960s, thought that this adversarial intention, which stands behind what he would later call the ideal of "authenticity," was and would continue to be definitive of artistic and intellectual culture, albeit in diminished form, for some time to come (*Sincerity and Authenticity*). "It is a belief still pre-eminently honored that a primary function of art and thought is to liberate the individual from the tyranny of his culture in the environmental sense and to permit him to stand beyond it in an autonomy of perception and judgment" (*Beyond Culture* preface). Insofar as hard-boiled detective novels and then film noir marked important advances for a popularized modernism, they strengthened the influence of this adversarial culture by weakening the restrictions of the larger culture at both the symbolic and the personal levels. Popular novels and films alike became significant symbolic forms for furthering the detachment and deinhibition of individuals from the prevailing Protestant and Victorian culture of respectability.

The popularization and spread of the adversarial culture through hard-boiled detective novels and noir films, which subverted and interrogated what was considered to be a philistine culture of respectability, may easily be traced through the rise of what John Burnham has called "conventional minor vices"—drinking, smoking, drug use, gambling, sexual misbehavior, and swearing—beginning approximately with the second quarter of the twentieth century. Of these, the prevalence of swearing, sexual misbehavior, drinking, and smoking are especially notable in Hammett's *The Maltese Falcon*, which was first published in 1930. Spade's recurrent profanity, in particular, is an obvious marker of working-class status and a minor vice in the midst of becoming more acceptable to mainstream society—what Burnham identifies as "the rise of lower order parochialism" (16–17). Likewise, Spade's cynical affair with Iva Archer, the wife of his partner, Miles; his acceptance of sexual favors from his client, Brigid O'Shaughnessy; and his incessant smoking and frequent drinking are all examples of minor vices which were increasingly no longer subject to condemnation by the larger culture. But in addition to the rise of vices associated with lower-order parochialism, Hammett's novel highlights two other "energizing factors" identified by Burnham as critical to overturning the waning culture of respectability and the inversion of cultural standards: greed and rebelliousness (15–20). Greed is, of course, omnipresent in the novel, and the definitive object of greed is all too obviously embodied in the camp symbol of "the black bird"—the Maltese Falcon (in the words of Huston's Spade, "the stuff that dreams are made of"). But Hammett's Spade also embodies rebellion against conventional morals and manners, specifically the morals and manners of the domesticated middle class. Spade is a born risk taker, a gambler (hence his name), a rebel of sorts who remains unapologetically undomesticated. Indeed, his lack of domestication defines his rebelliousness. Hammett's Spade is the antithesis of the family man, a loner with no home. He is notable for his lack of impulse control: his violent temper, his physical forcefulness, and his brutishness and sadism. Of these, Spade's violent temper may be the most telling in Hammett's novel because it stands in stark contrast to the depiction of Spade in Huston's film in which Spade is equally a risk taker, a loner, and also capable of violence; defined not by his periodic lack of self-control, but by his complete self-possession, his mastery of himself and others.

Huston's Spade overlaps with Hammett's Spade in many respects, of course, especially considering the constraints of the Production Code at the time of the film, which prohibited, in particular, explicit sexuality and profanity. But in addition to Huston's Spade lacking the rough edges of Hammett's character, Huston's film also omits what has been variously referred to as the modernist story or parable of the Flitcraft case, which Spade tells to Brigid O'Shaughnessy at the beginning of chapter 7 without any introduction or explanation:

> A man named Flitcraft had left his real-estate office, in Tacoma, to go to luncheon one day and had never returned. He did not keep an engagement to play golf after four that afternoon, though he had taken the initiative in making the engagement less than half an hour before he went out to luncheon. His wife and children never saw him again. His wife and he were supposed to be on the best of terms. He had two children, boys, one five and the other three. He owned his house in a Tacoma suburb, a new Packard, and the rest of the appurtenances of successful American living. (62)

As Spade continues, he explains that Flitcraft was eventually discovered five years later living in Spokane, remarried with a child, once again living a comfortable suburban life. When confronted by Spade, who was the detective on the case, Flitcraft had explained that he had been nearly killed the afternoon of his disappearance by a beam falling from a building under construction and had come to recognize in that moment that the life he knew as "a clean orderly sane responsible affair" was "fundamentally none of these things," that "he, the good citizen-husband-father, could be wiped out . . . by accident." As a consequence, he had immediately come to recognize that his life was "out of step" and decided to "change his life at random by simply going away." For Spade, the implicit irony is that Flitcraft then proceeded once again to adjust to a new life as a "good citizen-husband-father." Spade concludes with the comment that "that's the part of it I always liked. He adjusted himself to beams falling, and then no more of them fell, and he adjusted himself to them not falling" (63–64). Hammett's Spade refuses to adjust to American middle-class life not simply domestically, but at a more fundamental level–existentially. The implicit moral of his story is that he self-consciously resists the fate of the philistines. As Spade says to Brigid during his final exchange with her just prior to turning her over to the police, he won't "play the sap" for her (213). Likewise, Hammett's Spade won't "play the sap" for the shallow American dream either.

Of Banked and Unbanked Fires

Huston's Spade also won't "play the sap" for Brigid (Mary Astor). Likewise, he resists the fate of the philistines, but in an entirely different manner. Indeed, for Huston's Spade, manner is everything—the signature trench coat and hat; the facial grimaces revealing carefully controlled tensions; the masterful dominance of every social encounter; the careful control of emotions, even in the midst of apparent outbursts of temper. As a master of self-possession, Huston's Spade is a spiritual descendent of Baudelaire's dandy, perhaps the single most influential ideal of aesthetic modernity. For Baudelaire, the dandy was an aesthetic model for living that opposed both the corruption of the bourgeoisie and the temptations of a disorderly bohemian life—what Baudelaire called "the cult of multiplied sensation" (qtd in Seigel 109). As Stanley Cavell has argued, Baudelaire's ideal of the dandy has been an instructive presence in American film for some time: "Our most brilliant representatives of the type are the Western hero and Bogart" (Cavell 56). Like Baudelaire, Cavell identifies the feature of a "hidden" or "latent" fire as essential to the character of the dandy—what Baudelaire describes as "an air of coldness which comes from an unshakeable determination not to be moved . . . a latent fire which hints at itself, and which could, but chooses not to burst into flame" (29). Hammett's Spade is distinguished from Huston's Spade by his failure to keep his fires banked.

These contrasting dispositions are quite evident in Spade's first meeting with Kaspar Gutman (Sydney Greenstreet) in Huston's film. Although the film closely parallels the novel, the former explicitly portrays Spade as much more clever and self-possessed in his dealings with Gutman. Huston's Spade engages in a "homoerotic ploy" with the obviously homosexual Gutman and then proceeds to feign losing his temper with melodramatic flair when he shatters a glass on the floor and then exits Gutman's hotel suite while making threats and giving Gutman an ultimatum (Greenberg 68). The critical scene occurs outside the suite as Spade moves toward the elevator: Spade's grin, the somewhat whimsical musical score, and Spade's amusement at his own shaking hand all indicate that he has intentionally staged the scene to throw Gutman off

Figure 11.1. Spade leaves Gutman's apartment after cleverly pretending to lose his temper.

balance in an effort to gain the upper hand. Spade knows little about the black bird and its whereabouts, but he leaves Gutman uncertain as to what he does know and what his next move is. With Hammett's Spade, the homoerotic ploy is not so obviously present, and Spade's anger is much more authentic, even though he too grins at his shaking hand and, in this case, makes a comment to the elevator operator. However, the entire scene is much more clumsily executed by Hammett's Spade because he has clearly lost his "cool," as indicated, for instance, by the handkerchief with which he wipes his face (112).

A similar contrast of the two Spades is also evident, for example, during the second visit of detectives Dundy (Barton MacLane) and Polhaus (Ward Bond) to Spade's apartment, when Lt. Dundy punches Spade in the face for his insolence in concocting a preposterous story in order to keep Brigid, Joel Cairo (Peter Lorre), and Spade from being taken to the police station for questioning and possible arrest. Although the scene on film follows the novel closely, with Huston's Spade quite angered over Dundy's provoked attack, the next film scene omits all reference to, let alone depiction of, Spade's uncontrolled outburst of anger in Hammett's text:

> Red rage came suddenly into his face and he began to talk in a harsh guttural voice. Holding his maddened face in his hands, glaring at the floor, he cursed Dundy for five minutes without break, cursed him obscenely, blasphemously, repetitiously, in a harsh guttural voice. Then he took his face out of his hands, looked at the girl, grinned sheepishly, and said: "Childish, huh? I know, but, by God, I do hate being hit without hitting back." (82)

Such discrepancies between the film and the novel help to clarify contrasting modes of modernist resistance to conventional society, but they also raise questions about conceptions of action and agency in hardboiled fiction and film noir. Specifically, they raise questions about not simply the presence or absence of agency, but rather degrees of agency, changing conceptions of agency over time in different sociocultural contexts, and the role of agency in modernism and film noir.

For Robert Pippin, although there are many different theories of action and agency, certain common features are agreed upon—"the simplest being that in acting I know what I am about and why I am about it . . . and that what I am doing is subject to some kind of deliberative control. Action is action because it is somehow inwardly directed." According to Pippin, film noir is of special interest precisely because "almost nobody significant in noirs behaves in a way that fits such a reflective model of action and agency, at least not with respect to the central actions around which the basic plot revolves" (14–15). *The Maltese Falcon*, in both its novel and film versions, complicates this picture even further: Hammett's Spade, despite his periodic loss of temper, is notable among hard-boiled detective protagonists for his relatively strong sense of agency, whereas Huston's Spade stands out even more for the almost sovereign agency of his dandyism. Both are in their respective ways agents of modernist resistance to the established social order: considering the Flitcraft case, Hammett's Spade appears to be a self-conscious agent of lower order parochialism acting against conventional middle-class society, whereas Huston's Spade is an agent of high modernism acting against the same. Neither is subject to the fatalism that later characterized both the development of hard-boiled detective fiction and film noir, but Hammett's Spade more closely approximates the impaired agency of later noir protagonists.

Palmer argues that "novels like Dashiell Hammett's *The Maltese Falcon* (1930) express a powerful disillusionment with contemporary culture but simultaneously validate the somewhat incongruous notion of a heroic individual, the private detective who lives by his own values and code." But he contends that as the hard-boiled detective novel developed during the 1930s and 1940s, we increasingly find protagonists trapped by the forces of circumstance and at the mercy of their own shortcomings and self-destructive tendencies (e.g., James M. Cain's *Double Indemnity* [1936], Cornell Woolrich's *Black Angel* [1946]) (Palmer 36). Likewise, we see a similar development in the case of film noir: the inestimable Spade in *The Maltese Falcon* stands as the first in a long lineage of American noir protagonists with progressively decreasing powers of agency that may be traced through the likes of the doomed Walter Neff (Fred MacMurray) in Billy Wilder's *Double Indemnity* (1944), Ole "Swede" Andreson (Burt Lancaster) in Robert Siodmak's *The Killers* (1946), and Jeff Markham (Robert Mitchum) in Jacques Tourneur's *Out of the Past* (1947) to its logical end with the defeated Scottie Ferguson (James Stewart) in Alfred Hitchcock's *Vertigo* (1958) during the classic noir period. In other words, Hammett's Spade and Huston's Spade are similar in that they are both transitional figures. Both redefine the figure of the detective and stand at the beginning of their respective genres as agents of modernist resistance. With the development of a full-blown noir worldview, the locus of modernist criticism shifted from individual agency to fatalism with the consequence that the failure of individual agency became the source of a new aesthetic critique of bourgeois modernity.

The relationship between the male noir protagonist and the classic femme fatale also reflects the declining efficacy of agency during the noir period. In fully developed film noir, the femme fatale frequently triggers self-destructive tendencies in the noir protagonist or is at least associated with fatalistic circumstances. The femme fatale may accept and then betray the protagonist's love (e.g., Kitty Collins [Ava Gardner] in *The Killers*), reveal herself to be ruthless and cold-blooded (e.g., Kathie Moffett [Jane Greer] in *Out of the Past*), or unintentionally precipitate fatal and fatalistic consequences (Evelyn Mulwray [Faye Dunaway] in *Chinatown*). In Huston's (and indeed Hammett's) *The Maltese Falcon*, Brigid (a.k.a. Miss Wonderly and Miss LeBlanc) is in the end revealed to be a ruthless killer, but she does not fit the typical model of a femme fatale. Brigid is not Kathie Moffett because her performance closely mirrors Spade's dandyism in its self-control. She adheres to Baudelaire's formulation that "it is the joy of astonishing others, and the proud satisfaction of never oneself being astonished," which is one of the hallmarks of a dandy (28). But Brigid is also a "vulgarian." In her "brutishness," Brigid is what Cavell characterizes as a "false dandy" (as are, to a less impressive degree, Joel Cairo and Kaspar Gutman) because she violates the dandy's aesthetic code and can only bring Spade to ruin if he allows her to do so (57). In the closing scene with Brigid just prior to Spade turning her over to the police for the killings of Miles and Thursby, Spade cites a host of reasons as to why he will not let her go free, but the critical one is revealed in the following passage (with text omitted from the film in brackets):

> If that doesn't mean anything to you forget it and we'll make it this: I won't because all of me wants to—[wants to say to hell with the consequences and do it—and because—God damn you]—you've counted on that with me the same as you counted on that with the others. (Hammett 215)

In Spade's determination not to be moved, not to give into his strongest impulses, he keeps his fires banked and thus vetoes the influence of his strongest rival. Fatalism does not prevail in either the novel or the film. Nor does the unrestrained greed and rapacity which the blackbird symbolizes go unchecked.

The Protonoir Worldview

In films such as *Double Indemnity* and Edgar G. Ulmer's *Detour* (1945), the critique of modernity is unmistakable. Each constructs a notion of fate (however contrived it might be) that is set within the cultural context of a modernist critique of twentieth-century capitalist civilization. In *Double Indemnity*, as Naremore has argued, the insurance agent Walter

Neff "is little more than a cog in a bureaucracy, and he cannot resist the blandishments of sex and money. Even the femme fatale, Phyllis (Barbara Stanwyck), is "visibly artificial . . . a soulless, modernized female" who is "affectless" (87–89). Similarly, Ulmer's *Detour* was clearly influenced by the Frankfurt School and may be read as a critique of the American wasteland in which the lives of the major characters are dominated by cultural and economic forces embodied in Hollywood. As Paul Cantor explains, "the characters in *Detour* seem incapable of generating authentic desires; they are always setting their goals on the basis of the models that American society offers them" (146). Consequently, as in the case of *Double Indemnity*, the theme of fate is specifically linked to a critique of late modern capitalist civilization. The grim fatalism of Walter Neff and Al Roberts (Tom Neal) is a manifestation of the sickness of mid-twentieth-century American society and, by implication, late modernity.

The rise of a *fatalistic*, hard-boiled noir worldview in literature and film is not simply a matter of modernist criticism of conventional society, but also a growing loss of faith in the entire modern capitalistic social order, and the effectiveness of individual agency in both supporting and opposing that order. Indeed, one cannot be separated from the other. Sam Spade's potency as an agent becomes less credible and less easily sustained in a social order that has begun to doubt its very existence. In fact, the rise of a bleaker noir worldview corresponds almost perfectly with what Peter Drucker called the failure of the "capitalist creed." In *The End of Economic Man*, Drucker contended that the worldwide depression of the 1930s marked the end of modern faith in both capitalism and Marxism because both were based upon the belief that economic progress would result in moral progress and lead to a more just society:

> Capitalism as a social order and as a creed is the expression of the belief in economic progress as leading toward the freedom and equality of the individual in the free and equal society. Marxism expects this society to result from the abolition of private profit. Capitalism expects the free and equal society to result from the enthronement of private profit as a supreme ruler of social behavior. (37)

According to Drucker, the vicissitudes of the economic and political spheres make sense only in relation to their social ends. The perceived senselessness of the Great Depression and the threat of war in Europe in the late 1930s were informed by doubts about the very purpose of modern civilization. According to Drucker, the senselessness of depression and war has nothing to do with "anything inherent in the character of war and depression as such. They are exclusively due to the disintegration of the belief in the foundations of society" (61). The depressions of the 1830s and 1873 were both more severe than the Great Depression of 1929, but the Great Depression was experienced as more irrational and senseless by the great majority of the populace precisely because individuals were no longer willing to make sacrifices in the name of future economic and moral progress. The modern belief that the trials of the capitalist economy would eventually lead to a more just society had failed for both capitalists and Marxists alike.

In short, behind the failure of faith in individual agency is the corruption and failure of the established social order itself. As transitional texts, the Hammett novel and the Huston film leave faith in the efficacy of individual agency intact and therefore keep a full-blown noir fatalism at bay. But the corruption symbolized by the figure of the black bird threatens to draw everyone who comes into contact with it, Spade included, under its spell. As mentioned earlier, the Maltese Falcon is an omnipresent and an all-too-obvious symbol of greed. If, as Gutman remarks to Spade during their second meeting, "we all know that the

Figure 11.2. Even Spade falls under the spell of the "black bird."

Holy Wars . . . were largely a matter of loot," then the assumption is that for anyone who is not a fool, modern life is also a quest for loot. Indeed, Gutman tells Spade that he has been on the trail of the black bird for seventeen years. But the spell of the bird is not simply a matter of unmitigated greed for the object itself. Rather, the characters attracted to the pursuit of the falcon, most of them criminals, are under the influence of what René Girard calls "triangular desire." They desire the black bird, and desire it ever more intensely, because other rivals and imagined rivals desire it, because there is no "external mediator" (1–52). Among the cast surrounding Gutman, Joel Cairo, Wilmer Cook (Elisha Cook Jr.), Brigid O'Shaughnessy, and of course Gutman himself, not to mention Captain Jocobi (Walter Huston) and Floyd Thursby, there is an intense and jealous competition, which Gutman would like to draw Spade into because he is not only a potentially valuable ally, but also a formidable rival whose mere yearning for the bird makes it more valuable in Gutman's eyes. In addition, the feverish desire for the black bird is intertwined with the erotic competition between Brigid, who has repeatedly secured male allies by seducing them, and the homoerotic entourage around Gutman (i.e., Wilmer and Joel). That Spade does succumb to Brigid and does not succumb to the feverish desire for the bird does not mean that he is not tempted by it, especially at the moment when it falls into his hands and Effie [Lee Patrick] exclaims that his grip is "hurting me." Likewise, although the more conventional figures (e.g., Effie, Tom Polhaus) seem for the most part unaffected by this feverish desire, there is the implicit implication that the entire social order is at risk of being seduced by a contagion of unchecked jealousy and greed.

Nonetheless, the threat of this contagion cannot be taken entirely seriously in the film version of *The Maltese Falcon* because it is, as Susan Sontag once commented, "among the greatest camp movies ever made." According to Sontag, camp is "the sensibility of failed seriousness, of the theatricalization of experience." It is characterized by artifice and exaggeration (287, 275). With Huston's film, the artifice and exaggeration begin, of course, with the highly stylized performance of Bogart himself, which transforms the tough and unsophisticated Spade into what Sontag might have called a sort of democratic dandy, while retaining the original Spade's streak of sadism (witness the pleasure both Spades take in punching out Joel Cairo). But Spade's theatrics are, in turn, matched by Greenstreet's Gutman and especially Astor's Brigid, both of whom are preposterous characters—Gutman with his flamboyant pursuit of the black bird and Brigid with her relentless fabrications. The stylized, ironic performances of Bogart, Greenstreet, and Astor, not to mention the nearly comic performances of Lorre and Cook as Gutman's boys and the at times almost whimsical musical score by Adolph Deutsch, serve to create some modernist distance on the melodramatics of the novel and to alert viewers that they are indeed watching a highly aestheticized performance. Most important, Huston's work avoids the near tragic implications of some of the best noir films in which, to paraphrase Palmer, someone or something is always coming out of the dark past. Huston's masterpiece is distinguished from the noir films yet to come by the fact that nothing comes out of the dark past to compromise the sovereign agency of his inimitable Sam Spade.

Note

1. I would argue that a much more convincing case can be made for Alfred Hitchcock's *Vertigo* as marking the end of the classic noir period. See Woolfolk.

Works Cited

Baudelaire, Charles. *The Painter in Modern Life and Other Essays*. Trans. and ed. J Mayne. New York: Da Capo, 1946.

Burnham, John C. *Bad Habits*. New York: New York UP, 1993.

Cantor, Paul. "Film Noir and the Frankfurt School: America as Wasteland in Edgar Ulmer's *Detour*." In *The Philosophy of Noir*. Ed. Mark T. Conrad. Lexington: UP of Kentucky, 2006.

Cavell, Stanley. *The World Viewed: Reflections on the Ontology of Film*. Enlarged edition. Cambridge, MS: Harvard UP, 1979.

Calinescu, Matei. *Five Faces of Modernity*. Durham: Duke UP, 1987.

Drucker, Peter F. *The End of Economic Man: The Origins of Totalitarianism*. New York: Harper and Row, 1969.

Girard, René. *Deceit, Desire, and the Novel*. Trans. Y. Freccero. Baltimore: Johns Hopkins UP. 1965.

Greenberg, Harvey Roy. *Screen Memories: Hollywood Cinema on the Psychoanalytic Couch*. New York: Columbia UP, 1994.

Naremore, James. *More than Night: Film Noir in Its Contexts*. Berkely: U of California P, 1998.

Palmer, R. Barton. *Hollywood's Dark Cinema: The American Film Noir*. New York: Twayne, 1994.

Pippin, Robert. *Fatalism in American Film Noir*. Charlottesville: U of Virginia P, 2012.

Seigel, Jerrold. *Bohemian Paris: Culture, Politics, and the Boundaries of Bourgeois Life, 1830–1930*. New York: Penguin, 1986.

Sontang, Susan. *Against Interpretation and Other Essays*. New York: Farrar, Straus and Giroux, 1966.

Trilling, Lionel. *Beyond Culture: Essays on Literature and Learning*. New York: Harcourt Brace Jovanovich, 1965.

———. *Sincerity and Authenticity*. Cambridge, MA: Harvard UP, 1972.
Woolfolk, Alan. "The Dread of Ascent: The Moral and Spiritual Topography of *Vertigo*." *Hitchcock as Moralist*, ed. R. Barton Palmer, forthcoming.

12

Camilla Fojas

Of Borders and Bandits

The Treasure of the Sierra Madre

It was not easy for John Huston to bring *The Treasure of the Sierra Madre* (1948) to the silver screen. After surveying eight thousand miles of the Mexican countryside in search of a suitable location for a story about prospecting Americans, he found a small town in the state of Michoacán where he would begin shooting. Yet rumors began to circulate that the film, the very first Hollywood production to be shot entirely in Mexico, would not depict the country well. Huston was forced to halt production for a government investigation that, after two long months, eventually concluded in his favor. Yet more intrigue and speculation would haunt the set. Huston agreed to hire B. Traven, the reclusive author of the novel upon which the film is based, as a technical advisor. At the last minute, Traven sent his "personal secretary," Hal Croves, in his place. Everyone involved in the film suspected that Traven was masquerading as Croves, and some even hounded him, causing the latter to leave the set precipitously (Grobel 285–91). Huston was not inclined to indulge the atmosphere of suspicion dogging Croves. Huston would later affirm, "Everybody thinks that Traven was the man who claimed to be Traven's secretary but I don't agree" (Studlar and Desser 218). The tone of defiance one detects here characterizes many of Huston's dealings during this period, especially his dealings with authority, whether that authority was the House Un-American Activities Committee or Hollywood studio heads. Huston was so outraged by the Communist witch-hunts of the House Un-American Activities Committee (HUAC) in Hollywood, which were taking place during the making of the film, that, soon after wrapping up filming for *The Treasure of the Sierra Madre*, he helped form Hollywood Fights Back which would become the Committee for the First Amendment (CFA).

This sense of defiance is a common strain in the often divergent story lines of the film and novel. Both stories are about resistance to the dominant order and its prevailing beliefs, and both share a fascination with figures defined by their individualism and mobility: US migrants in Mexico and Mexican bandits. Yet what distinguishes the film from the novel are the diverse contexts of national reception and the attendant cultural fantasies around each figure. Indeed, the cinematic bandit, Gold Hat (Alfonso Bedoya), would generate a lasting legacy as the iconic figure of the bandit in US popular culture in a manner that Huston could not have anticipated. The bandit transcends the story line for the way he syncretizes a number of fantasies, anxieties, and fears about US national identity in relation to Mexico during the Cold War period, a time of paranoia and fear mongering. As a figure of ambivalence, Gold Hat is both derided and idealized for his defiance; his defiance will become a defining characteristic of US exceptionalism after the Cold War.

Both the novel by B. Traven and the film directed by John Huston follow the Western tradition in which lone men traverse a frontier that is less geographical than it is a symbolic marker of various kinds of differences and distinctions. In this case, it is about the cultural and economic incursion of the North into the South, represented by Anglo Americans seeking economic opportunities in Mexico. Huston's film did not follow the generic conventions of the Western; it featured no major heterosexual relationship and was the first Hollywood studio film to be shot entirely in Mexico with a large number of Mexican actors and actresses often speaking untranslated Spanish dialogue. Although after the Mexican Revolution, there were limited employment prospects for non-Mexicans, the idea that a better life might be found south of the border still held sway. The story is an allegory about capitalism and alternate forms of association and social organization, set as a border story after the Mexican Revolution and the US financial crisis of 1929, events that foregrounded the figures of the Mexican bandit and the down-and-out Anglo American.

The Treasure of the Sierra Madre highlights a migration trend of poor Americans from the North seeking work and possible wealth in Mexico during a boom in oil production and natural mineral extraction. The novel, more than the film, shows how this era produced the "bandit" as a similarly impoverished and dispossessed figure, albeit one that captured the US imagination as an abiding symbol of Mexican primitivism and savagery. The visual depiction of the bandit is in keeping with a long history of US popular cultural images and descriptions of Mexican bandits as a racialized other who hinders the full occupation of former Mexican territories within the US sphere of influence, a role similar to that of the ravaging Indian of the Western. Yet, the bandit is a modern figure and a figure of modernity, as an effect of modern social struggles and the impact of industrialization in Northern Mexico and the Southwest of the United States. Whereas the novel complicates the figure of the bandit and puts them on the same or similar ground as the Anglo heroes, the film resonates within a history of Hollywood depictions of Mexican bandits—while its overall story line is critical of US hegemony. Nonetheless, the spectacle and image of the bandit transcends its narrative context and resonates within the visual history of the motion picture bandit in the United States.

B. Traven actively cultivated mystery and confusion about his identity. According to some sources, he was an anarchist German expatriot, Ret Marut, living in Mexico when he wrote the novel. The novel has mysterious history linked to its author and his shifting identities and attributions of national origin. A detective-critic discovered that his original name was Otto Wienecke and that he was born in the small town of Schwiebus, Poland, before moving to Germany. He moved to Mexico in 1924 where, claiming to be a US citizen, he went by different names, including Hal Croves—though Huston would disagree. He published *The Treasure of the Sierra Madre* [*Der Schatz der Sierra Madre*] in Germany in 1927, eight years before it appeared in English in the United States. The novel was incredibly popular on a global scale and circulated widely in numerous editions. It was translated into at least thirteen languages and was adapted as a series of books for young adults (Farmer 3).

Traven was immersed in the radical anti-institutional anarchist traditions of turn-of-the-century Germany. In *The Treasure of the Sierra Madre*, he details the destructive force of capitalism and the dehumanizing lust for gold on the part of Dobbs, one of the three main Anglo characters. While Dobbs represents the materialism of the American capitalist system, the remaining two protagonists, Howard and Curtin, offer possible futures within an alternative community of indigenous Mexicans. The main difference between the novel and the film hinges on the role and function of the Mexican bandit in this dichotomy.

In the novel, the bandit has a flexible significance and is applied indiscriminately to diverse national representatives who are seemingly agents, rather than victims, of capitalist exploitation. *The Treasure of the Sierra Madre* in both film and novel begins with the plight of Dobbs (played by Humphrey Bogart in the film), a down-and-out Anglo American in search of enough money to buy his next meal as he seeks employment. He meets a fellow American, Curtin (Tim Holt), working for an oil company run by yet another American, Pat, who regularly cons his workers out of their pay—and whom Curtin refers to as a "bandit" in the novel (36). Curtin and Dobbs band together to extract their earnings from Pat by force, taking only what is owed them, establishing their maverick application of justice. While hatching up an entrepreneurial plan to mine for gold, they meet Howard—played by Huston's father, Walter Huston—an old-timer and savvy speculator, a fellow Anglo American. Together they begin their trek to the Sierra Madre, where they interact with groups of bandits, indigenous villagers, and a lone Anglo American, Lacaud, referred to as "the stranger," who happens upon their camp. He never gets beyond his status of an outsider and must endure the ridicule and suspicion of the three other Americans and is eventually sacrificed, thus becoming a sign of the potential exclusiveness of a community based on shared materialism. Each of the three main characters reacts differently to his accumulation of wealth, as the story becomes an increasingly powerful allegory of the ravages of capital.

Many film scholars have noted that the film created the popular image of Mexican bandits and banditry. This is partly because of the line, "Badges, we don't need no stinking badges," that has circulated widely in popular culture and in diverse contexts. In fact, the misquoted line is number 36 on the American Film Institute's (AFI) rigorously chosen list of "100 Greatest movie quotes of all time." AFI has a jury of over fifteen hundred leaders in the film community including film artists, critics, and historians. They are charged with selecting "quotes from American films which circulate through popular culture, become part of the national lexicon and evoke the memory of a treasured film, thus ensuring and enlivening its historical legacy." The popular adaptation of these lines is edited for brevity and impact, which intensifies the sense of depravity of the bandit character. In the oft-quoted line taken from the novel, Gold Hat, the leader of one of the bandit outfits, expresses his refusal to be identified: "Badges, to god-damned hell with badges! We have no badges. In fact, we don't need badges. I don't have to show you any stinking badges, you god-damned cabrón and ching' tu madre" (145). The line in the film, however, is shorter and more emphatic: "Badges? We ain't got no badges! We don't need no badges! I don't have to show you any stinking badges!" Although in the novel, the bandit speaks with profanity, his English is without the ungrammaticality attributed to him in the film. The latter enhances their criminality and adds to the overall negative portrait of the bandits.

Traven, moreover, depicts several different groups and types of bandits. The line under discussion is spoken by the leader of a band of Mexicans trying to relieve the main characters of their firearms by convincing the Anglos that they are actually *policía montada*, mounted police. And indeed, it was a common practice for the state to employ known bandits as federal police who would then work both sides of the law to their advantage. However, social bandits fighting for a religious cause and seeking arms and funds to advance their cause also appear in the novel. Most are drawn into the cause and are exploited by the bandit leaders. For Traven, these bandits are less a target of criticism than they are the victims of the institutions for which they labor and the social order that exploits them.

Traven's representation of differing types of bandits is in keeping with Eric Hobsbawm, who cautions against the simple collapse of the distinction between bandit and criminal. The bandit figure, according to Hobsbawm, challenges and upsets the social order and reveals its power structures. Similarly, in Travern's novel, the bandit is a symptom of an imperial legacy who exposes the fissures in Spanish claims to power. The history of banditry is, in short, a history of political power (Hobsbawm 13). Bandits are not simply robbers or criminals but outsiders who resist the imposition of hegemonic forms of power through violent means. Moreover, they emerge during times of economic and political crisis. Describing the bandits that Dobbs, Curtin, and Howell happen upon, Traven remarks:

> In certain countries whenever banditry occurs on such a large scale, it is not always possible to determine who profits by what bandits do. The bandits may get all the booty for themselves, but often they may not know for whom they are fighting. A man high up in politics, a general hot after the seat of the president, a dismissed secretary of commerce, may use these bandits, whom he calls rebels, to destroy the reputation of the government before foreign nations and before their own. (127–28)

Bandits are curious and confusing figures. They are instrumentalized as pawns of various forces in power, often to different and sometimes opposing ideological ends and sometimes acting in pure self-interest. In this case, the forces in control use the bandit to execute their own power while simultaneously dismissing their charges as "rebels."

Traven also shows how another power structure, the Catholic Church, works to exploit the bandit:

> The bandits in this case made it quite clear that they were fighting for their king, Jesus. Fighting on behalf of the Roman Catholic Church, for religious liberty. The fact is that they have only a vague idea as to who Cristo was. It would have been quite easy to make them believe that Bonaparte, Columbus, Cortés, and Jesus were all identical. The Roman Catholic church during its four hundred years of rule in Latin America, of which three hundred and fifty were an absolute rule, has been more interested in purely material gains for the treasures and coffers in Rome than in educating its subjects in the true Christian spirit. (128)

The bandits defend what they presume to be a higher cause. Yet, often the ultimate aim of this cause, whether religious or imperial, is the accumulation of wealth. In this case, the bandits responsible for a terrifying train attack included two Catholic priests who liken their actions to those of Father Hidalgo and Father Morelos, who fought against Spanish colonialism for Mexican independence. Traven writes that the Mexican government took swift action against these priest-bandits to ensure to "American tourists" that the country was safe for visitors (128–29). For Traven, there is no hierarchy of law and order or privileging of the United States in what he implies is the corrupt "influence of the atmosphere of the continent" (76). The Anglo characters are the protagonists in an allegory in which capitalism is a function of colonialism.

The social bandit and its community of outlaws, however, are not deemed an alternative to state power. Traven does not mythologize them as holdouts against an arbitrary and oppressive state. Instead, they represent the mere reversal of state power masquerading as its representatives, the *policía montada*. The bandit clan approximates a hierarchical state formation in which a leader, the man with the golden hat (where gold is metonymic of capitalism) holds absolute power over his men. Referred to as his "followers," they follow his direct orders and move only when commanded. Ironically, their acculturation to power and discipline is attributed to their Catholic training:

> These men are never at a loss about what to do and how to do it; they are well trained in their churches from childhood on. Their churches are filled with paintings and statues representing every possible torture that white men (Christians, inquisitor, and bishops) could think of. These are the proper paintings and statues for churches in a country in which the most powerful church on earth wanted to demonstrate how

deep in subjection all human beings can be kept for centuries if there exists no other aim but the enlargement of the splendor and riches of the rulers. So it is not the bandits who were to blame. They were doing and thinking only what they had been taught. Instead of being shown the beauty of this religion, they had been shown only the cruelest and the bloodiest and the most repulsive parts of it. (146)

Bandit cruelty finds its origin in the paintings, statues, and visual texts of Catholicism. Thus, from the church, they learned how to instill terror and were simply enacting its teachings, including accruing wealth in ill-gotten ways. They prayed to the church not simply for protection, but also for impunity for the crimes they committed. The narrator attacks the violent imperialism of the church through its victims, those trained in its practices, the dispossessed peasantry steeped in religious superstitions, who would carry out the bidding of the church against and outside the law. Their position outside the legal system is less a sign of freedom than a sign of their persistent marginalization. The Mexican legal system is hardly any better than the church. The Texas Rangers' infamous practice to shoot first and ask questions later is emulated by Mexican officials in the novel.

The bandit in Mexico, particularly after the revolution, was a sign of the failure of the state to provide adequate economic conditions for its peoples. In the novel, the bandits are indigenous small farmers who are "more peasants than farmers" and who are able to use their knowledge of the terrain in their craft (129). Traven makes a distinction between the leaders of the cause, mostly priests, and the bandit recruits. The followers are peasants exploited by yet another powerful institution, the Catholic Church, and rather than pursue the cause, return home to their land and families. For this reason, Hobsbawm notes that the cycle of banditry follows the "rhythms of agriculture" and is at its height in the spring and summer (35). They are not the rootless, landless figures typically associated with the career bandit. The majority of *federales* that pursue bandits are likewise from indigenous tribes trained in war after years of struggle to defend their peoples. The bandits originate from the same social class as those who police them, such that indigenous peoples are pitted against each other's genocidal self-destruction. In another ironic twist, these peasant farmer bandits use the same firearms they used during the revolution to fight feudal lords for redistribution of land. Now they are fighting against their own interests, serving a religious cause that ultimately would lead to structural conditions that would delegitimize their claims to land.

Furthermore, Mexican bandits were often complicit with the very social structures that deemed them outsiders. Although their mythic identity suggested freedom and social protest, they were also a terrifying presence besetting anyone they might encounter on Mexico's roads and trails (Vanderwood 13). In *The Treasure of the Sierra Madre*, the bandits mount a vicious train attack and impose a class-based expression of violence. The train itself is used to reflect the social stratification upheld by the bandits. The team, ironically dressed as *mestizo* farmers, enter the train under the cover of wide palm hats. After throwing off their disguises, they begin to indiscriminately massacre passengers of the second-class car. In the first-class car, however, they merely pick off a few resisters. Their murderous desires are fueled by class consciousness: "It seemed that their thirst for blood had been satisfied with the killing of the poorer people" (Traven 123). Far from defenders of the poor, they are depicted as perpetrators of violence.

In a manner that ignores the complexities of the bandits that Traven depicts, the bandit has always held fascination for Hollywood audiences as both a sign of Mexican depravity that justifies the southwestern land grab and as a hero who resists the forces of modernity. It is the most abiding icon of Mexican culture for the United States particularly in the image of the socially rebellious revolutionary figure of Pancho Villa. The Hollywood bandit is a mix of racial and ethnic stereotypes with some heroic and mythic contours. Huston's own depiction of the bandit is more nuanced than this. Following Tavern's model, Huston at first establishes visual and characterological parity between the bedraggled Americans and their bandit captors and then goes further by making the American Dobbs the true bandit.

The image of the bandit in the film falls neatly into the historical trajectory of such images, and as Luis Reyes and Peter Rubie note, the reemergence of the bandit in the film marks the end of the Good Neighbor Policy and internal US censoring of negative images of Mexicans (275). However, Charles Ramírez Berg notes that the film is unlike others of its ilk for its critique of US imperialism, one that is much more incisive than the novel for the linking of the various imperialisms experienced by Mexicans. He argues that the film shows much more of Mexico than bandits, representing a wide swath of its social life. Moreover, Huston employs Mexican actors, including Julián Rivero as an artistic barber and Martín Garralaga as a railway conductor. The Mexican actors speak untranslated Spanish both to the main characters, especially to Howard, who translates their speech, and to each other. For Ramírez Berg, the film is an example of "counter-stereotyping" and anti-imperialism by showing how the US oil companies exploit their

Figure 12.1. Gold Hat's persona adds to a negative portrait of Mexican bandits.

workers and revealing the negative impact of US greed for Mexican resources (85–86).

Although the story line is critical and opens up a space for the critique of US-Mexican relations, the icon of the bandit ostensibly persists beyond the story line and resonates within a history of Hollywood filmmaking. With a limited range of affect and emotion, Gold is strongly representative of a negative stereotype. He is a buffoon whose lines are played for comedy. Juan J. Alonso notes the bandit has a "narrative economy" that precedes his individual appearance. But although we already know his story and the dimensions of his character, Alonzo argues that room is left open for the possibility of a revision of the bandit type, partly accomplished by the audience who might critically engage the bandit in a complex reading of the film. Moreover, the stereotype is so overdone in the film that it begins to undo and maybe even unhinge the image of the bandit. Alonso reads this as a possible consequence of Huston's ironic sense of playful humor. Actor Alfonso Bedoya, known as a solid character in Mexican films of the 1940s, stole the scene with his roguish performance. John Huston met Bedoya during location shooting and immediately cast him in the role of Gold Hat. After working with Huston, he went to Hollywood, where he played a number of roles often as darkly menacing Mexican villains, mostly bandits, as in *Border Incident* (1949), *California Conquest* (1952), and *Ten Wanted Men* (1955) (Berumen 246–47). He brought a sense of defiance to the role of Gold Hat, perhaps reflecting Huston's own defiant character. But, although Gold Hat and his crew appear only twice in the film, when they detain the prospectors in the attempt to extract them from their hiding place, and at the end when they attack and kill Dobbs, Huston has them return as the perpetrators of every attack in the film. In the novel, different groups of men attack the protagonists, and John Engell describes how Huston's choice heightens the narrative tension and locates a clear antagonist in Gold Hat and his crew. By concretizing the antagonist in an individual and his followers, the film diverts from the ideological aims of the novel that frame these characters within a larger historical and sociopolitical context. The story becomes one about individual responses to the lure of gold rather than a critique of the social world that generated these impoverished North Americans. In this way, Engell notes that the radical political critique of the novel becomes nothing more than a melodramatic and traditional "moral fable" in the classical Hollywood tradition (248).

This double vision of the film, one that critiques and concurrently participates in Hollywood stereotyping, persists in other issues that both the book and film address. Similar to Traven's novel, the film critiques capitalist materialism and in addition offers an alternative. Huston's film ends with a possible solution for the ravages of a modern industrial system that accords dubious value to gold. In Howard's first scene in the film, he discourses on the power of gold to transform men into murderers. He cautions the others about how gold elicits an unquenchable desire for more gold, which he likens to playing roulette. Yet, unlike gambling, in which the player may expect high returns for little investment and no labor, Howard warns that gold is worth only the labor invested in it. He warns that gold does not have a value in itself, but it is a sign of initiative and work. In fact, we witness the months of hard labor that drive these men to the edge of exhaustion. As the gold accrues, their attitudes begin to change. Dobbs, and to a certain degree Curtin, become more and more suspicious of each other to the point of paranoia, fearing that they will be robbed of their riches by the other. Howard, the old-timer, is the only character that does not fall prey to suspicions and doubt since he has seen the ravages of gold on the prospector's psyche. In fact, when he realizes that what they thought was gold was really worthless sand, he erupts in "a roar of Homeric laughter" suggesting the ludicrousness and ultimate dead end in the greed for gold (Traven 273). He deepens this explanation in the novel, remarking that all seekers after gold are ultimately the butt of a joke: "Anyway, I think it's a very good joke—a good one played on us and on the bandits by the Lord or by fate or by nature, whichever you prefer. And whoever or whatever played it certainly had a good sense of humor. The gold has gone back where we got it" (273). His laughter marks the absurdity and contradictions of capitalism, a system that devalues labor over that which it produces.

Dobbs eventually falls into the very trap that he earlier said he was determined to avoid and loses his life at the hands of Mexican down-and-outers in the novel and Gold Hat in the film. Curtin and Howard, however, realize that the quest for wealth leads to a dead end, as it literally does for Dobbs. After losing their riches, they are faced with the choice between setting up a small grocery store or a movie house with a small remainder of gold dust found in the mule saddle packs or continuing to live with the native community. The characteristics of that community diverge from the novel in significant ways. Traven explicitly promulgates a different form of social organization, idealizing precapitalist communal forms of society in Mexico that are represented under a more touristic gaze in the film.

Both Traven and Huston shared an interest in the possibilities of the different cultural and social life in Mexico, and both perhaps share in the idealization of this colonized culture. Postrevolutionary Mexico in the 1920s, when Traven arrived, was hospitable to those critical of US capitalism and who sought social and political alternatives to it. Writing about US travelers in 1920s Mexico, Dennis Merrill describes them as "lone eagles" who imagine they are "traversing a vanishing frontier." By the 1930s, Mexico was a popular destination for travelers seeking immersion in the ideals of revolution and tourists seeking refuge from their workaday lives. For many from the United States, Mexico was deemed a preindustrial rural place offering respite from the ravages of capitalist modernity. Huston's adaptation is replete with these itinerant Anglo-Americans, some seek work, others leisure—like the rich man from whom Dobbs begs money, ironically played by John Huston himself. In the end, Curtin and Howard are recipients of the bounties of Mexico. In repayment for his aid in helping a sick village, Howard is offered the hospitality of the villagers. In the novel, a villager tells Howard:

> I have good milpas, very fine acres. Lots of corn. I have many goats and quite a number of sheep. I am not so poor as I may look. Each day I shall have a turkey roasted for you, and as many eggs and as much goat's milk and roast kid as you can eat. I have already ordered my wife to make you at least three

times a week the very best tamales she can make. In fact, she has been hard at work since long before sunrise to prepare a great feast for you . . . The prettiest girls will come and be pleased to dance with you. I will make them because you are my guest. Why worry about your business? There is only one business on earth, and that is to live and be happy. What greater thing can you gain from life than happiness? (202–3)

Howard is reluctant to indulge this hospitality, but he eventually capitulates. In the film, this is conveyed in a scene in which indigenous women cater to Howard's every desire as he reclines in a hammock against a verdant backdrop. He enjoys a virtual cornucopia of offerings: fruit, animals, tequila, and women. His place among the indigenous is visually congruent with the promotional campaign of the 1938 Mexican Tourist Association, which featured the image of a native woman's profile framing the bounties of a colorful paradise—also the cover image of Merrill's book on US tourism in Latin America (94–95). The film, even more than the novel, conveys tourist fantasies of the offerings of a pre-industrial Mexico as an escape from the evils of capitalism and redemption through a feminized landscape, one passively awaiting to serve the weary sojourner. Although both film and novel are critical of the forces of capitalism and other institutions exerting power over people, they nevertheless contribute to prevailing ideas about Mexico as a land of plenty in which the outcast might find not only redemption but also hospitality and comfort in a dynamic that resonates with Mexico's colonial legacies.

Huston's adaptation of *The Treasure of the Sierra Madre* is largely considered an important exploration of the complexities of cross-border relations, but, intended or not, it functions as a cornerstone of the creation of the image of the Mexican bandit in American culture. These two perspectives exist in the film in a tense relationship. Nevertheless, to varying degrees, both verbal and visual texts remain indictments of capitalism in which the bandit is a victim of oppressive socioeconomic systems of power. Traven's novel, more so than Huston's film, is emphatic in its anti-institutional leanings and philosophical disposition. Traven conveys his ideological position in his assessment of the difference between dogs and donkeys, the latter being independent free thinkers unhitched to any master or engineering mission; "Dogs often show a real interest in what men do, even when the men in question are not their masters. Dogs even like to meddle in the affairs of men. Burros are less interested in men's personal doings; they mind their own business. That's the reason why donkeys are thought to have a definite leaning toward philosophy" (241). Huston highlighted the defiant critical mindedness and maverick individualism of Traven's work in a manner that would shape the mood of a generation cynical of Cold War politics in the United States. And in doing so, he inadvertently created an image of the bandit that would emblematize the ambivalent relationship of the United States to its southern neighbor.

Works Cited

Berg, Charles Ramírez. *Latino Images in Film: Stereotypes, Subversion, Resistance.* Austin: U of Texas P, 2002.

Berumen, Frank Javier Garcia. *Brown Celluloid: Latino/a Film Icons and Images in the Hollywood Film Industry* 1 (1894–1959). New York: Vintage, 2003.

Engell, John. "The Treasure of Sierra Madre: B. Traven, John Huston and Ideology in Film Adaptation." *Literature/Film Quarterly* 17.4 (1989): 248.

Farmer, David. *Catalogue of the Collection of B. Traven's* Treasure of the Sierra Madre. Austin: Humanities Research Center, U of Texas at Austin, 1968.

Grobel, Lawrence. *The Hustons.* New York: Charles Scribner's Sons, 1989.

Hobsbawm, Eric. *Bandits.* New York: New P, 2000.

Merill, Dennis. *Negotiating Paradise: U.S. Tourism and Empire in Twentieth-Century Latin America.* Chapel Hill: U of North Carolina P, 2009.

Reyes, Luis, and Peter Rubie. *Hispanics in Hollywood: A Celebration of 100 Years in Film and Television.* Hollywood: Lone Eagle, 2000.

Studlar, Gaylyn, and David Desser. "Ecounter with Rui Nogueira and Bertrand Tavernier." *Reflections in a Male Eye: John Huston and the American Experience.* Washington and London: Smithsonian Institution, 1993.

Traven, B. *The Treasure of the Sierra Madre.* London: Prion Books, 1999.

Vanderwood, Paul J. "Nineteenth-Century Mexico's Profiteering Bandits." *Bandidos: The Varieties of Latin American Banditry.* Ed. Richard W. Slatta. New York: Greenwood, 1987.

13

Nathan Ragain

"The Thing behind the Mask"

Period, Pacing, and Visual Style in John Huston's *Moby Dick*

My title, "The Thing behind the Mask," is of course drawn more or less from Herman Melville's Captain Ahab from the famous "Quarter-Deck" scene. Ahab fixes his doubloon to the mast, meditates on "visible objects [. . .] as pasteboard masks," and then whips the crew into a frenzy of "maledictions against the white whale" (Melville 144–46). Ahab uses the image of the mask to vent his hatred against the inscrutable "behind," but he does not use the phrase "the thing behind the mask." Those words come from John Huston's film, a scene in Ahab's cabin that conflates moments from "The Quarter-Deck" with other chapters. I foreground this line because I like to imagine Warner Bros. using it to retitle Huston's 1956 adaptation, much as it had retitled Melville's novel as *The Sea Beast* in its 1926 adaptation in order to market Melville's classic to an audience more interested in 1950s "It" and "Thing" monster movie and science fiction films like *The Thing from Another World* (1951) or like *Moby Dick* screenwriter Ray Bradbury's *It Came from Outer Space* (1953). I engage in this marketing fantasy in order to foreground my central interest in Huston's adaptation: the way it creates a relay between 1850s' and 1950s' anxieties. Throughout, I will argue that Huston presents *Moby Dick* as a Cold War allegory, but given that the novel was often already understood as an allegory of liberal democracy versus totalitarianism, I will trace the ways that Huston's engagement with the visuals and thematics of nuclear disaster destabilizes contemporaneous geopolitical readings of the novel. While Huston does not exactly subvert what Donald Pease describes as "the Cold War drama that [had] appropriated" Melville's novel, he does recast its characters away from a drama of the totalitarian Other, and, by drawing on the period styles of science fiction and monster movies, toward a nuclear drama in which an aberrant nature functions as an ambiguous other that mirrors the American self ("*Moby-Dick* and the Cold War" 117).

There are certainly details in the film that foreground its Cold War context. Most notably, Ahab uses his extensive map of whale sightings to predict that the *Pequod* will meet the white whale at Bikini Atoll. In his reading of the film, Walter C. Metz notes this detail as well as what I take to be perhaps the most significant context for Huston's adaptation, which is the very canonization of Melville's novel in the Cold War. Metz quotes Pease's argument that the novel's "final cataclysmic image of total destruction motivated [F. O.] Matthiessen and forty years of Cold War critics to turn Ishmael . . . [into] the principle of America's freedom and . . . surviving heritage" and suggests that this formulation "can be made resonant with Huston's film's Cold War activation of Richard Basehart-as-Ishmael's ideological survival of the United States in its conflict with the Soviet Union" (222). While I agree that Huston's film does indeed resonate with the period's ideological canonization of *Moby-Dick*, I am not convinced that it maps neatly onto a U.S.-Soviet opposition. For one, as Geraldine Murphy points out, there was not exactly a single Cold War reading of *Moby-Dick*, but rather *Moby-Dick* became a site on which Popular Front intellectuals (most notably Matthiessen) and anti-Communist New York intellectuals (most notably Richard Chase) staged their own Cold War battles with one another.

With the exception of Metz, most critics have considered Huston's adaptation to be an ambitious failure. David Lavery's assessment is perhaps the most damning. He catalogues several discrepancies—for instance Bradbury's decision to break "The Quarter-Deck" into separate above- and below-deck scenes—but his central complaint is that the film does not "make the slightest attempt to render Ishmael as the novel's central intelligence, capture even a trace of the book's wicked, blasphemous humor, or fully engage Melville's complex metaphors" (95). While Margaret Vasey finds the film's presentation of Ahab fairly faithful, she similarly questions its backgrounding of Ishmael's voice, noting that "the camera with its seemingly neutral perspective, stealthily draws attention to the film's star, Gregory Peck, as Ahab—and away from Ishmael" and that "character

Ishmael is often lost in the action, while narrator Ishmael's commentary is limited to linking the action of the film together" (143–44). Linda Costanzo Cahir echoes the common complaint that "Basehart's Ishmael is blank-faced, boyish, and good-natured, without a hint of the deep brooding, silent yearning, and sportive self-mockery that individuates Melville's Ishmael" (16), and she adds that "Huston's film [. . .] lacked the technical mastery and imagination necessary to render a cinematically credible form of the white whale" (15). In addition to this critical consensus, the film was hardly the success Huston had hoped for. Lawrewnce Grobel quotes Huston's disappointment at the film's reception—"I thought it would have a big audience . . . but the fact that there wasn't a multitude clambering to see *Moby Dick* was a great disappointment"—and one can detect this disappointment throughout his interviews (429).

I want to take the idea of Huston's failure seriously, and I want to link that failure to the ambition of adapting, not only Melville's multivalent novel to the screen, but just as importantly, Melville's 1850s for Huston's 1950s. Given that Huston's film, despite *Moby-Dick*'s canonical status, was not in fact a success in a climate that should have made it an easy success, I want to suggest that the film was dissonant with its moment and that this dissonance goes beyond assessments that would stress its unfaithfulness to the text. As noted above, many critics see Huston's failure as a failure of fidelity, most consistently to Ishmael's voice, but also to the depiction of Ahab and to the way a special-effects whale in an action sequence visualizes Melville's complex symbolism. Many of these elements, though, resonate with what Susan Sontag calls "the imagination of disaster" in the period's genre films, especially science fiction monster movies, and this resonance with the 1950s in turn produces a dissonance with the 1850s, even as the film's treatment of Ahab, Ishmael, and Starbuck is itself dissonant with Cold War readings of the novel. One way of resolving this would be to suggest that anachronisms like Bikini Atoll bespeak a fidelity to the text that filmic transcription would not, in that one cannot faithfully adapt a novel like *Moby-Dick*, which is so embedded in its late-Jacksonian period, without also embedding itself in its own postwar period. In other words, Huston is faithful to the text by being unfaithful, and to return to my opening marketing fantasy, by visually retitling the film *The Thing behind the Mask*. But in doing so, he does not obey the postwar US script. He makes the liberal democrat Ishmael ineffectual. He makes the totalitarian Ahab an uncomfortable American hero. And he uses 1950s imagery to foreground Melville's own anxieties about scientific rationality and aberrant nature.

To get at Huston's dissonance with the period's casting of Ahab and Ishmael, it is worth noting that the same year that Huston began production of *Moby Dick*, 1953, Trinidadian Marxist historian C. L. R. James wrote his own adaptation of Melville's novel while in a detention cell at Ellis Island, *Mariners, Renegades, and Castaways*, a book that shifts focus from the standard opposition between Ahab and Ishmael to the crew of the *Pequod*. James's revision of *Moby-Dick* into a narrative of occluded Third World labor is unfaithful both to Melville and to Cold War readings of Melville, and this unfaithfulness helps put Huston's own into relief. Both James and Huston shift focus away from Ishmael. Whereas standard Cold War readings rely on an opposition between Ishmael and Ahab, James undermines this opposition by equating the two characters. Pease notes that James "generalized [totalitarian rule] to include Ishmael, whom he described as 'an intellectual Ahab'" (*Arizona* 96), and in his own "*Moby Dick* and the Cold War," Pease similarly argues that Ahab and Ishmael share a "compulsion at work in their rhetoric" (141). Pease describes Ishmael as "turning virtually all the events in the narrative into an opportunity to display the powers of eloquence capable of taking possession of them" and then asks whether this power is "any less totalitarian, however indeterminate its local exertions, than a will to convert all the world into a single struggle" (145). Pease's argument is significant for Huston's film because, in backgrounding Ishmael, Huston largely does away with that same indeterminate eloquence that critics read as freedom and that Pease equates with totalitarian compulsion. Likewise, there is one key feature that both Huston's and Pease's Ishmael share, which is that Ishmael does not act: his "form of freedom does not oppose Ahab but compels him to need Ahab . . . as a cure of his boredom" (147). Where Pease's Ishmael is ineffectual, Basehart's is friendly but bland. Huston's failure to represent Ishmael's voice not only runs counter to the ideological investment in that voice as the novel's liberal center, but the resulting blandness of the film's Ishmael also presents Cold War liberalism as similarly bland, hardly oppositional to totalitarianism. When Ishmael does indeed survive, it is difficult to read this as also a surviving heritage; Ishmael is fully under Ahab's charismatic spell throughout the film.

But if Huston's Ishmael is not "our surviving heritage," his Ahab is even less clearly the totalitarian Other. For one thing, it is difficult to allegorize Stalin or Krushchev when you look like Lincoln, as Gregory Peck's Ahab most certainly does, and for which he was nearly universally criticized. Likewise, Peck's Ahab was criticized as being insufficiently mad. Huston consistently defended Peck, and his various defenses reveal the ways his casting of Peck creates dissonance with the Cold War's casting of Ahab. Like the totalitarian Ahab, Huston's is charismatic, but that charisma does not suggest the proper madness that would render it other for most of the film. Huston notes that he "was afraid of a melodramatic approach to Ahab, someone fiery and pyrotechnic," that "Ahab was not insane, his was a terrible sanity," and that it "was important for a charismatic American to have played him, not merely because he is a uniquely American character, but the role required that sort of soulful depth" (Long 28). Huston describes a particular form of charisma—one that does not rant, is not fiery—as particularly American. Bradbury agrees, calling Ahab "the most American character in all our literature" (qtd. in Grobel 416). And while their Ahab may ultimately be totalitarian—Ishmael refers to him as "our supreme lord and dictator"—he is certainly not a totalitarian Other. We can see this in Huston's handling of the "Quarter Deck" scene. It replaces the compulsive Shakespearean rhetoric with a delivery that is sane, slow, and perhaps even plodding. This is all to say that Huston's casting of a "uniquely American" and ambiguously totalitarian Ahab and a largely irrelevant Ishmael blurs the period's allegorical divisions between democratic self and totalitarian other. But this is not to say that Huston does not understand the novel as Cold War allegory, or even that he does not understand the novel in terms of a basic self/other opposition that underwrites such allegorical readings; it is just that there are no clear absolute others among the human characters. The clearest other in the film is that "thing behind the mask," both alien and nature. Huston gets at this by drawing on the filmic conventions of those key genres of science, nature, and the other, science fiction and horror, and in doing so, he both blurs the allegorical positions of the human characters and uses 1950s visuals to disrupt "the continuist and homogeneous time reproduced within U.S. literature and history" that underwrite the period's allegorical readings of Melville (Pease *Arizona* 14).

Allegorical readings like Matthiessen's and Chase's assume a certain transhistorical equation (or "continuist and homogeneous time") between distinct periods, and in many ways, Huston is visually attempting to be faithful not only to Melville, but to the 1850s as a distinct period. For instance, the film achieves a kind of realism (and fidelity to the novel) with its surprising visual attention to the stuff and the labor of whaling, much of it shot on location. Other choices are more ambiguous. Huston's title sequence consists of reproductions of nineteenth-century etchings and whaling books. Grobel notes that the "look [Huston] wanted was the harsh, masculine tones based on the steel engravings of nineteenth-century sailing ships" (423). It is significant in terms of realism, though, that the film does not first show us the nineteenth century by reproducing characters, settings, costumes, and the like, but through a series of images drawn directly from the period itself. The opening credits evoke the period realistically by reproducing its images, but they also suggest the mediated nature of period representation by reproducing pages from books. This ambiguity is reinforced through the film's use of Technicolor. Technicolor has a strained realism in that it is, like the real world, in color, but it also tends to foreground its color unrealistically. Huston had cinematographer Oswald Morris desaturate the film's color by combining it with a black-and-white negative, which, while correcting the hyper-realism of Technicolor, was aimed at recreating the look of the period's whaling books.[1] These initial engravings and the overall look of whaling books in the film foreground visual mediation, where historical period is signified through visual style. As we will see, a visual split between 1851 and 1956 emerges in a set of key scenes that seem very much informed, both visually and thematically, by the overlapping genres of science fiction and monster movie so key to the 1950s Cold War period style, in both their Technicolor and black-and-white B-movie varieties.

Grobel reports that when Huston approached Bradbury to write the screenplay, Bradbury asked, "Are you a Freudian? A Jungian? A Melville Society man?" to which Huston replied, "I want Ray Bradbury's *Moby-Dick*" (417). In 1953, the young Bradbury was already famous for his many science fiction, monster, and weird tales, especially *The Martian Chronicles, Fahrenheit 451*, and two films from that year based on his work: *The Beast from 20,000 Fathoms* (loosely based on his story, "The Fog Horn") and *It Came from Outer Space* (for which he contributed considerable screenwriting). Huston, then, seems to have wanted a *Moby-Dick* that shared some aspect of the visual or thematic language of science fiction. Further, in his introduction to the screenplay, William F. Touponce reports that Huston chose Bradbury "on the strength of Bradbury's poetic style" in "The Fog Horn" specifically (8). The story is certainly poetic in that its evocation of both the sea and the monster's loneliness makes heavy use of Bradbury's signature lyrical repetition, but it is also a story of a sea monster who falls in love with a lighthouse, which it then destroys, and one can imagine how a love story between a monster and a lighthouse might have appealed to a director making a film about the perverse psychic identification between human and beast. I do not want to suggest that Huston simply turns *Moby-Dick* into a 1950s science fiction, monster, disaster film. For one, Bradbury's approach to science fiction significantly resists the standard mapping of self/other onto human/alien that the genre writ large connotes. Grobel quotes Huston as admiring "something of Melville's elusive quality in [Bradbury's] work," and that elusive quality might refer to the latter's consistent troubling of self/other dichotomies. However, science fiction's language of both disaster and the other is a crucial context for his visual adaptation of what is, after all, a novel that ends with monstrous havoc and disaster and that meditates deeply on the relationship between self and other. At four points in the film, at least, Huston engages with genre conventions associated with science fiction and horror, and these involve subtle but significant revisions to Melville's novel: Ishmael's first encounter with Queequeg at the Spouter-Inn (ch. 3); the scene in which Ahab shows Starbuck his whaling charts (a conflation of chs. 36, 44, and 109); the long period of waiting before the final chase (culminating in chs. 119–20); and then the final chase that concludes both novel and film. The elements I will discuss are not, for the most part, in the writer's script Bradbury delivered to Huston in February 1954, which means that Huston himself either added the elements that one might associate with Bradbury, or at least added them in dialogue with the latter as the two produced the shooting script.

I will not dwell over Huston's treatment of the Spouter-Inn, and indeed Huston is pretty faithful to the bait-and-switch this chapter performs, from Ishmael's initial curious fear of the cannibal, to their quick

Figure 13.1. Queequeg's shrunken head looms in a way that suggests earlier B-film horror movies.

bonding as "bosom friends" (27). However, in executing this bait-and-switch, Huston relies on some of the genre conventions of horror, and while these are more associated with 1930s horror, they fit into a pattern of drawing from B film to highlight Melville's blurring of otherness. First, Huston's casting of his friend, the aristocratic Austrian, Friedrich von Ledebur, as the tattooed Pacific Islander Queequeg may seem like an odd choice—and Peter Viertel has noted this among the film's purported failures—but it is also not unlike casting the English Boris Karloff as Imhotep's mummy or the Swedish Warner Oland as Fu Manchu (Viertel 210). That is, the mismatch between character and actor places this scene in a long-standing tradition of using white European actors for exoticized horror, even if here, as in Melville, the scene moves from horror to fraternity, a fraternity perhaps underwritten by the actors' shared whiteness. So too do the scene's visuals trade in horror. Melville's New Bedford is certainly dreary and cold, but in both Bradbury and Huston, it is horror's "dark and stormy night," lit by lightning flashes through rain-streamed windows and soundtracked with only rain and thunder until Queequeg's entrance. In Melville, the only lightning we get is internal, metaphorical, when Ishmael's thoughts about tattooing "pass . . . through [him] like lightning" (29). And finally, while Huston is visually interested in Queequegs's tattoos (reportedly reproducing them faithfully from the novel's descriptions), he introduces him first through the shrunken head he carries. In Melville, of course, there is plenty of discussion of the "New Zealand head" that his bedmate is out peddling, but most of this is with the innkeeper, and the head does not provide the visual interest to the bedroom scene that the tattoos do. Ishmael first merely notes that Queequeg is carrying "that identical New Zealand head" in one hand, and then, after a much longer description of Queequeg's tattoos, he shows us the head one more time, briefly, as Queequeg takes "the New Zealand head—a ghastly thing enough—and cram[s] it down into the bag" (28–29). In Huston, this "ghastly thing" is highlighted. Its revelation follows a crescendo in both the thunder and the ominous soundtrack that had commenced upon Queequeg's entrance, and we then see the head, lit by alternating lightning and shadow, in a sudden close-up zoom, sustained for several seconds, while Ishmael cowers in bed. At this moment, Huston obeys the genre conventions of any number of zombie, mummy, and monster movies in fetishizing the exotic horror object. The dramatic energy of the scene quickly moves away from horror, but the significant point is that Huston visually foregrounds and subtly parodies B-film horror conventions and iconography in order to reproduce Melville's movement from exoticism to fraternity, and this tendency to lean on B-film when adapting the novel's meditations on self/other continues throughout the film.

While the Spouter-Inn sequence draws from B horror, later moments draw more from science fiction monsters, and especially from the visual iconography of the monster as it develops after the exploding of the atomic bomb. Huston's film references its own nuclear context in its chart scene. Ahab's chart centers on Bikini Atoll, the site of US nuclear weapons testing between 1946 and 1958 (and thus ongoing during the film's production and release). In Melville, Ahab's chart solves a problem—how to pursue the "absurdly hopeless task thus to seek out one solitary creature in the unhooped oceans of the planet"—and it does so instrumentally, by calculating tides, seasons, food migration, and the like (171). In the film, it functions in essentially the same manner, although Huston's chart is both more expansive, collating all the whaling knowledge of all whalers, and more precise: it predicts that the Pequod will meet Moby Dick at precisely "the new moon and April" at Bikini Atoll. And while the dialogue here does not mention Bikini, that location is visually highlighted—the camera zooms to a close-up of Ahab's finger pointing at Bikini—and in case we missed it, both Ishmael and Ahab later mention Bikini. Furthermore, Bradbury's screenplay makes no mention of Bikini. It does, however, revise Melville's depiction of the charts, tweaking his mid-nineteenth-century image of a rationalized chaos with a gothic image of mutation and monstrosity. Melville shows us Ahab's nightly "pencil mark . . . threading a maze of eddies and currents"—his interest is in calculation and instrumentality—whereas Bradbury's charts look like this:

> Great half-human winds blow across some of them with terrible pouched faces. Others are inhabited by nightmarish beasts. For a moment we look at the finned and gilled and scaled monstrosities in the illumination shed by the lantern which creaks from the beams overhead and casts a constantly reshifted light upon the paper continents, seas, and great nightmares therein. (84)

As with the early move from Ishmael's "ideas passing . . . like lightning" to the dark and stormy night, this is first of all an externalization of something Melville describes as internal—Ahab's own nightmares—and in this it relies on an expressionism associated with horror, producing an uncanny, gothic sense of nature as both self and other. As Touponce notes, "Bradbury's prose film links Starbuck's and our gaze at the charts with Ahab's nightmare-ridden sleep" (10). Touponce goes on to regret that Huston did not film the scene exactly as Bradbury had scripted it, and indeed Huston's chart does not reproduce Bradbury's visuals of "nightmarish beasts," but Huston does make a similar move in replacing Bradbury's gothic revision with a nuclear revision.

In place of Bradbury's monsters, Huston adds Bikini, which is in effect what Warner Bros. had added to Bradbury's "The Fog Horn" when they made *The Beast from 20,000 Fathoms*. To be sure, Huston's whale is not unleashed by the nuclear bomb, as it frequently is in many films of the genre, but it is implicitly made into a nuclear monster. Further, it recodes Melville's chart into the charts that frequently accompany scientists—mad or otherwise—in the period's disaster films. In her survey of the genre, Sontag notes that in many of these films, "there is a comparatively old-fashioned looking conference room, where the scientist brings charts to explain the desperate state of things to the military" (44). The scientists that Sontag is referring to here are mostly sane if desperate, while Ahab's sanity is entirely the question at this point in the film. He is the epitome of instrumental reason, and although he awakes from a nightmare when Starbuck enters, he seems completely reasonable as he explains the charts. However, after Starbuck's charge of blasphemy (which comes immediately after the visual of Bikini), as Ahab moves from the chart itself to his speech about the "thing behind the mask," he is slightly above camera and underlit, his eyes nearly flipped back in his head, so that the slow zoom to his face during this speech presents him through the expressionist angling and lighting of a horror villain or mad scientist.

This visual coding of Ahab as the mad scientist is especially significant when we consider that his monologue is loosely adapted from the "Quarter-Deck" chapter. For one, as noted, the line "the thing behind the mask" is not exactly from Melville and is reminiscent of science fiction film titles. For Sontag, science fiction's predilection for it/thing titles is significant because those films constitute "a popular mythology for the contemporary *negative* imagination about the impersonal. The other-world creatures which seek to take 'us' over are an 'it,' not a 'they' . . . Their movements are either cool, mechanical, or lumbering, blobby. . . . If they are non-human in form, they proceed with an absolutely regular, unalterable movement (unalterable save by destruction)" (47, emphasis in original). In Huston's chart scene, Ahab is clearly tracking a lumbering, blobby, regular, unalterable, and mechanical it/thing to the scene of destruction. But the Cold War "negative imagination about the impersonal" is also an imagination of totalitarianism, in which "we" become likewise "mechanical" things, whereas the signal chapter of *Moby-Dick* for totalitarian allegories is precisely "The Quarter-Deck," and precisely for the compelling rhetoric that Bradbury and Huston excise from that scene and move here, below deck, surrounded not by a frenzied crew but by a scientist's charts. This restaging suggests a shift from anxieties surrounding the rhetorical compulsion of totalitarian leaders to anxieties surrounding scientific rationality in the atomic age, anxieties dramatized two years before the film's release in the J. Robert Oppenheimer hearings, and in this light we should recall Huston's observation that Ahab's is "a terrible sanity." But it would be too simple to say that this simply recodes the mad scientist as the nuclear age totalitarian. For one, Ahab's chart is not only about control; it is also about a strong identification between the scientist and the nature he studies, and an exchange with Starbuck is revealing on this point:

> AHAB: I know their hidden journeys as I know the veins in my arm.
>
> STARBUCK: You mean their journeys can be foretold?
>
> AHAB: Aye, like the blood pumping in my veins, from heart to hand.

Melville's text simply notes that whales travel in "veins," so the addition of Ahab's simile here foregrounds the identification of the scientist's self with the malevolent other of nature through the instrumentality of the chart. It is also at this point that Starbuck charges Ahab with blasphemy, and the charge is twofold, both seeking vengeance on a dumb brute (which is from Melville) and wasting oil and money (which is not). Ahab's response, taken from "The Quarter-Deck" and lit as a mad scientist, continues to correlate that chapter's concerns with totalitarianism and "The Chart"'s concerns with science, but it also figures the atomic scientist as a sort of tragic hero, and again Oppenheimer seems resonant:

> All visible objects are but as pasteboard masks. Some inscrutable, reasoning thing puts forth the molding of their features . . . Yet [the whale] is but a mask. It is the thing behind the mask I chiefly hate, the malignant thing that has plagued and frightened man since time began, the thing that mauls and mutilates our race, not killing us outright but letting us live on, with half a heart and half a lung.

In some ways, Ahab's goals seem humanitarian here, to track and kill "the malignant thing," the principle of destruction. And so too are anxieties about the impersonal (all those undead pod people of science fiction) suggested in the final line (the language of which is adapted from ch. 41, *Moby-Dick*). That is, the chart scene uses the scene of totalitarianism,

Figure 13.2. Ahab tames St. Elmo's Fire.

"The Quarter-Deck," to register both nuclear and totalitarian anxieties in the unstable figure of the mad scientist as tragic hero.

While the film's allusions to Bikini remain far subtler than the sometimes crude nuclear allegories of monster movies, they do nevertheless inform the film's resolution, both the period of waiting in still waters that precedes the sighting of the white whale and then the final, climactic chase. In the film, the period before the chase culminates in the St. Elmo's fire scene (ch. 119, "The Candles"), and David Lavery has noted that this involves revisions to the climax's pacing and plotting. For one, Lavery notes, "[Bradbury] delayed Ahab's [. . .] taming of St. Elmo's Fire [. . .] until after his refusal to aid the captain of *The Rachel*'s hunt for his lost son," and for another, "Queequeg's realization of his coming death likewise departs substantially from the novel" in that Queequeg does not succumb to a fever but instead "reads the signs of his death while casting bones [. . . and is] roused from his deathwatch only when his friend's life is threatened" (97). While Lavery sees these revisions as needless, they actually make a good deal of sense once the setting for the film's climax has been marked as Bikini. In the novel, Queequeg has the carpenter build the coffin before the *Pequod* reaches the Pacific, whereas here the scene is reframed as part of the ship's waiting at Bikini, making Queequeg's coffin more emphatically a response to doomsday prophecy. Likewise, moving "The Candles" nearer to the end makes that scene more of a climax and makes the period that precedes it characterized by waiting. On purely dramatic grounds, Lavery might be justified in questioning whether this "enhance[s] the drama," but the revision of the novel's pacing also needs to be understood in a Cold War context, in which time was frequently described as wavering between "unremitting banality and inconceivable terror" (Sontag 42). The film's clearer division between the period of waiting and the final image of destruction repaces Melville's climax according to a Cold War temporality, one that shifts at the moment of St. Elmo's fire and the typhoon. The visuals in the scenes up to and including "The Candles" depart most from the film's use of desaturated Technicolor and its corresponding realism. The crew members, mostly shirtless, perspiring in the heat, are scattered and slumped about the deck. This is a period in which Ahab keeps a long, sleepless watch for the whale, his pacing leg marking time while the crew members comment on the fact that nothing is moving. Quite different from the rest of the film, the scene, in key recurring shots, looks bombed out, bathed in a red-orange haze, lit by an equally hazy sun superimposed against a radiating doubloon. While this is not solely an expression of the period's radiation anxiety, these shots, set so close to Bikini, do radiate, and the way they mark the pacing of the sequence connects radiation to temporality. The slow doomsday of radiation, then, seems to inform much of the action of the scene, which is keyed toward low-level madness. I have already mentioned that this setting frames Queequeg's premonitions of his own death, and it is worth noting that, as a Pacific Islander, he is closer to the deaths of the Bikini islanders than are the other characters. Likewise, he is jarred from his death reverie when Ishmael gets into a knife fight, which Ishmael initiates after another crew member begins carving new tattoos into Queequeg's chest. That is, the setting and its pacing seem to have occasioned a sort of generalized madness that parallels Ahab's own, but that also seems to proceed from the setting and pacing, making the crew as much subject to Bikini and aberrant nature as to Ahab's totalitarian rule. For instance, Pip's madness seems to proceed not from the experience of earlier of being thrown overboard but from the "unremitting banality" of this scene's setting and pacing. So too is Ahab's own madness confirmed only after this period, in the scene with the *Rachel*, when Ahab refuses to aid in the search for the captain's son. Whereas lighting had suggested his madness in the chart scene, Peck had nevertheless played the part with the slowness and "terrible sanity" described earlier. When he turns from the *Rachel*'s captain, though, he seems visibly pained, as if repressing a final impulse toward humanity, and in the following scene, baptizing the harpooners' lances, he is indeed the wild-eyed, twitchy madman that Bradbury had scripted from the outset.

This madness is then visually linked to science fiction when, in the middle of the typhoon, Ahab extinguishes a very green, very Technicolor St. Elmo's fire. The green light that Ahab extinguishes does not come from either Melville or Bradbury. Bradbury's light is, true to Melville, "a pallid fire," a "supernatural color," and a "pale forked flame" (156). Melville's light is pale, ghostly, and described numerous times as linked to whiteness. Huston's fire comes instead from the science fiction films of the period. It uses the same technology, for one thing, a superimposed Technicolor animation all the more obtrusive in its color, given that it is superimposed over the already desaturated color negative. It is also the same shade of green as the Martian nuclear rays in *The War of the Worlds* (1953). It is the same green light that bathes the crew throughout *Forbidden Planet* (1956). It is not God's ancient "clear spirit of clear fire," that is, but God's atomic fire, tied visually to the Technicolor of the period's big-budget science fiction films. The green St. Elmo's fire disrupts the film's period realism in several ways: it calls attention to its status as a 1950s effect; it includes a visual associated with the futuristic in its depiction of the 1850s, thus inserting further temporal dissonance; and it draws from a visual iconography closely associated with nuclear power, thus reframing the scene's anxieties about nature and charisma as particularly nuclear anxieties.

As in the chart scene, this scene also ties the totalitarian allegory to the figure of the mad scientist harnessing nuclear power. The scene includes one of the several lines that suggests Ahab's totalitarianism more overtly. He says to the crew, "You be the cogs that fit my wheel," and his charismatic performance, coupled with that line's mechanical metaphor, brings together the two major tropes of discourse about totalitarianism: the impersonal and the charismatic leader. So too does his single-minded pursuit resonate with any number of science fiction scientists' destructive, single-minded pursuits. However, Ahab does not unleash the monster, nor does he harness St. Elmo's fire except to quench it, to "put out the last fear," as the film has it. Starbuck reads his performance in a way that bridges the scene's nuclear and totalitarian anxieties, when he remarks, immediately after Ahab extinguishes the flame, "Where are the crew of the Pequod? There is not one face I know among thirty. He has snatched their souls . . . I see a madman beget more madmen." The film came out the same year as *Invasion of the Body Snatchers*, so I am suggesting resonance, not influence, when I note that Starbuck's lines about "snatching men's souls" are not in Melville but are very much in 1956 with their concern about "the negative imagination about the impersonal." However, whereas body snatchers are usually alien others (Communists), Ahab is "uniquely American," and it is worth noting the obvious point that only the United States used nuclear weapons.

This nuclear iconography, in turn, informs the "imagination of disaster" that is the whale itself. Melville's whale is obviously a multivalent symbol—of the phallus, of whiteness as an ideological construct, of nature's unreasoning malevolence—and while critics have tended to see Huston's interest in the whale as primarily about the action of the hunt, interviews reveal that he was clearly drawn to it as a multivalent symbol as well. Elaborating on Ahab's "terrible sanity," Huston remarks that "his arrogance was the naked fist raised against the deity. Melville saw the Almighty as a malignant being and the whale as the symbol of God" (28). In a somewhat different formulation, Grobel reports that Huston considered the novel "a blasphemy. The message of *Moby-Dick* was hate. The whale is the mask of a malignant deity. Melville doesn't choose to call the power Satan, but God" (423). The slippage between God and Satan in these formulations resonates with the film's broader blurring of self and other, an ambiguity that seems all the more charged in a nuclear context, in which the split atom seems a malignant other at the heart of both nature and the national self, and in which the mad scientist "putting out the last fear" courts destruction. Thus the whale, as in Melville's final three chapters, is also a giant beast who wreaks seemingly purposeful havoc, rendered as a monster movie era special effect, although he is also not quite wholly other. As Grobel reports, the whale was done with huge, moving models—three of them, ultimately, since the first two were lost at sea, considerably running up the budget. And while other critics have charged that the film reduces Melville's multivalent symbol into "a rubbery special effects whale," I do not want to overemphasize the crudeness of the whale model construction.[2] I do want to call attention to the way those whales are technically, and thus visually, linked to the monster movie as a period style, although they certainly do not rely on the jerky stop-motion animation of B films. That is, they are using contemporaneous technology to work toward both realism and symbolism, and they are doing so in open seas, which both increases the film's realism while making the realism of the whale's motion harder to control. In this they visually cannot help but foreground the failure of verisimilitude, which is to say they cannot help but foreground the technological limitations of period reproduction. Huston noted his own sense of failure regarding the look of the whale after seeing Steven Spielberg's *Jaws*:

> I wasn't imaginative to dream of doing what Spielberg and Lucas and those guys do today . . . You could hardly see the teeth of our whale. In *Jaws* you couldn't help seeing anything *but* the shark's teeth. It was gory, and if you could have had some of that gore and action in *Moby Dick*, it would have made the film work better . . . [The technology] wasn't there because no one invented it . . . *I should have invented it.* (Grobel 429, emphasis in original)

Huston's jealousy of *Jaws* is a jealousy of verisimilitude, but in his description of this jealousy, he betrays a conflict at the heart of visualizing period. He casts this jealousy as his own failure to be technologically forward looking, when in fact his regret is more complicated: in not being technologically forward looking, he failed to capture his desire for a backward-looking film (to recreate the 1850s whale hunt in all its realistic violence), while his own depiction of the 1850s, in drawing on science fiction and monster movies, is therefore drawing on a genre that foregrounds its own forward-looking technology.

In order to see this, we must look not at the big-budget science fiction films that share with *Moby Dick* both Technicolor and a larger budget, but at the lower-budget B films like the already-noted *The Beast from 20,000 Fathoms*. The giant lizard in that film is rendered through Ray Harryhausen's stop-motion animation, and the film stars Kenneth Tobey. Tobey plays an air force pilot who eventually tracks and kills the monster, a role which basically reprises his roles in 1951's *The Thing from Another World* and *It Came from Beneath the Sea* (1955). In addition to the resonance of all of these film titles with *Moby Dick*, the last of them centers around a (completely sane, if chauvinistic) navy captain hunting and killing a giant octopus. Released by Columbia Pictures the year before Huston's film, it frequently draws on both the language and the visuals of whaling, noting many times that the octopus is "bigger than any whale" and calling its hunt Operation Sea Beast, in a possible allusion to Warner Bros.' 1926 adaptation of *Moby-Dick*. Operation Sea Beast ultimately kills the octopus after the heroine, Prof. Lesley Joyce (Faith Domergue) talks with some "old whalemen" and designs a nuclear torpedo modeled on a whaling harpoon. Although the torpedoes do not ultimately hit their mark, the beast is finally killed when the men of the crew, after the beast's extensive destruction of San Francisco, catch it resting underwater and stab it in the brain with nuclear harpoons. The climax of this film resembles that in *Moby Dick*, in that in both films, we are shown protagonists stabbing at a vast visual expanse of monster centered around the monster's eye. In *Moby Dick*, this involves one of the film's most significant revisions, when Ahab leaps atop the whale and literalizes his "from hell's heart I stab at thee" speech. While this scene is sufficiently effective as both revision and climax, I am particularly interested in the attention to the whale's eye. That attention seems to have been a sticking point for contemporaneous critics. William Murray remarks, "[By] this time I think I've heard all the objections [including] the one about the close-up of the whale's malevolent blue eye."

During the chase scenes in Melville, the whale's eye is not in fact mentioned. In these chapters, Melville's visual interest is in the jaw and the battering ram–like forehead. (Huston pays visual attention to these as well, his jealousy of *Jaws* notwithstanding.) Melville does discuss the whale's eyes in ch. 74, "The Sperm Whale's Head," but there the eye is notably hard to locate, and it is presented as a prelude to Ishmael's phenomenological meditation on the difference between human and whale vision. In the film, besides a couple of incidental, long-distance glimpses, the whale's eye is shown twice in close-up, both times through shot/countershot with Ahab, and in both of these, shot/countershot and angling suggest that Ahab is the object of the whale's gaze. The first of these is when the whale first rises: we see his eye, then Ahab looking, then a closer shot of the whale's eye, and then Ahab throwing his harpoon. The second is as Ahab climbs onto the whale after his boat has been smashed, and Ahab's climbing is again framed by two shots of the whale's eye, in the second angled (and sustained) to watch Ahab. Further, these shots follow almost immediately after a scene between Ahab and Starbuck (adapted from the "mild, mild day" speech in "The Symphony") in which an emphatic and sustained shot/countershot of Starbuck's and Ahab's eyes, in extreme close-up, follow Ahab's request to "look into a human eye" and visualize the ambiguous opposition between Ahab and Starbuck. In both Huston and Melville, to "look into a human eye . . . is better than to gaze into sea or sky," but the parallel between "The Symphony" eye shots and the "Chase" eye shots knits them together in a visual meditation on otherness (Melville 444). For one, it makes the whale more of a subject, which he is throughout the novel, although interestingly not in Melville's final chapters. But in doing so, it also enforces an identification with the thing behind the mask, the malevolent nature, and the unfeeling wall of destruction figured in the whale's expanse, teeth, jaws, and battering ram–like forehead. That is, it produces a blurring of the self/other distinction at work in nuclear allegory.

The film's whale eye is then true to the novel's broader rendering of the whale as both subject and other, but in this it is also true to the visual iconography of monster movies, especially those associated with Bradbury. Most significantly, the horror of Bradbury's own *It Came from Outer Space* centers on the alien's single, almost human eye in an otherwise monstrously nonhuman form, and the advertisements for the 3D version of the film feature the eye prominently. Further, the drama of that film revolves around a complicated play of self and other, in that the aliens are in fact benign and only assume human form because they recognize that humans cannot tolerate the image of the other. Besides the shots of the alien eye, the film also makes use of subjective camera shots from the aliens' perspective, an effect that Bradbury himself proposed. This is all then very similar to the way Huston frames the whale's eye with Ahab's and Starbuck's "human eye" and then frames Ahab with the whale's own eye (where shot/countershot effects a move like Bradbury's subjective camera), and it likewise recalls the line that ends Ishmael's opening monologue in the film: "the sea, where each man as in a mirror finds himself."

As I have argued, the film's casting of Ahab and Ishmael consistently avoids or blurs the geopolitical self/other dichotomies that inform those Cold War readings of *Moby-Dick* most interested in democracy and totalitarianism, and it does so in part by shifting focus to a malevolent nature, figured in the whale, as its key other. However, there is also a final turn, and one that seems at least in part informed by the nuclear anxieties surrounding Bikini and the figure of the mad scientist, by which the whale cannot be wholly other if Ahab is not wholly other. These turns in Huston's drama of self and other, finally, produce an interesting and fairly complex relay between Melville's text and 1956, in that the film's nuclear iconography, seemingly most unfaithful to Melville in inserting the Cold War into an 1850 text, is also what allows Huston to remove *Moby-Dick* from the contemporaneous Cold War critical framework and to foreground the novel's own complex blurring of self and other, democracy and compulsion, and scientific rationality and aberrant nature.

Notes

1. See Laws 126.
2. See Metz 222.

Works Cited

Arnold, Jack, dir. *It Came from Outer Space*. 1953. Universal, 2002. DVD.
Bradbury, Ray. *Moby Dick: A Screenplay*. Burton, MI: Subterranean, 2008.
Cahir, Linda Costanzo. "Routinizing the Charismatic: Melville and Hollywood's Three *Moby-Dick*s." *Melville Society Extracts* 110 (1997): 11–17.
Gordon, Robert, dir. *It Came from beneath the Sea*. 1955. Sony, 2003. DVD.

Grobel, Lawrence. *The Hustons: The Life and Times of a Hollywood Dynasty*. New York: Scribner's, 1989.
Haskin, Byron, dir. *The War of the Worlds*. 1953. Paramount, 1999. DVD.
Huston, John, dir. *Moby Dick*. 1956. MGM, 2001. DVD.
Lavery, David. "Melville's *Moby-Dick* and Hollywood." *Nineteenth-Century American Fiction on Screen*. Ed. Barton Palmer. New York: Cambridge UP, 2007. 94–105.
Laws, Page. "King Adapter: Huston's Famous and Infamous Adaptations of Literary Classics." *John Huston: Essays on a Restless Director*. Ed. Tony Tracy and Roddy Flynn. Jefferson, NC: McFarland, 2010. 123–35.
Long, Robert Emmet, ed. *John Huston: Interviews*. Jackson: UP of Mississippi, 2001.
Lourié, Eugène, dir. *The Beast from 20,000 Fathoms*. 1953. Warner, 2003. DVD.
Melville, Herman. *Moby-Dick*. 1851. Norton Critical Edition. Ed. Harrison Hayford and Hershel Parker. New York: W. W. Norton, 1967.
Metz, Walter C. "The Cold War's 'Undigested Apple-Dumpling': Imagining *Moby-Dick* in 1956 and 2001." *Literature/Film Quarterly* 32.3 (2004): 222–28.
Murphy, Geraldine. "Ahab as Capitalist, Ahab as Communist: Revising *Moby-Dick* for the Cold War." *Surfaces* 4.201 (1994):. Web. 16 June 2014.
Murray, William. "Movies: *Moby Dick*." *Village Voice* (17 Oct. 1956). Web.
Nyby, Christian, dir. *The Thing from Another World*. 1951. Turner, 2003. DVD.
Pease, Donald E. "C. L. R. James, *Moby-Dick*, and the Emergence of Transnational American Studies." *Arizona Quarterly* 56.3 (2000): 91–123.
———. "*Moby Dick* and the Cold War." *The American Renaissance Reconsidered*. Ed. Walter Benn Michaels and Donald E. Pease. Baltimore: Johns Hopkins UP, 113–55.
Sontag, Susan. "The Imagination of Disaster." *Commentary* (Oct. 1965): 42–48.
Vasey, Margaret. "Perspectives on Narration: When Word Becomes Action in *Moby-Dick*—Text to Film." *Varieties of Filmic Expression*. Ed. Douglas Radcliff-Umstead. Kent, OH: 1989. 142–47.
Viertel, Peter. *Dangerous Friends: At Large with Hemingway and Huston in the Fifties*. New York: Doubleday, 1992.
Wilcox, Fred McLeod, dir. *Forbidden Planet*. 1956. Warner Home Video, 2010. DVD.

Part III

Theory and Psychoanalysis

14

David Sigler

Huston's *Freud*

Adapting the Life of Psychoanalysis

Though ostensibly a biopic about Freud, John Huston's film *Freud: The Secret Passion* (1962) is also an adaptation of Freud's landmark study coauthored with Josef Breuer, *Studies on Hysteria* (1895). Huston creates characters named Cecily Koertner (played by Susannah York) and Carl von Schlossen (played by David McCallum), who, in being analyzed by Freud and Breuer, disclose their secret desires. Over the course of the film, the sessions give rise to the concepts of transference, dream analysis, the Oedipus complex, infantile sexuality, and the unconscious.[1] In Cecily and Carl, Huston brings together elements from the five case studies in *Studies on Hysteria*, as well as some later works by Freud. The integration of later Freudian concepts into these case studies, however fictionalized, may be problematic for literalist viewers—it's not like Anna O. was actually treated by Freud or that her case involved dream interpretation. Yet I would like to suggest that Huston's handling of these concepts is not as anachronistic as it may initially appear and that some of the film's inventions represent Huston's effort to confront complex problems that arise out of the material in *Studies on Hysteria*. The film adapts Freud and Breuer's work with admirable care—Marie-Andrée Charbonneau is right to say that "no *lèse-majesté* is committed here. Freud's life and work are not really misrepresented"— and reveals the difficulties, conceptual and narrative, that interfere with

Figure 14.1. Freud bends over a waking patient as Breuer looks on.

all attempts to discuss psychoanalysis through the conventions of biography (Charbonneau 88). Huston's film seeks on the one hand to rehearse a life story, and on the other to introduce psychoanalytic concepts to a mass audience. Caught between biography and theory, Huston chooses theory. He does not merely simplify and stylize Freud's life story, as would be expected with a biopic; instead, he largely turns his back on Freud's biography to grant psychoanalytic ideas biographies of their own. Yet as theory makes its own narrative demands, Freud's life here proves inseparable from his ideas.

As an adaptation of *Studies on Hysteria*, Huston's film is immediately interesting for several reasons. For one, it's highly unusual to adapt works of theory into Hollywood feature films, this one for Universal Pictures and starring big-time actor Montgomery Clift, whose career was temporarily ruined by the box-office failure of the film (Holland 286). Second, Huston is working with ideas that had from the start been conceptualized cinematically. Much has already been written about the ways that cinema and psychoanalysis intersect and sustain each other (Metz; Žižek; Lebeau). One might also note that *Studies on Hysteria*, which was published in the same year that cinema made its public debut in the United States, occasionally draws upon the nascent language of film, or film-like concepts, to conceptualize hysteria (Lebeau 1). Freud describes Elisabeth von R., for instance, in the following way: "It was as though she were reading a lengthy book of pictures, whose pages were being turned before her eyes" (*Studies* 153). Theorizing the formation of hysterical symptoms, Freud describes a process that closely resembles film editing: "The whole spatially-extended mass of psychogenic material is in this way drawn through a narrow cleft and thus arrives in consciousness cut up, as it were, into pieces or strips" (*Studies* 291). Thus Huston can be said to be giving direct technological expression to hysteria as Freud first construed it. A third source of interest resides in the competition between two source texts within the adaptation. Huston, working with screenwriter Charles Kaufman, who famously took over the project from Jean-Paul Sartre, draws upon the standard biography of Freud, Ernest Jones's *The Life and Work of Sigmund Freud*, but emphatically and unexpectedly shifts the focus of the film away from Freud to *Studies on Hysteria* and, thus, to the psychoanalytic concepts themselves. Although Clift-as-Freud appears onscreen constantly, he is primarily there to announce new ways of thinking. The film eschews biography in any traditional sense, preferring to treat the formulation of theoretical concepts as its plot points. The gesture is, in itself, I think, a particularly Freudian one: Freud's own *Autobiographical Study* similarly avoids details of its author's life, electing instead to trace the history of psychoanalytic reason.

Nevertheless, Huston's film, in narrating the life of a theoretical notion rather than that of a human being, does so in the film genre least equipped to recognize and maintain that distinction: the biopic. Huston embraces many of the clichés of the Great Man film, as per Dennis Bingham's discussion of the genre: it employs an opening voice-over to position Freud within a line of transformational figures (Copernicus and Darwin); it begins just at the moment when Freud is about to make his intervention, as he leaves the hospital to study under Charcot; it makes extensive use of flashbacks; its protagonist overcomes his meddlesome family, especially his mother, wife, and late father; it gives its hero a sidekick-mentor Breuer, and difficult mentor, Theodor Meinert (4–5). However, the overall tone of the film challenges the Great Man formal structure. Huston is conflating two familiar modes of biopic, the idol of production and idol of consumption film, such that Freud's meteoric brilliance is his very willingness to appreciate himself as damaged goods (Custen). *Freud* tells an old-fashioned hero-scientist story, but only through the excavation, revelation, and narration of its subject's hideous flaws and ugly wishes. Huston's Freud learns the mechanisms of the unconscious by hypnotizing and, later, psychoanalyzing patients, and then applying the lessons learned to his own childhood. Freud's derivation and testing of psychoanalytic insights, one after the next, constitute the plot of the film. It is here that Huston begins to collapse the boundaries between analyst and hysteric, and between psychoanalytic concept and biographical event.

Any project seeking to curate a history of psychoanalytic thought will be frustrated by a structurally necessary "internal contradiction," argues Jacques Derrida (19). This is because not everything that pertains to Freud personally would necessarily be pertinent to psychoanalysis. Yet the nature of psychoanalysis—its insistence upon investigating forgotten family histories or tracing intersubjective networks, as experienced through ancillary objects and heirlooms—ensures that Freud's life remains embedded in the theory (Derrida 20). To complicate this question yet more, psychoanalysis avers the possibility, even necessity, of repression, even as it maintains itself as an archive of deeply personal case histories. In this way, the archive that is psychoanalysis is illimitable, and there is no space outside of psychoanalysis through which to chronicle its development or offer biographical accounts of Freud's life. Derrida has claimed that although historians of psychoanalysis must, if they are to remain historians, approach Freud from an unpsychoanalytic perspective, they nevertheless "cannot have this exteriority," given the illimitability of psychoanalysis and the way that Freud is embroiled in it personally (53–55). Having traced this double bind, Derrida concludes his book *Archive Fever: A Freudian Impression* by expressing "compassion" for Freud: "We will always wonder what, in this *mal d'archive*, he may have burned. We will always wonder, sharing with compassion in this archive fever, what may have burned of his secret passions, of his correspondence, or of his 'life'" (101). By putting "life" in scare quotes, Derrida suggests that Freud may not have been capable of having a biography, given his "secret passions." Although the phrase recalls the title of Huston's film, I don't sense that Derrida was necessarily aware of Huston's film—he doesn't ever mention it. Nonetheless, the double bind destabilizing "life" in *Archive Fever* reminds us that *Freud: The Secret Passion* is, in just this way, "exquisitely tormented": to fulfill its audacious plan of developing the biopic of an idea, it quickly encounters the impossibility of separating Freud from psychoanalysis (Derrida 55).

As Huston's Freud develops his psychoanalytic method, he discovers that his life and work are inseparable: "I invented a theory to dishonor my father," he tells Breuer, who is played by Larry Parks. (The casting of Parks was itself an affirmation of the return of the repressed: this, Parks's final role, came after a decade and more of his blacklisting from

Hollywood.) In the film, as in psychoanalysis, the dead father is pervasive and uncompromising. The film posits its ultimate truths at the grave of several fathers—especially Freud's, but also the fathers of the film's fictional hysterics. The film ends with Freud attending his father's grave, having finally grasped that he has resented his father's response to anti-Semites. Because the film explains its concepts with recourse to Freud's early childhood, the life and work of Sigmund Freud here remain wedded, as they are in Jones's title, awkwardly and tenuously (a point I will return to momentarily). The film is embroiled in archive fever. In the attempt to adapt theory to life writing, the film vacates theory as such, relying instead on the biographical details of Freud's imagined past. In this sense, Jones's work—the biographical material—becomes a lost object, really even a MacGuffin, in this film, no matter how assiduously Huston turns to Freud and Breuer's text for alternative paths.

The task of writing Freud's life is always, Jones says, "a dauntingly stupendous one," even without the need to navigate a Hollywood Production Code or satisfy its expectations for marketability (1.xiii). Describing his project, Jones emphasizes how he is attempting to co-implicate Freud's work and life, "to try to relate his personality and the experience of his life to the development of his ideas" (1.xi). Yet Jones plots Freud's life and work onto overlapping but separate timeline through the construction of "periods," such as "The Breuer Period, 1882–1894," which particularly serves as source material for Huston's film. One is struck, after a while, in Jones's work, by the multidimensionality of Freud's output: it is hard to know which events of 1885 would belong to Freud "the neurologist, 1883–1897," say, as opposed to "The Breuer Period, 1882–1894." Jones has separate chapters for Freud's "Personal Life, 1880–1890" and "Marriage, 1886," as if marriage weren't even part of Freud's "personal life." The structure produces fractures, enabling Freud's life never to impinge upon his work in Jones's telling; they are separate and parallel experiences. One is, in Jones, always reading of either the life *or* work of Sigmund Freud.

Freud, notes Gertrud Koch, was "continually hostile to the idea of being made the subject of a biography" (3), and, as J. B. Pontalis notes also in the editor's preface to *The Freud Scenario*, he specifically dreaded that a film would be made of his discoveries (xvi). Freud valued his privacy and resisted attempts to tell his story. In sharing information with Jones, Freud felt that he had already been quite candid in his published work, and "he had a right to keep private what remained" (1.xi). Hence, although the archive of psychoanalysis seems in many ways illimitable, it finds its limit at the moment of life writing. Archive fever is the name for these limits, which, says Derrida, contain their own transgression within them. Once Breuer makes the revolutionary claim that "*unconscious ideas exist and are operative,*" the boundaries of the archive have been breached irreparably (*Studies* 221). The *Freud* screenplay—both as originally written by Sartre and then, after his resignation, as it was rewritten by seasoned Hollywood screenwriters Kaufman and Wolfgang Reinhard—draws upon elements from Jones's *Life and Work* but emphasizes the intellectual content of *Studies on Hysteria*. It is the tension between these two source texts and the different modes of storytelling they entail—the biographical in Jones, the theoretical in Freud and Breuer—that consumes the film in archive fever. As *Studies on Hysteria* inaugurates the archive delimitation problem in Freud's oeuvre, it's appropriate that Huston encounters the archive contradiction in adapting Freud and Breuer's work for the screen. In this sense, to adapt *Studies on Hysteria* responsibly is to wrestle with the double binds of archive fever, as Huston does.

As Freud reveals his process for developing psychoanalytic concepts in his *Autobiographical Study*, he describes his theoretical progress as the result of a deliberate tradeoff: "This experiment cost me, it is true, my popularity as a doctor, but it brought me convictions which to-day, almost thirty years later, have lost none of their force" (24). One has no choice, then, but to separate Freud's life from his ideas, if one is to respect the Faustian bargain given as the basis of Freud's career. Huston's Freud, too, pits his ideas (or "convictions") against his professional and personal well-being, suggesting that they are inversely related. Huston embraces, as a result, the romantic image of the lone scientist, unappreciated and alone—despite the highly collaborative nature of Breuer's work with Anna O. and Freud's with Breuer.

Cecily and Carl are fictional but combine elements from the case studies of *Studies on Hysteria*. Their cases seem complex when analyzed in the film—there are many twists and turns in the analysis of each—but they are less ambiguous, less vexing than the cases taken up in *Studies on Hysteria*. Cecily and Carl are vehicles through which to show the development of Freud's thinking, and thus the development of the psychoanalytic conceptual apparatus, as clearly as possible. This is itself a Freudian gesture. Freud liked that the Anna O. case was clear-cut. He was pleased about how thoroughly it eliminated the ambiguities so often found in case histories, likening her to a "sea-urchin" in which "the protoplasm of the eggs is transparent" (*Studies* 41). For Freud, the importance of the Anna O. case resides in how unmistakably it illustrates certain psychic mechanisms. Not being beholden to the actual cases, Huston can go yet further in the same direction. He creates fictional cases to illustrate the concepts all the more "transparently"—offering the principles of Freudian theory without the principals. Thus we have Carl, who exemplifies the Oedipus complex with utter, even comic, clarity: the son of a general, he has assaulted his father, saying, "I will bleed you, you filthy swine!" as his father carves the meat for dinner. During analysis, he attacks his father's military uniform with a saber. He explains under hypnosis that he did this because his father "raped a young girl at seventeen, every night"—his mother. This would seem to be one of Huston's most radical departures from *Studies on Hysteria*: the real Freud would not discover the Oedipus complex until *The Interpretation of Dreams* five years later. But Huston delivers clear examples, tidying up the complexity of Freud's world and Sartre's sprawling screenplay in a way that Freud actually might have preferred, were he given license to invent fictions.

Cecily combines many of the case studies from *Studies on Hysteria* and the period just following. She especially resembles Anna O., Freud's patient Elisabeth von R., and, through her "animal deliria," Emmy von N. (62). Her name seems to allude to Cäcilie M., an important patient of Breuer and Freud in the years following the publication of *Studies on Hysteria*, but Huston's Cecily does not suffer from any of Cäcilie's symptoms, and their cases are very different. Cecily is much more akin to Anna O.; it is Carl who is here a poet, as Cäcilie was. Sartre's original scenario, which was far too long to ever become a film, splits out these characters—Dora, Cäcilie, Anna, Mathilde—in a way much more faithful to psychoanalytic history. In the film as it was rewritten after Sartre's resignation, Cecily represents all of these cases. She is disgusted when her dachshund drinks from a golden cup, specifically "one my father gave me." This recalls Breuer's case study, in which Anna can't drink water and is disgusted that her Newfoundland dog drank water from a glass, yet the dachshund seems to be a reference to Emmy von N., whose small dog was important to her case. Cecily is haunted by a dream of her father's carcass being devoured by cats in Naples, which further recalls Anna O., who was afraid of cats leaping on her, equating that with rape (213). Cecily also shares Anna O.'s preoccupation with snakes (217). By making Cecily a patient first of Breuer and then Freud, Huston draws from the Emmy von N. case (53–54).

Huston very often, with his account of Cecily, ignores Jones's work. It was Jones who revealed Anna O.'s real existence as Bertha Pappenheim, for instance. Jones explains that Pappenheim was a friend of Freud's wife, Martha, and a groundbreaking social worker and women's rights activist (1.225). Huston does not incorporate these elements into the character Cecily, which suggests that his source material for Cecily is primarily *Studies on Hysteria*. Yet Huston includes some elements from Jones: Huston's Breuer becomes ensnared in countertransference with Cecily, just as Jones explains what happened in Anna O.'s case.

With the analyses of Cecily and Carl, Huston calls attention to repressed desire for parents and the mental processes of condensation and displacement. Both of these concepts were actually first outlined in *The Interpretation of Dreams*, but here they get applied to cases clearly derived from *Studies on Hysteria*. In the film, these desires, once finally acknowledged, lead Freud to reflect upon his own parents and the impression they made on him—and, by extension, the impression they have made upon psychoanalysis. The film does not really sympathize with the patients or hope for them to suffer less. Rather, Huston emphasizes the reasoning process by which Freud, through analysis of Cecily and Carl, develops many of the key early psychoanalytic concepts. In this way, the film isn't so much about Freud or his patients directly, but rather about how Freud learned to interpret his patients' desires. Freud is on a journey of self-discovery here, but to learn about himself he must first understand his patients. (At the very end of the film, the scene fades to the grave of Freud's father, where Huston personally intervenes in a voice-over to remind the viewer that the oracle at Delphi instructed her visitors to "know thyself.") The incidents that comprise *Freud* are arranged into levels, which seem distinct but turn out to be embedded in each other even as they remain parallel. It shares the narrative structure, then, of Dante's *Divine Comedy*—indeed, when planning his film, Huston famously wrote in his autobiography that "Freud's descent into the unconscious should be as terrifying as Dante's descent into Hell" (330). As the film progresses, Huston increasingly suggests that the definitive answers to the riddles of psychoanalysis involve the death and burial of Freud's father.

The scene in which Freud and Breuer see Freud's father at his deathbed—a pivotal one, given the logic of the film—visually and thematically recalls an earlier scene, in which Cecily remembers seeing her father's corpse at a brothel. Cecily had thought it was a hospital, but Freud's evolving technique roots out the more unseemly truth. Through the visual and thematic similarities of the scenes, Huston places Freud's father at a metaphorical brothel as well, aligning him implicitly with Carl. Freud, in a sense, becomes part of his patients. The same thing happens as Freud remembers his mother: Cecily's saying the word "bracelet" makes Freud remember his mother's snake bracelet, which recalls an earlier flashback in which young Sigmund watches his mother dress. In interpreting Cecily's case, for instance, Freud returns us, in flashback, to the scene of her father's death repeatedly, each time changing the details in revelatory ways. Freud learns about his own childhood through flashbacks occasioned by Cecily's testimony. The film assures the viewer that Freud's life has always already been structured according to the logic of repression, forgetfulness, and archive fever, yet to discover hidden aspects of Freud's life one must have already mastered the theoretical apparatus of psychoanalysis.

Flashbacks are typical for a biopic but are particularly emphasized in Huston's film. Freud argues in *Studies* that, although hysteria follows "an unmistakable linear chronological order," still "the logical chain corresponds . . . to a ramifying system of lines and more particularly to a converging one. It contains nodal points at which two or more threads meet and thereafter proceed as one" (288, 290). These convergences, as theorized by Freud, form a pattern that is crucial to the visual logic of Huston's film. The goal of analysis, says Freud in *Studies*, is to document "the existence of hidden unconscious motives," and Huston's film goes to elaborate lengths to demonstrate this (293). It does so at the level of content, plumbing Carl and Cecily's repressed desires, but also in its imagery, which often implies that Freud is complicit in hysterical patients' desires. In one early scene, for instance, Freud, along with a room full of other male physicians, is watching his mentor, Jean-Martin Charcot, induce through hypnosis new symptoms in a hysterical patient. The patient, previously psychosomatically paralyzed and veiled, is instructed to mimic the hysterical symptoms of another patient. She thus begins to shake her hands in a way that suggests manual sex. In the scene immediately after, Freud marries Martha. As Martha lifts up her bridal veil before a field of male well-wishers, she too shakes slightly and involuntarily under the gaze of a room full of fascinated men. Freud's personal life thus becomes marked by Charcot's sexual and scientific experimentation, and his marriage takes on the character of a perverse and hysterical sexuality, in which sex acts are performed involuntarily, as a matter of obedience and in mimicry of someone else. The Freuds' wedding, seemingly depicted only for context and to show the boundary between research hospital and private life, becomes compromised by the sexualities that his theory is supposed to have mastered. Meanwhile, Freud's biography has proven inseparable from his ideas in ways that undermine the central wager of this film. What might have seemed, at first blush, like a way for Huston to connect Freud's personal life to his clinical work ends up subordinating both to a greater, more totalizing master: the theory. The film in this sense embodies Breuer's theory from *Studies on Hysteria* that in hysteria, all simultaneous things become linked, so they must be analyzed together (208). In this way of thinking, there is no division possible between text and context, as contextual material is always the thing to be directly analyzed. In making a movie according to this principle, Huston foregrounds, in both the film's form and content, the development of psychoanalytic concepts, minimizing the development of psychoanalytic technique and turning away from the biographical material of Freud and the case histories. The film is literally hysterical: Huston seems to have taken to heart Freud and Breuer's warning that the act of telling a nonfictional story is inevitably so, in that "*hysterics suffer mainly from reminiscences*" (7).

There are multiple acts of reminiscence at work in Huston's film. While Freud is remembering his fictional childhood, Huston is memorializing Freud's collaboration with Breuer. This too is part of Huston's adaptation of *Studies on Hysteria*. Freud speaks in *Studies on Hysteria* of "my honoured teacher and friend Josef Breuer" (266), while much later in the *Autobiographical Study*, he describes Breuer merely as "my friend and helper" (19), whose friendship he had to sacrifice for the development of psychoanalysis. This division was already apparent in *Studies*, where the schism seems to emerge from Freud's sense, which Breuer did not share, that all hysterical symptoms have sexual causes. Freud notes in *Studies* that "in so far as one can speak of determining causes which lead to the *acquisition* of neuroses, their aetiology is to be looked for in *sexual* factors" (257). But he distances his coauthor, Breuer, from this opinion, saying: "It would be unfair if I were to try to lay too much of the responsibility for this development upon my honoured friend Dr. Josef Breuer. For this reason the considerations which follow [e.g., the emphasis on sexual explanations] stand principally under my own name" (256). Huston takes this disagreement, subtly traced in *Studies*, and turns it into the climax of his film. The film is bookended by scenes, almost identical, that begin and end Freud's collaboration with Breuer. In the first scene, Freud presents his findings at a conference only to be mocked by his scientific peers, except for Breuer, who is impressed enough to introduce himself. He expresses enthusiasm for his younger colleague's hotly controversial ideas and offers to collaborate. Near the end of the film, Freud stands in a very similar lecture hall to present his work to the Medical Society. Freud is again ridiculed, this time for his work with Breuer on infantile sexuality and the Oedipus complex, which actually would only become part of Freud's published work with *The Interpretation of Dreams* and *Three Essays on Sexuality*. This time, Breuer's reaction is pointedly different. The Society members, laughing at Freud, turn to Breuer and ask him: "Do you share your collaborator's view?" and "What do you think of infantile sexuality, Dr. Breuer?" He responds: "I do not believe in it. I can never accept it," and everyone claps. It's a heartbreaking scene, as Breuer literally and figuratively turns his back on Freud, ensuring that Freud will stand alone as a historical figure.

These scenes directly contradict Jones's biography, but they exaggerate the tensions apparent in *Studies on Hysteria*. It is true that *Studies* was, in actual fact, poorly received in the medical community (Jones

1.252–53). Breuer and Freud did have a falling out over the latter's perceived overreliance on sexual explanations. Yet Jones, recounting Freud's actual first presentation to the Society, emphasizes the indifference with which Freud had been greeted. The real-life Freud made the presentation on 26 November 1886. He was outlining the case of a male hysteric—the patient was a metal worker, not, like Carl, the son of a general—and Freud's remarks produced mild applause and very limited discussion (1.231). The challenging questions that did ensue took Freud to task for his belief that there could be male hysterics, given the etymology of the word. Despite the generally favorable reaction to his presentation, Freud, Jones says, was always sensitive about that presentation—even strangely sensitive, given the lack of actual hostility expressed (1.229–31). Huston elects to dramatize this as Freud imagined it rather than as it was, but also reimagines it as the occasion when Freud first met Breuer. Huston makes three of the six hysterics in the film male, though this is never presented as controversial in the film. Instead, Huston sensationalizes the division between Breuer and Freud. Although Meyers sees the latter Medical Society scene as Huston's "pedantic way of explaining [Freud's] basic psychological principles in the movie," these scenes are not as straightforward as that (196). My sense is that Breuer is dramatizing tensions quietly explored in *Studies on Hysteria*, and, in so doing, externalizing the encounter with archive fever. Consider how Breuer, in this scene, finds Freud admirable but his ideas repellent. By having Breuer say, "I do not believe in it . . . [and] can never accept it," Huston denotes the unconscious nature of the fantasy at the conclusion of the film: the phrasing is contradictory, in the sense that one would never have to "accept" something that one didn't "believe in." By positing that he won't accept infantile sexuality, Breuer backhandedly acknowledges the soundness of the concept. Once Breuer commits to Freud's personality but not his ideas, the viewer, who has been encouraged to side with Freud, is left to accept Freud's ideas without regard for his personality. Yet Breuer's rebuke signals a shift from the scenario at the beginning of the film; as roughly reminiscent of Freud's "A Child Is Being Beaten," Breuer is no longer merely "looking on" while Freud is being humiliated by his intellectual "fathers," the senior scholars standing in judgment, but is now beating Freud, his intellectual "son," himself.

Huston's film, in this way, takes on the very structure of hysteria, as per *Studies on Hysteria*: it teaches us to read hysteria through flashbacks, free association, and parallel asynchronous story lines; it seeks clear and unambiguous cases; it is made out of reminiscences; it shifts its procedures into the unconscious as it reaches its climax. In this way, the film is a very subtle and sophisticated adaptation of *Studies on Hysteria*, even while it seems to eschew both the particular case histories and the theoretical reflections from that book. Generally, the film is not as anachronistic as it may at first appear. Dream analysis, which is important to the film, actually debuts in *Studies on Hysteria*: Breuer observes that dreams are a "neighboring condition" to hysteria, so one must read them similarly, and Freud presents a long footnote on dream analysis in his discussion of Emmy von N. (19203, 67–70 n.1). *Studies* also introduces the word "overdetermined," a concept central to Cecily's symptoms, into the psychoanalytic lexicon (213). Although Holland claims that Huston's depiction of transference is anachronistic (168), Freud first uses the term in *Studies on Hysteria*—"Transference on to the physician takes place through a *false connection*," he says—and the concept informs Breuer's analysis of Anna O. (*Studies* 302–304, 34). As Holland observes, most of the film's psychoanalytic concepts were actually developed from 1885 through 1897, even if they only became influential later, after *The Interpretation of Dreams*, *A Case of Hysteria*, and *Three Essays on Sexuality* (167–68). By dwelling on these concepts in the cases of Cecily and Carl, Huston emphasizes the groundbreaking work contained in *Studies on Hysteria*: it contains the seeds of a whole clinical vocabulary yet to come. Huston also dramatizes two of the most important arguments of the book, specifically the development of "the talking cure" out of Breuer's work with Anna O. and the claim that hysteria is the cause, not the result, of feminine weakness (*Studies* 231). A careful reading of the text, performed with the benefit of hindsight from the later developments in psychoanalysis, could (and, I am arguing, did) produce *Freud: The Secret Passion* as an adaptation. Still, the film shies away from several of the chief innovations actually featured in *Studies on Hysteria*, such as Freud's technique of pressing on patients' foreheads (110. 270) or the realization by Freud that Breuer's concepts of "retention hysteria" and "hypnoid hysteria" are merely guises for "defense hysteria" (211,286). Huston is reading selectively but carefully, so as to focus on the concepts that would prove foundational for psychoanalysis. Yet he completely avoids the process of their development. It is a film about the concepts as they develop, not about Freud's work in developing them.

Freud especially features hypnosis but elides the actual procedure. Hypnotism is instant: Freud waves a cigarette in front of Carl's eyes, and Carl is hypnotized. It works unfailingly, despite how Freud in *Studies on Hysteria* emphasizes that not everyone can be hypnotized and that the process is tenuous (267–68). The period after the publication of *Studies on Hysteria* led to vast changes in Freud's technique: Freud stopped hypnotizing patients in 1896. He gradually, in the years between then and

1900, also stopped pressing on heads, cajoling patients to remember details, and closing patients' eyes (Jones 1.244). Huston's film, which focuses on the years right before and after 1895, doesn't much meditate on any of these innovations, even as they are introduced. Cecily makes good progress with Freud under hypnosis until, at a crossroads of the analysis, Freud simply informs her, "We found a better method." The film does not explain how Freud and Breuer arrived at this new method or why they thought it better. It does not credit Cecily, as Breuer credits Anna O., with any enthusiasm for "the talking cure." The improvement is simply announced, and immediately it opens up new levels of interpretation: Cecily, resistant, demands to be hypnotized, but Freud sits behind her and simply asks her to free-associate. Cecily calls Freud "Freuer," a portmanteau of Freud and Breuer, to signify her sense that she is being unfaithful to Breuer, her former analyst; she begins a chain of dense multilingual associations—her controversial fondness for wearing makeup as a child, the accusations that followed, of being like a prostitute, the real and fake words "pretty" and "prettifer," which Freud here connects to the French *prostituée* and the biblical name Potiphar, the wife of whom tried to seduce Joseph, as in Josef Breuer. *Studies on Hysteria* does not explore such chains of association—such work was years away for Freud. Parapraxis is theorized most famously in *The Psychopathology of Everyday Life* (1901). Here again, Huston highlights the conceptual innovation at the expense of actual technique or any attempt at capturing Anna O.'s story. It is not that Huston is being reductive—rather, the case of Cecily is exceptionally complex and multifaceted, by any standard but especially for a film—but that he is reinventing Freud's case studies to better illustrate multiple aspects of psychoanalytic thought. The case is solved, so to speak, once a large corpus of psychoanalytic concepts—hysteria, hypnosis, free association, condensation, displacement, parapraxis, the Oedipus complex, infantile sexuality, the defiles of the signifier, transference, and countertransference—can be marshaled out, one at a time, for use, even if only a few of these concepts were actually features of Anna O.'s case, or Elisabeth von R.'s, or Emmy von N.'s.

Freud also elides the major incidents of Freud's life during this period: none of Freud's six children born during this era is included in the film, for instance, and his other research beyond hysteria isn't discussed (Holland 167). His letters to Fleiss were part of Sartre's screenplay but cut from Huston's film. Holland notes that this is simply "the necessary trimming in a biopic," but that "the film is more accurate in the difficult task of rendering Freud's psychoanalytic discoveries" (168). Indeed, biopics inevitably streamline or simplify their subjects' lives as they "attempt to discover biographical truth," rather than attempting "a simple recounting of the facts of someone's life," as Bingham explains (7). The film anthropomorphizes Freudian concepts in the figures of its fictional hysterics, when it might have been simpler to adapt the actual case histories. Freud's process is elided, but the idea is born and traced through its infancy: the discovery of the Oedipus complex here takes place not through dream analysis or literary analysis, as it does in Freud's work, but through the fictional personal history of Carl. Later in the film, Freud adapts this same technique to his own case to discover the motives behind his (apparently compulsive rather than professional) tendency to psychoanalyze. Psychoanalysis is no longer, in Huston's hands, an epistemology, but its own conglomerate formation of hysterical symptoms. This is what embroils the film in archive fever: Huston traces the development of psychoanalytic reason with recourse, in flashbacks, to Freud's childhood. Huston presses the biopic into service to meet the demands of another twentieth-century technology of autobiography—psychoanalysis—and then using psychoanalytic premises—that all of Freud's ideas must be traceable to his early relationship to his parents—to create a satisfactory narrative for his biopic.

Derrida, in *Archive Fever*, criticizes scholarly attempts to read psychoanalysis through the detritus of Freud's personal life. Huston, conversely, supposes that Freud's personal life, once fictionalized, can take on the character of his ideas. Thus "archive fever" becomes "secret passion." Freud's life between 1895 and 1900, as depicted in Huston's film, takes on the very character of an intellectual breakthrough, while characters like Cecily and Carl separate the concept of hypnosis from the historical conditions of its actual discovery, and thus from the facts of life. Naturally, these are condensations required by and conducive to the biopic genre. The flip side of this process, however, is that the structural limitations compel the film to describe Freud's collaborative intellectual breakthrough in terms of his personal life in ways that render unrecognizable both the personal life itself and the text adapted.

Note

1. The film's treatment of seduction theory is controversial: Janet Walker and Diane Waldman, building on Jeffrey Masson's work, take the film to task for cutting Cecily's testimony of childhood abuse to Freud and for the film's implication that the theoretical breakthrough was learning to ignore these allegations and blame the victim; Leslie Brill, however, sees this as the work of the studio bosses who "mutilated" Huston's vision. Walker and Waldman 174–75; Brill.

Works Cited

Bingham, Dennis. *Whose Lives Are They Anyway?: The Biopic as Contemporary Film Genre.* New Brunswick: Rutgers UP, 2010.
Brill, Lesley. *John Huston's Filmmaking.* Cambridge: Cambridge UP, 1997.
Charbonneau, Marie-Andrée. "The Freud Scenario: A Sartrian Freud—A Freudian Sartre?," *Sartre Studies International: An Interdisciplinary Journal of Existentialism and Contemporary Culture* 13.2 (2007).
Custen, George F. *Bio/Pics: How Hollywood Constructed Public History.* New Brunswick: Rutgers UP, 1992.
Derrida, Jacques. *Archive Fever: A Freudian Impression.* Trans. Eric Prenowitz. Chicago: U of Chicago P, 1995.
Freud, Sigmund. *An Autobiographical Study.* Trans. James Strachey. *The Standard Edition of the Complete Psychological Works of Sigmund Freud.* Vol. 20/24. London: Vintage, 2001. 1–74.
Freud, Sigmund, and Josef Breuer. *Studies on Hysteria.* Trans. James Strachey. *The Standard Edition of the Complete Psychological Works of Sigmund Freud.* Vol. 2/24. London: Vintage, 2001.
Freud: The Secret Passion. Dir. John Huston. Universal Pictures, 1962.
Huston, John. *An Open Book.* New York: Random House, 1980.
Jones, Ernest. *The Life and Work of Sigmund Freud.* 3 vols. New York: Basic Books, 1955.
Kaplan, E. Ann, ed., *Psychoanalysis and Cinema.* New York: Routledge, 1990.
Koch, Gertrud. "Sartre's Screen Projection of Freud." *October* 57. Cambridge: MIT P, 1991.
Lebeau, Vicky. *Psychoanalysis and Cinema: The Play of Shadows.* London: Wallflower, 2011.
Metz, Christian. *The Imaginary Signifier: Psychoanalysis and the Cinema.* Bloomington: Indiana UP, 1982.
Meyers, Jeffrey. "The Making of John Huston's Freud: The Secret Passion." *Kenyon Review* 33.1 (2011).
Pontalis, J. B. Preface. *The Freud Scenario.* By Jean-Paul Sartre. Ed. J. B. Pontalis. Trans. Quintin Hoare. Chicago: U of Chicago P, 1985.
Sartre, Jean-Paul. *The Freud Scenario.* Ed. J. B. Pontalis. Trans. Quintin Hoare. Chicago: U of Chicago P, 1985.
Walker, Janet, and Diane Waldman. "Huston's Freud and Textual Representation: A Psycoanalytic Femanist Reading." *An Anthology of New Film Criticism.* Ed. Peter Lehman. Gainesville: UP of Florida, 1990. 282–99.
Žižek, Slavoj. *Everything You Always Wanted to Know about Lacan (But Were Afraid to Ask Hitchcock).* New York: Verso, 1992.

15

Kyle Stevens

Queer Movements

Color, Performance, and Rhythm in John Huston's *Reflections in a Golden Eye*

About Carson McCullers's novella *Reflections in a Golden Eye* the great playwright Tennessee Williams writes: "[It] is one of the purest and most powerful of those works which are conceived in that Sense of the Awful which is the desperate black root of nearly all significant modern art" (McCullers 134). Williams's attribution of a color to this affective condition seems particularly apt when thinking about this work. Here, the black root nourishes golden fruit: golden in that the novella is a gleaming work, and golden in another way, a way named cloying, suffocating, punishing by the text. Indeed, the novella specifies several golden eyes and reflections—in people and pictures and things. It does so from a position of knowledge, outside of these specific instances; there is a novella eye that contains the reflections. Similarly, in John Huston's 1967 film adaptation, we do not see the world through the eyes of a central character. It, however, is itself golden. There is no question of an outside to the chromatic ideology in this world picture, no forgetting that it is an unsettling fantasy, an ambiguous metaphor. In fact, this golden world was so disturbing to viewers upon its release that the studio overrode the director's wishes and redistributed the film in conventional color.

Now that the film has been released on digital formats that restore Huston's original vision, I want to ask what was so obscene about this difference from its literary source. Looking at the film with McCullers's text in mind throws Huston's stylistic choices into relief, allowing us to see how he translates word to image. The story shared by both iterations of *Reflections* is diffused across six characters, though it emphasizes Weldon Penderton (Marlon Brando), a closeted army captain, and Private Ellgee Williams (Robert Forster), the object of Weldon's fascination. McCullers's subject matter sparked controversy in midcentury America, not least from influential literary critic Leslie Fiedler, who declared that McCullers (along with authors such as Eudora Welty and Flannery O'Connor) "emasculated the powerful Faulknerian literary heritage by producing a feeble offspring: 'the true Magnolia Blossom or Southern homosexual style'" (Westling 4). Despite the objectionable values subtending this view, it gets something right about the connection between McCullers's style and sexual politics, a relatively new sexual politics concerned with the treatment of women and paranoia over the behavior of men. (Significantly, readers knew that Fiedler clearly did not mean a lesbian stylistic.) I will argue that one cannot separate an analysis of the style of Huston's *Reflections* from its sexual politics. By analyzing the movie's rhetorical strategies, especially its color, rhythm, and performances, I will elucidate the way that Huston formally constructs an ideological critique through modes of contrasting stasis and movement, a contrast tied to specific characters' identities as aesthetic and sexual subjects. In doing do, I will ultimately reveal that Huston was significantly ahead of the historical-political curve.[1]

In fact, the impulse to distinguish *Reflections*' political agenda from its form is the primary reason the film remains underappreciated. It has received the most attention from scholars of Huston's aesthetics and historians of queer identities in Hollywood history, but these two groups have essentially ignored each other.[2] In the 1990s, Lesley Brill and Stephen Cooper sought to recuperate the historically dismissed film in books on Huston, but neither seriously addresses its depiction of "deviant" sexualities. Conversely, those interested in the history of the representation of onscreen sexualities tend to misconstrue the film as a conservative cog in Hollywood's heteronormative dream factory—not least of all because of Huston's "masculinist" reputation.[3] Homosexuals were not yet banned from US military service when McCullers wrote her story (the prohibition resulted from a series of policy revisions in the 1940s), and now, after the "Don't Ask, Don't Tell" military policy has been repealed, perhaps we might see *Reflections* afresh, without avoiding the formerly taboo subject matter when considering its cinematic form.

Magnolia Blossom Style

From the very start of McCullers's contribution to late southern gothic, the notion of masculinity is indivisible from aesthetic notions of patterns and repetition, and from feelings about them. In short, clipped sentences, the novella begins:

> An army post in peacetime is a dull place. Things happen, but then they happen over and over again. The general plan of a fort in itself adds to the monotony [. . .] All is designed according to a certain rigid pattern. But perhaps the dullness of a post is caused most of all by the insularity and by a surfeit of leisure and safety, for once a man enters the army he is expected only to follow the heels ahead of him. (3)

Change and movement battle stasis in this place. Even if events themselves are not traumatic, the incessant, boring recurrence of male privilege leaves a sort of scar. A gloomy tediousness results from the ties that bind patriarchy and military, for the expectation to follow is also one not to lead. Originality, invention and creativity are ranked lower than unthinking obedience. Thus, with remarkable efficiency, McCullers creates a setting as much about "rigidity" and conformity as about the army.

At the same time, the next sentence marks her tale as one of rupture, of a break in the flow of history: "things do occasionally happen [. . .] that are not likely to re-occur." *This* story begins at the end of the first paragraph: "There was a fort in the South where a few years ago a murder was committed. The participants were: two officers, a soldier, two women, a Filipino, and a horse." Dayton Kohler observes, "Everything that happens—domestic infidelity, brutality, the frozen hate of impotence, sexual frenzy flows as if under inner compulsion from that opening statement" (6). Besides establishing our expectations of the violence to follow, this statement cues us to a politics of identity that was endemic to twentieth-century American history and that would only become more intense in the decades to follow the novella's publication. Within American racial logic of the time, in singling out one race, this omniscient narrator implies that the officers and women are white. Race distinguishes nonwhite males, sexual difference distinguishes women, and military status distinguishes white men from other white men. This opening salvo also establishes McCullers's style, a style in which brevity reigns. The narrator's voice is cold, observational; it has a ring of the ethnographic. This detachment from the action "and the clean, bare prose with which he (or she, for McCullers in no way discloses the gender of her narrator) tells the story," Virginia Spencer Carr writes, "impose an ironic sense of understatement upon the tragedy that ensues" (40).

This sense of understatement stands in dynamic tension with the complexity of the interlocking narrative arcs of the characters. McCullers's story is not as simple as her prose might suggest. One of the "two officers," Weldon, is married to Leonora (Elizabeth Taylor), who has affairs with other officers. Her current beau is Morris (Brian Keith), the other of the two. Morris is married to Alison (Julie Harris), who is bedridden and damaged from years of emotional abuse. We learn that she cut her nipples off with garden shears three years prior, after the death of their child. The "Filipino" is Anacleto (Zorro David), Alison's companion and servant (their economic arrangement is never made clear). Ellgee is the soldier, a practically mute private who communes with horses and who takes to stealing into the Pendertons' home each night to watch Leonora sleep. No happiness is in store for these characters. Alison dies, after which Anacleto simply disappears, and Morris cannot bring himself to continue his affair with Leonora. The novella ends as Weldon finds Ellgee at his unnerving nocturnal ritual and shoots him.

But "*Reflections* is more than a simple chronicle of violence," according to Kohler; "the real thing is not the effect of horror [McCullers] creates but the enveloping moment which reveals man's capacity for error, cruelty, guilt, self-deception, self-destruction" (7). Kohler directs us to see, rightly, the extent to which *Reflections* is a "planned novella"—how "every detail and symbol [is] deliberately created and plotted"—in the service of investigating darker aspects of the effects of postwar sociality on the Southern-American psyche (7).[4] Yet, although the book is deeply concerned with the psychological pain of the inevitable "loneliness and isolation" from others, McCullers shies away from elaborate descriptions of psychic states (Kohler, 7). She provides rather matter-of-fact statements, even sketchy ones, allowing readers to suture themselves into the story through the labor of their own investments as they "flesh out" psychic trajectories.

Given that McCullers's characters are in pain and isolated, perhaps it is not surprising that they are also disturbed, neurotic, and even mad. We can see in the novella a taxonomy of abnormal mental states and conditions: Weldon is homosexual (which was considered a mental illness at the time); Anacleto is also coded as a sexual deviant and as overly attached to Alison; Leonora is feebleminded and barely literate; Ellgee is sociopathic; Alison had a breakdown and is widely considered "crazy," as Leonora puts it. However, McCullers goes on to critique each of these categories, to blur the already gray borders between sanity and insanity within the ironically copacetic military base. Madness has often been seen to be a renunciation of reason, a divine mania, defined in opposition to and by arbiters of reason, and uncatchable by natural language. It is no coincidence that the sanest of them, Alison—the one who sees that Ellgee infiltrates the Pendletons' home, that Leonora and Morris are having an affair, that Weldon is a thief, that the military's firing of her friend Captain Weincheck is a result of antiaesthetic prejudice—is the one who is committed to an asylum.

Thus, McCullers's text is an especially interesting case with which to think about performance and the expression of mindedness onscreen. Performance can be, among other things, the art of suggesting how a mind attaches to a body, and then to the world. But stories of repressed homosexual desires in a homophobic context can also present difficulties for a largely visual medium. For example, McCullers's narrator states early on that "sexually, the Captain obtained himself within a delicate balance between the male and female elements [. . .] and had a sad penchant for becoming enamored of his wife's lovers" (11). It is more difficult for Huston to portray this information through a line of dialogue or character action, lest it no longer remain repressed. That is, the novella's narrator is free to say the things that *must* go unsaid within the diegesis.

Beyond the Period

From its opening, Huston's film identifies itself as interested in what goes unsaid.[5] The first image that appears is of McCullers's germinal prose: "There is a fort in the south where a few years ago a murder was committed." The words are in gold and on a golden background, only discernible because of the shadows each letter casts. Thus, the film is set not just on a military base, but, in a different way, in McCullers's text. That shadows—which denote blockages, reflections, and absences—determine the text's very legibility advises us, as spectators, to be aware of meaning as a function of such impasses. Furthermore, onscreen, unlike on the page, there is no period at the end of this exposition. The sentence remains unfinished, inviting spectators to consider matters of continuity and ellipsis, of what lies beyond the writing, of what exceeds the limits of language. It invites us to consider relations of word and image and prepares us for the way that the adaptation will ground the abstractness of language in the concreteness of images. It prepares us to move from our minds' eyes as readers to *this* fort in *this* south, and the absence of punctuation propels us forward into the movie without stopping.

The quotation gives way to a beautifully desolate landscape, diagonally striated by a dirt road, along which ambles a slim soldier. The film, like the novella, foregrounds the theme of isolation, capturing "the oddly dreamlike quality pervading [McCullers's] work" (Kohler 2). As we are introduced into this world, we realize that the golden color of the title sequence will remain, and so, in contrast to the promise of fidelity made by Huston's initial images, we must confront the fact that McCullers's prose is not golden, while his world is. More precisely, his images are rendered torrid sepia through a technique developed for the film that desaturates color in postproduction—save for pinks and reds, which serve as accents in multiple shots.[6] Although we might see Huston as participating in a tradition of cinematic color that dates back to *The Wizard of Oz* (Victor Fleming 1939), in which color is not a condition of the world, but the world is conditioned by its color, this new process received much attention upon the film's release.[7] The enormous changes in film culture of the 1960s created a new context for thinking about the use of color. Early in the decade, key European New Wave films bestowed an almost pious reverence for black-and-white fare (an attitude that was perhaps reinforced by the pop art movement's coincident commentary on the use of color in commodity culture). Yet by 1964, the Beatles' hip *A Hard Day's Night* (Richard Lester) was shot in black and white and within two years, *Who's Afraid of Virginia Woolf?* (Mike Nichols, 1966), also in black and white, was nominated for a Best Picture Oscar.[8]

After audiences flinched at *Reflections*' chromatic scheme, the brass at Warner Bros.–Seven Arts pulled it from theaters about a week after its release and replaced it with "a conventional, Technicolor version" (Cooper 111). Huston defended his alternative technique, writing that "when we are dealing with material of psychological content [conventional, fully saturated, spectacular color] becomes invariably distracting as it gets between the viewer and the mind he is trying to search into" (Cooper 111). He disparages dogmatic approaches to color—"This night and day difference is no longer the only choice"—and implies that desaturation provides him with a middle ground between the aesthetics of black and white, so often associated with documentary and a reality effect, and fully saturated color, what he called "literal beer-ad color" that was "fine for extravaganzas" (Cooper 111). *Reflections*' color thus conveys the almost ethnographic feeling of McCullers's prose, while disavowing aspirations to verisimilitude or to a documentary sensibility. The ethereal quality places it firmly in the realm of fiction. In this way, Huston's desaturated color encourages audiences to identify with the film, or with the camera as observing agent, not with the moral judgments of any particular character. Indeed, Huston has been outspoken that he would "rather have an audience identify with the picture itself than with a character in the picture" (Brill 56).

In this light, the golden complexion of Huston's film seems to embody McCullers's title (and, in fact, that is how the effect was chiefly understood upon its release), but I want to dwell for a moment on the curious complexity of the titular phrase. It is conventional to talk about reflections *on* surfaces, but "reflections on a golden eye" suggests a strange tale, one in which eyes do not see but act as mere reflective surfaces. Rather the preposition "in" is reserved for speaking about reflections in mirrors, or water: surfaces that we think of as having depth. So "reflections *in* an eye" directs us to consider the eye as deep, as an agent of perception, proof of a mind with a worldview. And what of this eye? The reflections are not golden; the eye is. One might claim that the world is golden, which then colors the looking eye—but then the reflections would again be *on* the eye, not in it. In McCullers's book, multiple, specific eyes are golden. In Huston's film, only two golden eyes exist: a close-up of Ellgee's eye and an eye of a peacock painted by Anacleto, but the whole world is golden. And just as the brown-eyed do not see a brown world, the golden-eyed would not see a golden world. Rather, Huston's technique stresses the sense that "golden" in the title refers to an *aspect* of the eye's perception, to the *way* it perceives, and to the world's acting upon the eye. "Golden" becomes descriptive of a mind, resonating, too, with the sense of "reflection" as contemplation. This eye sees the world *as* golden, and hence we, the spectators, are seeing the seeing-as of Huston's camera eye/I.

I will return to Huston's golden eyes in my reading of the film below, but it is important to note that the tea-stained tint is not exactly golden. True "golden," the reason the word refers not just to appearance but to a value judgment, requires opacity; it shines, as much texture as color. Huston's tint evokes the history of sepia photography, suggesting a nostalgic perspective, a world whose present is drained. It also evokes humidity and heat, steamy dusks that glow like the burn of a modest cinder. Given Huston's intentions, I am reminded of Rudolf Arnheim's belief that artists think in sensation. Brian Price points out that "color disrupts order: it promises to undo the Gestalt effected by line and form. The closer we look at color, the less legible forms become, the less able we are to comprehend the narrative and its moral message" (79). Because of the traditional emphasis on verisimilitudinous color, Huston's unusual effect draws attention to color and away from line, making the screen space freshly ripe with possibility. It nudges the visual track toward the abstract and away from the figural.

By echoing the impressions of warmth and nostalgia, this ochre also conjures up an idea of the American South. (It is, I think, telling that the Coen brothers will turn to a similar palette when telling a story set in the South during roughly the same time period: *O Brother, Where Art Thou?* [2000].) Thus, Huston's technique suggests a world already lost, one that was perhaps never golden to begin with, and if it was, it is no longer. Huston thus conveys not the presence of a real world, but loss and absence. Being sensitive to the color may remind us that within the American imaginary, the South is most often regarded not as a place to be explored but fled, suffered, embarrassed about, and guilty of. From the nation's inception until today, it has functioned as the geographical locus of conservativism, with a desire for things to remain the same and a resistance to the forward movement of (Hegelian) history. When *Reflections* was released in 1967, this reputation was painfully evident as racial enmity—and the rhetoric of color, of black *and* white—continued to intensify during the civil rights movement. Hence, if the novella participates in midcentury existentialist malaise and the "sense of the awful" (Williams sets works in the South, too, remember), Huston extends this to the formal level, where, as we will see, stasis threatens movement, the *élan vital* of cinema.

Staccato Movements

The color was not the only thing that troubled audiences about Huston's *Reflections*. Brando's performance was singled out as a failure, and, in this section, before returning to the issue of color, I want to look closely at Brando and Huston's collaboration on Weldon.[9] By analyzing its rhythm and contrasting it with the other male characters in the film, I will argue that the characterization of Weldon is not only highly stylized, but that it occupies an essayistic register, one concerned, too, with movement and stasis. While the great film critic Roger Ebert believes that "Brando regains the peak of his magnificent talent," the rest of the theater "laughed, perhaps because it's supposed to be 'funny' to see a man cry." Foreseeing that history would want an account of why the film was poorly received, he explains that "the audience was perhaps the greatest problem with this very good film." Ebert recounts that audiences' homophobia prohibited them from properly seeing the text, especially Brando's performance:

> [The audience] was filled with matrons, who found it necessary to shriek loudly and giggle hideously through three-quarters of it, and their husbands, who delivered obligatory guffaws in counterpoint. They had never seen anything funnier in their lives, I guess, than Brando nervously brushing

down his hair when he thinks a handsome young private is coming to see him.[10]

We might see in the audience's response evidence of more than bigotry, though. Their response rightly connects Brando's expressions—not just the narrative events involving Weldon—to the sexual politics of the film.

Weldon is introduced in his bedroom, lifting weights. He finishes a set and then eyes his barbell, challenging himself to a one-handed lift. He tries but cannot raise his laden arm. Weldon then considers his reflection in the mirror before suddenly and repeatedly punching himself in the gut with the side of his fist, testing his solidity as he stares at his weightless image. These short bursts are more self-flagellation than strikes of pride in his physique. During this assault his face remains still, which, as a foil to his sharp punches, effects a montage of corporeal movement that reinforces the sense already established through his struggle to lift his metal burden that this character is caught between wanting to move and remaining still.

Brando's body language when Weldon publicly self-presents resists movement altogether. Even his speech borders on the unintelligible as his mouth and tongue seem to barely move. We next see the captain instructing Ellgee to do some landscaping. Especially clear in his posture, Brando commits fully to a militant sensibility, to the quality of presentational stiffness, making a show of rigidity and the fetish for regulation. He stands with shoulders squared, his back braced, and his chin pushed toward the back of his lengthened neck. When he returns home he is incensed to find that the soldier has cleared too much brush. Ellgee has overexposed the Pendertons. We then see Weldon installed at his desk. The planes and angles of Brando's face are utterly motionless and belong to this static composition of lamp, pens, and toy cannons, all rigid lines and angles. His meditation is interrupted by the shrill laughter of Leonora and the cook telling a joke about "little queers" as they bustle about in the kitchen, all fluttering movement, waving hands, floral wallpaper, and rounded, flowing hair. Weldon directs Leonora to get ready for their guests and follows her into the living room, where she calls him "prissy," and he tells her that she disgusts him for going about in her tight riding breeches.[11] As a retort, Leonora disrobes, exposing the voluptuous curves of her body.

In book and movie, this action taunts Weldon. It is a clue not only to his inclination for male sexual object choices, but that he is uncomfortable with bodies and with the ways that bodies communicate—nudity functions here (and in many contexts where confinement reigns) as an expression of the body. Leonora's exposure hits pay dirt, and Weldon

Figure 15.1. A weakened Weldon grips the banister railing while hopelessly caught between stillness and the desire to move.

seethes. He follows her to the staircase and declares, "I will kill you!" But he remains still, anchored at the bottom of the steps. In juxtaposition to Weldon, Leonora moves freely physically while remaining emotionally "unmoved." She nonchalantly turns and asks him if he has "ever been collared and dragged out into the street by a naked woman." Brando's gestures make clear that he is angrier at himself than at her. He holds on to the banister not to bar himself from what he might do if he runs after her, but to support himself. He is weakened and clings to it, clutching it with both hands in front of him, as supplicating as it is threatening, showing them both that he isn't about to go anywhere. She refuses to help, though, and his head collapses onto the railing. Again, he is caught between wanting to move and remaining still.

This image of immobility collides with what we see next: Ellgee outside watching. In an extreme close-up, Leonora's nude form ascending the staircase is reflected in Ellgee's eye, which Ellgee's overtakes the screen and appears inhumanly still, unblinking, mindless in its sight. This insert shot surprises us with a body that is not at rest or watching, but photographic in its stasis. It contrasts sharply with Leonora's mobile reflection. Ellgee is transfixed and helpless before Leonora's image. Leonora again enjoys freedom of motion as she climbs to the top of his iris; she turns right at the summit and retires into his head where she will reside, for him, for the rest of his short life. Like the title and color suggest, seeing here is not the active, male, voyeuristic conception of vision so often discussed in film studies.[12] Perception is still ideologically conditioned, though. We will later learn from a barracks mate that Ellgee is a virgin who was told as a child that "women carry a terrible disease and you mustn't ever touch them." Ellgee's gaze upon Leonora is, rather, not about shaping the world but about suffering the world's assault.

In a continuation of this theme of looking and reflection, movement and stasis, desire and repulsion, after Ellgee becomes entranced with Leonora, the film cuts to Anacleto and Alison. Anacleto is at Alison's bedside, spooning medicine into her mouth. McCullers describes Alison and Anacleto as twinned: "Their voices and enunciation were so precisely

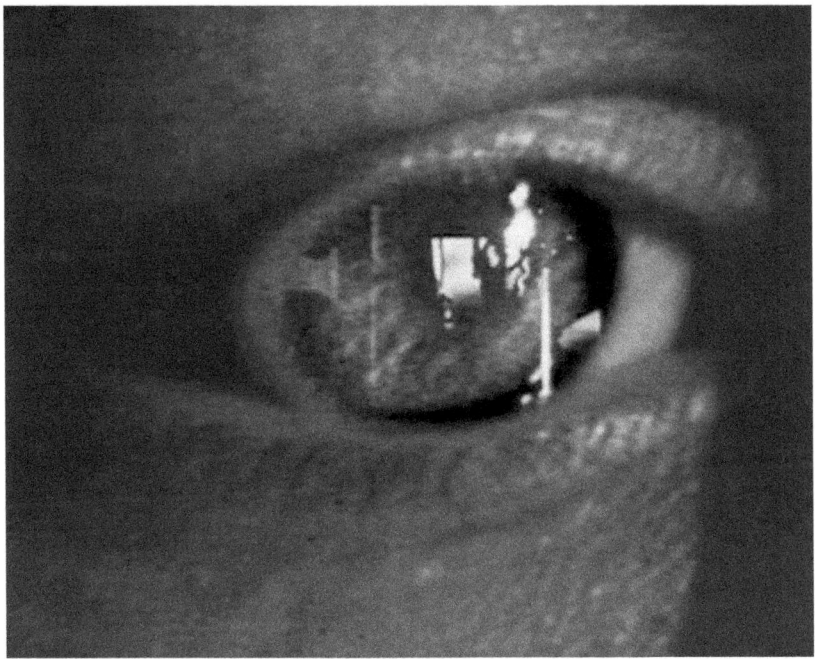

Figure 15.2. The nude figure of Lenora is reflected in an extreme close-up of Ellgee's eye.

alike that they seemed to be softly echoing each other," a conjunction that Huston achieves here by refusing the conventional, expected shot/reverse shot pattern (42). We see only Anacleto's face contort as Alison swallows. He moves, and she may or may not be still; we can't be sure. But we do know that he serves as her reflection and expresser, her visual echo. From the previous scene, in which the two couples played cards, we know that Alison struggles to express herself. (She abruptly left after seeing Leonora fondle Morris under the card table, although no one grasped that she was upset.) Anacleto is thus a different kind of reflection, a necessary one, like a shadow or a screen onto which Alison's expressions are projected; they are a joint apparatus.

That Anacleto is Alison's "moving picture show" is reinforced by performances he creates to amuse her. But they are also for himself, and he needs her to be his audience. We know Alison is sympathetic to the plight of aesthetically sensitive men since the only interjection that she is willing to make in the previous scene is to defend Captain Weincheck, who is mocked on the base, because, as Alison puts it, "he plays the violin and reads Proust." Anacleto's personality conveys the sort of performative flavor typically called "camp." There is no mention of a sexual object choice for Anacleto, but it is clear from the reception of both McCullers's and Huston's texts that—precisely because of his coded gender performance, which is to say, his freedom of movement—there was no question of Anacleto's sexual orientation at the time of the film's release. Such a reading conflates gender behavior and sexual object choice, though, so it is more accurate to describe Anacleto as queer—a term and category not available except as an epithet in late 1960s American culture.[13]

Anacleto floats around the room, gesturing widely with his hands, even involving his shoulders when he talks. His command of movement marks him as powerful within the logic of *Reflections*, and Huston highlights this by filming Anacleto with a continuously mobile, seemingly hand-held camera, constantly reframing him even when he is seated. This is a marked contrast to the stationary camera and largely static frames of the other characters, especially apparent in the stagnant shots of Alison in the same scenes. Anacleto's freedom directly contrasts with Weldon's confinement in the next scene, in which Weldon repeatedly practices his salute in the mirror. He stands stock still until the sudden, crisp movement of a salute erupts. Unlike Leonora or Alison, Weldon lacks a human to reflect him. He is private, rehearsing his masculinity for himself.

If we are in any doubt about Huston's composition of Anacleto as legato and Weldon as staccato, he cuts back to Anacleto, who impulsively decides to "compose a ballet" for Alison. The wonderful thing about Anacleto's dance is that he does not try too hard. He makes no pretense to be more than an amateur, nor does Alison need him to be. He dances for their pleasure, simply, dreamily. Zorro David contributes a brave performance, endowing flamboyance with gravitas. His features are round, while Brando's are jagged. Fluidity and expansive gestures—arms outsretched, hands outsretched—are feminine; stillness and violent bursts where hands come into the body, as when Weldon punches his gut or salutes, are masculine.

In the next scene, Huston further underscores the difficulty of movement for Weldon and brings Ellgee into this dynamic as a third term. The captain goes riding with Leonora and Morris. Weldon's discomfort with movement prohibits him from being a good rider, betraying his failure at masculinity, which is also understood to pertain to his sexual activity: "If the captain could see himself from behind he wouldn't ever get on a horse" a nearby soldier declares of Weldon's backside bouncing up and down. The trio comes upon Ellgee riding naked in a glen, "Barebacked and bare-assed," as Leonora puts it. Ellgee sits upright, barely moving as he canters the horse in circles. His form is as classically ideally proportioned as Leonora's, and his smooth, deliberate riding clashes with the prior image of Weldon's awkward bobbing. While Leonora and Morris ride away, Weldon remains, having now become the transfixed and helpless one staring. We see in Brando's performance of Weldon's struggle to both stay and leave that Weldon's life is disarranged by this moment.

Ellgee may be *au naturel*, but the proscenium formed by the trees marks him as a beautiful object with a theatrical artifice, his form's form accentuated by the high-contrast lighting. At the same time, Ellgee's placement in nature, fused with the horse, suggests that he stands apart from other civilized humans. McCullers's narrator repeatedly describes Ellgee as animalistic. His "mute expression," for example, "is found usually in the eyes of animals" (4). Ellgee's nonhumanity also extends beyond the animalistic, as when McCullers's narrator notes that Ellgee had "[never] been known to laugh, to become angry, or to suffer in any way" (4), that "there were in his mind no plans or thoughts of which he was aware" (28), and that "the mind of Private Williams . . . was without delineation, void of form" (90). While Forster excels at depicting Ellgee's inexpressivity, once performed, we see a face onscreen as frozen, impassive, even inscrutable, rather than lacking expression, which McCullers is able to depict in prose. Nevertheless, Huston finds ways to visually convey Ellgee's beastliness. In the film's first sequence, for instance, we are introduced to Ellgee as he enters the horse stables. Huston cuts so as to show Ellgee through the bars of the stalls as if he were sharing the space of horses.

As Weldon watches Ellgee ride in circles, the film returns to Anacleto and Alison. Huston's mobile camera continues reframing Anacleto as he shows Alison his latest opus, a gold, green, and pink watercolor painting of a peacock, all swirls and rolling curlicues. Despite its apparent innocence, he describes it in ghostly terms, as "ghastly green with one immense golden eye, and in it these reflections of something tiny, tiny and . . ." Alison finishes the thought: "grotesque." Perhaps with a touch of shame, Anacleto makes the peacock in his own image, and this preening creature, famous for its flamboyant males, sees the world playing out before it as Anacleto sees it, as grotesque. Unlike Ellgee and Weldon, who desire what they see, Anacleto's aesthetic sensibility affords him repulsion, a judgment that is warranted by this sad world. This is confirmed as Huston dissolves into the next shot so slowly that the peacock's eye is superimposed on the next scene: the terrifying, rapt stillness of Ellgee as he watches the oblivious Leonora sleep.

This brief interlude of Ellgee in Leonora's room reminds us of his stillness, his utter inexpressiveness, and the consequent mystery of his bestial gaze. Indeed, we, as spectators, are unsure whether to fear for Leonora's safety. Huston then cuts back to Anacleto, now extending the opposition between movement and stasis into something deeper, a struggle between aesthetes and militants. "Madame Alison," he inquires, "do you yourself really believe that Mr. Sergei Rachmaninoff knows that a chair is something to be sat on and that a clock shows one the time? . . . I myself find it hard to realize." For Anacleto, aesthetic talent determines one's beliefs, which distinguishes types of people, and Anacleto aspires to Rachmaninoff's category. His conviction that Rachmaninoff—known for the *movement* of his music, for its intricate rhythms and chromatic ornamentation—does not word the world like others do suggests that he thinks that the aesthetically sensitive express themselves differently because they see the world differently.[14] The longing in Anacleto's voice indicates that his wish is not simply to create beauty but to exist at this level of remove from the world, where one is free to believe in a reality beyond the linguistic.

Riding the Stallion

Establishing this contrast between the levels of movement and expressivity among Weldon, Ellgee, and Anacleto prepares the spectator to understand the scene that functions as the narrative's tipping point: Weldon takes Leonora's headstrong horse, Firebird, out for a ride. Firebird is the final participant in "the murder" of McCullers's opening statement, and, as his name suggests, he is a wild creature. Leonora earlier impugned her husband's manhood by pointedly asserting that "Firebird is a stallion." Once alone on the horse, Weldon lets loose, spurring it to gallop. He set this frantic movement in motion, but he cannot contain it in the short bursts to which he is accustomed. Firebird refuses to slow down. Weldon has failed his own test. His decision to ride Firebird, and to relax his guard against movement, is his undoing. The floodgates open as he hurls through the forest, and the branches that whip him become another method of self-flagellation. Huston's camera follows alongside the rushing steed, keeping apace and conveying frenzied speed in magnificently fast tracking movements. Then, suddenly, Weldon passes Ellgee sunning naked on a rock, and time seems to slow. His gaze upon a distant object shows the *relativity* of rapidity; as experienced within a mind, movement and stasis need not be opposed at all.

Weldon eventually slides off of Firebird and is dragged a considerable distance. When he stands, branch-whipped and dazed—his red blood standing out from the otherwise monochromatic frame—Weldon ties Firebird up and beats him mercilessly (and, by proxy, himself and Ellgee). On one level, the scene follows the book exactly, from the way he "slowly and methodically [ties] the horse to a tree" to the tears that follow when his "anger [is] unappeased" (70–71). McCullers writes, "Out in the forest there, the Captain looked like a broken doll that has been thrown away. He was sobbing aloud" (71). The narrator then proceeds to tell us that Weldon loses consciousness and, to provide his backstory, how he was raised by five aunts and had "never known real love" (71). Onscreen, there is no flashback, only Brando, who gives a poignant, practically silent, portrait of a man disintegrating. But how does one account for such adaptive work? What does a broken doll-man really look like? Brando breaks Weldon before us, and the ambiguous madness of his hysteria might look a lot like bad acting, as Ebert informs us at least some audiences thought (acting consists of actions, which for narrative purposes are usually depicted as having clear motivations and intentions). Weldon's face is indeed difficult to attribute a psychic state to. The widened mouth, one eyebrow pulling in toward the bridge of the nose, nostrils flared, chin into neck. It is the beginning of a cry, yes, but why? Part disbelief, part guilt, but mostly shame, probably. His is not the downcast head and lowered lids of easy shame, but the intense pain of shameful realization, self-contempt deeper than a sneer. Bound by self-fear, he seems not to know where to go, so he mutters, "Please," to himself before emitting a high-pitched staccato howl and dropping to the forest floor. He weeps less into his hands than as though he is trying to force the sob back down his throat. He does not allow himself to cry, even alone. As in McCullers's text, Weldon curls into a fetal position and soon discovers that he is not alone. Ellgee appears, quiet, naked, deliberate. He moves slowly to the horse and leads it away, which we see in long shot, sharing Weldon's ground-level view.

After this scene, in which Weldon crashes headfirst into his psychological blockage, he only has eyes for Ellgee. There can be no doubt that the drama of the scene arises from the rapid, petrifying, galloping through space, and not the embarrassment of getting thrown from a horse. *That* we barely see. In the book, this event manifests a hatred for Ellgee in Weldon, as though Weldon views Ellgee as a rival, as though the two compete to win Leonora. This is, of course, masked attraction for Ellgee, but, as we know, the captain has always fancied Leonora's beaux. It is with Ellgee that his desire turns to repulsion, perhaps because of the aura of amorality that hovers above Ellgee due to his animalistic aspect, his remove from civility, and his comfort with nature. If the captain were to forego regulated morality, then he might have to face the fact of his desires, to look at them rather than simply "have" them. Onscreen, however, Weldon's infatuation reads as a more traditional form of desire. Huston, rather shockingly for the time, parallels Weldon's desire for Ellgee with Ellgee's for Leonora and aligns our perception with Weldon's as he wanders the base searching for glimpses of the private among privates, transfixed by Ellgee, who frequently appears utterly still and seductively posed (his poses suggest the then-new subcultural style of homoerotic imagery that emerged in the 1950s in physique magazines).

Because of the novella's focus on Weldon's hatred for Ellgee, when the foretold murder scene finally arrives, it carries more sinister ambiguity than onscreen. Weldon sees Ellgee approach the house, and he goes into his room, fixes his hair, and fearfully, giddily awaits the soldier's approach. When he realizes that Ellgee has gone into his wife's room, he follows him, armed. Shocked, he fires his gun, and Huston's camera swiftly and repeatedly wipes between the shocked Weldon, screaming Leonora, and lifeless Ellgee, blurring our vision before alighting on each and visually incriminating all three in this event with its incessant triangular alternations.

The Unorthodox Square

I trust that it is becoming clear that *Reflections* should interest both scholars of Huston's form and of the history of gender and sexuality onscreen. The film establishes dichotomies between movement and stasis, expressivity and stoicism by opposing Anacleto's flamboyant effeminacy—read, too, as queer sexuality—and Ellgee's masculine gender performance, a performance inseparable from his heterosexual desire for Leonora. Anacleto enjoys expressive freedom, and Ellgee expresses nothing; he lacks the ability to express. The repressed Weldon is stuck between these poles, and that is his flaw, a flaw that resonates particularly in the late 1960s when second-wave feminism was just beginning to enjoin the country to rethink its strictures regarding gender behavior. Ellgee's sociopathy is inextricable from the fact that he is taught to hate and fear women and treats them as only things to look at. Weldon may appear to be a wretched, suffering cuckold, but his suffering is proof of his humanity, his struggle against the demands gender places on him to be masculine, inhuman. When movement and expression are prohibited, one must do so ironically, as Anacleto does. Anacleto reminds us that playacting can be a critical tool, a tool for making sense of being in the world, for trying on alternative ways of being, and for venting one's anxieties, even if one is only camping or playing a heightened version of one's self.

Not only does Huston articulate a connection between repression and the masculine virtues of stillness and stoicism, but he also through these formal contrasts identifies queerness as movement. Cinema consists, of course, of moving images, and Huston's use of color and discussion of aesthetic pictures could be seen as reflexive. (As I mentioned above with regard to the film's use of color, Huston wants his audience to identify with the film.) Moreover, when Ellgee or Weldon (and, to a lesser extent, Alison) watches in *Reflections*, they are not only still as they gaze upon others, but they see unseen—reminiscent of the very situation that Stanley Cavell calls the magic of cinema, and of our own position as we watch *Reflections*. Hence, if queerness is conceptualized as movement, and the situation of being still and undetected while watching others is cinematic, then Huston suggests that his movie is itself queer.

In this light, Huston's *Reflections* emerges as a better, more deliberately made film than historians have recognized, and as an extremely significant moment in the history of American queer cinema. Unfortunately, scholars of queer cinema have not only failed to appreciate it, but have rejected the movie as homophobic. In his seminal *The Celluloid Closet*, Vito Russo takes *Reflections* to task. He charges Huston with confusing homosexuality with "being like a woman" (196) through his "simplistic rendering" of Weldon as "a constipated closet case" and of Anacleto as "a screaming queen" (166). For Russo, the very presence of a flamboyant male can only be a homophobic gesture on the part of an author. He ignores film form and interprets a line from Morris, about the army "making a man" of Anacleto, as a demonstration of the film's "pro-closet philosophy," because it "suggests that men can indeed be 'made' . . . and that homosexuality is merely a matter of effeminate behavior that can be altered" (166). But we are never encouraged to agree with Morris. Russo, contemporaneous critics, and other scholars of queer cinema since, such as Richard Barrios, see Anacleto as not just queer but homosexual, comporting with the objections about the conflation of gender and sexuality that Russo inveighs against Huston for. This is telling, indicating that *Reflections* may have seemed too tame or ineffectual when confronting such a "horrifying" subject. Treating effeminacy in men simply and with respect could, at the time, only be seen as a failure of craft.

Russo also misremembers the film's moral climax: the moment of Weldon's conversion. He writes that the captain lectures to soldiers that "it is morally honorable for the square peg to keep scraping around in the round hole rather than to discover and use the unorthodox one that would fit it" (166).[15] In fact, this moment occurs at the end of the film, in the Pendertons' home. Weldon speaks up against Morris's proclamations that the military would have benefited Anacleto. In words directly from the novella, he accuses Morris of meaning

> that any fulfillment obtained at the expense of normalcy is wrong, and should not be allowed to bring happiness. In short, it is better, because it is morally honorable, for the square peg to keep scraping about the round hole rather than to discover and use the unorthodox square that would fit it? (114)

Morris replies that it would, and, after a long, touching pause, Weldon disagrees. During this temporal suspension, we might see Brando performing the novella's description: "With gruesome vividness the Captain suddenly looked into his soul and saw himself. For once he did not see himself as others saw him; there came to him a distorted doll-like image, mean of countenance and grotesque in form" (114–15). Recall that the novella's narrator describes Weldon as "a broken doll" when he sobbed in the forest, so, we might see this description of him as a moment of self-realization. "Grotesque" is also the word Alison gives to what is reflected in the golden eye of Anacleto's peacock, an implication that art sees this world accurately. Indeed, we are now positioned to see just how radical Huston's film was, and is. It is Anacleto, the queer Filipino servant, who paints the key to seeing the film. His aesthetic expression appears golden with a red accent, just like the images of the film before us. By "disappearing," Anacleto escapes the South, and the film suggests that we, too, might escape if we see as Anacleto sees, or as Rachmaninoff speaks: to revise one's beliefs about reality through refashioned representation.

Notes

1. Chronicling the history of depictions of homosexuality on US screens is beyond the scope of this chapter, but *Reflections'* depiction of homosexual desire was timely. The late 1960s and early 1970s were a transitional but still dark time for queer characters: "Many of [the films of the late 1960s] created confusion about their intended messages [and] reviews in the popular press usually failed to make distinctions between homosexuality and [the dangers of] repressed homosexuality" (Benshoff and Griffin 137). In 1967 Abby Mann (screenwriter of, among other things, *The Detective*) told the *New York Times* that "it's easier to be accepted in our society today as a murderer than as a homosexual"—a view born out in his script for *The Detective* (1968) (Russo 169). For more on the history of queer representation in US cinema, see Benshoff and Griffin.

2. Stephen Cooper's essay on *Reflections* only touches on issues of gender and sexuality. His emphasis is on seeing the film as an antiwar statement during the Vietnam War. Aside from Cooper, Lesley Brill offers the most trenchant examination of the film. Brill uses a psychoanalytic lens to see the film as an ironic statement on romance and the dilemma of being a human that feels "at once social and isolate" (168). Both wrote before the desaturated color version was made available again via digital formats. I will address *Reflections'* inclusion in history of queer representation below.

3. For more on this reputation, see DeBona.

4. Similarly, Louis Rubin claims that "of all [McCullers's] fiction it is probably the most bizarre, the least pleasant. It is a *tour de force*, a sustained exercise in pure pain, without respite or humor" (268).

5. Francis Ford Coppola wrote a script, which circulated for some years, but with which Huston was ultimately not happy (Philips 28). Huston instead employed his own assistant, Gladys Hill, and Chapman Mortimer—both unproven screenwriters.

6. For more on this process, see Cooper 110–11.

7. Huston consistently worked through Hollywood's transition to color, and he selected Frederico Fellini's cinematographer, Aldo Tonti, for *Reflections*.

8. This was the same year that the Academy of Motion Picture Arts and Sciences decided to do away with separate Oscars for color and black-and-white cinematography.

9. There is arguably no more influential actor in Hollywood history regarding styles of performance. Brando is famous for bringing the method school of performance to Hollywood, an approach to performance that drew from an actor's personal history in order to manifest "authenticity." For more on Brando's style, see Naremore.

10. http://www.rogerebert.com/reviews/reflections-in-a-golden-eye-1967.

11. There are unmistakable shades here of *Who's Afraid of Virginia Woolf?*. Taylor won an Oscar as Best Actress for her role, and it, too, begins with an embittered husband and wife preparing for guests, and features Taylor's character pursuing the husband not her own.

12. This conception, built from Freudian and Lacanian theory, defines the male gaze as an intentional mode of seeing, whereby the objectification of women serves as a palliative for the threat their bodies (as lack and threat of castration) pose.

13. In considering Anacleto's gestures within the context of the sexual politics of Hollywood and US history, I neglect to attend to the complexity of Filipino gender markers, such as Anacleto's sarong, or to broader, significant implications of his multiple identities. For example, one might consider that, in 1940, there was an American colonial presence in the Philippines, or that the Philippines and the US South are both plantation-based economies.

14. The romanticist Rachmaninoff famously wrote: "Interpretation demands something of the creative instinct. If you are a composer, you have an affinity with other composers. You can make contact with their imaginations, knowing something of their problems and their ideals. You can give their works *color*. That is the most important thing for me in my interpretations, *color*. So you make music live. Without color it is dead."

15. Interestingly, both Barrios and Russo write that Weldon tries on Leonora's makeup. In fact, as he approaches the height of his obsession/breakdown, he smears on "rejuvenating cream," a somewhat pathetic and obvious metaphor.

Works Cited

Arnheim, Rudolf. *Visual Thinking*. Berkeley: U of California P, 1969.
Barrios, Richard. *Screened Out: Playing Gay in Hollywood from Edison to Stonewall*. New York and London: Routledge, 2003.
Benshoff, Harry, and Sean Griffin. *Queer Images: A History of Gay and Lesbian Film in America*. New York: Rowman and Littlefield, 2006.
Brill, Lesley. *John Huston's Filmmaking*. Cambridge: Cambridge UP, 1997.
Cavell, Stanley. *The World Viewed*. Cambridge: Harvard UP, 1979.
Carr, Virginia Spencer. *Understanding Carson McCullers*. Columbia: U of South Carolina P, 2005.
Cooper, Stephen. "The Undeclared War: Political *Reflections in a Golden Eye*." Ed. Gaylyn Studlar and David Desser. *Reflections in a Male Eye: John Huston and the American Experience*. Washington and London: Smithsonian Institution, 1993.
DeBona, Guerric. "Masculinity on the Front: John Huston's 'The Red Badge of Courage' (1951) Revisited." *Cinema Journal* 42.2 (Winter 2003): 57–80.
Kohler, Dayton. "Carson McCullers: Variations on a Theme." *College English* 13.1 (Oct. 1951): 1–8.
Mayne, Basil. "Conversations with Rachmaninoff." *Musical Opinion*. Oct. 1936.
McCullers, Carson. *Reflections in a Golden Eye*. Boston and New York: Houghton Mifflin, 2000.
Naremore, James. *Acting in the Cinema*. Berkeley: U of California P, 1990.
Philips, Gene. *Godfather: The Intimate Francis Ford Coppola*. Lexington: U of Kentucky P, 2013.

Price, Brian. "Color, the Formless, and Cinematic Eros." Ed. Angela Dalle Vacche and Brian Price. *Color: The Film Reader*. New York and London: Routledge, 2006.

Rubin, Louis D. Jr. "Carson McCullers: The Aesthetic of Pain." *Virginia Quarterly* 53 (1977): 265–83.

Russo, Vito. *The Celluloid Closet: Homosexuality in the Movies*. New York: Harper and Row, 1987.

Westling, Louise. *Sacred Groves and Ravaged Gardens: The Fiction of Eudora Welty, Carson McCullers, and Flannery O'Connor*. Athens: U of Georgia P, 2008.

WESLEY KING

Flannery O'Connor's Symbolic Motif and the Psychoanalytic Objects of John Huston's *Wise Blood*

In Flannery O'Connor's 1952 novel, *Wise Blood*, she describes how Enoch Emery lost part of his two front teeth. Enoch, a misguided but earnest zoo worker who attaches himself to the mysterious and troubled protagonist Hazel Motes, received a gag gift from his father at the age of four. O'Connor writes: "It was orange and had a picture of some peanut brittle on the outside of it and green letters that said, A NUTTY SURPRISE! When Enoch had opened it, a coiled piece of steel had sprung out at him and broken off the ends of his two front teeth" (178). Enoch's nutty surprise is, on the one hand, one of the many occurrences in the novel where the characters encounter—often in consumer culture—conflicting levels of representation. The picture of peanut brittle on the canister deliberately tricks Enoch, while the lettering on the package, "A Nutty Surprise!," misleads by proclaiming an unexpected truth. That is, the gift, by its coiled spring, delivers on its promise of surprise. On the other hand, this is also a moment that is indicative of O'Connor's use of symbolism, more generally. In her essay collection, *Mystery and Manners*, she points out that "the writer of grotesque fiction" (which she classifies herself) aims to locate "the image that will connect or combine or embody two points; one is a point in the concrete, and the other is a point not visible to the naked eye . . . but just as real" (42). With regard to Enoch's nutty surprise, the manifestly concrete situation is one of false signs and misreading, while its invisible point, unconscious to Enoch, is in the significance of the arrangement or structure that otherwise exceeds its concrete elements. The themes of temptation, punishment, and the loss of innocence center on the cruel gift from the father with its serpent-like, coiled spring. As an invisible but real point of O'Connor's religious faith, the situation restages elements of the Eden myth.

Enoch's childhood memory is not depicted in John Huston's 1979 screen adaptation, *Wise Blood*. Although the film is set in 1974, and its naturalistic style strips some of the novel's more bizarre and grotesque imagery from the story, the film is largely a faithful adaptation. Most of its dialogue is from the novel, and most scenes feature actions and visual details explicitly described by O'Connor. But, as Matthew Bernstein notes in his important reevaluation of the film, the screenwriter Benedict Fitzgerald, with direct input from Huston, deliberately avoided many of O'Connor's symbolic motifs. Fitzgerald explained that, otherwise, "we might have found ourselves getting bogged down and thinking too much about the symbolic and allegorical aspects of the story" (qtd. in Bernstein 147). Huston's film does indeed close off certain representational ambiguity that O'Connor otherwise cultivates, if for no other reason, by the fact that film more directly "literalizes the verbal text" (Demory). Additionally, as we will see, Fitzgerald and Huston chose to portray certain moments in the novel in such a way as to provide more explicit psychic motivations for Hazel Motes (played by Brad Dourif). These choices create a pathology for the character that O'Connor's novel avoids articulating.

Nevertheless, the story of *Wise Blood* is a quest for meaning, for divine revelation in its final moments, and even in its more subtle and seemingly incidental departures from the novel, the film consistently reflects upon the logic of the symbol and on ambiguities and gaps in representation. For instance, the film's opening credits present, in the style of a documentary, a series of black-and-white still photographs that depict O'Connor's "Christ haunted" South (44). As has been pointed out by Michael Klein, many of these stills show "spiritual inscriptions [to be] linked and subordinated to the signs of a commercial, commodity-oriented culture" (232). For example, one of these stills shows a sign that juxtaposes a Dairy Queen logo with the message, "Repent, be baptized, in Jesus name." This suggests a central theme of the story in which religion has become a set of empty slogans, and commodities have come to bear people's hopes and desires in its place. More broadly, though, what ties many of these black-and-white stills together is in the way that they illustrate instabilities within and alienation from symbolic structures. The photograph of the porch floods us with representational images and a wide array of competing visual codes, from novelty items that have images of animals, to icons such as the Confederate flag, to a tapestry that presents a replica of Leonardo's da Vinci's *Last Supper*, and to a stuffed bear with a black face that is reminiscent of the racist imagery of the minstrel stage. In another still, the film pointedly and comically emphasizes a gap between the name and the thing: signs that read "peaches" and "plums" stand above a fruit stand that is itself filled with used tires. One photograph—over which appears the misspelled credit "directed by Jhon Huston"—depicts a gravesite that has a freestanding wreath into which is incorporated a memorial collage, featuring the words "Jesus called" and an amateur sculpture of a rotary phone. If O'Connor's method with Enoch's nutty surprise was to locate the concrete object that would combine with or embody an invisible (but real) meaning, the photograph of the grave seems to portray an inverse method in the way it literalizes its own verbal text. The euphemism for death, "Jesus called," is made concrete in an object in such a way that redirects the intended meaning of the euphemism—"Jesus called" . . . on the phone.

Despite the filmmakers' professed avoidance of O'Connor's symbolic motifs, this framing at the outset points to other, more consequential, divergences in the film which open directly onto central questions concerning the logic of O'Connor's symbolism: namely, what is the relationship between the object and meaning in her story? In what sense are these invisible points, as she describes them, "real"? In what follows, I am going to focus on three scenes or sets of scenes, which reflect on these questions, while they, in varying respects, depart from the novel: an early scene in the film of Motes purchasing his suit, one of the dream/daydream sequences when the young Motes enters the carnival tent, and, last, a visual motif—the color blue—that is threaded throughout the final scenes. Each of these sequences treats differently the underlying relationship between concrete objects and their meanings. In the scene at the store, which is not depicted in the novel, the objects in question—Motes's suit and hat—are especially significant insofar as they are in a psychic economy of loss and compensation, presence and absence, which embodies the logic of several of O'Connor's symbols and figures. While the objects of the early store scene are portrayed as meaningful in a way that is interior to the film and its characters, the later daydream, which is an important revision to O'Connor's novel, features symbols that speak to the more universal dimensions of sex and death, a sequence that intends to illustrate Motes's unconscious drives. The last example, the use of the color blue in the final scenes, is a minimalistic gesture that is of much greater consequence than one might expect; entirely within the spirit of the novel, it helps us to better understand how in O'Connor's work she represents the relationship between contingency and grace.

My approach to understanding the logic of the symbol in Huston's film, and the film's interpretation of O'Connor, is influenced by the relationship between three objects of psychoanalysis as articulated by Jacques Lacan, especially in his *Seminar 20*: *a* (the object cause of desire), Φ (phallus, the signifier of *jouissance* or the signifier for [subjective] lack), and S(A) (the signifier for the lack in the Other). A psychoanalytic approach to the film seems particularly appropriate with regard to Huston not only because he directed *Freud: A Secret Passion* (1962) and because Huston's *Wise Blood* adds a more recognizable oedipal dimension to O'Connor's novel, but also because of the way Huston treats centralizing objects in films such as *The Maltese Falcon* (1941). The meaning of the falcon is not primarily a function of its allegorical content but rather in the way it plays a structural role both in the characters' psyches and in how the film treats the relationship between reality and fantasy. The falcon's role changes in accordance with the three phases of the film that Leslie Brill has identified. In the first phase, the falcon is a fantasy object sustaining the characters' lies and distortions, or as Brill puts it, the "unstable appearances, plots, and identities, none of which seem anchored in reality" (144). In the film's second phase, toward the end, the falcon is shown to be valueless, an empty placeholder. Brill describes this second phase as "a sudden validation of a stable world of truth," in which some characters, such as Sam Spade (Humphrey Bogart), "accept the reality of reality" by deciding to turn over Brigid O'Shaughnessey (Mary Astor) to the police. I would modify this description of the concluding scenes to call it, instead, a psychoanalytic "traversing of fantasy" (Fink 72), in that Spade, in a Kantian gesture, releases his pathological attachments (the possibility for love, even) and adopts or takes responsibility for his desire—"you'll never understand me," he says to O'Shaughnessey—as the desire of the Other, in the form of moral law. Suspending his dislike and previous infidelities to his partner (Sam was having an affair with his partner's wife), he expresses the motivation for his decision as a categorical imperative: "When a man's partner is killed, he is supposed to do something about it. It doesn't make any difference what you thought of him. He was your partner, and you are supposed to do something about it." Brill, however, identifies a third phase that corresponds with the final line of the film (and that resonates beyond its ending), when Spade takes the otherwise valueless falcon, describing it, almost reluctantly, as "the stuff that dreams are made of." For Brill, this "makes ambiguous the dichotomies" of the second phase's accepting of the "reality of reality," almost immediately after those dichotomies were established. Here, I would suggest that this final movement in the film points to the fantasy behind reality, where the falcon, though recognized as only a placeholder (a "dingus" as Spade refers to it), is nevertheless upheld as a necessary placeholder sustaining the constructed nature of reality. *Wise Blood*, we will see, articulates more pointedly the underlying way that fantasy supports reality, and in its final scenes attempts to find an object as placeholder that would shift the coordinates of fantasy and thus both the structure of subjectivity and the way in which meaning and reality are constructed. To illustrate this, we need to better understand the psychic places in which the different objects of the film are positioned to occupy: a, Φ, $S(\cancel{A})$.

a, Φ, $S(\cancel{A})$

O'Connor's titular figure, "wise blood," gestures toward a psychoanalytic or split subject, in that it combines being, "blood," with meaning, "wise." Applied to Enoch Emery, it is a figure for the unconscious, especially as the "unconscious is structured like a language" (*Seminar 11* 69). O'Connor writes that Emery's blood "wrote doom all through him, except possibly in his brain, and that the result was that his tongue . . . knew more than he did" (*Wise Blood* 129–30). In psychoanalytic thinking, the subject is split because of its entry into the imaginary and symbolic orders, which prevents its direct access to the real. In Lacan's model for understanding the formation of subjective experience, the imaginary is the order of the image, including the body image, an order where the subject's relations are essentially specular. Lacan calls this process that forms the ego, best known as "the mirror stage," a "transformation that takes place in the subject when he assumes [*assume*] an image" (*Écrits* 76). The subject "assumes" both because the image is in the subject's place and because the subject is submitted to knowledge, recognition: seeing oneself is mediated through being seen by others.[1] For Lacan, these arrested images of the imaginary order, though they promise fullness and completion to the subject in a way fundamental to fantasy, are fraught both from within the imaginary and from without: identifications are retroactively dependent on the symbolic, which is the order of language and cultural transmission, an alienating medium through which the subject must articulate demands.[2] If in the imaginary, the subject assumes the image, in the symbolic, the subject is replaced by a signifier—a name, for example. As Lacan formulates it, "A signifier is what represents the subject to another signifier," implicating the subject within a symbolic chain and placing the subject into the field of social meaning, the field of the absent Other, S(A̶) (694). Entering the symbolic is the state of castration, which can be defined as the state of lack in the symbolic for an imaginary object.[3] There is no full speech, and the symbolic object, S(A̶), designates "the impossibility of telling the whole truth" (*Seminar 20* 93). There is always slippage between signifier and signified, and speech does not materialize its referents. Language is, in a primal way, dissociated from the real: *jouissance*, radical enjoyment, is "unavowable" (92).

In *Seminar 7*, Lacan casts the relationship between the symbolic and the real as a dynamic between the (superegoic) Law and the Thing (*Das Ding*). The split subject negotiates its relationship to "primary affect" by developing an "emotional distance" from the threatening Thing of the real by means of the pleasure principle (54). Under this conception, the Law is "the presence of the moral agency in our activity, insofar as that it is structured by the symbolic" (20). While structured by the symbolic, Law, nevertheless, "is that through which the real is actualized." The real is actualized through the Law, because, at its root, the Law is a system of directing the good and the bad, and these "exist . . . as clues to that which orients the position of the subject, according to the pleasure principle" (63). In other words, the Law is the symbolic structure through which the subject can partake in a partial *jouissance*, as the subject is regulated by pleasure and unpleasure. The Thing, on the other hand, is the (absent) object of radical enjoyment. It is the "beyond-of-the-signified" that provides the lure of the real (54), and "the strange feature around which the whole movement of *Vorstellung* [the imaginary-symbolic network] turns" (57). The key point here is that the Thing of the real sustains the constructed nature of reality, while also threatening its dissolution. In its feature as the lure, the real appears as *objet a*, the object cause of desire. In its threatening dimension, it is Φ, the signifier of *jouissance*.

For Lacan, these psychoanalytic objects—*a*, Φ, S(A̶)—represent impasses and lacks between psychic registers. These are gaps that things—in the most generic sense—could come to occupy. The concept *objet a*, though "apparently something" and a piece of the real, represents the lack in the real of a symbolic object (*Seminar 20* 95). That is, as a real cause of desire, it is not truly nameable; it is something of a present absence, a "there-being" that "is not nothing" (92). Lacan refers to it as a "semblance" (93), which refers to its role in the mirror-play of the imaginary, egoistic constructions, and the body image (the imaginary "has a lot to do with 'anatomy.'" [94]). In terms of motivational objects in cinematic narrative, Slavoj Žižek suggests Alfred Hitchcock's use of the MacGuffin is a manifestation of *objet a*, an absence which "set[s] in motion the symbolic movement of interpretation" (*Sublime Object* 185). Where *a* is a lack between the symbolic and real registers, Φ, the signifier of *jouissance*, represents an impasse between the imaginary and the real. Pointing to the birds from Hitchcock's *The Birds* (1963) as an example, Žižek describes Φ as "the impassive, imaginary objectification of the Real, an image which embodies *jouissance*." For our purposes, though, it is important to note that, while Φ has a kind of imaginary, fantastical presence, even an overwhelming presence, for Lacan, it is also a signifier that "serves the function of signifying the lack of being . . . that is wrought in the subject by his relation to the signifier" (*Écrits* 594–95). That is, by signifying lack, it is excluded from the normal set of signifiers. As Lacan writes, "A church bell tower can symbolize the phallus, the phallus will never symbolize a bell tower" (594). Its exclusion is necessary for the subject to come into being both under the symbolic order and the partial *jouissance* of the pleasure principle (described together as "Law," above). Φ, in this regard, reflects the dynamics of Immanuel Kant's account of the "negative pleasure" involved in the sublime (129). The sublime presents itself as an overwhelming presence, whether mathematical or dynamic, but as Kant reveals, this presence is entirely imaginary insofar as it is not to be attributed to be a quality of the object in itself. In a sense then, with the sublime, the imaginary is lacking a real object. For Kant, this lack of a real object points back to the inherent qualities of the subject, once the subject has reestablished a proper psychic distance from the threat of the sublime. This subjective elevation established, the sublime ultimately points to the subject's freedom as a subject of the moral law.[4] Lacan, however, would not characterize this process of subjectivization under the sublime Φ as freedom, precisely, insofar as the signifier indicates "that everything we are allowed to approach by way of reality remains rooted in fantasy," or rooted in the imaginary presence of the phallus (*Seminar 20* 95). Finally, where *a* and Φ represent an "open set" of the real, S(A̸), or the signifier of the lack in the Other, represents lack in the symbolic for an imaginary object, one the effects of which I characterized as the nonidentity between signifier and signified. S(A̸) is in a fundamental way cut off from the real, and the objects that could come to occupy this psychic place seem to be of a quite different order. We will discuss this in more detail later in relation to the ending scenes of *Wise Blood*.

objet a

In the film, we see something akin to *objet a*, in both its real aspect as the absent cause of desire and its role in the imaginary construction of the ego, in Mote's relationship to his suit and hat. In a departure from the novel, the film early on places us with Motes and a shopkeeper. Motes has just emerged from a dressing room, wearing a new suit, and he begins trying on various hats. As Motes tries one hat after another, pausing each time to check himself in the mirror, we learn through his conversation with the shopkeeper that he had earned a purple heart but had refused to wear it. As he states, "I did not want people to know where I was wounded." It is unclear what location of the body he is referring to, or whether he is referring to Vietnam as the place he was wounded, or whether, metaphorically, the purple heart might signify to others a wounded heart, psychic wounds. In any case, Motes's refusal to wear the purple heart is indicative of his general rebellion as to what he perceives as the Other's demands, whether those of "people," in this instance, or God's, the state's, and everyone else's throughout the film. For example, when he first emerges from the dressing room, he deposits his army uniform, which he was wearing in the previous scenes, in the trash.

By juxtaposing Motes's invocation of his unnamed wound with the purchase of his suit and his meticulous search for a hat, the film positions the suit and hat as a compensation for Motes's deficiency or incompleteness. This suggests a duality between, on one hand, the present absence of a more fundamental object, a "not nothing" that structures desire or a psychic lack (*Seminar 20* 92), and, on the other, the generic things that might serve in its place as the concrete props of fantasy. For Motes, this suit and hat seem to indicate a vague promise outside of his symbolic universe, a promise of remaking his identity, which he is barely able to articulate. As he says to the shopkeeper: "I'm going to do some things. I'm going to do some things that I ain't never done before." It is noteworthy that during the scene we do not get a subjective shot of Motes in the mirror (which might possibly suggest wholeness or completion) or a shot where we might see Motes beside his mirror image—one or both might be expected in a moment like this—instead we remain static as he looks off to our right. This arrangement effects a displacement of Motes on several levels. His identity is both externalized into an imaginary space—a mirror image that is outside of the screen—and objectified through the wardrobe. That is, with regard to the suit and hat, he "project[s] onto them the avatar of his narcissistic image," his ideal ego (*Écrits* 685). In miniature, the scene, in staging an externalized, objectified ego, establishes a motif that, in the novel, is taken to a psychotic extreme in the case of Enoch Emery. Emery, who is obsessed with primates, becomes fascinated with Gonga, played by an actor in a gorilla suit, who is promoting a children's film. Emery eventually steals the suit, and when he rids himself of his own clothes to put it on, he loses "his former self" (198). In fact, Emery seems to lose selfhood altogether, and O'Connor registers this dramatic shift in identification in the narration by exchanging "his" for "it": "[A] black heavier shaggier figure replaced his. For an instant, it had two heads, but after a second, it pulled the dark back head over the other. . . . It began to growl and beat its chest" (199).

Motes's ideal ego constructions are certainly tamer at this moment in the store, only hinting, perhaps, at the way he will transform his body later through self-torture. Instead, the scene adds a different kind of complication to the dynamic between object and meaning that effects a displacement of his ideal ego. When Motes reaches to adjust the hat that he is ultimately to purchase, while staring off at the mirror, the price tag on the sleeve of the suit jacket is large and conspicuous. This price tag remains on the sleeve for several subsequent scenes—there is a tight shot of it when Motes is on the train, for instance—until Motes notices it in the restroom at the train station and tears it off in disgust. While we may have expected to encounter his mirror image, the price tag

Figure 16.1. In the restroom scene and elsewhere, Huston's use of mirrors complicates the relationship between subject and object.

serves as his double, instead. By having us view Motes viewing himself in this way, the film positions, against Motes's imaginary identification, his symbolic identification; if Motes is viewing himself with reference to his ideal ego, we view him with respect to his ego-ideal, "the point from which [one is] observed" (Žižek, *Sublime Object* 108). That is to say, we are not simply looking at him as an unseen voyeur, but rather the film positions us to see him as subject to larger symbolic structures and meanings, in this case economic value.

This "point from which [one is] observed" is reinforced and expanded upon in two brief scenes a few moments later in the film, after Motes arrives at the train station. The scene in the restroom and the scene in the cab, subsequent to one another, feature two mirrors that mediate three points of observation: one in the real, one in the imaginary, and one in the symbolic. In the restroom of the train station, Motes washes his hands, removes the price tag, and notices the name and address of a prostitute that has been written on the wall. While Motes washes his hands and face, we are positioned behind him and off to his left in a medium shot. Complementing the store scene where the mirror was positioned offscreen, the camera once again avoids framing Motes in the mirror (at first). Instead, it is Motes's hat that fills the reflected image as he looks down into the sink. Motes then dries his hands and looks back in the direction of the mirror; however, the subjective shot reveals that he is not looking at the mirror but the address on the wall near the mirror. Immediately following this, though, the camera frames a close-up of Motes in the mirror in such a way to suggest the perspective of the gaze, a manifestation of "objet a *in the field of the visible*" (*Seminar 11* 105), the object of the scopic drive. For Lacan, this is a structural gap in the visible and a point of the real from which the object (phenomenologically) observes. While it is perhaps impossible to truly represent the perspective of a subjective structural gap, visually or otherwise, the shot suggests such a thing in the following way. Motes's face is fully framed in the mirror, which gestures toward a subjective shot, but it is not quite subjective: we are slightly off-center and Motes, again, looks off to his right—the image of Motes, to its left—rather into the mirror, directly. We are observing Motes from a point that is within his subjective purview but on the margins of his visual field. Additionally, the shot captures part of the wall beside the mirror, which is a necessary frame for us to be aware that we are getting the mirror's perspective. Importantly, this inclusion of the wall establishes a "parallax gap" or the "confrontation between two closely linked perspectives between which no neutral common ground is possible" (Žižek, *Parallax View* 4). That is, the wall signals that we are (almost) in Motes's subjective position, while, at the same time, we observe him from the position of where the object might observe. Although *objet a* (the gaze, in this case) is not truly representable as a point of observation in the real, it is implied in the difference between these two perspectives.

If the scene in the abject setting of the restroom offers the zero point of subjective observation in the real, the subsequent scene, mediated again through a mirror, features points of observation from the imaginary and symbolic orders. Motes enters a cab and requests to be taken to the address of the prostitute. By Motes's hat, the driver mistakes him for a preacher and treats him like one despite Motes's protests. During the entire scene, the driver has his back to Motes, and their conversation takes place through the virtual space of the rearview mirror. Offering another variation in a continued theme, we do not see Motes looking into the mirror and seeing himself. Rather, he sees the driver's face, which is almost fully framed by the mirror. When the driver speaks, our perspective is Motes's perspective who himself speaks to the driver by making eye contact in the mirror, suggesting the possibility of rapport. The scene as a whole evokes an imaginary, egoic point of observation not only because we are offered the objectified image of another's look (by way of the mirror), but also because the substance of their conversation is almost entirely within the "dialectic of jealousy-sympathy" that Lacan situates in the virtual space of ego-relations (*Seminar 2* 52). The driver, who knows of the address that Motes has given him, and despite thinking that Motes is a preacher, nevertheless tries to build a sympathetic rapport: "I understand that it ain't anybody perfect on this green earth—not preachers, not nobody." The conversation comes to rivalry, however, as Motes continues to reject this identification: "Listen, get this . . . I don't believe in anything." The driver responds: "That's the trouble with you preachers. You've all got too good to believe in anything." The driver's dismissal comically highlights that what is ultimately at stake for Motes in this mirror-play of egos is his unshakeable symbolic identification, his ego-ideal, and the way that Motes's image has been transformed by the signifiers that he himself has nevertheless chosen. In the driver's last statement, the meaning attributed to the hat—of Motes's being a preacher—persists and even supersedes the conditions of being a preacher—the condition of believing in something.

The driver's statement proves prophetic, since Motes soon starts preaching "The Church without Christ," suggesting the inevitability of his role. Nevertheless, this early sequence in the film, from store to cab, dramatizes both the psychic position of *objet a* as a present absence and the objects that serve in this place as props of fantasy and ego construction, especially insofar as the fantasies that these objects sustain come into conflict with broader social meanings. Throughout O'Connor's novel, and the film, there are many variations on this dialectic of place and object. For instance, a figure such as "The Church without Christ" points to the possibility of a social structure or system of meaning emerging around a lost object. Indicative of O'Connor's novel, there is something of a present absence when O'Connor writes of Motes in a different context, "He was not waiting on the Judgment because there was no Judgment, he was waiting on nothing" (160)—but waiting, nonetheless. Conversely, Emery's "new jesus" serves as placeholder that might sustain meanings and desires, even when the concrete thing itself does not seem to provide the right conditions for meaning. The "new jesus" is a mummified corpse the size of a baby, a corpse which Emery stole from a museum.

Φ

In Motes's dreams, the logic of the symbol—the relationship between concrete objects and meaning—is considerably different. The film's greatest departure from O'Connor's novel is in its arrangement of several dream sequences which are used in order to tell the story of Motes's childhood, how he grew up under oppressive religious guilt. Interspersed as they are throughout the film, and framed by showing Motes either tossing in his sleep or staring out into space, they provide a depth of interiority to which O'Connor's novel never truly grants us access, in that they illustrate drives and motivations for Motes (despite being portrayed as largely unconscious to Motes). As dream sequences, the film breaks from its naturalism to a kind of expressionism—the scenes are more darkly lit, and the bare landscapes and backgrounds of the dreams provide a site through which sparse individual elements stand out and suggest symbolic importance. One dream, in particular, provides a symbolic motif that places us on the terrain of Φ, phallus (the signifier of *jouissance*), and introduces a different dialectic, one between the Law and the Thing, which I suggested earlier is analogous to dynamics of "negative pleasure," which Kant associates with the sublime (129). The scene in question portrays a threatening, sublime dimension of the real as something to be negotiated through the pleasure principle and the conventional, oedipal arrangement of male sexuality.

After visiting the prostitute, Motes falls asleep with her in her bed. In the following dream scene, a much younger Motes enters a carnival tent and sees a raised coffin. In order to view what is on display, he climbs the adjacent pole. From this pole, which is now between his legs, hangs a single light that illuminates the object on display. From this elevated position, Motes looks down into the coffin at a seminude woman. From Motes's perspective, we see her lie still for a brief moment, but once

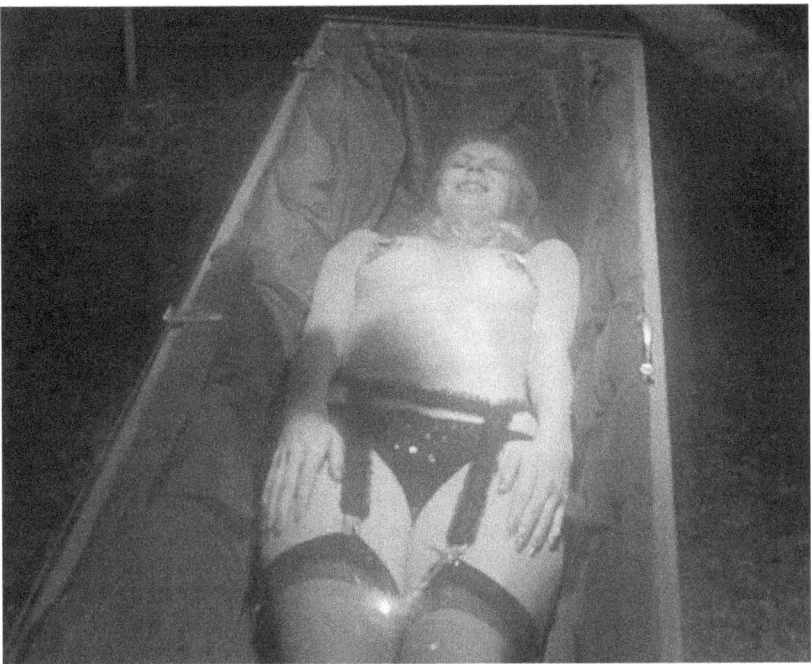

Figure 16.2. During Motes's dream, Huston pairs sexual desire with death.

she sees the young Motes she begins to gyrate and laugh hysterically set to garish brass instruments. Although she is smiling, the threatening laughter is fantastical in that it seems to be emanating both from the woman and from elsewhere as she holds a frozen smile. This laughter echoes as we return to a shot of Motes tossing in his sleep.

By way of comparison, O'Connor treats this moment in the following way:

> He slid the money on the platform and scrambled to get in before it was over . . . All he could see were the backs of the men. He climbed up the bench and looked over their heads. They were looking down into a lowered place, where something white was lying, squirming a little, in a box lined with a black cloth. For a second he thought it was a skinned animal and then he saw that it was a woman. She was fat and she had a face like an ordinary woman except that there was a mole on the corner of her lip, that moved when she grinned, and one on her side. (57–58)

Among the differences in these portrayals, O'Connor's offers distance and misdirection, where Huston's film provides something of the immediacy of *jouissance*. By describing the casket as "a box lined with a black cloth," and the woman, not as her idealized portrayal in the film, but as ordinary, O'Connor avoids elements of cathexis—anxieties and desires—that the film instead tries to emphasize. In the novel, Motes's look is focused on contingencies, the mole on the corner of her lip, the mole on her side, which are objective and contingent elements of her body that are not particularly sexualized. Most certainly, her body is not elevated to the status of the Thing as the object of "primary affect" (*Seminar 7* 54). In the film, Motes's view takes us elsewhere—specifically, to a close up of the woman's crotch. For the young Motes, however, this is portrayed as too close. The scene, while offering up the woman's body as a sexual object (in a way that is dramatically distinct from the novel), also more emphatically overlays sex and death to produce—for Motes, at least—the first moment of Kant's negative pleasure, the sublime Φ as the threatening Thing of *jouissance* without the second moment—subjectification under the Law. From Motes's perspective, there is not enough psychic distance for pleasure. In representing sex and death as a seminude woman in a coffin, there is little symbolic distance in the scene, whatsoever.

Nevertheless, the film, through this dream and other dreams/daydreams, takes us down the path of the Oedipus complex and its familiar coordinates: the father as a function of the Law and castration anxiety. For example, in a later scene, when Motes's car has stalled on the road, he has a flashback to his grandfather's preaching. While sitting terrified in the audience, the young Motes urinates himself. In the next scene, a truck driver startles Motes from his daydream, stating that his car "smells like an outhouse," as if Motes has repeated the embarrassment of his younger self. More important for us, though, is whether the meanings associated with Φ, in its dialectic between the Law and the Thing, are presented as the ultimate horizons of meaning for the film—or for that matter, the novel. Motes, like Oedipus, blinds himself, and in the novel, the situation just before he makes this decision features the motifs of Law and transgression. Motes, while driving, has been stopped by the police. After it is revealed that he has been driving without a license, and after a brief altercation, the officer asks him to drive his car to the top of an embankment. After Motes steps out of the car, the cop pushes it off the top of the embankment, destroying it. Though sparing, the description of Motes in the aftermath portrays this moment as an epiphany. O'Connor writes: "Haze stood for a few minutes, looking over at the scene. His face seemed to reflect the entire distance across the clearing and beyond, the entire distance that extended from his eyes to the blank gray sky that went on, depth after depth, into space" (211). Just after this moment, Motes walks into town to purchase the quicklime with which to blind himself.

We can interpret this moment and Motes's subsequent blinding in several (ultimately related) ways. This invocation of space and distance shares qualities with the Kantian sublime not only because of its gesturing to infinity, "depth after depth," but also because it points back to the subject, in that this is an image reflected in Motes's face. Unlike the earlier dream in the film version, this is less the first aspect of the sublime, that of the object's overwhelming excess and its threatening dimension—a threat due in large part to the fear of death—than it is the second moment. Earlier, I characterized this second moment of the sublime as lack in the imaginary for a real object, where the subject experiences the sublime to be not a quality of the object in that the object recedes and the subject takes its place. As opposed to Φ as the signifier of *jouissance*, I liken this moment of the sublime, within the dialectic of Φ, to the phallus as the signifier of lack. In O'Connor's description, Motes's experience is of a structure without content: "depth," "space," and "blank[ness]." For Kant, this would be the space where freedom can take place, freedom in relation to the moral law, and Alenka Zupančič describes this psychic space in Kant's account as the subject viewing from the position of the superego.[5] For Lacan, as well, the excluded signifier Φ "names the as yet empty space that the subject will come to be" as a subject unto the Law, or "the moral agency in our activity, insofar as that it is structured by the symbolic" (Fink 103; *Seminar 7* 20). This is to say: should we see Motes's epiphany and blinding as symbolic castration, an act in which, as Zupančič has characterized the common reading of Oedipus's act, "the subject accepts his contingent . . . destiny as something necessary, recognizing in it the meaning of existence" (175)?

The novel would suggest that we should not. At the precise moment when the novel skirts the idea that Motes's self-blinding is to pay for his more foundational transgressions, thus becoming more fully subject, the novel shifts perspective away from Motes's subjectivity altogether. The final chapter is from the point of view of Motes's landlady, Mrs. Flood. As Bernstein points out, the film, too, "visualize[s] O'Connor's decisive shift in point of view . . . We remain with Mrs. Flood for the final ten minutes of the film" (154). Neither novel nor film shows us Motes in the act of blinding himself, and thus resists treating this action as having tragic pathos. As opposed to Sam Spade's assertion of a moral imperative at the end of *The Maltese Falcon*, Motes's act has no clear universal dimension. In the final ten minutes of the film, the pacing of the action slows considerably as Motes, through the effects of his self-torture, becomes increasingly abject. It seems as if we, the audience, are waiting in some sort of leftover time, as if we are "waiting on nothing" (*Wise Blood* 160).

$$S(\cancel{A})$$

And it is in the concluding moments of the film where we encounter a different order of meaningful object, one which seems to accord with the subjective impasse of $S(\cancel{A})$, the signifier of the lack in the Other. As described earlier, this designates the lack in the symbolic for an imaginary object and implies that the symbolic is foundationally disassociated from the real. Fink suggests that $S(\cancel{A})$ may be understood as the "loss of a 'first signifier' . . . when primal repression occurs" (114). Although discourse is commonly grounded upon master signifiers, and, in theory, any word could be elevated to having this psychic status, there is no ultimate symbolic guarantor that makes meaning epistemologically complete. In terms of concrete things that might occupy this place, Žižek offers that such an object would embody a kind of paradox as a "leftover of the Real, an 'excrement'" that "functions as a positive condition of the restoration of a symbolic structure" (183), a "radically contingent" thing "through which symbolic necessity arises" (185). Such objects would seem to speak directly to O'Connor's aims in her use of symbolism. For instance, the example of Enoch Emery's "nutty surprise," with which this chapter opened, showed O'Connor to cultivate distance between the concrete thing and its invisible but real meaning, creating symbolic arrangements whose significance far exceeds the objects themselves. As Denise Askin points out, O'Connor's symbolism was influenced by the theologian William Lynch, who posited that "the 'mud in man' is nothing to be ashamed of. It can produce . . . the face of God" (qtd. in Askin 49). Throughout the novel, O'Connor's meaningful objects are either abject (like Emery's "new jesus"), spontaneous (like the "nutty surprise"), or contingent (like the moles on the woman that the young Motes views in the coffin). While these categories are not the same, they point to her looking to find a minimal threshold of materiality that can still sustain meaning, perhaps as a way of testing the void that Lacan would put at the center of the symbolic, $S(\cancel{A})$.

Detecting the face of God in the mud in man, or more precisely, the way that contingency gives rise to symbolic necessity, seems to structure the way that the film treats the ending of the novel. By the end of the story, Motes leaves the house where he is staying, presumably to die, and Mrs. Flood has called the police to search for him. The police, who are on the lookout for a missing person in a blue suit, come upon Motes where he has fallen beside the railroad tracks. Following O'Connor's novel, instead of rushing to the aid of an obviously dying man, the police discuss whether they have properly identified the color of the suit. The way that Motes is framed at this moment, between the two police officers, between the one's prominent gun and the other's nightstick, suggests that there is no escape for Motes. Whether or not he intends to repay his symbolic debt to God through his self-torture and death, he will be taken back to Mrs. Flood's to "pay his rent." Although the brief argument about the color of the suit might seem primarily meant to indicate the officers' blasé attitude to Motes's suffering, it importantly recalls an earlier scene in the film where the authority of Law is also mediated through a conversation on the meaning of color. Motes and Enoch are attempting to cross the street and are stopped abruptly by a cop, loudly blowing on his whistle. After lecturing them on obeying the light the cop adds, "Now you tell all your friends about these lights. Red is for stop, green is for go," and he goes on from there to explain the universality of this meaning. The officer says that this meaning is the same for "white folks and niggers." There is a deep irony in his appeal to universal meaning in his statement, since it asserts color-based distinctions and hierarchies while lecturing on the meaning of the color of the lights.

Nevertheless, both this earlier scene at the light and the ending are significant because of the way that color is a figure for the contingent. There is nothing intrinsic to red and green that means "stop" and "go"; rather their meanings are more clearly a result of social construction. Both film and novel in these scenes allude to the violence that might be necessary to stabilize these meanings. On the other hand, while color is not an object precisely, it is a phenomenal quality that might lay claim to a greater stability between name and thing, "blue" and the color blue. That is, as a phenomenal object, it can serve as a kind of symbolic guarantor of meaning, while resisting any specific ethos or pathos projected onto it.

At the end of the film, the color blue, though contingent, becomes a structuring, visible motif. Just previous to the police officers' discussion of whether the suit is blue, we witness Motes in blue walking by a blue house, and, a few moments later, the camera is positioned just outside the driver's side window of the police cruiser, filming its blue interior and the blue of the officers' uniforms. When the cruiser stops, the shot frames, through the passenger window, a blue dumpster which is near the center of the screen. When the police exit the vehicle, a faded blue building takes up most of the background. We see the blue of Motes's suit as they carry him to the car, the blue of the flashing police light through a barred window of Mrs. Flood's house, and then the blue of her patterned dress when they carry Motes in. Within this sequence, the shot of the dumpster seems particularly deliberate and significant: the framing of the dumpster suggests the logic of leftover, remainder, and excrement, and it reinforces the abject state that Motes is in. So, too, the brief flash of the blue light that we view from the barred window seems—to a reader of the novel—to suggest O'Connor's final image of "a pin point of light" (236).

Nevertheless, as a conventional symbol, blue is not particularly significant in its having metaphorical content—I do suppose Motes is sad, which perhaps is a meaning for blue—rather that what we see taking shape, though subtle, is an element of contingency generating a larger structure around an absence in meaning. In *Mystery and Manners*, O'Connor suggests that such subtle gestures "between the violences that precede and follow them" are "almost imperceptible intrusions of grace" (112). That is, unlike Motes's attachment to his suit and hat, or the objects of his dreams, there is something to the color blue that both escapes meaning and produces a formal space for meaning. It is in this formal space where O'Connor would place the possibility for faith.

Notes

1. See "Aggressiveness in Psychoanalysis," *Écrits* 96.
2. See "The Situation of Psychoanalysis:" "Man is, prior to his birth and beyond his death, caught up on the symbolic chain, a chain that founded his lineage before his history was embroidered upon it . . . [M]an is in fact considered to be a whole, but like a pawn, in the play of the signifier, and this is so even before its rules are transmitted to him" (*Écrits* 392).
3. See *Seminar 17* 124–28.
4. See *Critique of Judgment*, section 27, 140–43.
5. See Zupančič 149–55.

Works Cited

Askin, Denise T. "Anagogical Vision and Comedic Form in Flannery O'Connor: The Reasonable Use of the Unreasonable." *Renascence* 57.1 (2004): 47–62.

Bernstein, Matthew. "John Huston's *Wise Blood*." *Twentieth-Century American Fiction on Screen*. Ed. R. Barton Palmer. Cambridge: Cambridge UP, 2007.

Brill, Lesley. *John Huston's Filmmaking*. Cambridge: Cambridge UP, 1997.

Demory, Pamela. "Faithfulness vs. Faith: John Huston's Version of Flannery O'Connor's Wise Blood." *The Journal of Southern Religion*. Vol. 2 (1999): *ATLA Religion Database with ATLA Serials*. Web. Nov. 2016.

Fink, Bruce. *The Lacanian Subject: Between Language and Jouissance*. Princeton, NJ: Princeton UP, 1995.

Kant, Immanuel. *Critique of the Power of Judgment*. 1790. Ed. Paul Guyer. Trans.

Paul Guyer and Eric Matthews. Cambridge: Cambridge UP, 2000.

Klein, Michael. "Visualization and Signification in John Huston's *Wise Blood*: The Redemption of Reality." *Literature Film Quarterly* 12.4 (1984): 230.

Lacan, Jacques. *Écrits*. 1966. *Écrits: The First Complete Edition in English*. Trans. Bruce Fink. New York: W.W. Norton, 2006.

———. *The Ego in Freud's Theory and in the Technique of Psychoanalysis 1954–1955*. *The Seminar of Jacques Lacan*. Ed. Jacques-Alain Miller. Book 2. Trans. Sylvana Tomaselli. New York: W. W. Norton, 1991.

———. *Encore: On Feminine Sexuality, the Limits of Love and Knowledge 1972–1973*. *The Seminars of Jacques Lacan*. Ed. Jacques-Alain Miller. Book 20. Trans. Bruce Fink. New York: W. W. Norton, 1998.

———. *The Ethics of Psychoanalysis 1959–1960*. *The Seminar of Jacques Lacan*. Ed. Jacques-Alain Miller. Book 7. Trans. Dennis Porter. New York: W. W. Norton, 1992.

———. *The Four Fundamental Concepts of Psychoanalysis*. *The Seminar of Jacques Lacan*. Ed. Jacques-Alain Miller. Book 11. Trans. Alan Sheridan. New York: W. W. Norton, 1981.

———. *The Other Side of Psychoanalysis*. *The Seminars of Jacques Lacan*. Ed. Jacques-Alain Miller. Book 17. Trans. Russell Griggs. New York: W. W. Norton, 2007.

O'Connor, Flannery. *Mystery and Manners: Occasional Prose*. New York: Farrar, Straus and Giroux, 1970.

———. *Wise Blood*. 1952. New York: Farrar, Straus and Giroux, 2007.

Žižek, Slavoj. *The Parallax View*. Cambridge, MA: MIT P, 2006.

———. *The Sublime Object of Ideology*. New York: Verso, 1989.

Zupančič, Alenka. *Ethics of the Real: Kant, Lacan*. New York: Verso, 2000.

Contributors

Robert L. Colson is assistant professor of interdisciplinary humanities at Brigham Young University in the Department of Comparative Arts & Letters. His work focuses on modernist and postcolonial fiction. He is published in *ariel: A Review of International English Literature* and *Research in African Literatures* and has work forthcoming in the *James Joyce Quarterly*. His current book project, *Novel Forms of Nationalism*, examines nationalism and narrative form in the work of Virginia Woolf, James Joyce, Salman Rushdie, and Ngũgũ wa Thiong'o.

Tom Dorey is a doctoral student in the Communication and Culture program at York University in Toronto. His research focuses on auteurism in contemporary Hollywood and indie cinema, cinematic paratexts, and American "Smart Cinema." His work has appeared in *The New Review of Film and Television Studies* and *A Companion to Robert Altman* (2015).

Camilla Fojas teaches in American studies and media studies at the University of Virginia. Her books include *Cosmopolitanism in the Americas* (Purdue UP, 2005), *Border Bandits: Hollywood on the Southern Frontier* (University of Texas P, 2008), *Islands of Empire: Pop Culture and US Power* (U of Texas P, 2014), and *Zombies, Migrants, and Queers: Race and Crisis Capitalism in Pop Culture* (U of Illinois P, 2017). She co-edited *Mixed Race Hollywood* (New York UP, 2008) with Mary Beltrán and *Transnational Crossroads: Remapping the Americas and the Pacific* (Nebraska UP, 2012) with Rudy Guevarra. Her articles have appeared in *Cinema Journal*, *Symplōke*, *Journal of Asian American Studies*, *Journal of Popular Film and Television*, and *Comparative American Studies*, among other journals and edited collections.

Jonathan C. Glance is the Benjamin W. Griffith Jr. Professor and chair of the Department of English at Mercer University. He received his

PhD from the University of North Carolina at Chapel Hill. His research interests are in the depiction of literary dreams in gothic, romantic, and Victorian novels. His work has appeared in *The Journal of the Fantastic in the Arts* and *Studies in Scottish Literature*.

Betty Kaklamanidou is a Fulbright scholar and an assistant professor in film and television history and theory at Aristotle University, Thessaloniki, Greece. She is the co-editor of *The Millennials on Film and Television* (2014), *HBO's "Girls"* (2014), and *The 21st Century Superhero* (2010), and the author of *Genre, Gender and the Effects of Neoliberalism: The New Millennium Hollywood Rom Com* (2013) and two books in Greek on adaptation theory and the history of the Hollywood rom com. Betty is currently co-editing a collection on political television shows and is publishing her new monograph on the construction of the contemporary political film genre in Hollywood.

Wesley King is an assistant professor of English at Flagler College. He received his PhD from the University of Virginia, and his research interests are in psychoanalysis and race. His current book project is on whiteness, aesthetic theory, and nineteenth-century American literature. Work from this project has appeared in *The Emily Dickinson Journal*.

Thomas Leitch teaches English and directs the Film Studies Program at the University of Delaware. His most recent books are *Wikipedia U: Knowledge, Authority, and Liberal Education in the Digital Age* and the forthcoming *Oxford Handbook of Adaptation Studies*.

Douglas McFarland is a professor and chair of the English Department at Flagler College. He has published pieces on the Coen brothers, Peter Bogdanovich, and Hitchock, as well as Montaigne and Rabelais.

R. Barton Palmer is Calhoun Lemon Professor of Literature and director of film studies at Clemson University. Among his many publications on literature/film adaptation are four edited volumes on Cambridge University Press: *Modern American Drama on Screen* (with William Robert Bray), *Modern British Drama on Screen* (with William Robert Bray), *Nineteenth-Century American Fiction on Screen*, and *Twentieth-Century American Fiction on Screen*. He has also edited *Hitchcock at the Source: The Auteur as Adaptor* (SUNY P). Along with Julie Grossman, Palmer serves as general/founding editor of the book series *Adaptation and Visual Culture* (Palgrave MacMillan). He wrote *To Kill a Mockingbird: The Relationship between the Novel and the Film* and, forthcoming, *60s Literary Cinema in Great Britain and the United States* (both Bloomsbury).

Dale M. Pollock is an associate professor in cinema studies and producing at the North Carolina School of the Arts, where he previously served for seven years as dean of the School of Filmmaking. He received his bachelors from Brandeis University and his masters in communications from San Jose State University. He is the president of Peak Productions of Los Angeles, CA, and Green Street Productions of Winston-Salem, NC. He has produced thirteen feature films, including *House of Cards* (in North Carolina), *Set It Off*, *Mrs. Winterbourne*, and *Blaze*. Films he produced were nominated for four Academy Awards and starred actors such as Paul Newman, Shirley MacLaine, Denzel Washington, Queen Latifah, Tommy Lee Jones, and Kathleen Turner.

Murray Pomerance is a professor in the Department of Sociology and director of the Media Studies Working Group at Ryerson University. His recent books include *The Eyes Have It: Cinema and the Reality Effect* (Rutgers, 2013), *Alfred Hitchcock's America* (Polity, 2013), *Tomorrow* (Oberon, 2012), and *Michelangelo Red Antonioni Blue: Eight Reflections on Cinema* (California, 2011). He has edited or co-edited numerous volumes, including *The Last Laugh: Strange Humors of Cinema* (Wayne State, 2013), *Hollywood's Chosen People: The Jewish Experience in American Cinema* (Wayne State, 2012), *Shining in Shadows: Movie Stars of the 2000s* (Rutgers 2011), and *A Little Solitaire: John Frankenheimer and American Film* (Rutgers, 2011). He is editor of the "Horizons of Cinema" series at State University of New York Press and the "Techniques of the Moving Image" series at Rutgers, and, with Lester D. Friedman and Adrienne L. McLean respectively, co-editor of both the Screen Decades and Star Decades series at Rutgers University Press.

Nathan Ragain received his PhD in English from the University of Virginia and is currently a postdoctoral scholar at the University of Nevada, Reno. His manuscript project, "Collective Subjects: The Aesthetics of Revolutionary Nationalisms," examines how ethnic US writers since the 1960s have developed experimental aesthetic forms to navigate between identitarian and universalist politics. Articles from this project have appeared in *Criticism* and in a 2013 special issue of *MELUS* on cross-racial collaboration.

Steven Rybin is an assistant professor of film studies at Minnesota State University, Mankato. He is the author of *Gestures of Love: Romancing Performance in Classical Hollywood Cinema* (SUNY P, forthcoming), editor of *The Cinema of Hal Hartley: Flirting with Formalism* (Wallflower, 2016,) and co-editor, with Will Scheibel, of *Lonely Places, Dangerous Ground: Nicholas Ray in American Cinema* (SUNY P, 2014).

David Sigler is an assistant professor of English at the University of Calgary. He is the author of *Sexual Enjoyment in British Romanticism: Gender and Psychoanalysis, 1753–1835* (McGill-Queen's UP, 2015). He has written about Freud and Lacan in journals such as *SubStance*, *Criticism*, *Interdisciplinary Literary Studies*, *Shakespeare Yearbook*, and *Studies in Popular Culture*.

Kyle Stevens is a visiting assistant professor of cinema studies and English at Colby College. He is the author of *Mike Nichols: Sex, Language, and the Reinvention of Psychological Realism* (Oxford UP, forthcoming), and his essays have appeared in *Cinema Journal*, *Critical Quarterly*, *Film Criticism*, and *World Picture*, as well as several edited collections. In 2016, he will become editor of *New Review of Film and Television Studies*.

Alan Woolfolk is vice president of academic affairs and dean of the faculty at Flagler College in Saint Augustine, Florida. He is a sociologist who has published extensively on contemporary culture, public intellectuals, film, and social theory. He has twice been a National Endowment for the Humanities Fellow and is a member of the editorial board of *Society*.

Index

Adorno, Theodor, 28
African Queen, The, xvii, 107–111, 113–122
African Queen, The (John Huston, 1951), xvii, 4, 8, 11–12, 107–123, 129, 141
Agee, James, 8, 12, 43–44, 141, 143, 145
Albee, Edward, 127
Ali, Muhammad, 153, 160
All Quiet on the Western Front (Lewis Milestone, 1930), 148
Allied Artists, 102
Alighieri, Dante, xvi, 47, 49, 240
Alonso, Juan J., 205
Altman, Rick, 9, 16
American Mercury, 165
Anderson, Christopher, 137
Anderson, Maxwell, 4
Anderson, Michael, 130
Andrew, Dudley, xiv
Andrews, Anthony, 45
Andrews, Geoff, 3
Annie (John Huston, 1982), 5–6, 8
Annie Get Your Gun (George Sidney, 1950), 31
Antonioni, Michelangelo, 133
Aragon, Art, 157, 160
Arnheim, Rudolph, 255
Arnold, Jack, 211, 216, 227–228
Around the World in 80 Days (Michael Anderson, 1956), 130

Askin, Denise, 286
Asphalt Jungle, The, 24–25, 34
Asphalt Jungle, The (John Huston, 1950), xv, xvii, 3, 4, 9–10, 23–40, 46, 143, 153, 168
Astor, Mary, 80, 83–84, 111, 173, 186, 193, 274
As You Like It, 115
Autobiographical Study, 235, 238, 242
Avildsen, John G., 154

Bacall, Lauren, 12, 172
Bachmann, Gideon, 93, 142, 146–147
Baker, Aaron, 165
Balio, Tino, 137
"Ballad of Boh Dah Thone, The," 95
Banita, Georgiana, 121
Barbarian and the Geisha, The, (John Huston, 1958), 3, 5, 8
Barrios, Richard, 266
Barry, Kevin, 57–58, 62, 65, 70–71
Basehart, Richard, 212–214
Batman Returns (Tim Burton, 1992), 172
"Battle Hymn of the Republic, The," 150
Battle of San Pietro, The (John Huston, 1945), 4, 5, 126–127, 143, 149
Baudelaire, Charles, 44, 53–54, 56, 182, 186–187, 190
Bauman, Rebecca, 169

Bazin, André, xiv
BBC, 2, 6
Beast from 20,000 Fathoms, The (Eugène Lourié, 1953), 216, 220, 226
Beat the Devil (John Huston, 1953), 5, 13, 14
Bedoya, Alfonso, 198, 205–206
Being and Nothingness, 52
Benshoff, Harry, 267
Berg, Charles Ramirez, 204–205
Bergman, Ingmar, xiii, 6, 133
Bergon, Frank, 144
Bernstein, Matthew, 272, 285
Berumen, Frank Javier Garcia, 206
Bible… In the Beginning, The (John Huston, 1966), 4, 130
Bicycle Thieves (Vittorio de Sica, 1948), 131
Bingham, Dennis, 235, 246
Birds, The (Alfred Hitchcock, 1963), 129, 277
Birth of a Nation, The (D. W. Griffith, 1914), 146
Bisset, Jacqueline, 45
Black Bird, The (David Giler, 1975), 4
Black Angel (Roy William Neill, 1946), 189
Blair, Betsy, 130–131
Bleak House (Justin Chadwick and Susanna White, 2005), 2
"Blue Hotel, The," 143
Boddy, William, 137
Boetticher, Budd, 3
Bogart, Humphrey, 9–10, 78–79, 83–86, 88–89, 107, 111, 118, 121, 141, 164, 173, 182, 193, 200, 274
Bogdanovich, Peter, 29
Bond, Ward, 84, 188
Bondanella, Peter, 169, 178
Boone, Pat, 127
Border Incident (Anthony Mann, 1949), 206
Bordwell, David, 133–135
Borgnine, Ernest, 131

Bradbury, Ray, 13, 211, 215–222, 224, 227–228
Brady, Matthew, 10, 146
Brando, Marlon, 250, 256–258, 261, 263, 266
Breen, Joseph H., 33, 147
Breuer, Josef, xviii, 233–244
Bridges, Jeff, 154–155, 157–159
Brill, Leslie, xiii, xv, 3, 58, 60, 67, 70–71, 77, 81, 108, 128, 250, 254, 274–275
Bringing Up Baby (Howard Hawks, 1938), 114–115, 120, 122
Bronfen, Elisabeth, 178
Brougham, George, 13–14
Brown, Clarence, 141
Brown, Norman, 34–35
Bull, Peter, 110
Buñuel, Luis, 6
Burnett, W. R., xv, 4, 24–25, 34
Burnham, John, 184
Burton, Richard, 128, 133
Burton, Tim, 172
Bush, George W., 178
Butch Cassidy and the Sundance Kid (George Roy Hill, 1969), 92
Byron, George, 8

Cahier de Cinema, xiv
Cahir, Costanzo, 213
Cain, James, 183
Caine, Michael, 9
Calhern, Louis, 26, 31–32
California Conquest (Lew Landers, 1952), 206
Calinescue, Matei, 182–183
Cameron, James, 111–112, 172
Cantor, Paul, 191
Carr, Virginia Spencer, 252
Cartmell, Deborah, 2
Caruso, Anthony, 26
Casetti, Francesco, 38
Cavell, Stanley, 181, 186, 265
Chadwick, Justin, 2
Chambers, John, 15

Chandler, Raymond, 183
Chaney, Lon, 13
Charbonneau, Marie-Andre, 233–234
Cheng, Vincent J., 57, 64, 72
Chaplin, Charlie, 4
Chase, Richard, 212, 215
Chayefsky, Paddy, 126
"Child is Being Beaton, A," 242
Church, Philip, 24
Clarke, Candy, 155
Clayton, Jack, 135
Clift, Montgomery, 4, 234
Codell, Julie F., 94–95, 97
Coen, Ethan, 256
Coen, Joel, 256
Cokes, Curtis, 159
Colasanto, Nicholas, 159–160
Cole, Bill, 34
Columbia Pictures, 113, 226
Committee for the First Amendment, 198
Condon, Richard, 4, 167–172, 178
Connery, Sean, 9, 100, 128
Cook, Fielder, 125, 133
Cook, Jr., Elisha, 85, 193
Cooper, Stephen, 250, 254
Coppola, Francis Ford, 178
Costigan, James, 126
Cowan, Jerome, 84
Crane, Stephen, xvi, xviii, 139, 141–151
Croce, Arlene, 3, 8
Crowther, Bosley, 12, 130, 134
Curtis, Tony, 13–15
Curtiz, Michael, 3, 5, 18
Custen, George, 235

Dangerous Liaisons (Stephen Frears, 1988), 176
Dano, Royal, 143
David, Zorro, 252, 261
Davies, Andrew, 2, 6
Davis, Bette, 113–114
Days of Wine and Roses (Blake Edwards, 1962), 133

"Dead, The," 57–73
Dead, The (John Huston, 1987), xvi, xvii, 1, 4, 9, 57–73, 111, 129
DeBona, Guerric, 140
De Laurentiis, Dino, 129
Delevantias, Cyril, 132
Demme, Jonathan, 178
Demory, Pamela, 272
Densham, Pen, 2
Derrida, Jaques, 236, 237, 246
De Sica, Vittorio, 131
Desser, David, 137, 197
De Stefano, George, 176
Detour (Edgar G. Ulmer, 1945), 190–191
Devine, Andy, 149
Dexter, Brad, 26
Diaghilev, Serge, 28
DiBattista, Maria, 114–115
Dickens, Charles, 8
Dierkes, John, 147, 149
Dieterle, William, 5
Dobbs, Fred C., 10
Domergue, Faith, 226
Dominik, Andrew, 178
Double Indemnity (Billy Wilder, 1944), 172, 189–191
Douglas, Kirk, 13–14, 127
Dourif, Brad, 165, 272
Dr. Ehrlich's Magic Bullet (William Dieterle, 1940), 5
Drucker, Peter, 191–192
"Drums of the Fore and Aft, The," 96, 102
Dubliners, 47, 49, 54
Duffy, Edna, 72
Du Maurier, Daphne, 3
Durant, Tim, 146
Dyer, Richard, 158

Ebert, Roger, 256–257, 263
Edgerton, Gary, 126–127
Edwards, Blake, 133
Eksteins, Modris, 28–29
Eliot, T. S., 45

Emma (Diarmuid Lawrence, 1996), 2
Engell, John, 206
Epstein, Jean, 38
Evan, Sara M., 170
Eyman, Scott, 168

Fairbanks, Douglas, 13
Farber, Manny, 77
Fahrenheit 451, 216
Farmer, David, 199
Fat City, xviii, 153–155, 161, 163
Fat City (John Huston, 1972), xviii, 5, 47, 153–165
Fellini, Frederico, 6, 133
Fiedler, Leslie, 250
"Figures of Fighting Men," 155
Film Culture, 142
Fink, Bruce, 274, 286
Finnegans Wake, 44
Finney, Albert, 45, 49–50
Fitzgerald, Benedict, xviii, 272
Fitzgerald, F. Scott, 8, 144
Fitzgerald, Michael, 11
Fleming, Victor, 141, 254
Flesh and the Spirit, The, 5
Florey, Robert, 5
Flowers of Evil, 53–54
"Fog Horn, The," 216, 220
Foreman, John, 92, 102
Forester, C. S., xvii, 4, 12, 107–111, 113–122
Forster, Robert, 250
"Fool," 155
Forbidden Planet (Fred M. Wilcox, 1956), 224
Four Hundred Blows, The (François Truffaut, 1959), 131
Frankenheimer, John, 125, 127–129
Frears, Stephen, 176
Freud, Sigmund xvi, xviii, 35, 233–247
Freud: The Secret Passion (John Huston, 1962), xvi, xviii, 3, 4, 102, 129, 233–247, 274

Freund, Karl, 50
From Here to Eternity (Fred Zinnemann, 1953), 128
Frye, Northrop, 45–46
Fuller, Graham, 2
Fultz, James R., 12
Furnace Harbor, 24

Gallo, Guy, 46
Gardner, Ava, 128, 133
Gardner, Leonard, xviii, 153–155, 160–161, 163
Garnett, Tay, 172
Garralaga, Martin, 204
Georgakas, Dan, 147
Gethryn, Anthony, 13–14
Giannetti, Louis, 168
Gibbons, Luke, 72
Gigot (Gene Kelly, 1962), 128
Giler, David, 4
Girard, René, 193
Gleason, Jackie, 128
Glenville, Peter, 125
Godard, Jean-Luc, 133
Godfather Part III (Francis Ford Coppola, 1990), 178
Gone with the Wind (Victor Fleming, 1939), 141
Gordon, Robert, 226
Grant, Cary, 114–115, 120
Green, Guy, 125
Greenberg, Harvey Roy, 187
Greene, Graham, 183
Greenstreet, Sidney, 78, 85
Griffin, Sean, 267
Grimes, Stephen, 12, 92, 102
Grobel, Lawrence, 197, 213, 215–216, 225–226
Guinness, Alec, 4, 13
Gunning, Tom, 29

Hagen, Jean, 27
Hall, Conrad L., 154, 161–162
Hall, Grayson, 132
Hammen, Scott, 140, 143

Hammet, Dashiell, xv–xvii, 3, 75–82, 126, 182–186, 188–190
Hands of Orlac, The (Karl Freund, 1935), 50
Hard Day's Night, A (Richard Lester, 1964), 254
Hardy, Thomas, 8
Harris, Julie, 252
Harris, Mark, 126
Harris, Oliver, 179
Harryhausen, Ray, 226
Hart, Clive, 72
Haskin, Byron, 224
Hathaway, Henry, 3
Hawks, Howard, 5, 18, 33, 114–115, 120, 122, 167
Hayden, Sterling, 26, 30
He Knew He Was Right (Andrew Davies, 2004), 2
Heaven Knows, Mr. Allison (John Huston, 1957), 5, 7, 11, 129
Helvick, James, 5
Hepburn, Katherine, xviii, 9, 12, 107–108, 113–122, 141
Heber, Reginald, 97
Hecht-Hill-Lancaster, 131
"Help Me Make It through the Night," 162
Hemingway, Ernest, 144
High Sierra (Raoul Walsh, 1941), xv, 5
Higham, Charles, 139, 143
Hill, The (Sidney Lumet, 1965), 128
Hill, George Roy, 92
Hill, Gladys, 91–102
Hitchcock, Alfred, xiii–xv, 1, 2–6, 8, 11, 16, 18, 29, 129, 189, 194, 276–277
Hobsbawn, Eric, 201
Holt, Tim, 200
Holton, Milne, 144–145, 149
Hornblow, Jr., Arthur, 24–25
House Un-American Activities Committee, 197–198
Humberstone, H. Bruce, 206

Huston, Anjelica, 4, 58, 111, 168
Huston, Tony, 4
Huston, Walter, 4, 151, 193, 200
Hutcheon, Linda, 67
Hyman, Elliot, 127

I Confess (Alfred Hitchcock, 1953), 29
In This Our Life (John Huston, 1942), 5
Independence (John Huston, 1976), 5
Inge, William, 126
Interpretation of Dreams, The, 239, 240, 242, 244
Invasion of the Body Snatchers (Don Siegel, 1956), 225–226
It Came from Beneath the Sea (Robert Gordon, 1955), 226
It Came from Outer Space (Jack Arnold, 1953), 211, 216, 227–228
ITV, 2

Jaffe, Sam, 26–27, 29
James, C. L. R., 214
James, William, 43, 50–51
Jameson, Richard T., 144
Jaws (Steven Spielberg, 1975), 7, 225–227
Jezebel (William Wyler, 1938), 5
Johnston, Hugh, 15
Jones, Ernst, 235, 237, 243, 245
Jost, François, 59–60
Joyce, James, xv, xvii, 4, 44–45, 47, 49, 54, 56, 57–73, 108
Juarez (William Dieterle, 1939), 5
Julius Caesar (Joseph L. Mankiewicz, 1953), 31

Kael, Pauline, 6
Kaminsky, Stuart, 143, 156, 162
Kant, Immanuel, 277, 282, 285, 288
Kaper, Bronislau, 149
Karloff, Boris, 218
Kaufman, Charles, 235, 238
Kazan, Elia, 125–127
Keach, Stacy, 154–159

Keaton, Buster, 120
Keith, Brian, 252
Kelley, Barry, 26
Kelly, Gene, 128
Kenner, Hugh, 58
Kerr, Deborah, 128, 133
Kessler, Harry Graf, 28
Key Largo (John Huston, 1948), 4, 168
Killers, The (Robert Siodmak, 1946), 13, 189–190
Killing, The (Stanley Kubrick, 1956), 32
Killing Them Softly (Andrew Dominik, 2012), 178
Kimball, George, 155, 160
King Lear, 49
Kipling, Rudyard, 10, 91–98, 101–102
Klein, Michael, 272
Koch, Gertrud, 237
Kohler, Dayton, 251–252, 254
Kohner, Paul, 140
Kraft Television Theatre, 126
Kramer, Stanley, 125
Kristofferson, Kris, 162
Krohn, Bill, 6
Kubrick, Stanley, xiii, 32
Kurosawa, Akira, xiii
Krushchev, Nakita, 214

Lacan, Jacques, xviii, 274–278, 280–281, 284–286, 288
Lake, Veronica, 172
La Mure, Pierre, 5, 10
Lancaster, Burt, 13, 14
Lancaster, Elsa, 113
Landers, Lew, 206
Lang, Fritz, 8, 16
"Lass of Aughrim, The," 68
Laughton, Charles, 113
Lavery, David, 212, 222–223
Laws, Page, 1, 228
Lawrence, D. H., 45
Lawrence, Marc, 26–27

Lebeau, Vicky, 234–235
Lehmann-Haupt, Christopher, 161, 163
LeRoy, Mervyn, 167
Lester, Richard, 254
Let There Be Light (John Huston, 1946), 126–127, 140, 143–145
Letters to Fleiss, 245
Lewis, Edward, 13
Lewis, Joseph H., 3
Life and Times of Judge Roy Bean, The (John Huston, 1972), 5
Life and Works of Sigmund Freud, The, 235, 237, 243, 245
Lincoln, Abraham, 214
List of Adrian Messenger, The (John Huston, 1963), 4, 12–16, 129
Little Caesar (Mervyn LeRoy, 1931), 167
Little Dorrit, 2
Litwak, Leo, 155
Lonely Passion of Judith Hearne (Jack Clayton, 1987), 135
Long, Robert Emmet, 215
Lorre, Peter, 85, 188, 193
Lourié, Eugène, 216, 220, 226
Lowry, Malcolm, xv–xvi, 4, 43–46
Lubitsch, Ernst, 17
Lumet, Sidney, 125, 128
Lynch, William, 286
Lyon, Sue, 132

MacDonald, Philip, 12, 13–14, 17
MacKenzie, Aeneas, 92, 102
Mackintosh Man, The (John Huston, 1973), 5
MacLane, Barton, 188
MacMurray, Fred, 172
Madsen, Axel, 92–93, 101–102
Magnificent Yankee, The (John Sturges, 1950), 31
Mahan, Wayne, 160
Mailer, Norman, 7
Main Attraction, The (Daniel Petrie, 1962), 127

Maltese Falcon, The, xvi–xvii, 75–82, 182–186, 188–190
Maltese Falcon, The (Roy Del Ruth, 1931), 76
Maltese Falcon, The (John Huston, 1941), xvi–xvii, 1, 3–5, 76–89, 111, 126, 164, 168, 173, 181–195, 274, 285
Mamoulian, Rouben, 18
Manganiello, Dominic, 72
"Man Who Would Be King, The," 91–95, 98
Man Who Would Be King, The (John Huston, 1975), xvii, 4, 6, 9–10, 43, 91–102, 135
Manchurian Candidate, The (John Frankenheimer, 1964), 129
Mankiewicz, Joseph L., 31
Mann, Anthony, 206
Mann, Daniel, 125
Mann, Delbert, 125, 130–131
Marnie (Alfred Hitchcock, 1964), 129
Married to the Mob (Jonathan Demme, 1988), 178
Martian Chronicles, The, 216
Marty (Delbert Mann, 1955), 130–131
Mathiessen, F. O., 212, 215
Mauldin, Bill, 147, 149
Mayer, Louis B., 33, 140–143
Mayne, Basil, 268
McBride, Joseph, 92
McCallum, David, 233
McCann, Donnal, 58, 111
McClory, Sean, 58
McCullers, Carson, xviii, 4, 108, 249–253, 259–266
McIntire, John, 26
McIntosh, Mary, 32
Melville, Herman, xv–xvi, 100, 211–228
Mencken, H. L., 165
Merlin, Jan, 15–17
Merrick, David, 135
Metz, Christian, 234

Metz, Walter C., 212, 228
Meyers, Jeffrey, 155, 157, 243
MGM, xviii, 24, 135, 139–144, 149–151
Middlemarch, 2
Milestone, Lewis, 148
Miller, Arthur, 126–127, 129
Miller, J. P., 126
"Minstrel Boy, The," 97
Misfits, The (John Huston, 1961), 5, 7, 120–121, 126, 129, 153
Mitchell, Kurt, 15
Mitchum, Robert, 13–14
Moby-Dick, xv–xvi, 100, 211–228
Moby Dick (John Huston, 1956), xv–xvi, 7, 10, 13, 43, 47, 100, 127, 211–228
Moll Flanders (Pen Densham, 1996), 2
Monroe, Marilyn, 26, 33, 120–121
Monta, Rudolf, 24–25
Morely, Robert, 116
Morris, Oswald, 216
Moulin Rouge (John Huston, 1952), 5, 9–10, 13, 47, 127
Mulligan, Robert, 125
Murders in the Rue Morgue (Robert Florey, 1932), 5
Murphy, Audie, 143, 147–149
Murray, William, 227
Mystery and Manners, 271–272, 288

Nabokov, Vladimir, 23
Naremore, James, 31, 57–58, 77, 84–85, 183, 267
Neill, Roy William, 189
Nietzsche, Friedrich, 35
New York Times, The, 17, 163
Nichols, Mike, 127–128, 176, 254
Nicholson, Jack, 169
Night of the Iguana, The, xvi, xviii, 127–128, 131–136
Night of the Iguana, The (John Huston, 1964), xvi, xviii, 4, 127–129, 131–136
Nin, Anaïs, 108

Index

Nolan, William F., 129, 141–142, 144–145
Norris, Margot, 67–68
Notorious (Alfred Hitchcock, 1946), 31
Now, Voyager (Irving Rapper, 1942), 114
Nyby, Christian, 226

O Brother, Where Art Thou? (Joel and Ethan Coen, 2000), 256
Oates, Joyce Carol, 153–155, 162
Obama, Barack, 178
O'Connor, Flannery, xv, xviii, 18, 108, 250, 271–275, 279, 281–288
Of Human Hearts (Clarence Brown, 1938), 141
Oland, Warner, 218
Open Book, An, xv, xvi, xvii 9, 12, 44, 78, 123, 140–142, 160
Oppenheimer, Robert J., 221
Osteen, Mark, 1
Out of the Past (Jacques Tourneur, 1947), 189–190
"Overture to Semiramide," 172

Palmer, R. Barton, 27, 137, 183, 189, 194
Palmer, William J., 168, 176
Parks, Larry, 236
Patterns (Fielder Cook, 1956), 133
Patrick, Lee, 83, 193
Pease, Donald, 212, 214–215
Peck, Gregory, 212, 214–215, 224
Perry, Frank, 125
Peterson, Lowell, 36
Petrie, Daniel, 127
Phobia (John Huston, 1980), 5
Philco-Goodyear Television Playhouse, The, 126
Phillips, Gene, 131, 267
Pierpoint, Claudia Roth, 114
Pitt, Brad, 178
Pizzello, Stephen, 162
Phaedrus, 35
Pippin, Robert, 181, 188–189

Place, Janey, 36
Plain Tales from the Hills, 95
Plato, 35
Playhouse 90, 126
Pollack, Sydney, 126
Pontalis, J. B., 237
Pope, Alexander, 56
Portrait of the Artist as a Young Man, A, 47, 58
Posnack, Ross, 51
Postman Always Rings Twice, The (Tay Garnett, 1946), 172
Pound, Ezra, 45
Price, Brian, 255
Pride and Prejudice, 2
Principles of Psychology, The, 51
Prisoner of Zenda, The (Richard Thorpe, 1952), 31
Prizzi's Honor, 167–172, 178
Prizzi's Honor (John Huston, 1985), xvi, xviii, 4, 167–178
Psycho (Alfred Hitchcock, 1960), 129
Psychopathology of Every Day Life, The, 245
Public Enemy, The (William A. Wellman, 1931), 167

Quintero, José, 127

Rachmaninoff, Sergei, 262, 266
Rapper, Irving, 114
Ray, Robert B., 80
Reagan, Ronald, xvi, 168, 170
Rebecca, 3
Red Badge of Courage, The, xvi, xviii, 139, 141–151
Red Badge of Courage, The (John Huston, 1951), xvi, xviii, 10, 12, 139–151
Red River (Howard Hawks, 1948), 18
Reflections in a Golden Eye, 108, 249–253, 259–266
Reflections in a Golden Eye (John Huston, 1967), xvi, xviii, 4, 7, 10, 111, 249–269

Reinhard, Wolfgang, 238
Reinhardt, Gottfried, 141–144
Report from the Aleutians (John Huston, 1943), 4, 5, 126, 143
Reyes, Luis, 204
Richardson, Lee, 175
Richardson, William P., 146
Ritt, Martin, 125
Rivero, Julian, 204
Roach, Janet, 167, 170
Robinson, David, 159
Rocky (John G. Avildsen, 1976), 154
Rodriguez, Sixto, 157, 160
Roman Spring of Mrs. Stone, The (José Quintero, 1961), 127
Roosevelt, Eleanor, 12, 121–122
Roots of Heaven, The, 3, 5, 8
Ross, Lillian, 12, 141, 143, 146–147, 150–151
Rossen, Robert, 125
Rossini, Gioachino, 173
Rosson, Harold, 26, 39, 146, 148
Rosson, Richard, 167
Rowland, Henry, 28
Rubie, Peter, 204
Rubin, Louis, 267
Ruskin, Joseph, 173
Russo, Vito, 265–266

Sarris, Andrew, 3–8, 11, 16, 18
Sartre, Jean-Paul, 52, 129, 235, 239, 245
Satan Met a Lady (William Dieterle, 1936), 3, 76
Scarface: The Shame of a Nation, (Howard Hawks and Richard Rosson, 1932), 167
Schary, Dore, 25, 140–143, 150
Schenk, Nicholas, 141, 151
Schivelbusch, Wolfgang, 28–29
Scholes, Robert, 47
Schlesinger, John, 125
Schrader, Paul, 36
Schulberg, Budd, 31
Schwarzenegger, Arnold, 158

Scott, George C., 13
Scott, Lizabeth, 172
Sea Beast, The (Millard Webb, 1926), 211
Seadler, Si, 150–151
Seigal, Sam, 114, 141
Seigel, Don, 225–226
Sergeant York (Howard Hawks, 1941), 5
Serling, Rod, 126–127
Seven Arts Productions, 127, 135
Seven Days in May (John Frankenheimer, 1964), 127–128
Shakespeare, William, 49, 81, 115
Shaw, Charles, 5
Shelley, Mary, 8
Shooting Montezuma: A Hollywood Monster Story, 15–16
Sidney, George, 31
Sight and Sound, 159
Simon, Neil, 136
Sinatra, Frank, 13–15
Sinful Davey (John Huston, 1969), 5
Siodmak, Robert, 13, 189–190
"Six O'Clock, Winter," 24
Sloan, John, 24
Smight, Jack, 125, 156
Smith, Julian, 178
Smith, Maggie, 135
Sobchack, Vivian, 178
Soldier's Three and Other Tales, 95–96
Some Like It Hot (Billy Wilder, 1959), 13
"Son of God Goes Forth to War, The," 97
Sontag, Susan, 193, 213, 220, 223
Spielberg, Steven, 7, 225–227
Splendor in the Grass (Elia Kazan, 1961), 126
Stalin, Joseph, 214
Stallman, R. W., 145–146
Stallone, Sylvester, 154, 158
Stanwyck, Barbara, 172
Stark, Ray, 127–129, 135–136
Stranger, The (Orson Welles, 1946), 13

Streetcar Named Desire, 131
Streetcar Named Desire (Elia Kazan, 1951), 127
Stresemann, Gustav, 28
Student Prince, The (Richard Thorpe, 1954), 31
Studies on Hysteria, xvi, xviii, 233–244
Studlar, Gaylan, 97, 101, 137, 156, 165, 197
Sturges, John, 31

"Taps," 149
Taubman, Howard, 131–132, 135–136
Taylor, Elizabeth, 252
Taylor, John Russell, 14
Taylor, Trey, 114
Teal, Ray, 30
Tempest, The, 81
Ten Most Wanted Men (H. Bruce Humberstone, 1955), 206
Terminator 2: Judgment Day (James Cameron, 1991), 172
Texas Carnival (Charles Walters, 1951), 143
Thatcher, Margaret, xvi, 168
Thorpe, Richard, 31
Thing from Another World, The (Christian Nyby, 1951), 226
This Property is Condemned (Sydney Pollack, 1966), 127
Three Essays on Sexuality, 242, 244
Tice, George, 26
Titanic (James Cameron, 1997), 111–112
Tobey, Kenneth, 226
Todd, Mike, 130
Tonti, Aldo, 267
Torres, José, 157
Touch of Evil (Orson Welles, 1958), 182
Tourneur, Jacques, 189–190
Train, The (John Frankenheimer, 1965), 129
Traven, B., 4, 126, 197, 197–209
Treasure of Sierra Madre, The, 197–209

Treasure of the Sierra Madre, The (John Huston, 1948), xviii, 4, 9, 10, 46, 126, 197–209
Trilling, Lionel, 184
Truffaut, François, xiv, 1, 8, 131, 133
Turner, Kathleen, 168, 170–172
Turner, Lana, 172
Tyrrell, Susan, 154

Ulmer, Edgar G., 190–191
Under the Volcano, 43–46
Under the Volcano (John Huston, 1984), xvi, xvii, 4, 43–56, 129
Unforgiven, The (John Huston, 1960), 5, 7
Ulysses, xv, 44, 46
Universal Studios, 102

Van Damme, Jean-Claude, 158
Vanderwood, Paul J., 204
Vanity Fair, 2
Varela, Manuel Barbeito, 71
Varieties of Religious Experience, 50–51
Vasey, Margaret, 212–213
Veiller, Anthony, 13, 92, 102, 128
Veirtel, Peter, 92, 102, 218
Vertigo (Alfred Hitchcock, 1958), 189, 194
Victory (John Huston, 1981), 5
Von Hofmannsthal, Hugo, 28
Von Ledebur, Friedrich, 218

Waldman, Diane, 246
Walk with Love and Death, A, 5
Walker, Janet, 246
Walsh, Raoul, xv, 5
Walters, Charles, 143
War of the Worlds, The (Byron Haskin, 1953), 224
Ward, James, 132
Warner Bros., 113–114, 211, 226, 254
Way We Live Now, The, 2
Webb, Millard, 211
Welles, Orson, xvi, 13, 29, 182
Wellman, William A., 167
Welty, Eudora, 250

Westling, Louise, 250
Westmore, Bud, 15
White, Susanna, 2
Whitmore, James, 26, 143
Who's Afraid of Virginia Woolf? (Mike Nichols, 1966), 127–128, 254
Wilcox, Fred M., 224
Wilder, Billy, 13, 17–18, 172, 189–191
Williams, Esther, 143
Williams, Tennessee, xvi, xviii, 4, 126–128, 131–136, 249, 256
Williams, William Carlos, 23
Willis, Gary, 153
Wise Blood, xvi, xviii, 271–275, 279, 281–288
Wise Blood (John Huston, 1979), xvi, xviii, 4, 6, 8, 11, 18, 47, 129, 165, 271–288

Wives and Daughters, 2
Wizard of Oz, The, (Victor Fleming, 1939), 254
Woolrich, Cornell, 189
Working Girl (Mike Nichols, 1988), 176
Wyler, William, 5

Yacowar, Maurice, 136
York, Susannah, 233
"Young British Soldier," 96–97, 101
Young, Vernon, 162

Zanuck, Darryl, 9
Zupančič, Alenka, 285, 288
Zinnemann, Fred, 128
Žižek, Slavoj, 111–112, 234, 276–277, 280, 286
Zolotow, Sam, 137

www.ingramcontent.com/pod-product-compliance
Ingram Content Group UK Ltd.
Pitfield, Milton Keynes, MK11 3LW, UK
UKHW021833140426
5217IPUK00021B/1416